The Modern Mercenary

The Modern Mercenary

*Private Armies and What They Mean
for World Order*

SEAN McFATE

OXFORD
UNIVERSITY PRESS

OXFORD
UNIVERSITY PRESS

Oxford University Press is a department of the University of Oxford.
It furthers the University's objective of excellence in research, scholarship,
and education by publishing worldwide.

Oxford   New York

Auckland   Cape Town   Dar es Salaam   Hong Kong   Karachi
Kuala Lumpur   Madrid   Melbourne   Mexico City   Nairobi
New Delhi   Shanghai   Taipei   Toronto

With offices in

Argentina   Austria   Brazil   Chile   Czech Republic   France   Greece
Guatemala   Hungary   Italy   Japan   Poland   Portugal   Singapore
South Korea   Switzerland   Thailand   Turkey   Ukraine   Vietnam

Oxford is a registered trademark of Oxford University Press
in the UK and certain other countries.

Published in the United States of America by
Oxford University Press
198 Madison Avenue, New York, NY 10016

Library of Congress Cataloging-in-Publication Data
McFate, Sean. The modern mercenary : private armies and what they mean
for world order / Sean McFate.
pages cm
ISBN 978-0-19-936010-9 (hardback : alk. paper); 978-0-19-062108-7 (paperback : alk. paper)
1. Private military companies.   2. Mercenary troops.   3. Mercenary troops—United States.
4. United States—Military policy.   5. Security, International.   I. Title.
U240.M224 2014355.3'54—dc232014000896

1 3 5 7 9 8 6 4 2
Printed in Canada
on acid-free paper

To the past—farewell

Epitaph on an Army of Mercenaries

These, in the day when heaven was falling,
The hour when earth's foundations fled,
Followed their mercenary calling,
And took their wages, and are dead.

Their shoulders held the sky suspended;
They stood, and earth's foundations stay;
What God abandoned, these defended,
And saved the sum of things for pay.

—A. E. Housman

CONTENTS

LIST OF TABLE AND FIGURES

Table

Figures

FOREWORD

In 2004, I found myself in a peculiar position. I was in Burundi, a small country in central Africa, sipping a Coke with the country's president, the US ambassador, a woman I presumed was from the Central Intelligence Agency (CIA), and the president's eight-year-old daughter. It was around nine p.m., and we were watching the local television news in his living room at the presidential palace, not speaking a word. There was nothing to say. The president's life was in danger. The United States had brought me in to keep him alive. I wasn't sure how.

Ten years earlier, the genocide of the Tutsis that began in Rwanda swept south through neighboring Burundi, leaving a wake of sorrow and ash. More than eight hundred thousand people were murdered in ninety days, which is nearly a soul a minute. The original genocide remained unfinished business for some, and a group of Hutu rebels called the Forces Nationales de Libération (FNL) yearned to conclude its grim work. When I arrived at Bujumbura, the capital of Burundi, the FNL was hiding out across the border in the "Wild, Wild West" of Kivu, the easternmost region of the Democratic Republic of Congo, which abuts Burundi to the west.

US intelligence organizations received credible information that the FNL planned to cross the border at night, travel the twenty kilometers to the capital, and descend on the presidential palace. Their target was the president. They knew his assassination could reignite the genocide, just as the 1994 genocide was triggered by the killings of the Burundian and Rwandan presidents.

My job was to prevent this genocide from happening. I was to keep the president alive and in public view and without anyone knowing it was a US program, including staff at the US embassy. This I did. Curiously, I was not a member of the CIA or part of a covert US military unit or even a government employee. I was from the private sector—a "contractor" to many and "mercenary" to some—working for a large company called DynCorp International. DynCorp provides a wide range of services for the US government, from repairing military jets to guarding the president of Afghanistan to flying counterdrug missions in Colombia to preventing a possible genocide in Africa.

This is increasingly how foreign policy is enacted today: through corporations. Superpowers such as the United States cannot go to war without contractors in places like Iraq and Afghanistan, which was not the case even a generation ago. Tasks that once would have been the sole province of the CIA or the military are routinely contracted out to firms listed on the New York Stock Exchange. The most disturbing aspect of this trend is the decision to outsource lethal force: paramilitary, armed civilians patrol the streets of Baghdad and Kabul for their employer, the United States of America. These small private armies are organized as multinational companies, the most infamous being Blackwater USA, which commoditize conflict. Since 9/11, this industry has exploded from tens of millions to tens of billions of dollars in the chum slick of war contracts.

For-profit warriors cause concern. I recall being lambasted as a "mercenary" and "morally promiscuous" by fellow graduate students at Harvard University, insinuating that my existence somehow imperiled world peace. Similarly, my paratrooper buddies from the US Army's 82nd Airborne Division, where I served as an officer, scowled and said that I had "gone mercenary" and was lost to "the dark side." Yet the work I was doing at DynCorp was similar to what I would have done had I remained in the military, and the pay and benefits were not that great, despite popular perceptions to the contrary. Why all the vitriol?

The critics of the private military industry do have a point: linking profit motive to warfare has frightening implications in modern times. The growth of this industry has received copious attention in scholarship and popular literature alike. But despite the volumes of ink spilled on the subject, rigorous analysis remains thin, because private military companies are notoriously opaque. Moreover, their employers are reluctant to share information with outside researchers because of the politically sensitive nature of the work.

The secrecy surrounding the private military industry has shrouded it in mystery, myth, and conspiracy theory. Knee-jerk left-wing and right-wing critiques permeate the debate, politicizing and polarizing it. Much is highly sensationalized. What genuine study has occurred is narrow and limited to a few aspects of the industry: the legal status of armed civilian contractors on the battlefield; accountability issues relating to monetary fraud, waste, and abuse; and the experiences of high-profile companies such as Blackwater in Iraq and Afghanistan.

Meanwhile, broader questions remain. Why have strong countries such as the United States elected to employ private military forces after centuries of their prohibition? Does the privatization of war change warfare, and if so, does it affect strategic outcomes? What does the privatization of military force augur for the future of international relations? As a veteran of this industry, I continue to be haunted by these questions, which is why I wrote this book.

Despite the many concerns, the private military industry has a bright future. This multibillion-dollar industry will not simply evaporate once the United States withdraws from overseas deployments such as Afghanistan. In fact, the opposite will occur: contractors will help fill the security vacuum left by US forces. The industry may also grow, become more competitive, and develop into a free market for force, where the means of war are available to anyone who can afford it. Already, private military companies of all stripes are seeking new opportunities in conflict zones in Africa, the Middle East, and Latin America.

Moreover, the marketplace will likely transform, as new private military firms emerge from countries such as Russia and China, offer greater combat power, and work for the highest bidder with scant regard for human rights. New consumers of private force are appearing worldwide, seeking security in an insecure world: oil and mining companies guarding their drill sites against militias, shipping lines defending their vessels against pirates, humanitarian organizations protecting their workers in dangerous locations, countries fighting civil wars, and guerrillas fighting back. Few would welcome an unbridled market for force in world affairs, yet it is already developing.

Other fears exist, too. Private military companies will increasingly use military robotics such as armed drones that are becoming ever more available and advanced, making even small companies lethal. Companies are already engaging in cyber-warfare, offering clients offensive "hack-back" capabilities against intruders. These cyber-mercenaries are currently illegal in many countries, including the United States, yet they have a growing market among people and organizations that need to protect critical information.

Another worry is that a private military company might start an armed conflict that others must finish. For example, a client hires a company to stage an armed humanitarian intervention in a war-torn country to save innocent lives, but the company's actions backfire and make the situation worse rather than better, necessitating an emergency follow-on intervention by the United Nations or the United States.

Finally, a new type of warfare may emerge—contract warfare—that encourages war. As with contract killing, wealthy clients would hire private armies to wage wars for their own interests. Consequently, other wealthy actors would employ different private armies in self-defense, creating a security dilemma as both sides escalate and possibly use their arsenals of mercenary force. Contract warfare is literally a free market for force, where private armies and clients seek each other out, negotiate prices, and wage wars for personal gain.

This book examines why and how the private military industry—called mercenaries by many—has reemerged in modern times. Chapter 1 questions the common assumption that profit and warfare are always evil. Sometimes they are not. I saved many lives as a private military contractor. However, linking profit motive to killing invites serious moral concerns, and a better understanding of today's industry is required to grasp its benefits and dangers.

Chapter 2 does this by analyzing the current market for force, which was largely driven by the US wars in Iraq and Afghanistan. This chapter penetrates this secretive business from an insider's perspective and explains what kinds of companies operate where, whom they work for and who works for them, and what they do. It also offers definitions for the different kinds of security firms working in the marketplace and provides a new typology to understand the industry.

Chapter 3 reveals a disturbing trend: there is a growing codependency between the United States and this industry. Short of a national draft, it is unlikely that the superpower could go to war without the private sector. If a military colossus such as the United States finds these firms valuable, others will likely follow suit, establishing a new norm in interntational relations.

Chapter 4 explains how this situation developed and finds that private armies, present throughout the course of history, never really went away. Instead, they were subdued by states over the past four centuries and are now returning after a mere four-hundred-year hiatus.

Chapters 5 and 6 analyze the timeless advantages and risks of employing private force and turn to the high Middle Ages in Europe for insights, since contract warfare and mercenaries were common back then. The *condottieri*, Swiss companies, *landsknechts*, and other "free companies" dominated war from the thirteenth to the fifteen centuries throughout much of Europe. One lesson from this era is clear: private warriors change warfare and therefore war's outcomes, altering the course of international relations.

To better understand the implications of this, chapter 7 explores the making of the modern world order and how private armies shaped it. The medieval world was messy, and a wide host of political actors—popes, kings, city-states, wealthy families, and so on—all made overlapping claims of sovereignty over the same parcels of land and society. Disputes inevitably erupted and frequently were settled on the battlefield, often fought by each side's mercenaries. From this medieval din, one political actor emerged victorious: states. Kings and other rulers of states monopolized the market for force by investing in their own standing armies, loyal only to them, and outlawing mercenaries, leaving their nonstate adversaries defenseless. Out of this arose a new and state-centric world order, where only states have the privilege of enforcing their political will through violence. This order still exists today.

However, this order is changing. The reemergence of private armies heralds the slow return to the status quo ante of the Middle Ages, when states did not enjoy primacy in international politics and instead shared a crowded world stage with other actors. Drawing on the scholarship of Hedley Bull and others, chapter

8 explains the features of this emerging order and describes it as *neomedievalism*: a non-state-centric and multipolar world order characterized by overlapping authorities and allegiances. It does not foretell the ruin of states or the onset of anarchy. Instead, this new global system will persist in a durable disorder that contains rather than solves problems.

Given the important relationship between authority and war, chapter 9 investigates neomedieval warfare and how it could shape world affairs. A key challenge of neomedievalism is the commodification of conflict. Offering the means of war to anyone who can afford it will change warfare, why we fight, and the future of war. If money can buy firepower, then large corporations and ultra-wealthy individuals could become a new kind of superpower.

Chapters 10 and 11 offer two glimpses into the industry's future through case studies. The first examines DynCorp International, a large private military company operating in Liberia, a small West African country. After I helped prevent genocide as a grad student in Burundi, raising an army in Liberia became my primary mission. This chapter explains how we did it. The second case concerns Somalia's budding market for force. Market actors are more like medieval mercenaries, fighting for the highest bidder and even becoming predatory. By contrast, DynCorp is a "military enterpriser," building an army for the client rather than deploying it. These different types of market actors create different kinds of marketplaces. Somalia is a free market for force, with "lone wolf" mercenaries, while Liberia is a mediated market, with the company working closely with its government client in a public-private partnership. The case studies conclude that private military actors worsen security in a free market such as Somalia but increase it in a mediated market such as Liberia and under the right market circumstances could even prove a powerful tool for the United Nations and others.

Chapter 12 draws insights from these case studies and identifies four mutually reinforcing trends in the private military industry: resilience, proliferation, indigenization, and bifurcation. The industry will endure after the United States withdraws from Afghanistan, seeking new clients. In fact, it is already doing so, globalizing as new customers and companies appear around the world. And as the industry goes global, it is concurrently indigenizing or "going native." Warlords and others have adopted the private military model to make a living, and international clients, including the United States, are buying. Finally, the industry is beginning to bifurcate between a mediated market with military enterprisers and a free market populated by mercenaries. Whichever trajectory wins the market in the coming years is important, because it will influence the future or war.

The world is at a crossroads, and if the industry is left on autopilot, it may morph into a situation of perpetual and predatory mercenarism similar to that of medieval Italy. However, other options exist that harness the industry's benefits while mitigating its risks. It is important that its evolution happen in a deliberate and nonreckless manner, because the private military industry is here to stay. As in the European Middle Ages, private warfare has the power to shape international relations and the world.

ACKNOWLEDGMENTS

I am indebted to the counsel of Christopher Coker at the London School of Economics, whose lucid work on the nature of war and society informed this book from its inception. I am grateful to Christopher Kinsey and his scholarship on the private security industry, which has influenced my thinking on the subject. Equally, I am thankful for the guidance of Gregory Mills, whose indefatigable work in fragile states as strategic adviser, scholar, journalist and occasional race car driver are an inspiration. I am also grateful for the indispensable assistance of Dave McBride at Oxford University Press, the help of Peter H. McGuigan and his team at Foundry Literary+Media, the thoughtful edits of Brian Slattery, and the support of Nadia Schadlow. Finally, I am thankful to my friends and colleagues at the National Defense University, the RAND Corporation, and the New America Foundation who provided me with invaluable feedback and friendship.

Washington, D.C., July 2013

ABBREVIATIONS

AFL	Armed Forces of Liberia
ARTEP	Army Readiness Training Evaluation Program
BTC	Barclay Training Center
CBO	Congressional Budget Office
COIN	counterinsurgency
COTR	contracting officer's technical representative
CPA	comprehensive peace agreement
DDR	disarmament, demobilization, and reintegration
DDRR	disarmament, demobilization, rehabilitation, and reintegration
DOD	US Department of Defense
DRC	Democratic Republic of the Congo
ECOWAS	Economic Community of West African States
GAO	Government Accountability Office
GDP	gross domestic product
ICC	International Criminal Court
ICJ	International Court of Justice
ICRC	International Committee of the Red Cross
IDIQ	indefinite delivery/indefinite quantity contract
IDP	internally displaced person
IET	initial entry training (military "basic training")
IMF	International Monetary Fund
INTERPOL	International Criminal Police Organization
ISAF	International Security Assistance Force
ISOA	International Stability Operations Association (formerly International Peace Operations Association, or IPOA)
LOGCAP	Logistics Civil Augmentation Program
LURD	Liberians United for Reconciliation and Democracy

MEJA	Military Extraterritorial Jurisdiction Act
MOD	Ministry of Defense or Ministry of National Defense
MODEL	Movement for Democracy in Liberia
MPRI	Military Professional Resources Inc.
NGO	nongovernmental organization
NTGL	National Transitional Government of Liberia
NTP	notice to proceed
ODC	Office of Defense Cooperation
OECD-DAC	Organization for Economic Cooperation and Development—Development Assistance Committee
PA&E	Pacific Architects and Engineers
PSD	personal security detail
PKO	peacekeeping operations
PMC	private military company
R2P	Responsibility to Protect
RFP	request for proposal
RUF	Revolutionary United Front
SAS	Special Air Services
SOW	statement of work
SSR	security sector reform
TCN	third-country national
TO&E	table of organization and equipment
TRC	Truth and Reconciliation Commission
UCMJ	Uniform Code of Military Justice
UNDP	UN Development Program
UNDPKO	UN Department of Peacekeeping Operations
UNHCR	UN High Commissioner for Refugees
UNMIL	UN Mission in Liberia
UNOSOM	UN Operation in Somalia
USAID	United States Agency for International Development
UAV	unmanned aerial vehicles
WPPS	Worldwide Personal Protective Services

1

Peace through Profit Motive?

> I'll get paid for killing, and this town is full of men who deserve to die.
> —Sanjuro, masterless samurai

The 1961 Japanese movie *Yojimbo*, directed by Akira Kurosawa, tells the story of Sanjuro, a masterless samurai, or *ronin*, who arrives at a small town that has been torn asunder by two competing criminal gangs. The *ronin* persuades each crime lord to hire him as protection from the other, and through skillful political manipulation and the bloody use of his sword, he successfully pits the rival gangs against each other. The gangs soon annihilate each other in battle, while the *ronin* enriches himself; he then moves on to the next crime-ridden town. By acting in his economic self-interest, the *ronin* brings peace to the town, albeit with much collateral damage.

Yojimbo may serve as an apt analogy for where today's private military industry is heading. Private military organizations—from ancient mercenaries to modern private military companies (PMCs) such as Blackwater USA—are expeditionary conflict entrepreneurs that kill or train others to kill. It is certainly conceivable that a PMC today could secretly and simultaneously serve two clients at war with each other, as did the *ronin* in *Yojimbo*, expanding the conflict for profit until both sides destroy each other, after which the company would move on to the next conflict and business opportunity.

More nuanced scenarios also abound. A human rights organization such as Amnesty International could hire a PMC such as Blackwater, currently rebranded as "Academi," to stage a humanitarian intervention in a place like Darfur to save lives and curb the ongoing genocide, which has claimed more than three hundred thousand lives. This, in turn, could prompt the Sudanese government to hire an opposing PMC sourced from countries such as Russia or China, which have troubled human rights records, to counter Blackwater and help Sudan "pacify" Darfur. If PMCs are truly profit-maximizing entities, like the *ronin* in *Yojimbo*, it is likely that these two PMCs would cut deals between themselves, either explicitly or implicitly, to promote their parochial business interests, namely, spreading and elongating war for the sake of profit.

The result would be two or more PMCs fighting an artificially prolonged proxy war in Africa for state and nonstate actors, with far-reaching implications for international relations. Combining profit motive with war will introduce a new kind of warfare—contract warfare—that will likely increase armed conflict worldwide.

Not Just Fantasy

The above scenario may sound like a movie script, but it is not. In 2008, I was asked to participate in such a plan. Millionaire actress Mia Farrow had approached Blackwater and a few human rights organizations to end the genocide in Darfur. The plan was simple. Blackwater would stage an armed intervention in Darfur and establish so-called islands of humanity, refugee camps protected by PMC firepower for civilians fleeing the deadly *janjaweed*, gunmen who massacred whole villages in Darfur. During this time, the human rights organizations would mount a global name-and-shame media campaign to goad the international community into ending the genocide once and for all with a muscular UN peacekeeping mission.

One of the human rights organizations approached me with this plan, given my background as a veteran of the private military industry who operated in Africa. The group wanted to know two things: Could Blackwater actually stage an armed intervention in Darfur? And if it could, was this desirable?

The answer to the first question was certain: Blackwater could feasibly stage a humanitarian intervention. In 2005, it had launched a subsidiary company called Greystone, which could rapidly deploy a military force anywhere in the world to create a more secure environment for its customers. In the words of the company, "Greystone is an international security services company that offers your country or organization a complete solution to your most pressing security needs.... Customer satisfaction is our primary focus, and we deliver superior services with professionalism and flexibility." The company website lists humanitarian peacekeeping as a primary service that "provides a light infantry solution that is self-contained and self-sufficient. The Greystone peacekeeping program leverages efficiency of private resources to provide a complete cost effective security solution."[1] Being familiar with western Sudan and Greystone's actual capabilities, I believed Greystone could stage a humanitarian intervention in Darfur for days and perhaps even weeks.

We also discussed other options for Greystone. One was the possibility of training and equipping Darfurians or African Union peacekeepers to better defend against Sudanese aggression. Another was using unarmed aerial drones to provide early warning to Darfur villages of impending attacks and also to document human rights atrocities for CNN and other global media outlets. Last was direct action: offensive combat operations such as commando raids or armed aerial drone strikes conducted by Blackwater personnel to scatter the *janjaweed* and disrupt the Sudanese military's ability to conduct the genocide.

The answer to the second question was less certain. Even though Blackwater could intervene in Darfur, there were doubts about whether it should. The action would brazenly violate international law, although some argued that it was justified by the international community's failure to enforce human rights laws and stop the genocide. There were other concerns, too. The intervention could undermine ongoing diplomatic efforts to resolve the conflict peacefully, even if those efforts were paltry, and might even drag the United States into a war with Sudan, since Blackwater and other principal actors were Americans. Owing to this, Blackwater fretted that its actions would anger its best client, the United States, which would be bad for business. Also, the Blackwater employees conducting the operation could be tried by the International Criminal Court at The Hague for war crimes in their effort to stop a genocide, which Blackwater and the human rights groups both found bitterly ironic. The human rights groups worried that it might trigger additional violence and reprisals in the region, worsening the situation for local Darfurians in the long run.

Finally, such an action would set a precedent that many would not welcome: the possibility of international vigilantism, which could undermine the world order. Today global governance and the use of military action are the exclusive purview of nation-states and the United Nations, which is made up of states. Only states are allowed to wage war, and corporations, human rights groups, rich people, and all other nonstate actors are forbidden to use military force to achieve their objectives. A humanitarian intervention organized and conducted by nonstate actors would blatantly challenge this norm and set a dangerous precedent.

However, this is exactly what the human rights groups were hoping to do, namely, to provoke the international community into action. If the United Nations condemned Blackwater, it would, in effect, be abetting genocide, yet if it did not stop the company, it would be encouraging mercenarism. The only solution would be for the United Nations to condemn Blackwater and intervene in Darfur to finish what the PMC had started, or so the planners of this plot hoped.

Ultimately, all parties decided not to pursue a private military intervention. They believed the risks outweighed the benefits. However, it is possible—even probable—that in the future, individuals and organizations will overcome such reservations and retain more aggressive PMCs to do their bidding. A tycoon seeking an altruistic legacy might hire a PMC from, say, Chechnya or El Salvador, both of which have a surplus of unemployed skilled fighters and a deficit of respect for the laws of war, to stage a similar operation for the purposes of posterity. If successful, this could encourage similar undertakings that would foster a free market for force, where PMCs and clients seek each other out, nego- tiate prices, and wage wars for personal gain—in other words, contract warfare.

The Return of Private Armies

Such a market for force is closer than many might suppose. Currently, the market is not truly free; it is a monopsony, where there is a predominant buyer—the United States—and many sellers. This is a result of the United States' insatiable need for security in Iraq, Afghanistan, and elsewhere. As the consumer-in-chief, the United States wields market power to shape private military business prac- tices and norms. For example, major PMCs today will not work for countries such as Sudan that are at odds with the United States. But this may change after the Iraq and Afghanistan bubbles burst and PMCs seek new buyers and proffer more forceful services to survive.

This new market for force will likely develop into a free one, unless the United States or a similar "superclient" has need of every PMC available, which is unlikely. Also, if trends of the past are indicators of the future, then the new mar- ket will be lightly regulated, and efforts by countries to change that will simply drive PMCs offshore or underground. Current domestic laws are inadequate, international law is ambiguous and difficult to enforce, and ultimately, a new Geneva Protocol is needed to regulate the private military industry. However, such efforts usually evolve over decades.

What would a free market for force look like? The supply and demand for security in an insecure world would logically seek each other out. Supply would expand as PMCs emerged from Russia, China, and elsewhere, offering greater combat-oriented possibilities and willing to work for the highest bidder, with scant regard for human rights or international law, in order to win new clients in a crowded marketplace.

Furthermore, the staff that make up the larger PMCs is drawn from all over the world. Companies such as G4S, Triple Canopy, and DynCorp International may have British or American headquarters but recruit much of their person- nel from places such as the Philippines, Colombia, South Africa, and so forth. These individuals have learned the trade, and some will likely return to their countries of origin and form their own, smaller PMCs, willing to work for who- ever pays them.

Other small firms already exist, empowered as subcontractors to bigger PMCs in Iraq, Afghanistan, and elsewhere. As the United States withdraws from these conflict zones and its large security contracts conclude, these small firms will spin off and seek new clients in the international marketplace as full-fledged PMCs. New firms have already sprung up in places like Afghanistan and Somalia, as this book will show, offering more combat-offense capabilities and taking risks that current industry leaders would never contemplate.

Supply can create demand in the context of security, and this will also diversify the marketplace. New capabilities provided by emerging firms will attract new clients beyond the United States: fragile states and tyrannical regimes augmenting their forces, UN missions requiring more peacekeepers, multinational corporations and shipping lines protecting their assets, humanitarian workers needing protection, opposition groups seeking regime change, and the whims of superempowered individuals. The near contract to intervene in Darfur may be the first of its kind but is probably not the last. Worse, unscrupulous PMCs can create demand through extortion, demanding "protection money" from anyone they can threaten and who can pay.

The future marketplace will be global hot spots and conflict zones such as the Middle East, Latin America, and Africa, because demand for security is high there. It is natural that supply should pursue demand and vice versa, yet introducing an industry vested in conflict into the most conflict-prone places on earth is vexing, given the possible consequences for the people who live there. Few would like to see an unbridled market for force emerge in the decades ahead. Yet such a world may already be upon us.

Since the end of the Cold War, PMCs have proliferated at an alarming rate. Surprisingly, the primary consumers of this new service are not weak regimes in the developing world looking to consolidate their grasp on power, although this has happened, but strong states like the United States of America in places like Iraq and Afghanistan. This is curious, because the United States is the greatest military power on earth and should not need hired guns. This book examines why this has occurred and what it means for the future of international affairs. It finds that private military force, a timeless phenomenon, is back after a four-hundred-year hiatus and is not likely to go away.

The Emergence of Neomedievalism

Even more disquieting, the reappearance of private military actors heralds a wider trend in international relations: the emergence of neomedievalism. In the modern world order, only states are sovereign, and only they can partake in international politics, make international laws, and legitimately wage war. But it was not always so. For example, during the Middle Ages in Europe, sovereignty was fragmented among different political actors—emperor, church, king, bishop, princes, city-states, chivalric orders, and so forth. Each vied for power, waged war (often through mercenaries), and made overlapping claims of authority over people, places, and things. Back then, rulers rarely retained absolute authority within a large territory, as a state does today.

This began to change over the centuries, as states eventually became the dominant actors on the world stage, crowding out nonstate actors. This conquest was, in part, guaranteed by their monopoly on the use of force, such as national police and military forces; those who did not comply with a state's orders were thrown in jail or worse. Armed nonstate actors, like mercenaries, were strictly outlawed because they could physically challenge the state—even defeat it. Hence private force was deemed a threat to states and the modern world order, which is based on states. This order is sometimes called the Westphalian system, named for the Peace of Westphalia in 1648, which ended the Thirty Years War and gave birth to the modern state system.

Now the situation is changing back. The growing willingness to employ private force and subsequent erosion of the taboo against mercenarism signal a return to the premodern norm of medieval times, when mercenaries were common and states did not enjoy the monopoly of force. Moreover, states are no longer the principal actors in international affairs as they were a century ago. Today they compete with others who also have political power: multinational companies such as ExxonMobil, international organizations such as the United Nations, and nongovernmental organizations such as Amnesty International. As in the Middle Ages, today's world order is polycentric, with authority diluted and shared among state and nonstate actors alike.

The gradual return to the status quo ante of the Middle Ages is best described as *neomedievalism*, non-state-centric and multipolar world order characterized by overlapping authorities and allegiances. It is a metaphor for a global phenomenon and is not intended to be Eurocentric. Nor does it imply worldwide atavism. States will not disappear, but they will matter less than they did a century ago. Nor does neomedievalism connote chaos and anarchy; like the medieval world, the global system will persist in a durable disorder that contains rather than solves problems.

As in the Middle Ages, a key challenge of neomedievalism will be controlling private military force. Offering the means of war to anyone who can afford it will change warfare, why we fight, and the future of war. The commodification of conflict could reintroduce contract warfare, which has the power to transform world politics back to the future.

This is a disturbing observation, that states soon may not be expected to retain a monopoly on the use of force. Instead, private armies may return, in which case a sharper understanding of today's industry is needed to grasp the scale of this danger and what it portends for the future of peace and security. Key questions include: Who are these new private military actors? How are they different from those of the past? Who is hiring them? What kinds of services do they provide? Where are they based, and where do they tend to operate? Answering these and other questions will explain the contours of today's market for force and suggest where it will go after Iraq and Afghanistan.

2

Understanding the Private Military Industry

The market economy as such does not respect political frontiers. Its field is the world.

—Ludwig Edler von Mises

The private military industry has surged since the end of the Cold War and is now a multibillion-dollar business. Today's military firms are sophisticated multinational corporations with subsidiaries around the world and quarterly profit reports for investors. These companies are bought and sold on Wall Street, and their stocks are listed on the London and New York exchanges. Their boards consist of Wall Street magnates and former generals, their corporate managers are seasoned Fortune 500 executives, and their ranks filled with ex-military and law-enforcement personnel recruited from around the world. They work for governments, the private sector, and humanitarian organizations. The industry even has its own trade associations: the International Stability Operations Association (ISOA) in Washington, D.C. the British Association of Private Security Companies in London, and the Private Security Company Association of Iraq. Despite the surfeit of coverage in recent years, the industry remains confusing, because it is notoriously impervious to outside investigators. Consequently, little is known about how and why these private military actors exist.

Why So Little Is Still Known

The private military industry has become a fashionable subject for study over the past decade, but knowledge about the industry is still thin. The primary obstacle to research is the lack of data available on the industry. The firms themselves can be more opaque than the US military or intelligence agencies, because they are not subject to the Freedom of Information Act or similar legislative tools that impose transparency. Even members of Congress do not have direct access to the contracts by which these firms are employed, even though Congress is writing the checks.

Journalists' and academics' analyses of PMCs are anemic, because the industry is media-phobic, owing to its roots in the military, which traditionally eschews public scrutiny. Reporters, who are typically not even allowed to interview members of, much less embed in, PMCs, can only record the events surrounding the industry. Academics depend almost entirely on the work of journalists for their analyses of these firms. Consequently, their mutual conclusions can be speculative and even factually erroneous. This has stultified understanding of the industry.

Government inquiry into the industry is limited and, at times, convoluted. Currently, there is little, if any, meaningful regulation of or reporting requirements from this industry, which is remarkable given that the firms are authorized to use lethal force abroad under the US flag. Reports produced by government watchdog agencies such as the Congressional Research Service, the Congressional Budget Office, the Special Inspector General for Iraq Reconstruction, the Special Inspector General for Afghanistan Reconstruction, and the Government Accountability Office offer excellent snapshots of discrete problems with the market but lack analysis of macro trends.

Remarkably, government investigators are often given limited access to the industry's internal workings, owing to issues over proprietary knowledge. What genuine investigation has occurred is narrow and limited to three areas: the legal status of armed contractors on the battlefield; monetary fraud, waste, and abuse; and experiences in Iraq and Afghanistan. Wider ramifications of this industry are left relatively unexamined, such as how the commodification of conflict might undermine long-term foreign policy objectives. Congressional hearings on PMCs, such as those held by Congressman Henry Waxman, spotlight problems with these firms but do little tangibly to resolve them and are often little more than political theater.

Much of the media discourse on the industry is framed in acrimonious and demonizing terms, owing in part to the sensationalistic lure of labeling PMCs as mercenaries and the promise of an audience. A sample of headlines from mainstream news outlets reveals some of this: "Dogs of War: From Mercenary to Security Contractor and Back Again," "Making a Killing: The Business of War," "Modern Mercenaries on the Iraqi Frontier."[1] Reporters-turned-authors fan the fire of conspiracy theorists by insinuating that PMCs represent a shadow government manipulating or coercing the national security establishment, with provocative books such as Jeremy Scahill's best-selling *Blackwater: The Rise of the World's Most Powerful Mercenary Army*, Stephen Armstrong's *War PLC: The Rise of the New Corporate Mercenary*, and Robert Young Pelton's *Licensed to*

Kill: Privatizing the War on Terror. Such distortions of the industry are more inflammatory than informative.

Industry defenders are equally problematic, as they tend to treat it as just another services industry, overlooking the moral, strategic, and policy complexities of the issue. They maintain that the private sector is more efficient and effective than the public sector at finding solutions to difficult security challenges but offer little evidence to outside researchers to corroborate these claims. They even inoculate the language used to describe the industry with euphemism. ISOA is disparaging of the terms *private military company* and *private security company* and promotes the softer phrase *contingency contractors.* Perhaps Erik Prince, founder and CEO of Blackwater, best articulates the industry's self-image: "Our corporate goal is to do for the national security apparatus what FedEx did to the Postal Service."[2] However, after a handful of Blackwater personnel killed seventeen innocent Iraqi civilians at Nisour Square in Baghdad on September 16, 2007, his company rebranded itself from the militaristic "Blackwater," a term used by Navy SEALs to describe covert nighttime underwater operations, to "Xe," which stands for xenon, an inert, noncombustible gas. Some might view this as disingenuous and even cynical. The company has changed its name once again, to "Academi," and Prince has since left the company and the country.

Amid the public debate, a broad range of scholarly literature has emerged on the private military industry within international relations, law, political science, and economics, mainly dwelling on a few aspects of the issue: vague regulatory options for the industry at national, regional, and international levels; normative challenges to the state's monopoly on force; and typologies that clarify the industry's organizational structure. The conclusions drawn are generally theoretical and speculative, however, pointing out not only the lack of data needed for rigorous analysis but even disagreement about how to define a PMC.

Theoretical Confusion

Despite the glut of attention lavished on this topic in recent years, there still is no common definition, typology, or understanding of who exactly is a member of the industry. Consequently, there is a range of terms used to describe these firms, further confusing the issue: *private military contractors, private security companies, private military companies, private security/military companies, private military firms, private security contractors, private military corporations,* and *military service providers.* Some analysts and organizations, such as the International Committee of the Red Cross (ICRC), use terms interchangeably—say, *private military company, private security company,* and *private military/security company* (*PMSC*)—sowing further conceptual disorder. The US government generally favors *private security company*, yet this term means wholly different things to different parts of the bureaucracy, as noted in a congressional investigation into the matter, which itself uses the term in an exceptional manner.[3] Still others use *PMSC* as a catchall definition, but such an all-encompassing category is not analytically meaningful. The lack of a common lexicon handicaps discourse on a topic already shrouded in secrecy.

Definitions range from the very narrow to the overly broad, and both ends of the spectrum are unsuccessful from a critical perspective. Not surprisingly, the industry defines private security too narrowly as the commercial act of physically protecting a person, place, or thing—or, in the words of Doug Brooks, former president of the ISOA, private security is any activity directly related to protecting a "noun." Similarly, the National Defense Authorization Act for fiscal year 2008 defines private security functions as the guarding of personnel, facilities, or properties and any other activity with armed personnel.[4]

These definitions may sound fairly comprehensive, but they fail to account for the many activities the industry's firms are involved in, such as intelligence analysis, military operational coordination, security force training, and logistical support in nonpermissive and hostile environments. Moreover, they ignore the moral aspects of conducting business when it comes to the application of lethal force.

Broad definitions also exist and tend to emanate from the academic community. The seminal book *Corporate Warriors* by Peter W. Singer catalyzed the debate over private military force in 2003 and remains one of the best analyses of the industry to date. Singer defines private military firms (PMFs) as "private business entities that deliver to consumers a wide spectrum of military and security services, once generally assumed to be exclusively inside the public context."[5] This definition provides a good baseline for study but ultimately depends on the subjective assessment of what military services are inherently governmental or "assumed to be exclusively inside the public context." This will vary greatly from observer to observer.

Another important book is Deborah Avant's *The Market for Force*, in which she divides the industry into two categories: external and internal security. External security consists of combat operations, military advice and training, and logistical support, whereas internal security includes policing, intelligence services, and static defense.[6] This is helpful, because it differentiates security based on what happens inside versus outside a state. External security deals with force projection and protecting national borders from invaders, while internal security maintains domestic order. One limitation of this approach is that it is highly state-centric in an era when national borders matter less and less; weak states have notoriously porous borders, while strong ones are plugged into a globalized world that frequently blurs the line between internal and external affairs.

Despite these difficulties, Singer and Avant represent some of the best scholarship on the topic. But, like many, they are challenged by a lack of industry data and insider knowledge, resulting in definitions that are too expensive to parse the complex private military industry. A new definition and a new taxonomy are needed, ones that provide analytical and theoretical coherence for modern private military actors.

The Market for Force Revealed

The organization of the industry reflects the market and how it evolved. At present, the market for force is not a free market but rather a monopsony, a market with a single buyer. The current market marker for modern force is the United States, as it has turned to the private sector in unprecedented ways to support its wars in Iraq and Afghanistan. While other outfits exist, such as the French Foreign Legion, they are not part of today's market for force, because they are not free-market actors, selling their services to different customers. The Foreign Legion is part of the French Army, is led by French officers, takes its orders exclusively from Paris, rewards its legionnaires with French citizenship, and only serves the French government at cut rates. It has little in common with the armed contractors operating in Iraq or Afghanistan.

The United States' insatiable need for security in Iraq and Afghanistan fueled the growth of today's private security industry. This also gave the United States market power as the consumer-in-chief to shape business practices and norms during the industry's formative years, as it grew from a multimillion-dollar to a multibillion-dollar market. Not surprisingly, market actors now look very American, as firms naturally pattern themselves after their biggest client to attract more business. Owing to this, a fitting typology for the private military industry is based on the US military.

Specifically, the mold of the modern private military industry is the US Army, for two reasons. First, these new firms are land forces and fundamentally private armies, as the United States has hired no private navies or air forces. Second, former US Army and Marine Corps personnel fill the management ranks of these companies to instill confidence in and ensure interoperability with the client, because they understand the operations and culture of the US military. The boards of directors for these corporations are stocked with retired generals to help win contracts from the US government, anticipate future government needs, and lend credibility to the firm for its chief customer. This produced a US-centric industry to appeal to its primary customer.

The categorization of activities required to support land warfare is similar regardless of private versus public providers, although different armies have slightly different approaches. Because combat can occur anywhere in the modern theater of war, the typology is based on function rather than location in the battlespace. For the US Army, military units fall into one of three general categories based on their function or mission: combat arms, combat support, and combat service support. The function of *combat arms* units is to kill or train others to kill the enemy in foreign lands, unless a foreign enemy is invading the homeland. Combat arms units include infantry, special forces, armed aviation, and armor (e.g., tanks). *Combat service* units provide operational support to the combat arms units, allowing them to engage the enemy more effectively, but they do not directly engage the enemy themselves unless in self-defense. These units include the military police and military intelligence. *Combat service support* units provide logistical and administrative support to combat arms and combat service units, thereby supplying and sustaining the force. Like combat service units, combat service support components are not expected to engage the enemy unless in self-defense. This category includes quartermaster, ordnance, transportation, adjutant general, finance, and medical services corps. The chief distinction between combat service and combat service support is that the former offers operational support while the latter offers logistical and administrative support to combat arms units.

Like the US Army, the private military sector consists of three categories of units or companies analogous to combat arms, combat service, and combat service support. The *private military companies* (PMCs, the focus of this book) are the private sector equivalent of combat arms, since their job places them in the line of fire. PMCs are expeditionary conflict entrepreneurs structured as multinational corporations that use lethal force or train others to do so.

Five characteristics distinguish PMCs from other armed nonstate actors in global politics. First, they are motivated more by profit than by politics. This is not to suggest that all PMCs disregard political interests and serve merely at the whim of the highest bidder, but they are fundamentally profit-seeking entities. Second, they are structured as multinational corporations and participate in the global financial system. These are not shady "lone wolf" mercenaries stalking the jungles of the Congo during the wars of African liberation. Third, they are expeditionary in nature, meaning that they seek work in foreign lands rather than providing domestic security services. There are exceptions to this, especially when it comes to homeland defense, but in general, these firms are foreign focused and are not domestic security guards. Fourth, they typically deploy force in a military manner, as opposed to a law-enforcement one. The purpose of military force is to defeat or deter the enemy through organized violence, while law enforcement seeks to deescalate violent situations to maintain law and order. This intrinsically affects how they operate. Fifth and most important, PMCs are lethal and represent the commodification of armed conflict. There will always be exceptions to these five features, but they serve as a good test of whether an armed nonstate actor is a PMC.

There are two kinds of PMCs: mercenary and military enterpriser. Mercenary companies are private armies that can conduct autonomous military campaigns, offensive operations, and force projection. At present, there are no large mercenary firms, but they have existed in the recent past. For example, the now-defunct firm Executive Outcomes, based in South Africa, conducted independent military campaigns in Africa during the 1990s. In 1993, the Angolan government hired Executive Outcomes to defeat the rebel group National Union for the Total Independence of Angola (UNITA), retake oil facilities in the harbor town of Soyo, and train government soldiers for $40 million a year. Two years later, Sierra Leone's government hired Executive Outcomes to defeat the Liberian-backed Revolutionary United Front (RUF), retake the Kono diamond area, and force a negotiated peace for $35 million.[7] Executive Outcomes provided its own combat units, air forces, global supply chain, and so forth, to defeat the enemy. The United States has shunned strong PMCs, and consequently, they are absent from today's market for force.

Distinct from mercenaries, military enterprisers raise armies rather than command them. Historically, this type of conflict entrepreneur trains, equips, and fields whole regiments to fight for their clients. Most modern PMCs are military enterprisers and make their money not by deploying their own armies but by making them for someone else. For example, the United States has relied on contractors to develop the Afghan National Army and the Afghan National Police, even awarding DynCorp International a contract worth up to $1 billion to train the police.[8]

Raising foreign forces is inherently a PMC function, because only combat arms units can transfer their unique skill sets from one to another. Only an infantry unit can train another country's infantry units, which is standard practice in military training. The reason is self-evident. Military professional training is derived from the knowledge and credibility of field experience, which cannot be duplicated by a textbook or imitated by a pretender. A quartermaster unit cannot train platoon patrol tactics, nor can an infantry platoon train brigade resupply operations. Nonveteran civilians are unqualified to train military units, which is why PMCs draw their personnel from the ranks of former military and police units worldwide. Furthermore, training others to kill occupies the same moral universe as killing itself and must be considered within the ambit of PMCs.

Military enterprisers are PMCs in another way, too. With their stronger mercenary cousins, military enterprisers share the same competences and could easily be transformed into mercenary firms. In other words, if one has the ability to raise an army, then one also has the aptitude to deploy it, since the skill sets are closely related. In fact, most modern PMCs blend the two categories. The

United States contracts PMCs to help raise Iraqi and Afghan security forces, but these firms also augment the US military there, using deadly force (mostly) for defensive purposes. Examples of these tasks include protecting fixed or static sites, such as housing areas, reconstruction work sites, or government buildings. Other tasks include providing armed escorts to convoys traveling through risky areas or offering bodyguards in dangerous places. Bodyguard teams, called personal security details (PSDs) in industry parlance, protect high-ranking individuals in conflict zones, such as Afghanistan President Hamid Karzai, who was protected by DynCorp International in 2002.

PMCs routinely deploy armed personnel, convoys, and helicopters to protect people and things for their clients. In 2005, the State Department's Worldwide Personal Protective Services II (WPPS) contract awarded up to $1.2 billion to Blackwater, Triple Canopy, and DynCorp International, which collectively provided some fifteen hundred "shooters," or armed civilians authorized to kill, in Iraq alone. This contract provided armed escorts for US government personnel around the world, with license to kill under limited circumstances. This contract, though lethal, is not equivalent to the military campaigns waged by Executive Outcomes in Africa, but it does demonstrate that mercenaries and military enterprisers are related and in the same category.

The *security support companies* are the private sector version of the US Army's combat services units and are generally unarmed. Examples of security support companies range from Science Applications International Corporation (SAIC), which provides intelligence analysis, to the Lincoln Group, which conducts strategic communication in Iraq, to CACI and Titan, which provide interpreters to the US military, to Total Intelligence Solutions, which runs spy rings for the US government overseas. Security support companies are as controversial as PMCs, even though they typically are unarmed and do not employ lethal force. CACI and Titan contractors were implicated in the Abu Ghraib prison scandal, and Lincoln Group instigated an uproar when journalists discovered that the US government had hired the company to propagandize the US cause in the Iraqi free press.

General contractors are equivalent to the US Army's combat service support units and provide logistical support through supply, maintenance, transportation, medical, and other services that combat units require. General contractors are not members of the private military or security industry, as they perform nonlethal tasks that are not uniquely military or security-related in nature. However, it is important to include them within this typology and acknowledge their presence and complicity in conflict-affected areas. Typical general contractor tasks include equipping soldiers, maintaining vehicles, constructing buildings, driving trucks with supplies, cooking meals, building bases, and performing routine administration. The bulk of contractors in conflict-affected areas fall into this category.

Table 2.1 Typology of the Private Military Industry

Functional Area	Public Sector Military Unit Type	Private Sector Equivalents	Typical Tasks and Missions
Combat Arms/Private Military Companies (PMCs) Expeditionary organizations whose primary function is to kill or train others to kill the enemy in foreign lands (and the focus of this book)	• Infantry • Special forces • Armed aviation • Armor • Artillery • Combat engineers	*Mercenary PMCs* • Executive Outcomes • Sandline International • Sterling Corporate Services *Military Enterprise PMCs* • Blackwater/Academi • DynCorp International • Triple Canopy	• Combat: Deploying military units to defeat the enemy and achieve wartime objectives. This includes military campaigning, force projection, offensive and defensive operations, reconnaissance, and special operations. In the private sector, mercenaries conduct these tasks. • Generating foreign forces: This involves demobilizing adversarial forces and/or raising new ones. This includes recruiting, training, equipping, and fielding new security forces and establishing the institutions that oversee them. In the private sector, military enterprisers conduct these tasks. *Note:* Some PMCs blend mercenary and military enterpriser functions.
Combat Service/Security Support Companies Expeditionary organizations that provide operational assistance to combat arms units	• Noncombat engineers • Intelligence and espionage • Communications • Information Operations & Psychological Operations • Civil Affairs	• Titan Corporation • SAIC • Lincoln Group • Total Intelligence Solutions • MPRI	• Operational coordination: Establishing and managing command, control, and communications operations in hostile environments. • Intelligence collection, analysis, and risk assessment: Gathering information and developing threat analysis. • Information warfare: Planning and disseminating propaganda and other psychological actions to influence the opinions, emotions, attitudes, and behavior of foreign groups. • Cyber-warfare: Hacking to conduct deception espionage or sabotage.

| **Combat Service Support/ General Contractors** Organizations that provide logistical assistance to combat arms units | • Quartermaster
• Ordnance
• Transportation
• Adjutant general
• Finance
• Medical services | • KBR
• DynCorp International
• Swift Global Logistics
• Parsons
• SOS International
• ITT Corporation | • Equipping and supplying soldiers and civilians in the field with food, water, ammunition, equipment, etc.
• Providing services that promote, improve, conserve, or restore the mental or physical well-being of personnel.
• Maintaining equipment such as vehicles, generators, buildings, etc.
• Transporting units, personnel, equipment, and supplies.
• Managing human resources.
• Constructing military bases and infrastructure.
• Demining. |

Focusing on function in relation to combat operations and recognizing the influence of the US Army's organizational and operational influence on the emerging private military industry produce a more logically coherent typology than earlier attempts, especially for typologies created before the wars in Iraq and Afghanistan, which shaped the industry in substantial ways. Table 2.1 depicts this new typology.[9] A few of the larger companies, such as DynCorp International, operate in all three categories, but this is exceptional; most companies specialize in only one category.

US military officers frequently discuss tooth-to-tail ratios in campaigns. *Tooth* refers to combat arms units, while *tail* refers to combat service and combat service support. How the private sector's tooth-to-tail ratio compares with that of the US military is unknown and worthy of further study. Based on preliminary numbers of armed contacts and trainers, such as the WPPS or security force assistance contracts, one would expect the private sector ratio to be overwhelmingly tail compared with that of the US national army. But as the Nisour Square and Abu Ghraib scandals demonstrate, numbers may not be the best measure of campaign significance, as the mistakes of a few contractors had a strongly negative strategic effect for their employer. Owing to these and other incidents, PMCs remain the most controversial component of private armies: they represent for-profit killing and the commodification of conflict.

Secrecy and lack of data have hobbled understanding of the private military industry, leading to confusing and conflicting accounts of who is and is not a member. The best way to comprehend the contours of the industry is in terms of the United States' own military. The United States birthed this industry for its wars in Iraq and Afghanistan, and, unsurprisingly, the industry mirrored the client's own army. PMC leadership, culture, and operational concepts are all derivative of the US military, which is very appealing to the client.

However, this raises disconcerting questions about the relationship between client and companies. Are the bonds between the United States and the private military industry too close? Do conflicts of interest exist? Does this relationship ultimately extend or limit American power? When the United States invaded Iraq, few imagined at the time that it would also introduce a new norm in modern warfare: the privatization of war. The next chapter explores the deepening dependency between the superpower and the private military industry and implications for the American way of war.

A Codependency Problem

To place any dependence upon militia, is, assuredly, resting upon a broken staff.

—George Washington

Contractors have been present on US battlefields since the American Revolution, but never before has the country relied so heavily on their services to wage war. Consequently, war has become big business again. In little more than a decade, the industry has expanded from a multimillion-dollar to a multibillion-dollar affair. The market's value remains unknown; expert estimates range wildly from $20 billion to $100 billion annually.[1] What is known is that from 1999 to 2008, the US Department of Defense (DOD) contract obligations—for both security and nonsecurity functions—increased from $165 billion to $414 billion.[2] In 2010, DOD obligated $366 billion to contracts (54 percent of total DOD obligations), an amount six times the United Kingdom's entire defense budget.[3] Moreover, this only entails DOD contract obligations and does not include contracts made by other government agencies, such as the State Department or USAID, through its "implementing partners." The actual amount the United States paid for purely security contracts remains unknown.

The manifestations of the new market are stark. Not surprisingly, the number of contractors supporting operations in Iraq and Afghanistan has reached historic proportions compared with earlier US wars (see figure 3.1). For example, in 2010, the United States deployed 175,000 troops and 207,000 contractors in war zones. During World War II, contractors accounted for only 10 percent of the military workforce, compared with 50 percent in Iraq today, a 1:1 ratio of contractors to military personnel. As the number of troops in Iraq has decreased, so, too, has the number of contractors. From 2008 to 2010, troop levels dropped by 57,400 (37 percent) and the number of contractors by approximately 67,000 (41 percent). However, this reduction is not uniform across the types of contracted personnel. Those providing base support and construction declined by approximately 27,400 (31 percent) and 34,000 (94 percent), respectively,

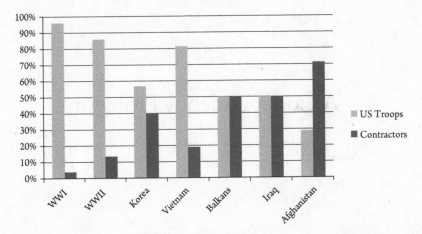

Figure 3.1 Contractors as Percentage of US Military Workforce in Theaters of War (as of March 2010).

whereas the number of armed contractors actually increased by 2,417 (26 percent), which is significant.[4]

Contractors are also paying the ultimate sacrifice, accounting, in a rising trend, for 25 percent of all US fatalities since the wars in Iraq and Afghanistan began. In 2003, contractor deaths represented only 4 percent of all fatalities. That number rose to 27 percent from 2004 to 2007, and from 2008 to 2010, contractor fatalities accounted for 40 percent of the combined death toll. In 2010, more contractors were killed than military personnel, marking the first time in history that corporate casualties outweighed military losses on US battlefields. In the first two quarters of 2010 alone, contractor deaths represented more than half, 53 percent, of all fatalities (see figures 3.2 and 3.3).[5]

The exact numbers are difficult to reach, as the US government does not track such data, and companies have a propensity to underreport their wounded and dead, as it is bad for business.[6] But overall, this trend suggests a growing US dependency on the private military industry in warfare, and unless the United States decides to significantly expand its public armed forces or reduce military engagement abroad, this trend toward the privatization of warfare will continue.

To address this development, the US Army commissioned an independent internal study led by top military logisticians, who issued their report in 2007, titled *Urgent Reform Required: Army Expeditionary Contracting*, also known as the Gansler Report after its chairman, Jacques Gansler. The panel found that the "Operational Army" is "expeditionary and on a war footing but does not yet fully recognize the impact of contractors in expeditionary operations and on mission success." Furthermore, panel members unanimously agreed that "acquisition failures in expeditionary operations urgently require a systemic fix of Army

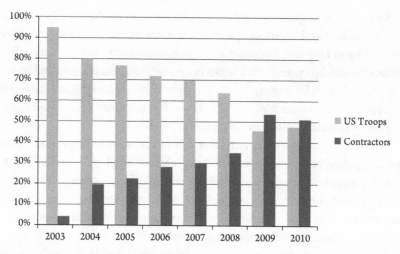

Figure 3.2   Percent Breakdown of Fatalities in Iraq.

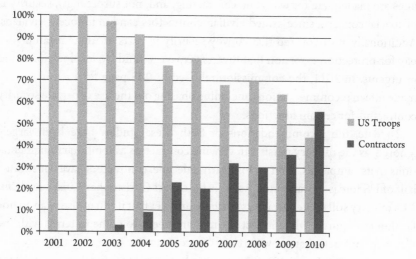

Figure 3.3   Percent Breakdown of Fatalities in Afghanistan.

contracting" and recommended sweeping changes in four broad areas: first, establishing effective laws, regulations, and policies to govern contracting, especially for expeditionary operations; second, fundamentally restructuring and reorganizing Army institutions to better manage and integrate contractors into operations; third, increasing the stature, quantity, and career development of military and civilian contracting personnel (especially for expeditionary operations), including introducing contract management into all levels of military education; and fourth, providing the training and tools necessary for overall contracting activities in expeditionary operations.[7]

A year later, Congress established the Commission on Wartime Contracting, an independent and bipartisan panel of eight senior experts, to study wartime contracting in Iraq and Afghanistan. Its purpose was to examine waste, fraud, abuse, accountability, and other issues in conflict-zone contracting and to make recommendations for improvement. The commission found that at least $31 billion, and possibly as much as $60 billion, was lost to contract waste and fraud in Iraq and Afghanistan, much of which was avoidable.[8]

The commission also discovered that contractors were often performing jobs that law, policy, or regulation required government employees to do. Excessive reliance on contractors also had other deleterious effects: creating unreasonable risks to mission objectives and other key US interests, eroding federal agencies' ability to perform core capabilities, and overwhelming the government's ability to effectively manage and oversee contractors.

One of the commission's central questions was what tasks are "inherently governmental" and should never be outsourced. It found that existing guidelines are inadequate for war-zone contracting, and, not surprisingly, security is of special concern, since armed civilian contractors can kill innocent civilians. Additionally, it discovered that convoy security in parts of Afghanistan invites pay-for-protection extortion that diverts taxpayers' funds to local warlords and insurgents. In 2011, the commission released its 248-page final report, which made fifteen recommendations, including phasing out the use of private security contractors for certain functions.

To date, the recommendations of both these studies have been largely ignored, as the military persists in viewing contractors as temporary augmentations to its campaigns, even as, for nearly a decade, contractors have constituted half of US forces in war zones. As industry expert Christopher Kinsey explains, "the military still sees contractors as a bolt-on asset that it can utilise in an ad hoc fashion as required, when in fact the military needs to come to terms with the idea that contractors are now part of its force structure."[9]

The 2010 Quadrennial Defense Review by the military finally acknowledged the military's "dependence" on contractors and its intention to reduce it through an "in-sourcing initiative." However, this program will not apply to contractors in conflict areas.[10] In a widely distributed memorandum, Secretary of Defense Bob Gates confirms that the number of contractors in war zones "well exceeded" military personnel and added, "I do not expect this to change now or in future contingency operations."[11]

In addition to the increasing US dependence on the private sector to wage war, the types of private actors are also expanding. The vast majority of contractors in Iraq and other places are unarmed and provide nonlethal logistical support, such as construction, maintenance, and administrative duties (see figure 3.4). Logistics is the traditional role of contractors on the battlefield, and today's

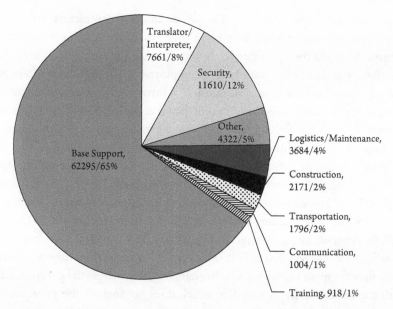

Figure 3.4 US Military Contractors in Iraq by Type of Service Provided (as of March 2010).

largest contracts remain logistical in nature, such as the US Army's Logistics Civil Augmentation Program (LOGCAP, worth up to $22 billion). What is new, and controversial, is the presence of armed contractors. To many, the decision to outsource lethality to armed civilians in foreign lands, who are tasked to kill people when necessary, smacks of mercenarism.

PMCs account for 12 percent, or 11,610, of the overall contracting force in Iraq in 2010 and 14,439 in Afghanistan, representing a minority of all contractors in theater.[12] But size does not matter when it comes to armed contractors. Even though they are fewer in number than their unarmed brethren, their actions resonate disproportionately more loudly, owing to the nature of their work: they kill people. When a handful of Blackwater personnel killed seventeen innocent civilians at Nisour Square in Baghdad on September 16, 2007, it created a firestorm of anti-US sentiment that undermined the US counterinsurgency strategy of "winning hearts and minds" in Iraq and generated such international ill will that Secretary of State Condoleezza Rice had to publicly address the shooting and launch an official investigation.[13] Despite the pandemonium, the Blackwater contractors walked free, because they are immune from Iraqi law, in accordance with Order 17 of the Coalition Provisional Authority.[14] Many were outraged, including Iraq Prime Minister Nuri al-Maliki, who angrily declared, "It cannot be accepted by an American security company to carry out a killing. These are very serious challenges to the sovereignty of Iraq."[15]

A common misperception is that private military contractors make enormous sums of money when they serve overseas. This is not necessarily true. Companies make their profit on "time and materials," meaning that they charge the client a premium for every hour an employee works or for every item purchased, no matter how small. For example, a firm may bill the government $40 an hour for an employee's time yet only pay that person $30 an hour. The difference between the "billing rate" and what a firm actually pays for the time or material covers the contractor's indirect costs, overhead, and profit.

In the past, some critics have claimed that private armies are more expensive than public ones. For example, Joseph Stiglitz and Linda Bilmes estimate that in 2007 in Iraq, "private security guards working for companies such as Blackwater and DynCorp were earning up to $1,222 a day; this amounts to $445,000 a year. By contrast, an Army sergeant was earning $140 to $190 a day in pay and benefits, a total of $51,100 to $69,350 a year."[16] However, this analysis is flawed, since they compare a company's billing rate—what it charges the government—with the annual salary of a soldier, which does not include the government's indirect costs and overhead, such as health care, the use of vehicles, housing, hazardous-duty pay, pension, and so forth. Fundamental confusion regarding how firms make their money has led to misleading conclusions about the private sector's efficiency.

Currently, most PMCs are headquartered in the United States, and members of the senior management are US citizens, but, like all multinational corporations, the companies maintain offices in several countries. Should one government, such as the United States or the United Kingdom, impose strict regulations on their trade, they could move offshore. Dubai is a favorite hub for the industry owing to its proximity to the markets (i.e., the Middle East and Africa) and its business-friendly laws.

In terms of personnel, these new military multinational corporations are comparable to the private armies of old. The people who fill their ranks are densely international. In Iraq, only 26 percent of contractors are US citizens. In Afghanistan, the number is only 14 percent.[17] Personnel who work for PMCs fall into one of three categories. The first is US citizens, who make up only 20 percent of the contractor workforce, according to the Congressional Budget Office.[18] They generally fill management positions and highly technical jobs, such as engineering or legal services, and receive the highest pay. A second category is local hires or local nationals, citizens of the country in which the firm is working (e.g., Iraqis working in Iraq). Local hires usually account for the bulk of contractors overseas, and they perform a wide range of mundane tasks, such as driving, food preparation, and interpreting. This is also the lowest-paid category. The last category is third-country nationals (TCNs), who are neither US nor local citizens. TCNs hail from countries as diverse as India, Fiji, Ghana, Ecuador,

Australia, Mexico, and South Africa.[19] They typically do not fill significant management positions and are almost always paid less than a US counterpart, even if the job is identical and the two are working side by side.

In other words, most American PMC personnel are not American. According to a DOD report, more than 85,000 contractors were working for U.S. Central Command in Afghanistan in 2013. Of these, approximately 16,000, or 18 percent, provided security and training, with the rest performing functions such as construction and base support. Less than 10 percent were American, and more than 80 percent were Afghan nationals. The DOD listed approximately 2,400 individuals providing private security services in Iraq, mostly TCNs.[20] What is significant for the future of the industry is that these TCNs and local hires are gaining valuable trade knowledge that they can use to found new PMCs that are less picky about whom they work for and how they do it.

The US penchant to lean on the private sector in war has produced the modern mercenary. Half of the country's military force structure was contractors in Iraq and Afghanistan, and, short of conscription, it is unlikely that the superpower could have sustained two multiyear wars simultaneously without them. This was a convenient political solution for the country's leadership at the time, since premature withdrawal from Iraq and Afghanistan would look like Vietnam-era defeat, and a national draft was unthinkable. However, this solution came at a cost. In the process, the superpower unleashed a new norm in international relations: the legitimate use of private military force, or what many call mercenarism.

4

How Did We Get Here?

And history with all her volumes vast, Hath but one page.
—Lord Byron, *Childe Harold's Pilgrimage,*
Canto IV (1818), Stanza 108

It is a familiar story. A superpower goes to war and faces a stronger-than-expected insurgency in distant lands yet has insufficient forces to counter it because of political and military constraints. The superpower decides to hire contractors, some of whom are armed, to support its war effort. The armed contractors prove to be both a blessing and a curse, providing vital security services to the campaign yet at times killing innocent civilians in their zeal, causing strategic setbacks and damaging the superpower's legitimacy. Without these contractors, it would be hard for the superpower to wage war, but with them, it is difficult to win.

The armed contractors in question are not in Iraq or Afghanistan but in northern Italy, and the year is not 2007 but 1377. The superpower in question is not the United States but the papacy under Pope Gregory XI, who was fighting the antipapal league led by the duchy of Milan.[1] The tragic killing of civilians by armed contractors did not occur in Baghdad but in Cesena, 630 years earlier. The military companies employed were not DynCorp International, Triple Canopy, or Blackwater but the Company of the Star, the Company of the Hat, and the White Company. Known as free companies, these for-profit warriors were organized as corporations, with a well-articulated hierarchy of subcommanders and administrative machinery that oversaw the fair distribution of loot according to employees' contracts. CEO-like captains led these medieval PMCs.

One of the most famous mercenary captains was Englishman Sir John Hawkwood, who led the transalpine White Company. He achieved international celebrity on the battlefield, earning fame and fortune. He served as England's ambassador to the Roman court, received angry letters from Saint Catherine of Siena, and joined English writer Geoffrey Chaucer, Flemish chronicler Jean Froissart, and Italian humanist Francesco Petrarch at a lavish wedding feast for King Edward III's son.[2]

Contemporaries admired and reviled him. According to fourteenth-century Italian storyteller Franco Sacchetti, two Franciscan monks encountered Hawkwood near his fortress at Montecchio. The monks greeted him with the standard salutation, "May God grant you peace." Hawkwood coldly replied, "And may God take away your alms." Shocked by this rudeness, the monks demanded an explanation. "Don't you know that I live by war," Hawkwood answered, "and peace would destroy me? And as I live by war so you live by alms." Sacchetti adds: "And so, he managed his affairs so well that there was little peace in Italy in his times."[3]

The parallels between earlier and modern PMCs are strong. Today the United States and other countries employ contractors to fulfill security-related contracts in Iraq, Afghanistan, and elsewhere. In the late Middle Ages, such men were called *condottieri*—literally, "contractors"—who agreed to perform security services described in written contracts, or *condotte*. Both modern and medieval contractors were organized as legal corporations, selling their services to the highest or most powerful bidder for profit. Both filled their ranks with professional men of arms drawn from different countries and loyal primarily to the paycheck. Both have functioned as private armies, usually offering land-based combat skills rather than naval (or aerial) capabilities and deploying force in a military manner rather than as law enforcement or police.

Both historical and contemporary PMCs have been international in composition. Although the mercenary companies in the high Middle Ages fought mostly in northern Italy, their ranks swelled with men from every corner of Europe and even Muslim Saracens from the Levant. Private armies today also gravitate to where the fighting is, such as Iraq and Afghanistan, yet they employ personnel and subcontractors from all over the world. Differences also exist, as ancient firms were private armies akin to Executive Outcomes rather than today's weaker PMCs, but suffice it to say that today's firms share DNA with their ancestors.

Private Military History

Mercenaries fight primarily for profit rather than politics, and the job is as old as war itself, often referred to as the second-oldest profession. The word *mercenary* comes from the Latin *merces* ("wages" or "pay"); today it connotes vileness, treachery, and murder. But it was not always so. Being a mercenary was once considered an honest albeit bloody trade, and employing mercenaries to fight wars was routine throughout most of military history: King Shulgi of Ur's army (2094–2047 BC); Xenophon's army of Greek mercenaries known as the Ten Thousand (401–399 BC); and Carthage's mercenary armies in the Punic Wars against Rome (264–146 BC), including Hannibal's sixty-thousand-strong army, which marched elephants over the Alps to attack Rome from the north. When Alexander invaded Asia in 334 BC, his army included five thousand foreign mercenaries, and the Persian army that faced him contained ten thousand Greeks. In fact, Greek mercenaries were core to his military campaign, on all sides of the conflict.

Rome relied on mercenaries throughout its thousand-year reign, and Julius Caesar was repeatedly saved, even at Alesia, by mounted German mercenaries in his war against Vercingetorix in Gaul. Nearly half of William the Conqueror's army in the eleventh century were mercenaries, as he could not afford a large standing army, and there were not enough nobles and knights to accomplish the Norman conquest of England. In Egypt and Syria, the Mamluk sultanate (1250–1517) was a regime of mercenary slaves who had been converted to Islam. From the late tenth to the early fifteenth centuries, Byzantine emperors surrounded themselves with Norse mercenaries, the Varangian Guard, who were known for their fierce loyalty, prowess with the battle ax, and ability to swill copious amounts of alcohol. In Europe, the *condottieri*, Swiss companies, *landsknechts*, Bretons, Gascons, Picards, and other mercenaries dominated warfare from the thirteenth to the sixteenth centuries. The list is long. For at least three thousand years, private military force has been a feature—often the major feature—of warfare.

Independent mercenaries foster a different kind of armed conflict: contract warfare. Contract warfare is literally a free market for force, where private armies and clients seek each other out, negotiate prices, and wage wars for personal gain. There were problems with this way of war, especially in the European Middle Ages, when bands of brigands sold their services to the highest bidder during wartime and became marauders in times of peace, raiding and ravaging the countryside. In extreme cases, such as medieval Italy, this attracted more fortune-seeking mercenaries, perpetuating a tragic cycle that resulted in ceaseless conflict.

Continuous wars combined with a lack of economic opportunity swelled mercenary ranks, which drew warriors of all stripes from across the continent. Italy was awash in free companies during this tumultuous era. In France, they fought in the Hundred Years War and were known as *routiers* or *écorcheurs* (literally, "skinners of dead bodies"). In Spain, they fought for both Peters in the war between Peter the Cruel of Castile and Peter the Ceremonious of Aragon. Hiring private armies was how war was usually fought.

This way of warfare gradually changed between the sixteenth and twentieth centuries, shifting from a free market for force dominated by mercenaries to a monopoly controlled by states and their national militaries. This transformation coincided with states' steady consolidation of power during the Middle Ages over political rivals such as the church, the Holy Roman Emperor, city-states, and aristocratic families, all of which used mercenaries to assert their sovereignty over one another. States invested in their own standing armies, loyal only to them, and outlawed mercenaries, eventually driving them out of business and leaving their nonstate adversaries defenseless.

States' monopolization of the market for force was gradual. In the hundred years leading up to 1650, warfare became increasingly violent as armies grew larger, weapons increasingly destructive, and consequences more grave. Power struggles such as those between Habsburg Spain and Holland, Habsburg Austria and the Ottomans, or French Huguenots and French Catholics, dragged on for decades, and the demand for force was great. The reliance on mercenaries was ubiquitous, and the overall cost of warfare was little more than the *solde*, or "pay," due to mercenaries, from which the word *soldier* is derived. Battles were fought mostly between hired units, and as one military historian explains, "by and large, the military forces of every country consisted of mercenaries."[4]

During the Thirty Years War (1618–1648), for example, the majority of Sweden's military was mercenary, a significant number given that Sweden was a military superpower at the time and that King Gustavus Adolphus was one of the great innovators of maneuver warfare. At the Battle of Breitenfeld, only 20 percent of Sweden's army consisted of Swedes, and at the Battle of Lützen, the figure was 18 percent. European armies were an amalgamation of mercenaries, and the concept of patriotism was unconnected to military service.[5]

By the middle of the seventeenth century, the conduct of violence was a capitalist enterprise no different from any other industry. According to historian Michael Howard, "war became the biggest industry in Europe," as each side bought and brought increasing numbers of troops to the battlefield.[6] Major engagements during this period typically involved fifty thousand soldiers, as evidenced by the battles of White Mountain (1620), Breitenfeld (1631), Lützen (1632), Nördlingen (1634), Wittstock (1636), and Rocroi (1643).

To meet the rising demand for troops, a new breed of conflict entrepreneur emerged, *military enterprisers*, who outfitted entire regiments and leased them to those in need of martial services. Distinct from mercenaries, military enterprisers raised armies rather than commanding them. These "rental regiments" or contractor armies allowed rulers to wage war on a grand scale without undue administrative or fiscal reform, effectively lowering the barrier to entry in war and encouraging ever-larger battles. Examples of the greatest military enterprisers include Count Ernest Mansfeld, who raised an entire army for the Elector Palatine; Amsterdam businessman Louis de Geer, who sourced for Sweden a complete operative navy; the Genovese marquis of Spinola, who managed the king of Spain's military affairs in the Netherlands; and Bernard von Weimar, who produced armies for Sweden and then France. Most famously, Count Albrecht von Wallenstein offered his services plus an army to Holy Roman Emperor Ferdinand II and eventually became the supreme commander of the Habsburg monarchy's armies and the richest man in Europe. By the end of the war, the market had moved beyond oligarchs like Wallenstein to smaller actors, such as mercenary colonels and merchant financiers, empowered by credit and supply networks based in Amsterdam, Hamburg, and Genoa.

Military enterprisers differ from mercenaries in significant ways and represent the median point in the gradual transition from private to public armies, as they were a hybrid of both. Like mercenaries, they are private sector actors involved in armed conflict and motivated chiefly by profit. Unlike mercenaries, they typically worked in monogamous public-private partnerships with a government client to build armies rather than deploying them. They are hybrids of private and public armies, imperfectly blending the profit motive of the former with the loyalty of the latter.

Military enterprisers were attractive to states for two reasons. First, having private military actors generate but not control armed force is less threatening to the client, as medieval mercenaries sometimes operated as a security racket. Second, demanding that private military actors work exclusively for the client was safer, too, as it discouraged defections to the enemy. By the seventeenth century, states were sufficiently powerful to demand such concessions from the market.

This arrangement also served private military actors, since they were often victims of faithless employers and preferred long-term, paying clients in perpetual need of armies. Military enterprisers had other reasons to remain faithful servants to their clients. According to historian David Parrott, they aspired to join the ranks of the military-obsessed European elite and therefore remained loyal to their aristocratic employers, because this bequeathed cultural and social benefits associated with military involvement. Such benefits would be nullified if they were perceived to act against the ruler in whose state they wished to enjoy these benefits. Also, unlike the *condottieri* captains, military enterprisers were often victims of their own success. Employers often made it treasonous for able enterprisers to abandon their contracts and had the power to enforce this clause, causing the enterpriser to lose both fortune and head.[7] Such was the case of Wallenstein, who was perhaps falsely accused of treachery and killed in 1634. His death remains shrouded in controversy.

Such public-private partnerships changed the business of war, transforming it from a free to a mediated market for force. In a free market, consumers and suppliers of warfare sought each other out, negotiated a price, and waged war. Both sides of the bargain were generally unconstrained, and the marketplace was laissez-faire in nature. For example, mercenaries such as *condottieri* often worked for the highest bidder, changed sides when it suited their purses, sought wars out, and occasionally started them. When business was slow, they often pillaged the countryside until they were hired by a client or paid to go away. In many ways, mercenaries and the free market for force perpetuated armed conflict.

This contrasts with a mediated market, which imbued a modicum of restraint into force providers and their patrons. Long-term and exclusive public-private partnerships aligned the interests of client and mercenary, making it harder for either side to defect and infusing stability into the marketplace. For example, Wallenstein was not incentivized to betray Ferdinand II, because the ruler was his main source of profit. Nor was Ferdinand II motivated to break his contract with Wallenstein, as the enterpriser was his primary supplier of armed forces during a war of survival. In other words, they were codependent in ways that medieval mercenaries and their clientele were not. Such relationships had existed in the past, as with Hawkwood and Florence, but by Wallenstein's time, they were dominant. The presence of shared, long-term interests restrained corrupt behaviors and therefore mediated the market for force.

However, this did not necessarily make the market safer. While monarchs found the loyalty of military enterprisers attractive, populations were less enamored with their contractor armies. The havoc wreaked by these behemoth forces was not limited to the battlefield. They sustained themselves by pilfering the countryside, sometimes violently and often lawlessly, and the tyranny of plunder wore heavily on civilian populations. Rectifying the social damage caused by en masse larceny was expensive for employers, who consequently attempted to station troops away from population centers and ideally to deploy them in offensive campaigns in foreign lands. However, this was not always possible. The inhabitants of Brandenburg complained bitterly that the mercenaries guarding them were far more terrible than the enemy Swedes outside the city walls, and they begged their ruler, Frederick William, the Great Elector, to disband the unruly companies. Assessing the situation, the elector wrote in April 1641: "We find that our military forces have cost the country a great deal and done much wanton damage. The enemy could not have done worse. We do not see that we have had, or are likely to have, the least benefit from their services. Therefore we have resolved to keep only what is necessary as a garrison for our fortresses."[8]

The elector's sentiments were not unique. The unrestrained actions of mercenaries caused widespread destruction and misery in the course of the Thirty Years War. These mercenary companies were often intractable and could usurp their employers if left unchecked. Additionally, because they were recruited only during a military emergency and dismissed immediately at its conclusion, they frequently roamed the countryside like brigands of the Middle Ages while awaiting new contracts. These and other bitter experiences taught both rulers and ruled that they could not entrust the protection of their homeland to unreliable mercenaries. At the conclusion of the Peace of Westphalia in 1648, leaders of all sides tacitly agreed that an open market for force was too destructive and expensive to continue and that public armies should replace private ones; that is, the state should take over.

The State Monopolizes Force

Shortly after the Peace of Westphalia, the Holy Roman Emperor Ferdinand III established the first peacetime field army in the history of the monarchy. He issued a decree in 1649 announcing that of the fifty-two regiments raised during the great war, nine infantry (including both pike and shot) and ten cavalry (one of dragoons and nine of cuirassiers) would not be demobilized with the rest but would remain as permanent units. Previously, there had been small attempts to create standing public armies. The force of King Charles VII of France in 1445 consisted of nine thousand French soldiers. Rudolf II of Austria had three winter regiments in 1598 at key fortifications along his frontier. Hungarian king Matthias Corvinus's Fekete Sereg, or Black Army, captured parts of Austria and Bohemia in the fifteenth century. However, these antecedents did not attempt to dislodge private armies and take over the market for force. The size, scale, and scope of Ferdinand's ambitions were unprecedented, as he sought to expunge the need for mercenaries and thus began the state's monopoly on violence, the end of private armies, and the beginning of modern public armies.

The transition from private to public armies was gradual, spanning centuries. It arguably began in the sixteenth century, and by 1650, it was clear that on-demand military services were no longer economical to rulers, given the destruction that mercenaries wrought upon the countryside and the threat they posed to their employers. What was needed was a public army of systematically trained and disciplined professionals, maintained in peace and war, winter and summer, with a regular means of obtaining supplies and replacements. Critically, this military force would be paid by and loyal to the state, unequivocally. Following the Thirty Years War, the Great Elector of Brandenburg-Prussia retained four thousand soldiers and increased that number to twelve thousand after the Northern War (1655–1660). Wurttemberg, Hesse, Saxony, and Bavaria undertook similar efforts.

France formed a standing army by absorbing most of Louis XIV's officers into the *gendarmerie* and establishing six standing infantry units that endured after the Peace of the Pyrenees (1659). These regiments enabled the Sun King to mobilize his armies swiftly in the War of Devolution and overrun the Habsburg-controlled Spanish Netherlands and the Franche-Comté, encouraging him to create an even larger standing army at the end of the war in 1668. Concurrently, in England, Oliver Cromwell's New Model Army was a prototype standing army, and after the Restoration of 1660, Charles II was permitted to retain five regiments from this force, totaling about three thousand men, to garrison his fortresses as royal guards.

These early efforts were the germ of the large national militaries centuries later. As military historian John Mears explains, "the nature of military conflict in the seventeenth century provided a further impetus for the creation of permanent armed forces ... giving them an appearance which men in the twentieth century can recognize as being distinctly modern."[9]

Technological improvements in weaponry helped make public armies possible. Previously, mercenaries provided not only on-demand military services but also highly specialized ones. The Swiss Guard delivered precision tactics in the heat of battle that required extensive training. Similarly, the heavy crossbow known as the *balestrieri*, with armor-piercing bolts, required a significant investment of time and training to use with any skill in combat, especially against moving or ranged targets.

The cost of developing similar in-house capabilities for states was simply too high, which is why they outsourced these needs in the Middle Ages. However, the need to outsource began to change with the advent of the musket, which allowed relatively unskilled infantry to punch holes in the armor of highly skilled knights, killing them from a safe distance. Also, the declining price of gunpowder made training musketeers cheaper and less time-consuming, giving rise to the possibility of the citizen-soldier. Combining this with the practice of conscription, rulers discovered that they could muster large national armies without the risks associated with mercenaries.

Napoleonic reforms also helped consolidate the states' monopoly of force. The armies that swept across Europe under Napoleon's command were mostly made up of French citizens, mustered under *levée en masse*, rather than professional soldiers. With the decisive French victory over and occupation of Prussia following the twin battles of Jena and Auerstedt in 1806, Prussia quickly adopted a citizen-soldier model and rejoined the campaign later to help defeat the French forces. As the Napoleonic wars continued, this model of national conscription eventually became the norm for all powers, and it survives today, as demonstrated by the modern draft.

Administrative changes also helped put private armies out of business. Sustaining a large standing army is complicated and expensive, requiring a considerable bureaucracy to collect taxes and administer revenue. Over time, large centralized state bureaucracies replaced feudal lordships in the machinations of governance and especially military administration. Louis XIV established a sophisticated bureaucracy to manage state affairs at the expense of the estates and the great nobles. Influenced by Swedish ideas and the reforms of Gustavus Adolphus, Secretary of State for War Michel le Tellier and his son the marquis de Louvois managed the *intendants de l'armée* that reorganized the French army into a pyramidal structure of responsibility and authority, led by generals and managed by bureaucrats. It eventually grew to four hundred thousand soldiers.

Modeling this bureaucracy, Great Elector Frederick William, ruler of Brandenburg-Prussia, created the *Generalkriegskommissariat* in 1655, with subordinate officials in each of his various territories. This bureaucracy eventually eclipsed the authority of local aristocrats on all matters of finance and taxation connected with the army. Paying for the new civil service and soldiers mandated an ever-increasing tax base built on an economy unfettered by marauding mercenaries, reinforcing the need to outlaw private armies. By the end of the eighteenth century, the bureaucracy and the army were so big in relation to the total population that the marquis de Mirabeau reputedly quipped, "Prussia is not a state with an army, but an army with a state."[10]

Enlightenment ideas and their accompanying political revolutions also spurred the demise of private armies by strengthening the bond between soldier and state. Previously, mercenary organizations were a conglomeration of nationalities bound by a desire for profit, a shared "command language" for issuing military orders, and perhaps loyalty toward colleagues. Although some private armies, such as the Swiss companies, consisted of a single nationality, most were a multinational lot, such as the *landsknechts*. This began to change when ideas of rationalism, the social contract, and natural rights emerged from the English, American, and French revolutions, ushering in a new era that transformed the individual from royal subject to national citizen and proclaimed that kings no longer ruled by the divine right of God but did so by the consent of the ruled, on pain of death. However, with new privileges came new responsibilities. Just as the state was obliged to protect citizens' rights, citizens were duty-bound to defend the state, as demonstrated by the *levée en masse* that swelled Napoleon's ranks. The revolutions cemented a bond between individual and state, giving rise to nationalism and linking military service to patriotic duty.

Over time, the state became the principal market actor for force and outlawed the competition, such as mercenaries, for fear that they could physically threaten the government's existence. The only exception to this was for states that wished to "rent" their armies to other states for a profit rather than a cause. During the American Revolutionary War, Great Britain hired nearly thirty thousand soldiers from German states, mostly from Hesse-Kassel, to quell the colonial revolt. The American rebels called these German soldiers Hessians. German states became factories of state-sponsored mercenarism, supplying tens of thousands of German soldiers to other national powers in the soldier trade (*Soldatenhandel*). In a sign of the times, what was once considered a legitimate practice became morally repugnant, attracting pejorative labels such as *Menschenhandel* (trade in human beings), *Menschenverkauf* (sale of human beings), or *Seelenverkauf* (sale of souls).

Similarly, although pirates were strictly outlawed and typically faced the gallows if caught, it was considered legitimate for states to hire private warships, or privateers, by issuing a letter of marque to attack enemy ships. Privateers were even allowed to pilfer as part of the prize. The key difference between a pirate and a privateer was normative. Acts of piracy were deemed illegal, because, as a nineteenth-century jurist explained, they were "done under conditions which render it impossible or unfair to hold any state responsible for their commission."[11]

States also delegated military affairs to quasi-state-run trading companies such as the East India Company, which commanded its own armed forces and governed India for Great Britain for more than two centuries. The last incident in which a state raised an army of foreigners was in 1854, when Great Britain hired 16,500 mercenaries for the Crimean War (although none saw battle, because the war ended before they arrived in theater). By 1900, the practice of utilizing private forces, even when state-sponsored, was defunct.

The Black Market for Force

In the twentieth century, the Westphalian order was at its zenith, and the free market for force was pushed underground. World War I, World War II, and the Cold War were emblematic conflicts of the period, waged between "great power" nations using huge public militaries as gladiators to settle political disputes. The privilege of legitimately waging war was arrogated exclusively to states and their militaries and was the view espoused in international relations theory, which arose during this period.

In fact, so Westphalian were the emergent "laws of war" that they sought only to regulate interstate warfare and largely ignored armed nonstate actors. Early laws of war, such as the Lieber Code (1863), the First Geneva Convention (1864), and the Hague Conventions (1899 and 1907), simply codified nineteenth-century customs of war as fought between national armies. States developed a positive legal regime through multilateral treaties that dictated appropriate behaviors on the battlefield between their armies. In other words, the laws of war codified battlefield custom originating in European religion, chivalry, and culture. Historian and legal scholar Geoffrey Best describes the period from 1856 to 1909 as the "epoch of highest repute" for war etiquette.[12]

By the middle of the twentieth century, Western powers declared that the laws of war applied to all armed actors everywhere. After World War II, the

Nuremberg War Trial pronounced that treaties such as the Hague Convention of 1907 "were recognized by all civilised nations" for half a century and were thus customary laws of war and binding on all parties, whether the party was a signatory to the specific treaty or not.[13] This is reaffirmed in the 1998 treaty known as the Rome Statute of the International Criminal Court, which claims universal jurisdiction.[14] Modern notions regarding the laws of war are what chiefly separate "regular" from "irregular" warfare, the former being "acceptable" killing by "legitimate" Westphalian powers, whereas the latter is typically the purview of nonstate actors and tantamount to dishonorable practices such as murder, torture, deception, and other "war crimes."

Despite the strong norm against mercenaries, state-sponsored mercenarism continued into the twentieth century.[15] The Flying Tigers—the popular name of the 1st American Volunteer Group of the Chinese Air Force in 1941–1942—consisted of some sixty Curtiss P-40 shark-faced fighter planes based in Burma, which flew missions against Japanese forces occupying China. The unit was staffed by mostly former US military personnel and pilots and its deployment was little more than a way for the United States to combat Japan before war was formally declared. Monthly salaries varied but were all substantially higher than those of the US public military: $250 for a skilled ground crewman, $600 for a pilot officer, and $675 for a flight leader.[16] Squadron commanders received $750 a month, or $11,486.65 in 2010 dollars. In many ways, the Flying Tigers were precursors of modern PMCs.

The first PMC was WatchGuard International, formed in 1965 and registered in island of Jersey by David Stirling and John Woodhouse. Stirling also founded the British Special Air Services (SAS) and staffed WatchGuard International with SAS veterans. The SAS is the United Kingdom's elite special forces regiment, highly trained in covert operations, guerrilla warfare, and counterinsurgency. The PMC operated mostly in the Gulf States but worked worldwide, and its services included training foreign forces, supporting operations against insurgents, and providing military advisory teams to governments in the Middle East, Africa, Latin America, and East Asia.

WatchGuard International followed the military enterpriser model, ostensibly working with the United Kingdom. It was the first of many British PMCs in an era when such firms were unknown. Following WatchGuard International, other British PMCs emerged to take its place, all led by ex–SAS officers and largely staffed with former SAS soldiers: SAS counter terrorism warfare team leader Ian Crooke ran Kilo Alpha Services (KAS); SAS squadron leader Arish Turtle managed Control Risks; SAS counterespionage specialist H.M.P.D. Harclerode ran J. Donne Holdings; SAS South American specialist David Walker; and SAS group intelligence officer Andrew Nightingale managed both Keenie Meenie Services and also Saladin Security. Like WatchGuard International, they worked in dangerous places with unpalatable regimes and conducted risky security operations that most Western governments would wish to avoid.

However, WatchGuard International and the SAS-PMCs are exceptional. Most mercenaries during this period led illicit lives, operating as private warriors in the shadows rather than as for-profit companies in the open market. Individual soldiers of fortune bounced between geopolitical hot spots in China, Latin America, and especially Africa. Their employers included rebel groups, weak governments, multinational firms operating in precarious regions, and former colonial powers that desired clandestine influence in the affairs of their past colonies. The decolonization that followed World War II offered particularly rich opportunities for these private warriors.

The Congo Crisis of 1960–1968 began with national independence from Belgium and ended with the seizing of power by Joseph Mobutu, causing the deaths of tens of thousands of people. During this maelstrom of conflict, international mining companies such as Union Minière hired hundreds of mercenaries known as Les Affreux ("The Frightfuls"), including Irishman "Mad" Mike Hoare and Frenchman Bob Denard, to support the Katanga secession. Later, Hoare attempted a coup d'état of the Seychelles Islands, and Denard fought in many African countries, including Angola, Zimbabwe, Gabon, and the Comoros Islands, where he participated in four coups, the last in 1995. Their exploits informed movies such as *The Wild Geese* (1978), for which Hoare was a technical adviser, and *The Dogs of War* (1980), based on a Frederick Forsyth novel inspired by the life of Denard. These and other treatments still shape mercenary stereotypes in today's popular" imagination, summed up by a scene in *The Dogs of War* when one mercenary makes a toast before the ad hoc team embarks on its mission: *"Vive la mort! Vive la guerre! Vive le sacré mercenaire!"*[17]

It was not until the 1970s that the laws of war noticed mercenaries, and only then as a response to the African wars of decolonization in the 1960s, where a black market for mercenaries thrived. This prompted the society of states to formally proscribe mercenaries in the Third and Fourth Geneva Conventions. The primary objection to mercenaries was that they were warriors without a state, fighting for money rather than national ideology. The most widely accepted definition of a mercenary in the laws of war is in Article 47 of Protocol I Additional to the Geneva Conventions, which states as follows:

1. A mercenary shall not have the right to be a combatant or a prisoner of war.
2. A mercenary is any person who:
    a. is especially recruited locally or abroad in order to fight in an armed conflict;
    b. does, in fact, take a direct part in the hostilities;

   c. is motivated to take part in the hostilities essentially by the desire for private gain and, in fact, is promised, by or on behalf of a Party to the conflict, material compensation substantially in excess of that promised or paid to combatants of similar ranks and functions in the armed forces of that Party;

   d. is neither a national of a Party to the conflict nor a resident of territory controlled by a Party to the conflict;

   e. is not a member of the armed forces of a Party to the conflict; and

   f. has not been sent by a State which is not a Party to the conflict on official duty as a member of its armed forces.[18]

However, this definition is so restrictive yet imprecise that almost no one falls into the category. As Best remarks, "any mercenary who cannot exclude himself from this definition deserves to be shot—and his lawyer with him!"[19]

The Return of Private Armies

Shortly after the Cold War, the world witnessed the resurgence of private military force. Perhaps it is not surprising that the first real mercenary firm emerged in Africa. With the fall of the South African apartheid regime, Lieutenant-Colonel Eeben Barlow left the South African Defense Force to establish the first combat-offensive PMC, the appropriately named Executive Outcomes. Its ranks were populated by soldiers from South African special forces units, such as the 32nd Battalion and the Koevoet ("crowbar" in Afrikaans), a special counterinsurgency police force. Unlike the SAS-PMCs, Executive Outcomes was not a military enterpriser but a true mercenary firm: a private army in the mold of the old *condottieri*. It was a fully functional, self-contained military organization, complete with its own air force, which would conduct full-spectrum combat operations for the right price.

In the early days of the Rwandan genocide, Executive Outcomes approached then–UNDPKO chief Kofi Annan and offered to help contain the violence as the United Nations generated a competent peacekeeping force, which normally requires several months. Annan refused Executive Outcomes' offer, claiming later that "the world may not be ready to privatize peace."[20] This view was costly, as more than eight hundred thousand people died within one hundred days, or eight thousand people a day, more than all those killed in the American wars in Iraq and Afghanistan combined. Later, Angola, Mozambique, Uganda, and Kenya also turned to Executive Outcomes for help. Some scholars suggested, with a fair degree of hyperbole, that Executive Outcomes represented the future of armed conflict, but this has not come to pass.[21] Executive Outcomes remains an exceptional phenomenon. Taking a cue from its progenitors 350 years earlier, the South Africa government outlawed mercenaries in 1998, and Executive Outcomes was dissolved as mandated by the Regulation of Foreign Military Assistance Act.

However, Executive Outcomes' legacy lives on. The firm was loosely linked to a London-based PMC known as Sandline International, managed by former British Lieutenant Colonel Tim Spicer, British Special Air Service (SAS) officer Simon Mann, and US Army Special Forces Colonel Bernie McCabe. Connecting these two PMCs were Mann, who had worked for Executive Outcomes, and Anthony Buckingham, a British army officer–turned–oil executive who helped Executive Outcomes secure contracts in Angola.

Fearing Executive Outcomes' imminent demise in the late 1990s, Buckingham turned to Sandline for services, although the exact relationship among Executive Outcomes, Sandline, and Buckingham remains unclear. In 1997, Papua New Guinea's prime minister, Julius Chan, contracted the firm to recapture copper mines held by separatists on Bougainville Island for $36 million.[22] Sandline subcontracted most of its personnel from Executive Outcomes, only to be rebuffed by the Papua New Guinea army, which arrested and deported the contractors without shots fired. Chan was forced to resign, and the entire spectacle made world news as the Sandline Affair.

Around this time, ousted Sierra Leone president Ahmad Tejan Kabbah contracted the firm to train and equip forty thousand Kamajor militia and members of a regional peacekeeping force to overthrow the military junta and secure diamond areas. Sandline was also to provide logistical and air support to the operation and launch a full countercoup from neighboring Guinea. This, too, ended in failure, resulting in the arms-to-Africa scandal in the United Kingdom.

Later, the private warriors found themselves working for different sides. Mann led a group of mercenaries with alleged financial backing from Mark Thatcher, son of the former UK prime minister, in an attempted coup d'état of oil-rich Equatorial Guinea in 2004, known as the Wonga Coup. The coup failed, and Mann was sentenced to thirty-four years in prison, but he was released on grounds of compassion. McCabe left Sandline to become the head of global security for the Marathon Oil Corporation, which invested heavily in Equatorial Guinea and would not wish to see the country change political hands. It would be interesting to imagine a reunion between these two brothers-in-arms on opposite sides of the cell door in Equatorial Guinea's notorious Black Beach prison. As for Spicer, shortly after the United States invaded Iraq in 2003, he founded a new PMC called Aegis Defence Services and won a lucrative contract worth $293 million over three years, providing armed protection, logistical support, and intelligence services to the US government.[23] Executive Outcomes' progeny lives on today.

Over the past millennium, European rulers first encouraged, then delegitimized, and finally all but eliminated mercenarism. During the Middle Ages, conflicts were often settled on the battlefield between both sides' mercenaries, and contract warfare was common. Over time, kings and other rulers of states monopolized the market for force by investing in their own standing armies, loyal only to them, and outlawed mercenaries in order to avoid the problems associated with mercenarism.

However, this did not occur quickly. The transition from a free market of mercenaries in the Middle Ages to a monopolized one of national armies in the nineteenth century was gradual, and in between, a mediated market existed, made up of military enterprisers that were a hybrid of mercenaries and national armies. These for-profit actors built armies rather than commanding them, usually for a single government client in a monogamous public-private partnership. In some ways, military enterprisers are "dogs of war" domesticated by states, as they are mercenaries incentivized to stay in one house and obey house rules, rather than wandering the wilderness and fending for themselves. Exceptions exist, of course, but the general arc of the market for force flows from free to mediated to monopoly.

Now mercenarism is returning. Since the end of the Cold War, private military actors have reappeared in force, some as mercenaries, others as military enterprisers. Strong PMCs such as Executive Outcomes and Sandline are mercenaries organized as multinational corporations. They seek out conflicts, negotiate a price with a customer, and deploy their private army to defeat their client's foe. Weaker PMCs such as Blackwater are more analogous to military enterprisers that build forces or augment a powerful state's own armed forces rather than deploying a stand-alone military. Not all strong PMCs are mercenary, nor are all weak ones military enterprisers. However, military enterprisers can grow into mercenaries if they have the requisite resources and clientele, since an entity that knows how to build an army probably knows how to use it.

The presence of a private military industry today is significant. It indicates that the market for force is shifting back to a mediated market and that the state's monopoly on force is loosening. If this trend continues, then the world will return to a free market of mercenaries and contract warfare. Some may find this shocking; however, private military force has been the norm rather than the exception in military history, and the last four hundred years are anomalous.

5

Why Private Armies Have Returned

Is it really true that political self-interest is nobler somehow than
economic self-interest?

—Milton Friedman

Observers of history should not be surprised by the return of private armies, as
they are ubiquitous throughout the history of warfare. Yet important questions
remain regarding exactly how and why this occurred. We know that weak states
lose their monopoly of force when they lack the military muscle to dominate
armed threats. But why would the United States, a military superpower, rely on
the private sector to wage war? And why now?

Faith in Free Markets

The move toward private solutions to public problems began during the Cold
War as a way to use business know-how to streamline government operations.
The intellectual roots for the logic of privatization originated in the Austrian
school of economics at the turn of the twentieth century in Vienna, and later
found fuller expression at the University of Chicago with economists Friedrich
Hayek, Milton Friedman, Ronald Coase, George Stigler, and others. The
Chicago, or "freshwater," school of economics advocates laissez-faire banking
rules, unfettered free markets, and minimal government intervention. It stands
in stark contrast to the "saltwater" school of economics based at coastal US
universities—notably, Harvard, MIT, and Berkeley—which espouses the mac-
roeconomic theory of John Maynard Keynes and others who believe that government intervention in markets is necessary to prevent market failure.

The ideas of the Chicago school found an enthusiastic champion in British
Conservative Party leader Margaret Thatcher. During the economically bleak
summer of 1975, a Conservative Party strategist proposed that the party should
take a pragmatic "middle way" between the liberal Keynesian policies of its

rival Labour Party and the free-market ideas of the Chicago school that many Conservatives backed. Interrupting him, Thatcher reached into her briefcase and pulled out a copy of Hayek's *The Constitution of Liberty*, held it up for all to see, and asserted, "This is what we believe." With this, she banged the book down on the table.[1] When Thatcher was elected prime minister in 1979, she had the opportunity to test Hayek's ideas and initiated a comprehensive and controversial program to denationalize and privatize many state industries. Despite enormous public resistance, her efforts helped achieve the unthinkable by turning around the British economy. The privatization revolution was under way.

Over the next three decades, fervor for free markets swept across the world. The Soviet Union and communism collapsed. State-managed economies from India to Latin America liberalized, and globalization led to an economic boom. At the core of this transformation was privatization, as states retreated from what Lenin called the "commanding heights" of the economy: large industrial plants, banking, foreign trade, and other key sectors of a national economy. International financial institutions such as the World Bank and the IMF helped turn the ideology into a normative reality by encouraging rulers to turn their backs on patrimonialism and liberalize not only their economies but also their political systems by embracing democracy. They found willing partners in nascent postcommunist countries that were eager to join the rising globalized economy.

Western ideologues and especially neoconservatives interpreted this as proof of a causal relationship between free markets, democracy, and freedom, a link Hayek had posited in his popular book *The Road to Serfdom*, written at the apex of totalitarianism in World War II. US President Ronald Reagan shared Thatcher's faith in free markets and was fond of saying that "the best minds are not in government. If any were, business would hire them away." He meant it. As Thatcher did, he introduced sweeping economic policies, christened Reaganomics, that opposed government regulations, tariffs, and other infringements on the marketplace. He pushed for massive tax cuts that favored business growth at the expense of government budgets to help stimulate the private sector and recover from the economic malaise of the 1970s.

Faced with ballooning federal deficits, Reagan established the Private Sector Survey on Cost Control to eradicate waste and inefficiency in the federal government. Its chairman, J. Peter Grace, unsurprisingly concluded that "government-run enterprises lack the driving forces of marketplace competition, which promote tight, efficient operations." The solution was privatization: "Turn government operations over to the private sector and you get innovation, efficiency, flexibility."[2]

Consequently, a number of areas previously considered inherently governmental were increasingly privatized, from the postal system to prisons, rationalized by the belief that businesses could find more efficient and effective solutions to public functions than the government. This faith in free market forces cleared the road for the eventual privatization of security.

Reagan's successors continued his privatization policy, as hundreds of billions of dollars' worth of government activities were outsourced to businesses. In 1993, President Bill Clinton announced the creation of the National Performance Review, an interagency task force led by Vice President Al Gore to identify problems and offer solutions and ideas for government savings, including privatization. Across the aisle, the Republican-majority Congress was equally dedicated to the cause. The result was "cost savings in a range of 20 to 50 percent when federal and private sector service providers compete to perform these functions," according to the Office of Management and Budget.[3]

By the time George W. Bush entered the White House, privatization was a well-established norm despite the fact that the relative cost saving associated with the private sector remains hotly debated among economists. During his tenure, he sought to privatize parts of the gigantic social security program, which paid out $675 billion in benefits in 2009, and nominated devout followers of Ayn Rand, the high priestess of unfettered capitalism, to the Securities and Exchange Commission, which polices Wall Street. It should not be so shocking that the US military also acceded to privatization.

The Post–Cold War Security Vacuum

The Cold War's end produced a perfect storm of market conditions that forged the private military industry. As the world became unstable, the United States was simultaneously downsizing its massive military by 40 percent in order to reap a "peace dividend." Almost immediately upon taking office in 1993, the Clinton administration implemented a 40 percent drop in the defense budget and reduced forces from 2.2 million to 1.4 million active-duty soldiers, sailors, airmen, and marines. The cuts affected the entire military. Army divisions were reduced from eighteen to ten, navy ships were decreased from 547 to 346, and air force fighter wings were dropped from thirty-six to nineteen. Overseas troop strength was especially targeted for reduction, as the United States no longer required a massive army standing watch over the Iron Curtain to guard against Soviet invasion. Troops stationed overseas shrank by more than 50 percent, from approximately six hundred thousand in 1990 to two hundred fifty thousand in 1999.[4] These dramatic reductions in force structure generated the labor pool of experienced ex–military personnel that the new private military industry needed to grow.

Just as military supply was shrinking, demand for military operations was on the rise. From 1960 to 1991, the US Army conducted ten operational events outside of normal training and alliance commitments; by comparison, from 1991 to 1998, the Army conducted twenty-six operational events. The US Marine Corps undertook fifteen contingency operations between 1982 and 1989 but conducted sixty-two such operations after the fall of the Berlin Wall.[5] US land forces found themselves surprisingly busier in the post–Cold War era than during the decades of Soviet Union nuclear threat.

The dwindling military force structure combined with the mission creep of stability operations created a post–Cold War security vacuum that the budding private military industry was eager to fill. The United States licensed MPRI to work for Croatia and Bosnia, which hired it to train and equip their forces for more than $150 million. The State Department contracted DynCorp International to provide "peace verifiers" in Kosovo, and to train Haitian police, and eradicate coca plants as a part of Plan Colombia, during which three of its American crop-duster pilots were shot down and killed.[6] Lacking its own full complement of forces, the United States permitted the private military industry to perform tasks traditionally associated exclusively with the national armed forces. As Tim Spicer of Sandline International explains: "The end of the Cold War has allowed conflicts long suppressed or manipulated by the superpowers to reemerge. At the same time, most armies have got smaller and live footage on CNN of United States troops being killed in Somalia has had staggering effects on the willingness of governments to commit to foreign conflicts. We fill the gap."[7]

Humanizing War

Another factor in the new market for force is what war scholar Christopher Coker calls "humane warfare." Following the Cold War, the Western way of war changed. It sought to humanize war by converting it into a humane endeavor that seeks to minimize casualties on all sides, even among enemy combatants. Perhaps the decades of living under the threat of mutually assured nuclear destruction had curdled the West's appetite for bloodshed; perhaps the rise of the human rights regime had a hand, as it required UN commanders on Balkan battlefields and elsewhere to fight with human rights lawyers by their sides to parse the excessively complex and convoluted rules of engagement on the use of force. Possibly, the effort to sanitize war of cruelty resulted from a collective amnesia regarding war's fundamental nature in the modern memory, or conceivably, it was the sight, captured on CNN, of four dead and mutilated US soldiers being dragged through the streets of Mogadishu by gloating mobs of AK-47-wielding Somalis in 1993. Maybe it was all of this and more.

In the almost twenty years after Somalia, the United States has introduced two significant innovations to realize "humane" warfare: armed unmanned aerial vehicles (UAVs, also known as drones) and the private military industry to do the dying for America. Technology such as precision-guided munitions launched from drone aircraft reduces the risk of civilian casualties and collateral damage, and it avoids the sticky situation of a US pilot being shot down and captured or killed by the enemy.

Contractors, meanwhile, are mostly disposable human beings. Although some evidence suggests that the public is just as concerned about the deaths of contractors as it is about military deaths, statistics on the former are much less likely to be known.[8] The United States reveres its fallen soldiers: the media pay tribute to the dead daily, politicians running for office reflexively invoke their sacrifices, and members of the public demonstrate their wide support—even if they do not support the wars—with bumper stickers, yellow ribbons and lapel pins (an old US Army tradition), and billboards. In stark contrast, no one even tallies the numbers of dead contractors, much less reveres them, despite the fact that research shows a significant number of contractors died in Iraq and Afghanistan (see figures 3.2 and 3.3).

Through technology and contractors, the United States could fight wars without tears. It need not spill much of its own blood, thereby giving the appearance of humanizing warfare and even making war seem virtuous when labeled "humanitarian intervention," as was the case in the Balkans. Such anodyne endeavors to humanize war are delusional, as Carl von Clausewitz, the great eighteenth-century Prussian war theorist, cautions: "Kind-hearted people might of course think there was some ingenious way to disarm or defeat an enemy without too much bloodshed, and might imagine this is the true goal of the art of war. Pleasant as it sounds, it is a fallacy that must be exposed: war is such a dangerous business that the mistakes which come from kindness are the very worst."[9] Nonetheless, private armies became an attractive option for the United States well before the wars in Iraq and Afghanistan.

The Utility of Private Force

The appeal of private force is understandable regardless of century. Even Sir Thomas More, the Renaissance humanist and author of *Utopia*, coining the word, advocated using mercenaries. Despite the protestations of Catherine of Siena in the Middle Ages or organizations such as Human Rights First today, private armies are big business for a reason: they work. As with many things in the world, the utility of private force varies from individual situation to individual situation. But for many, the military advantages that mercenaries provide to employers are significant and timeless, which is why they remain an enduring facet of history.

First, mercenaries offer on-demand military services to execute whatever plans their employers please, whether buttressing national security, furthering a commercial interest, settling a dispute, self-glorification, or self-preservation. In an insecure world, there will always be a demand for security services. The *condottieri* made their livelihoods surfing the maelstrom of armed politics that pervaded northern Italy during the high Middle Ages, so much so that some mercenary captains became political actors in their own right, such as Braccio da Montone and Sigismondo Malatesta, who ruled lands in addition to private armies. Others, such as Francesco Sforza of Milan, became so strong that they took over the states they served, as warlord became lord.

On-demand soldiers also allow rulers to swell their armies' ranks with mercenaries when volunteers or conscripts are lacking. Examples are numerous: Persia in the fifth century BC; William the Conqueror in the eleventh century; Sweden and the Holy Roman Empire in the seventeenth century; England, France, and Prussia in the eighteenth century; and the United States in Iraq and Afghanistan today. In each of these cases, for-hire soldiers made up one-third to one-half of the overall military strength. On-demand force also allows a surge capacity to serve the immediate strategic needs of rulers who fail to plan. When England found that it did not possess enough ground troops to suppress its rebellious colonies during the American Revolution (1776–1781), England doubled its army by hiring thirty thousand German soldiers. Two hundred years later, the United States is in a similar position to its former foe: half of its military force structure is made up of contractors, and the United States cannot fight without them.

Second, private armies can be cheaper than public ones, as maintaining a year-round professional standing army is expensive regardless of era. The tax revenue required to field, maintain, and manage such a force is sizable, involving capital costs such as barracks and siege engines and sustaining costs such as salaries and upkeep. Removing citizens from economically productive jobs such as farming or factories to stand in the ranks of an army is a significant opportunity cost to the country's economy, as the military does not produce a commodity that can be sold for profit and taxed. Many economists view military expenditure as essentially inflationary. Finally, governments tend not to be as innovative or efficient as business in operations, as companies keep costs down out of existential necessity.

The cost saving of private armies is confirmed in modern times. Examining the cost-effectiveness of PMCs in Iraq, the US Congressional Budget Office (CBO), an official government agency charged with reviewing congressional budget issues, found private military contractors to be cheaper than the US Army. According to CBO estimates, the Army's total cost of operating an infantry unit in Iraq was $110 million, while hiring the same size unit from Blackwater to perform the same tasks during the same time period was only $99 million. In peacetime, the cost differential jumps even more. The cost of maintaining an army infantry unit at home is $60 million, whereas the cost of Blackwater is nothing, since the PMC's contract would be terminated.[10] As Secretary of Defense Donald Rumsfeld explained:

> It is clearly cost effective to have contractors for a variety of things that military people need not do, and that for whatever reason other civilians, government people, cannot be deployed to do. There are a lot of contractors, a growing number. They come from our country but they come from all countries, and indeed sometimes the contracts are from our country or another country and they employ people from totally different countries, including Iraqis and people from neighboring nations. And there are a lot of them. It's a growing number.[11]

Mercenaries are also cost-effective for long-term engagements; historically, some employers used the same private military organization for more than a century to wage war on the cheap. Mercantile firms such as the East India companies were licensed to raise armed forces and war in service of their countries' economic interests while sparing their governments the headache of managing global military and trade operations. By the turn of the nineteenth century, the British East India Company boasted an army of one hundred fifty thousand soldiers and 122 ships of the line, the larger ones mounting up to forty guns, a match for all but the most powerful enemy warships. However, maintaining this immense private military proved costly, both operationally and politically, and contributed to the company's eventual demise in the late nineteenth century.

Third, mercenaries can sometimes prove safer than public armies, as they reduce the risk of *praetorianism*, a term deriving from the infamous Praetorian Guard, the imperial bodyguard of the Roman emperors established by Augustus Caesar. During its three-hundred-year existence, it assassinated fourteen emperors, appointed five, and even sold the office to the highest bidder on one occasion. Rulers may feel safer with transient mercenaries, such as the Varangian Guard in Byzantium, than with an institutionalized security force that serves only its own interests.

Furthermore, mercenaries' bought loyalties may prove more reliable than public armies in the case of internal conflict and civil war. King Henry II of England engaged mercenaries to suppress the great rebellion of 1171–1174, because their devotion lay with their paymaster rather than with the ideals of the revolt. In 2011, Libyan president Muammar Qaddafi adopted the same approach and hired foreign fighters to violently quash national protests and fight rebellious army units.

Mercenaries may be appealing when a ruler does not want to arm an aggrieved populace that could potentially mutiny or menace other members of society. As the medieval Venetian poet Christine de Pizan makes clear, "there is if I may dare so no greater folly for a prince, who wishes to hold his lordship freely and in peace, than to give the common people permission to arm themselves."[12] Likewise, there was rich debate among the American founding fathers in the discussions over the US Constitution in the 1780s regarding the wisdom of standing armies. Antifederalists feared that an unemployed army could become a public menace by preying on the populace it was tasked to protect, and even federalists such as Alexander Hamilton acknowledged the danger.[13]

The relative security of mercenaries, of course, relies on the ruler and the mercenaries both honoring their contracts. Princes who do not pay their bills may become victims of their own mercenaries, and greedy mercenaries may treacherously wish to renegotiate their contracts with violence. Although praetorianism by PMCs is not a real risk for the United States today, despite the frenzied forebodings of Pulitzer-winning journalists and Hollywood, it remains a threat for fragile states that dabble in the market for force.

Fourth, mercenaries provide specialized military skills and services that are too expensive for ordinary public militaries to sustain. Like all market actors, private military organizations seek out gaps between supply and demand and attempt to fill them, taking advantage of economies of scale to develop capabilities such as armor-piercing crossbow soldiers known as *balestrieri* in the fourteenth century and Mi-24 heavy attack helicopters flown by Executive Outcomes in the late twentieth century. The costs associated with equipping, training, and sustaining these specialized military units are too great for all but the wealthiest public armies, making it more efficient to outsource these capabilities when needed.

In addition to exotic military units, private military organizations also provide rare skill sets. The *ninja* and *shinobi* of feudal Japan were uniquely trained in unorthodox warfare, and MPRI has specific expertise in restructuring modern armed forces in developing countries. As T. X. Hammes, a retired US Marine Corps officer, affirms, "contractors can execute tasks the United States military and civilian workforce simply cannot."[14]

Private force has reentered the arena of world politics owing to a constellation of factors: market thinking in policy circles, the post–Cold War security vacuum, the desire to humanize war, and the high utility of private force. By the time the United States invaded Iraq in 2003, the market infrastructure was already in place to support the private military industry. The industry holds many timeless benefits, including the essential fact that on-demand force remains an attractive option for rulers, from King George III to President George W. Bush. The United States has opened the proverbial Pandora's box, releasing mercenarism back into international affairs. Now that the industry is back and unlikely to go away anytime soon, the next chapter explores some of its dangers and risks.

6

The Murky Side of Private Force

> The sinews of war are unlimited money.
> —Cicero

On April 27, 1522, two armies faced each other at dawn across a soggy field ready for battle at a manor park of Bicocca, a small town six kilometers north of Milan. On one side stood the combined forces of France and Venice, numbering more than twenty thousand troops, including the mercenary captain, or *condottiero*, Giovanni de' Medici's Black Bands and sixteen thousand dreaded Swiss mercenaries. For two centuries, Swiss companies were the scourge of the European battlefield, overtaking superior forces with deadly twenty-one-foot steel-tipped pikes and precision formations that could run down heavily armored knights—as the doomed duke of Burgundy could attest to—making them the most sought-after private armies on the market.[1]

Opposing the combined army were the comparatively meager Spanish imperial, Milanese, and papal forces, which numbered only sixty-four hundred but included *landsknechts*, or German mercenary pikemen. The Swiss companies and *landsknechts* were more than mere business rivals and held special contempt for each other. Holy Roman Emperor Maximilian I had formed the first *landsknechts* regiments several decades earlier and patterned them after the Swiss companies, which regarded them as cheap copies purloining their brand. Consequently, no quarter was given when these mercenary rivals met on the battlefield.

The attack commenced at dawn. The French advanced on the outnumbered Spanish imperial forces with two columns of Swiss mercenaries, numbering a few thousand each, bearing down on the *landsknechts* and the Spanish *arquebusiers*—soldiers using a predecessor of the musket—who stood behind a sunken road and an earthen rampart. As the Swiss advanced, their French masters ordered them to halt and wait for the French artillery to bombard the imperial defenses first, but the Swiss did not. Perhaps the Swiss captains doubted that the artillery would have any effect on the earthworks; perhaps the Swiss did not trust the French, owing to an earlier pay dispute regarding their contract;

perhaps it was the aggressive Swiss push-of-pike strategy that advanced without support of firearms; perhaps it was rivalry between the two Swiss columns, one from the rural cantons and the other from Bern and urban cantons; or perhaps it was their "blind pugnacity and self-confidence," as a French eyewitness later remarked.[2] Either way, the Swiss moved swiftly across the open field without regard for consequence.

As soon as the Swiss were in range of the enemy cannons, they began to take massive casualties. With nowhere to go but forward, they moved toward the Spanish positions but came to a deadly halt when they reached the sunken road that acted as a ditch and the tall rampart behind it. Atop that rampart were the *landsknechts*, who mercilessly attacked their trapped rivals, while the *arquebusiers* fired downward into the sunken road, massacring the Swiss. Retreating back across the field, they lost more men to cannon barrage. By the time they reached French lines, they had suffered more than three thousand casualties, including twenty-two captains and all but one of the French commanders who accompanied the Swiss assault.

The battle was lost, and three days later, the Swiss abandoned the campaign altogether, marching home to their cantons and marking the end of Swiss dominance in the mercenary market. As Francesco Guicciardini, a contemporary historian, wrote, "they went back to their mountains diminished in numbers, but much more diminished in audacity; for it is certain that the losses which they suffered at Bicocca so affected them that in the coming years they no longer displayed their wonted vigour."[3] From this battle comes the Spanish word *bicoca*, meaning a bargain or something acquired at little cost.

The problems of contract warfare are as timeless as the benefits. The unexpected departure of the Swiss mercenaries left their French masters powerless to carry on their campaign, and the French lost the war. Better, Machiavelli would have counseled, to have one's own troops than to hire mercenaries, which cost the French everything. Although today's nascent market for force is tame compared with the medieval market, the *condottieri* have much to teach us about how privatized warfare alters strategic outcomes.

Dispelling Common Myths

The mercenary market has long received bad press that has reified into truism. While history is replete with tragic examples of private military exploits, they are not always representative of the overall industry yet are often taken as such; hence the word *myth*. Before any cogent analysis of the industry's troubling aspects—and there are many—it is first necessary to dispense with some common myths about mercenaries.

Probably the most pernicious perception, made famous by Niccolò Machiavelli's bitter pronouncements, is that they are faithless. And he would know. Machiavelli was no stranger to mercenaries in Renaissance Italy and worked with them as the minister in charge of Florence's defenses, from 1503 to 1506. His native city suffered serial humiliations at the hands of its own mercenaries during its protracted war against Pisa. In his book *The Art of War*, he explains that a rift between military and civil life converts the former into a trade, turning soldiers into beasts and citizens into cowards, and makes his opinion on mercenaries plain in his famous treatise *The Prince*: "They are disunited, ambitious, without discipline, unfaithful; gallant among friends, vile among enemies; no fear of God, no faith with men." While there are certainly examples of faithless mercenaries, perfidiousness is hardly unique to the private military industry, although the consequences are more lethal than in other sectors. Additionally, according to some scholars, Machiavelli's claims about mercenaries may be overstated, ahistorical, or a misreading.[4]

In an open market for force, mercenaries are incentivized to honor their contracts in order to build a positive professional reputation and attract future business. Many mercenaries enjoyed long and esteemed relations with their employers: Hawkwood was faithful to Florence for decades, and the city honored him with a funerary monument at the Basilica di Santa Maria del Fiore; the Varangian Guard was fiercely loyal to the Byzantine emperors for centuries; and the Dutch and British East India Companies served their respective nations' interests admirably for well more than a hundred years. Private military actors tend to meet their contractual obligations when they are held accountable and when it serves their long-term interest.

Another myth is that mercenaries are lone-wolf adventure seekers. Although there are individual mercenaries or small bands of private warriors, most of the successful private armies are sizable and sophisticated organizations: Xenophon's Ten Thousand, the free companies of the *condottieri*, and PMCs such as Triple Canopy. These private armies are well organized, with clear chains of command, in-house codes of conduct and discipline, and internal machinations to handle administrative tasks such as personnel, logistics, and accounting. The *condottieri* formed expeditionary corporate military units made up of international personnel with itemized budgets for battle gear, compensation for loss of horse, ransom-based revenue detailed, and other costs of war. They also had company policies regarding the democratic distribution of loot, bonuses for victories, and a standardized war feast should victory be won. They even formed their own trade association of "confederated *condottieri*," much like today's International Stability Operations Association (ISOA) based in Washington, D.C.[5]

Finally, the stereotype that mercenaries are little more than murderous thugs is unfair. The marketplace tends to discipline bad mercenaries, as it did in the

Middle Ages. When the famed Hawkwood switched sides one too many times during the War of Eight Saints, Bernabo Visconti of Milan passed a decree promising thirty florins to anyone who "took or killed" a member of Hawkwood's company. Similarly, Blackwater saw its business with the United States plummet after the Nisour Square incident, and in 2009, the State Department did not renew the PMC's contract.

While these problems still haunt the private military industry today, they are still the exception rather than the rule. And those who cavil too much about ethical issues surrounding mercenaries ought not avert their eyes from the obvious. There is plenty of evidence that private armies are more disciplined and effective than public forces in Sudan, Somalia, Myanmar, Belarus, Chad, Zimbabwe, the DRC, Iraq, Afghanistan, Guinea, Kyrgyzstan, the Central African Republic, Tajikistan, or Côte d'Ivoire, to name a few. Some even await the day when the United Nations hires qualified PMCs as peacekeepers, a rational choice given that peacekeeping needs rise each year while national troops available for such missions dwindle. Today, such missions are often undermanned and staffed by soldiers from poorer countries, who are often badly trained. Private military force is a high-utility commodity, which is why the market for force has thrived for most of human history.

For-Profit Killing

Myths aside, there are profoundly disturbing problems with an industry that is paid to kill. Many cringe at linking armed conflict to profit motive, because it incentivizes private armies to prolong and expand war for financial gain. Worse, markets fail, and in the context of war and the market for force, failure may mean impunity for mercenaries—violence without constraint—because no credible police force exists to control them. Under these conditions, mercenaries devolve into marauders and prey on the weak for survival, as was often the case in the Middle Ages.

Moreover, the market for force does not behave like other markets. A surplus of military supply does not necessarily correspond to lower private military prices or insolvent weaker mercenary companies. Instead, unemployed mercenaries can weather tough economic times by plundering local lands to feed themselves. This makes security a commodity that is not strictly demand-driven but also self-directed, generating bloody market distortions. Pope Urban V described marauding mercenaries in the fourteenth century as a "multitude of villains of various nations associated in arms by the greed to appropriate the fruits of labor of innocent and unarmed people, let loose to every cruelty, to extort money, methodically devastating the countryside."[6] When mercenaries fight in times of war and pillage in times of peace, for civilians, the line between war and peace may disappear.

Even when the market for force is functional, security is a commodity for which supply can artificially create demand through extortion. Like a mafia, a private military organization can arrive at a community and extort payment in exchange for not attacking it. The *condottieri* made a lucrative living this way, as the most common response for communities was to purchase reprieve. In 1342, Werner of Urslingen and the Great Company made a tour of Italy and successfully extorted payment from Cesena, Perugia, Arezzo, Siena, and several Lombard communes. Eleven years later, the Great Company, by then numbering some ten thousand, returned under the leadership of Montreal d'Albarno, whom the Italians called Fra Moriale, and extracted tribute from Pisa, Arezzo, Florence, Siena, and the Malatesta of Rimini. True to their name, *condottieri* entered into a no-sack contract with local cities. The October 1381 agreement between the city of Siena and John Hawkwood stipulated that his company would not attack the city and its local lands for eighteen months in exchange for four thousand florins. Often, it was cheaper for both mercenary and target to negotiate a price for peace rather than face the expenditure of a siege and sacking.

However, such payments only encouraged more mercenaries, either as rack-eteers or as hired defenders of cities, revealing the true nature of the market for force: expansion. Consistent with the logic of both markets and war, competition in the market for force escalates until one market actor emerges victorious with the monopoly of force, eliminating all rivals. This produces constant war, since monopolies are difficult to attain. In the late thirteenth and early fourteenth centuries, Florence and its mercenaries were continuously at war with someone: Pisa (1362–1364), the pope (1374–1375), and Milan (1389–1390, 1399–1400, 1423–1424, 1430). Luckless Siena was obliged to buy its freedom from enterprising *condottieri* thirty-seven times between 1342 and 1399. This endless fighting attracted more mercenaries from every corner of Europe, compounding the problem.

The dynamic of the market for force presents a counterintuitive conundrum for modern observers. Private warfare actually swells rather than depletes the ranks of private armies. Wars fought by national armies, such as World War I and II, often devolve into conflicts of attrition that terminate when one side runs out of citizens to conscript. As the Allies marched on Berlin in 1945, the German army had insufficient soldiers left to defend the city and had to rely on old men and young boys. Japan went even further. Low on soldiers, the government extended the logic of its kamikaze program to the entire populace, arming people with bamboo spears to repel the expected US land invasion, in what critics called "collective suicide."

Inversely, wars fought by mercenaries evolve into conflicts of amplification. Unlike states, private armies can recruit soldiers from around the world and are not restricted to limited labor pools, such as a state's citizenry. In fact, battle between mercenaries can enlarge the labor pool as the lure of well-paying contracts, rich booty, career progression, and other opportunities attract private warriors from around the world. Medieval mercenaries in northern Italy hailed from all over Europe, just as PMCs in Iraq and Afghanistan are packed with foreigners, and intrastate conflicts in Libya and Côte d'Ivoire have attracted mercenaries from all over Africa. During the Thirty Years War, some forty thousand Scotsmen—perhaps 15 percent of the total males in Scotland—journeyed to central Europe to fight for both sides of the conflict.[7] As in all markets, supply seeks demand, and supply in this case is private warriors, and demand is armed conflict.

Unconstrained by nationality in their recruitment, private armies can endure wars of attrition, as long as there is a paying client and enough willing men-at-arms on the planet. Such conditions only propagate private warfare. More war means more mercenaries, which gives private armies more resources to ply their trade, fostering more war. This self-feeding and ever-escalating cycle of violence generates the perpetual war that is the market for force.

Encouraging War

On-demand military services make it easier and subsequently more tempting to go to war, in several ways. The option of private warriors lowers war's barrier to entry for consumers. For the United States, using contractors saves the government from more painful political solutions, such as a national draft, courting unwilling or unsavory coalition partners or a premature withdrawal from Iraq and Afghanistan. Proponents and opponents of the wars admit that without contractors, the United States would require a total force of 320,000 in Iraq and a force of more than 210,000 in Afghanistan.[8] Hiring contractors in domestically unpopular wars also allows the government to dodge national political debate over whether the wars should end, since few Americans care about contractor casualties.[9]

Similarly, when a policy is politically too risky, outsourcing it to the private sector offers employers a layer of plausible deniability in the event of failure. Not surprisingly, the origins of plausible deniability are tightly bound to nonstate violence. State rulers invented the concept at the turn of the seventeenth century to give themselves political cover for dubious ventures. If a private undertaking authorized by the ruler met with success, he or she could claim a share of the profits, but if it met with failure, the ruler could claim that he or she was not responsible.

Plausible deniability was especially useful when using private forces could accidentally draw the state into war with another state. Since the end of the Cold War, governments have relied on the industry for clandestine and covert operations. Clandestine operations are those that the United States hopes will remain secret, but if they are exposed, it will either admit to or simply remain silent on them; covert operations are ones that the United States will always disavow. Typically, the United States only uses PMCs for clandestine operations, which is a legal gray area, whereas only the CIA is authorized under federal law to conduct covert operations.

However, this trend may be changing, as the United States has increasingly employed private spy firms for intelligence collection. These firms are typically founded by ex–CIA personnel, such as Cofer Black, the chairman of Total Intelligence Solutions, a subsidiary of Blackwater. Similarly, former CIA spy Duane Clarridge runs a network of contracted spies in Pakistan and Afghanistan to collect information on militant fighters, Taliban leaders, and the inner workings of Kabul's ruling class. Michael D. Furlong created a private spy ring to track militants in Afghanistan and Pakistan for $22 million, although senior Pentagon officials claim that Furlong "deliberately misled" senior generals when journalists questioned the contract—a safe claim for the United States to make if a politically embarrassing operation fails or is exposed.

Plausible deniability also allows the government to hide secrets from itself, especially official oversight mechanisms. The United States' use of contractors allows the executive branch a method of circumventing congressional oversight, because there is (at present) little requirement to report on the activities of contractors. The State Department, DOD, and intelligence agencies all have dedicated congressional oversight committees. Members of Congress are continually concerned with the deliberate lack of executive branch transparency regarding contractors; according to a 2008 Congressional Research Service investigation, "as oversight hearings have demonstrated, the executive branch either has not kept sufficient records to produce or has been unwilling to present basic, accurate information on the companies employed under United States government contracts and subcontracts in Iraq."[10] More generally, the White House can exploit the oversight loopholes to prosecute war while politically insulating itself with plausible deniability.

Plausible deniability fosters moral hazard among decision makers, making it easier to enter and remain at war. Moral hazard is a concept used by economists to describe a situation in which a person or institution does not have to face the full consequences of its decisions and therefore acts in a reckless manner. For example, people might be more likely to steal a car if they knew the police would not catch them, or a bank may make riskier loans if it knew the government would bail it out if the loans defaulted. Economist Paul Krugman describes moral hazard as "any situation in which one person makes the decision about how much risk to take, while someone else bears the cost if things go badly."[11]

In contract warfare, moral hazard encourages war. The plausible deniability provided by contractors allows democratic regimes to circumvent their own checks and balances, established to prevent rash decision making such as declaring war and risking the survival of the nation. In the cases of Iraq and Afghanistan, the private military industry allowed the White House to wage war without the full supervision of Congress. Moreover, contractors are easier to blame in the event of failure than one's own military. This situation invites moral hazard, because decision makers are not fully held accountable for their actions, lowering the threshold to go to war.

Exploiting Gaps in Knowledge for Profit

The moral hazards in the market for force extend beyond plausible deniability. As with many business transactions, the market for force is plagued by asymmetries of information, which also encourage moral hazard. In economic theory, information asymmetry arises when one party has more critical information than another in a business transaction, which can be leveraged for advantage. This is especially true when an employer needs to hire a specialist who is far more expert in the situation than the employer and is tempted to exploit this gap in knowledge for profit.

This leads to a related challenge that economists call the principal–agent problem. Take the example of a leaky roof. The home owner calls a carpenter to fix it, and the carpenter tells the owner that the entire roof must be replaced, when, in fact, only a small hole requires repair. The unscrupulous carpenter is incentivized to lie, because he will make substantially more money replacing the whole roof than repairing a small hole. The home owner innocently agrees to the costly roof replacement, because he lacks the expertise to know better. In economic theory, the employer is the principal, and the carpenter is the agent. The agent, who should act in the principal's interest, instead acts in his own interest because of moral hazard.

Similarly, in contract warfare, the employer is the principal, and the private military organization is the agent. Dishonest PMCs can exploit this asymmetry of information for profit, since it is difficult for the employer to observe and understand what the PMC does during a campaign. To alleviate this problem, medieval customers would have representatives, called *provveditori*, travel with and monitor the hired mercenary companies during the campaign and even goad them into battle to ensure that they did not shirk their obligations.

However, this was a defective system, as *condottieri* could manipulate key information, such as intelligence on the enemy that only the *condottieri* knew, to unduly influence the *provveditori* to make business decisions in favor of the *condottiero*'s interests rather than the client's. Or *condottieri* could simply ignore the *provveditori* and allow themselves to be outbid on the field of battle, turning against their original employers. This is precisely what happened to the Milanese at Canturino in 1363, when Milan's entire Hungarian contingent went over to the enemy. During their war with Pisa in 1364, the Florentines successfully bought off Pisa's mercenaries amassed before its walls. Who was managing whom?

Similar asymmetries of information exist between the United States and the private military industry that the industry can exploit for profit. The bureaucracy needed to competently oversee contractors did not grow commensurately with the industry during the Iraq and Afghanistan boom years, and as a result, the government lacks the capacity to manage the industry, as the Gansler report and other government studies repeatedly show. A 2010 US inspector general's investigation found that the State Department did not adequately supervise the PMCs that were paid $1.6 billion to build the Afghan National Police.[12]

To avoid this problem, the United States deploys modern *provveditori*, called contracting officers' technical representatives (COTRs), into the field to oversee the government's interests, but, as in the Middle Ages, this system is deficient. There are insufficient numbers of COTRs, those that exist receive inadequate training, and they lack the needed tools and authority to manage multimillion-dollar contracts in conflict zones. Owing to this, COTRs are vulnerable to manipulation in the same manner as *provveditori*, because they are often too reliant on contractors' specialized knowledge and access to key information to make important decisions regarding the contract. This represents a clear conflict of interest. Contractors, like the *condottieri*, are incentivized to share only expert opinion or information that lengthens or expands their contract for profit.

That the mercenaries can themselves be cheated is another type of moral hazard; if a manager cannot be fired because he or she is protected by nepotism or cronyism, then that manager can treat his or her employees unprofessionally with impunity. Strong employers in the market for force can renege on paying their mercenaries without fear of consequence. In the Middle Ages, a scammed mercenary company could attempt to attack its unfaithful employer but may have been too weak to do so after a long military campaign. Furthermore, the employer could hire a fresh company at a fraction of the price to chase off the remnants of the war-weary company.

Some employers were also relatively untouchable. Pope Gregory XI was infamous for lack of payment during the War of Eight Saints and drove Hawkwood and half of the Breton companies to defect to his enemies. As in the Middle Ages, there are at present few options for PMCs whose customers have backed out of their contracts. The market for force is inherently a distrustful environment that encourages both principal and agent to behave in treacherous ways, which is dangerous in the context of war.

Weak Contract Enforcement

Doug Brooks, president of ISOA, once made a case for the privatization of warfare this way: "write a cheque, end a war."[13] While appealing, it is obviously simplistic, even if there are some examples, such as Executive Outcomes' involvement in Sierra Leone. Generally, contract warfare is fraught with difficulties, especially in contract enforcement. According to military historians Jurgen Brauer and Hubert van Tuyll, the challenge of holding parties to contractual promises eventually put the *condottieri* out of business.[14] There was not—nor is there today—an effective judicial system to enforce contracts in the market for force.

Weak contract enforcement is a central flaw in the market for force, because it allows both the client and the mercenary to double-cross each other, leading to traitorous outcomes. Private military force operates in places with little governance, such as fragile states or war zones, where it is difficult to enforce contracts; there are no war police, judiciary, or prisons for deceitful employers or private armies.

Even superpowers such as the United States have trouble disciplining errant PMCs. When Blackwater personnel killed seventeen Iraqi civilians at Nisour Square in 2007, they were simply sent home without punishment. Or, as Erik Prince, then CEO of the firm, said during congressional testimony, "they have one decision to make: window or aisle" on their return flight home.[15] Other than being fired, PMC personnel face little, if any, punishment for mistakenly killing civilians, whereas members of the US armed forces or Iraq security forces could be court-martialed and imprisoned.

For contracts to work without law enforcement, there must be trust between the seller and the buyer. But trust is a rare commodity in the market for force. As fourteenth-century Italian novelist Franco Sacchetti put it, in mercenaries, "there is neither love nor faith."[16] The principal-agent problems in contract warfare breed treachery and tragedy for consumers, providers, and bystanders alike in the market for force.

Conspicuously absent from the list of concerns is the question of legitimacy, which presupposes that only states and international organizations such as the United Nations can rightfully wield military force. This is a modern bias that demands exposure. To understand this prejudice, we must first delve into the origins of the contemporary world order and its special antipathy toward mercenarism.

7

The Modern World Order:
A Brief History

War made the state, and the state made war.
—Charles Tilly

The morning of November 19, 2005, started just like any other for the US marines of Kilo Company. It was Kilo's third tour in Iraq, and many of its marines were veterans of the initial invasion, in the spring of 2003, and the hard-fought battle for Fallujah in the fall of 2004. A convoy of four Humvees rolled out of the base that morning for a routine patrol in the city of Haditha. They traveled in a line, well spaced out and heavily armed. Unknown to them, insurgents had planted a large roadside bomb in their path, probably weeks before, and at 7:15, it blasted the fourth Humvee, lifting it into the air and splitting it in two. One marine was killed instantly, and the other two were seriously injured.

What happened next is unclear. According to reports, the marine leader stopped the convoy and ordered five Iraqi men—a taxi driver and four teenagers—out of their car and shot them dead in the street. Next, the marines attacked four adjacent houses and over the next few hours killed nineteen more civilians, ranging in age from three to seventy-six. Many were shot multiple times at close range while unarmed, some still in their pajamas and in their bedrooms. One was in a wheelchair, and four were children.

Many believe that the marines' killing spree was revenge for the death of their squad mate, similar to the My Lai massacre of the Vietnam War. However, we may never know what actually happened, because the only investigation—conducted on the military by the military—did not fully address the core issue: the killing of unarmed civilians. Instead, it blamed "an unscrupulous enemy" that used unconventional warfare tactics, focused on procedural and bureaucratic processes, and dismissed the entire incident as a "case study" that illustrates "how simple failures can lead to disastrous results."[1] After the massacre of twenty-six civilians, the military quietly dropped all charges against the marines except for the squad leader, who was acquitted in a court-martial. The world did not seem to notice or care much.

Haditha stands in stark contrast to Nisour Square, a Baghdad traffic circle where Blackwater employees killed seventeen Iraqi civilians under similar circumstances while escorting a US diplomatic convoy on September 16, 2007. Like the marines, the Blackwater personnel went unpunished, but unlike the case with the marines, the world took notice and was outraged.

Iraqis cursed Blackwater, and a firestorm of anti-US sentiment swept through the country, undermining the United States' counterinsurgency strategy of "winning hearts and minds." Radical Shi'ite cleric Muqtada al-Sadr, leader of the Mahdi Army that spearheaded the first major armed confrontation against the United States–led occupation forces, demanded the expulsion of these "criminals" from Iraq. Iraqi Prime Minister Nuri al-Maliki bluntly declared that "it cannot be accepted by an American security company to carry out a killing. These are very serious challenges to the sovereignty of Iraq."[2]

The outrage spread beyond Iraq's borders and generated such international ill will that Condoleezza Rice, the US secretary of state, had to publicly address the shooting and launch an official investigation. Shortly afterward, the US government initiated four additional independent investigations led by the Department of Defense, the FBI, and other agencies. Congress also launched its own investigation, and Congressman Henry Waxman, the chair of the House Committee on Oversight and Government Reform, held hearings "to understand what has happened and the extent of the damage to United States security interests" and concluded that "the controversy over Blackwater is an unfortunate demonstration of the perils of excessive reliance on private security contractors."[3]

The investigations and outrage did not stop there. The Iraqis conducted their own investigation and banned Blackwater from operating in Iraq, demanded that the US government end its contract with the company, and called on Blackwater to pay the families $8 million in compensation. Private organizations also carried out inquiries and published their findings in reports such as Human Rights First's *Private Security Contractors at War: Ending the Culture of Impunity*. The United Nations used the occasion to release an ongoing two-year study into the "tremendous increase" in armed contractors and concluded that even though they were hired as "security guards," they were, in fact, performing military duties, making firms like Blackwater a "new form of mercenary activity" and illegal under international law.[4]

Both the marines and Blackwater personnel committed the same crime with the same outcomes, yet international reaction was radically different. In the case of the marines, there was almost no reaction—a single internal investigation, and the charges were quietly dropped. Few around the world seemed to notice, and fewer today remember. By contrast, Nisour Square immediately sparked international ire and multiple high-level inquiries, and it remains seared in the global imagination as a nadir of the Iraq War, analogous to the My Lai massacre of the Vietnam War. Why this major disparity in reaction? What accounts for the stigma against private military organizations? The answer lies in the origins of the modern world order, and to understand this, we must go backward in time.

The Medieval World Order

Life in the European Middle Ages was chaotic. If you were a peasant, you likely had several masters who demanded your allegiance: the local feudal lord, the king, the neighboring Franciscan monastery, the Holy Roman Emperor, the pope, to name a few. Worse, they often feuded, simultaneously claiming rights to you, your land, and your soul under pain of death. Unlike today, there was no single supreme authority within your territory, as in the modern state, and this led to overlapping authorities and divided loyalties.

Political scientists describe this situation as "fractured" or "fragmented" sovereignty, and it was the central feature of the medieval world order, where popes, emperors, kings, bishops, nobles, city-states, monastic orders, chivalric orders, and vassals frequently made concurrent and conflicting claims to the same parcel of land and the people upon it. Not surprisingly, this led to a lot of war.

Like most of history, the Middle Ages knew no taboo against mercenaries. Despite Machiavelli's protestations, the mercenary profession was considered a legitimate trade, and often the lesser sons of nobility, such as Duke Werner of Urslingen, Count Konrad von Landau, and Giovanni de' Medici, sought careers as mercenary captains. There was no stigma attached to hiring a private army; it was considered no different from employing an engineering company to repair one's moat or commissioning an artist to paint portraits of one's family. The commodification of conflict resulted in a thriving market for force, as the services of private armies, or "free companies," as they were known, went to the highest or most powerful bidder. Contract warfare was common in the Middle Ages, especially in northern Italy.

The medieval world order traces its roots back to the fall of the Roman Empire and perhaps reached its zenith during the "high Middle Ages," about 1000 to 1300. It slowly declined in the centuries that followed. Historians conventionally peg the end of the medieval era around 1500, but the reality is less clear. The centuries between 1400 and 1700 witnessed the gradual consolidation of political authority from the fragmented sovereignty of the Middle Ages—where church, emperor, king, princes, city-states, monasteries, and the like all made competing and overlapping claims of authority—to a centralized system of states that became the modern world order. But there is one date especially associated with this transition.

1648

In 1618, an uprising in Bohemia turned into a war throughout central Europe between Catholics, Protestants, and political opportunists that lasted thirty gruesome years. The devastation of this Thirty Years War was irrevocable. Nearly a third of the populations of what are now Germany and the Czech Republic were wiped out. The armies of Sweden, then a superpower, destroyed up to two thousand castles, eighteen thousand villages, and fifteen hundred towns in Germany alone. The economy was in tatters, and many small villages and cities would take a hundred years to recover. Disease and famine were rampant, and tens of thousands of people became refugees, wandering the plains of Europe. In terms of sheer destruction, the Thirty Years War was comparable to the World Wars for central Europe.

Out of the Thirty Years War emerged the modern international system, or so we are told. The war ended in 1648 with the Peace of Westphalia, named after two peace treaties signed in the Westphalian cities of Osnabrück and Münster, in modern-day Germany. All the continental great powers were party to this peace that redrew the map of Europe and rewrote the rules of power. The standard reading of this event holds that 1648 delivered humanity from the anarchy of the Middle Ages by creating a new world order, sometimes called the Westphalian order, which should look familiar to modern readers. Some scholars trace the origins of the modern order back to the Peace of Lodi (1454), which founded the Italian Concert, or developments in late medieval France, but 1648 is conventionally seen as the establishment of the modern world order.[5]

The Westphalian order has three primary characteristics. First, unlike in the Middle Ages, it vests all power into a single political actor: the state. The victors of the Thirty Years War resolved the medieval problem of overlapping authorities and allegiances by declaring that only entities that controlled land may legitimately rule. Certainly, land-based authorities existed before—empires, kingdoms, dukedoms, and so on—but the modern state is different, in that it claims *absolute* power over all people and resources within its territorial boundaries to the exclusion of nonstate actors, such as the pope.

Second, states must recognize other states as equals, and third, states should not interfere with the internal affairs of other states. Unlike in the Middle Ages, this drew a clear line between domestic and foreign politics. For domestic politics, states were free to govern as they wished, so long as they could persuade or compel their populations to obey their rule. Over the coming centuries, states increasingly participated in constructing citizenship and nationalism, so much so that by the twentieth century, most Europeans and others identified first with their nationality and second with their religion, ethnic group, or other affiliations.

States also forcibly compelled dissident citizens to obey their rule and sought a monopoly of violence so no one could fight back. They outlawed their armed competition, such as mercenaries, who could physically threaten the government's existence. The state's exclusive claim to violence to uphold its rule of law is, according to many, the very essence of statehood. For instance, in 1919, the eminent German sociologist Max Weber defined the state as "a human community that (successfully) claims the monopoly of the legitimate use of physical force within a given territory."[6] This definition remains widely used today, and states that cannot maintain a monopoly of force and endure civil war or frequent violent crime are routinely described as "weak," "fragile," or "failed" states.

For foreign politics, states made treaties with other states, sometimes sought to expand forcibly into their neighbors' territory, and prevented other states from interfering in their internal politics. Over time, states developed stronger controls over their own borders and built standing national armies—not present in the Middle Ages—to wage war against other states. The great seventeenth-century Prussian war theorist Carl von Clausewitz describes the use of militaries by states as "a duel on a larger scale" to resolve interstate disputes. For him, war is simply the "continuation of politics by others means."[7] His seminal book *On War* remains the best rationale of the Westphalian way of war, which is fundamentally between states and best exemplified by World Wars I and II.

Westphalian sovereignty demanded that states put private armies out of business. First, if a state were to govern as the sole authority within a given territory, it needed a monopoly of force to uphold its rule of law; all threats to this enterprise, such as mercenaries, were proscribed. Second, the Westphalian system held that each state was responsible for transborder violence that emanated from its territory, even if the regime did not support that violence. Owing to this, states prohibited private armies out of fear that they might start a war with a neighbor and drag both states into armed conflict with each other. The medieval market for force came to an end with the expansion of the Westphalian system, as public armies replaced private ones and mercenaries were outlawed. So powerful is this stigma against mercenarism that it still haunts the world order today, as evidenced by international reaction to the Haditha versus Nisour killings.

"Legitimate" Violence

Given the state's interest in violence as a means of control, it is not surprising that the rise of the modern state is closely related to war. The development of states and the subsequent state system that makes up the Westphalian order was gradual and complex, with a thick scholarly literature on the topic. A full review of this research is beyond the scope of this book, but one thing is clear: the state's superiority at wielding violence, both domestically and abroad, allowed it to stamp out internal dissidence and conquer nonstate rivals.

According to historical sociologist Charles Tilly, states arose as a sort of security racket, akin to the Mafia, providing "protection" to citizens for a fee, or tax. Over time, states grew powerful through a violent cycle: they created strong security forces to extract wealth from the population in order to pay for those security forces. Additionally, states required security forces to eliminate rivals, both foreign and domestic. Armed force was a significant factor in states' rise to power, or, to paraphrase Tilly, violence makes states, and states make violence.[8]

American economist Mancur Olson describes the rise of states another way, using the metaphor of banditry. Bandits survive by plundering the goods of others and moving on to their next victims. At some point, the bandit decides that roving the countryside in search of loot is too fatiguing and chooses instead to "loot in place" by forcibly taking over a community and extorting the locals for wealth under the heavy hand of tyranny, like a warlord, while enjoying a stable life not "on the run." However, this gives the stationary bandit an incentive to provide some semblance of government to ensure that people continue to produce wealth and also protect them from roving bandits.[9] In this way, a state is a "stationary bandit" that evolved from "roving bandits."

For Tilly and Olson, states arose from their superior ability to use force and eliminate nonstate rivals, rendering the distinction between "legitimate" and "illegitimate" force ambiguous, elastic, and invented. For them, might made right, and states were the mightiest. Monikers such as *legitimate* and *just* used to sanction state force were probably only internalized once states became the dominant political authority in Europe, recognizing no other authority except other states.

Many and perhaps most international relations scholars believe the modern world order is inherently stable. They describe Westphalian sovereignty as a "system" or "society" of states that govern the world, and a good example of this today is the United Nations, whose voting members are states alone. Stability is sustained by natural balancing within the system, as rival powers cooperate to prevent any single state from gaining too much power. States check one another's power through the Machiavellian calculus of national interests and balance-of-power politics, with military might as the ultimate arbiter. Hence the Westphalian order maintains global governance with the state as the prime actor of international relations.

From Peace Treaty to World Order

The implications of 1648 are profound for international relations, because it served as the beginning of a new world order, ruled by states. It resolved the medieval problem of overlapping authorities and allegiances by marrying sovereignty to physical territory, organized by state, and stateless authorities such as the papacy retained no authority at all. Perhaps this is why Pope Innocent X referred to the Peace of Westphalia as "null, void, invalid, iniquitous, unjust, damnable, reprobate, inane and devoid of meaning for all time."[10]

Unfortunately for Innocent, the following four centuries saw the Westphalian order grow from a European model to a worldwide one, partly because European powers exported it through colonization. Gradually, the state dominated all other forms of international authority. The papacy, once the powerful adversary of kings and princes in the Middle Ages, lost all territorial control by 1870, and its authority was largely relegated to the sphere of morality. By the end of the nineteenth century, the Westphalian state system had completely replaced the medieval order.

At the beginning of the twentieth century, European states were empires of such strength that they could successfully make claims to controlling territory and monopolizing violence beyond their borders and into Africa, Asia, and the Americas. From 1880 to 1914, European state politics played out on a global scale, in the crises of Fashoda, various Balkans wars on the Habsburg-Ottoman frontier, the Great Game of Anglo-Russo rivalry in central Asia, economic competition in China, and the Berlin Conference of 1884–85 that settled the scramble for Africa. New and non-European states also sought a place in the new world order, as the United States and Japan embarked on colonial conquests and even bested European powers on occasion, in the Spanish-American War (1898) and the Russo-Japanese War (1904–1905). European state hegemony went so far that France, under the Second Republic, declared Algeria an integral part of its own territory.

World Wars I and II remain the greatest expression of Westphalian war, in both scope and destruction, and their battlefields spanned the globe, by then mostly colonized by European states. In addition to the horrific losses of life, World War I also claimed the Habsburg and Ottoman empires as casualties, and the Treaty of Versailles seriously enfeebled Germany. However, this destructive test of the Westphalian order did not invalidate it. In one generation, Japan's imperial pursuits put it in direct competition with the United States, Italy's imperial conquests took it deep into northeast Africa, and Germany rebounded to threaten European powers once more under the Nazi regime.

On September 1, 1939, World War II erupted and perhaps marked the zenith of the Westphalian order. The Axis countries of Germany and Japan suffered total defeat and occupation by other states, and Italy was rendered ineffectual as a world power. The Allied countries of Britain and France were also grievously wounded and retreated from their colonies in the decades to follow. The Suez Canal crisis in 1956 demonstrated that Britain and France, the last of the old

European powers, were no longer leading actors on the world stage, replaced by the younger United States and Soviet Union. However, international relations had changed, because warfare had changed. Armed with world-destroying nuclear weapons, the US and Soviet superpowers sought power without tempting direct confrontation and therefore fought a cold war through allied states, proxy wars, and economic competition.

State-Centricity

Today the normative biases of the state-centric Westphalian order are so strong that they form the DNA of international law, politics, and scholarship. For instance, the primacy of states is ensconced in *international law*, a term literally meaning "law between states." The three tenets of Westphalian sovereignty are codified in the 1933 Montevideo Convention on the Rights and Duties of States, Article 2 (1) of the UN Charter, rulings by the International Court of Justice,[11] and other legal documents.

In the Westphalian world order, states are the only actors in international politics, the only subjects of international law, and the only entities that can legitimately use force to impose their authority. Consistent with Tilly and Olson, nonstate actors who employ violence are criminalized as "rebels," "terrorists," "insurgents," "mercenaries," and so on, despite the fact that some states use similar tactics, as frequently seen by government crackdowns on dissidents. If captured, these nonstate fighters are not afforded any privileges, such as "prisoner of war" status, as outlined in the Geneva Conventions, because they are not "lawful combatants." Such privileges are reserved exclusively for the club of states and their soldiers.

The Westphalian order is also the dominant paradigm of global politics. The primacy of the state is so ingrained in policymakers' understanding of world affairs that after the tragic events of September 11, 2001, many in the United States found it inconceivable that a nonstate actor, al-Qaida, could orchestrate such an attack without help from a state. No less a figure than James Woolsey, the former director of the CIA, said it was unlikely—if not impossible—for al-Qaida to act alone and without state sponsorship. In an interview with the television show *Good Morning America*, he said, "We particularly need to look hard at whether there may be some state—in my mind, most likely, Iraq—that is working together with bin Laden's group."[12]

Nor was the CIA director alone. Others at the highest levels of the US government spent years misguidedly looking for links between al-Qaida and states like Iraq, but to no avail. The United States invaded Iraq in part because of suspected ties between the regime and the terrorist organization. For example, in the lead-up to the Iraq War, US President George W. Bush alleged that Iraq President Saddam Hussein and al-Qaida had "high-level contacts that go back a decade" and that "Iraq could decide on any given day to provide a biological or chemical weapon to a terrorist group or individual terrorists. Alliance with terrorists could allow the Iraqi regime to attack America without leaving any fingerprints."[13] Many policymakers remain paradigm prisoners of the Westphalian order.

In terms of scholarship, the canonical reading of the Westphalian world order has dominated international relations theory in Europe and North America for the last fifty years. In 1948, on the three-hundredth anniversary of Westphalia, legal scholar Leo Gross published a widely read article that described the treaty in utopian terms as "the majestic portal which leads from the old into the new world" and credited it with "the outstanding place... [in] the evolution of international relations."[14] Hans Morgenthau, a leading scholar of international relations in the twentieth century, explained that the "rules of international law were securely established in 1648," and "the Treaty of Westphalia...made the territorial state the cornerstone of the modern state system."[15] According to *The Penguin Dictionary of International Relations,* "a number of important principles, which were subsequently to form the legal and political framework of modern interstate relations, were established at Westphalia. It explicitly recognized a society of states based on the principle of territorial sovereignty."[16] The list of quotes goes on.[17] Such is the strength of the Westphalian orthodoxy and fervent bias toward states as the central political unit of international relations in law, politics, and scholarship.

The End of an Order

In 1989, the Berlin Wall fell, and the Cold War ended, leaving only a single superpower standing, the United States. To some observers, this signified the everlasting triumph of the liberal-democratic state over all others and the Darwinian resolution of the Westphalian system. In a best-selling book, *The End of History and the Last Man,* scholar Francis Fukuyama asserted that the end of the Cold War was nothing short of the "end of history." Inspired by Hegelian dialectics, referring to nineteenth-century philosopher Georg Hegel and his idea of history, Fukuyama argued that the United States' Cold War victory signaled "the end point of mankind's ideological evolution and the universalization of Western liberal democracy as the final form of human government."[18] World peace was finally at hand.

Unfortunately for Fukuyama's argument, the future also had a say. With a single victor under the Westphalian order, the world grew more chaotic. The liberal-democratic enterprise did not spread to weaker states within the

international system, naturally buttressing it; instead, many weaker states fal-
tered even more. Some states lost control of their territory, as in the conflicts in
the Balkans, Indonesia, and Sudan. Other states, such as Liberia and Somalia,
failed altogether. Many lost their monopoly of force, resulting in civil wars and
large swaths of ungoverned spaces in which armed nonstate actors—separatist groups in northern Mali, warlords in eastern Congo, and violent extremists
in Yemen—have almost free rein. Some states, such as Guinea Bissau in West
Africa, are co-opted by drug cartels and become "narco-states," a literal mani-
festation of Olson's stationary bandit. Transnational terrorists such as al-Qaida
threaten weak and strong states alike, and in 2013 declared the Islamic State in
Iraq and Sham, an independent emirate that spans across Iraq and Syria. In fact,
so worrisome was the rise of weak states by 2002 that the United States declared
it was "now threatened less by conquering states than we are by failing ones."[19]

Sovereignty is not only eroding inside states, but it is also being corroded
from outside them. After the Cold War ended, nonstate actors such as the UN
began to interfere in the domestic politics of countries in direct contravention of
its own charter, which enshrines the core Westphalian principles in Article 2.[20]
In theory, the UN and similar institutions represent the collective will of states,
which make up the UN's membership. But in reality, some of these international
organizations have transcended into global actors in their own right, in a "sum is
greater than the parts" trend.

For instance, a year after the Soviet Union formally capitulated, then–UN
secretary-general Boutros Boutros-Ghali boldly declared that "the time of absolute sovereignty...has passed; its theory was never matched by reality." Here
the word sovereignty is code for "states," referring to the Westphalian order. His
solution was a new order managed by a muscular UN that administrated above
states, and cautioned: "The Organization must never again be crippled as it was
in the era that has now passed."[21] Since then, the UN has authorized military
interventions into a state's territory against its will—a violation of Westphalian
sovereignty—as seen in northern Iraq, Rwanda, Somalia, the former Yugoslavia
(Bosnia), Haiti, Liberia, Kosovo, and Sierra Leone. From 1945 to 1989, the UN
authorized seventeen such interventions, yet from 1990 to 2006, it approved
more than twenty per year.[22] Such actions would be unthinkable in a strong
Westphalian system.

In the twenty years since Fukuyama's end of history, it seems that state sovereignty is eroding on most fronts, and thus, the Westphalian order with it. This
has spawned a surge in debate among experts. Some have pronounced the state
dead, while others dismiss this, like reports of Mark Twain's death, as an exaggeration.[23] Many have begun to question the orthodoxy of 1648. Some, like Philip
Bobbitt and Robert Jackson, argue that the state is transforming from a land-based
authority into something else.[24] Others, such as Jörg Friedrichs and S. J. Korbin,

suggest that the Westphalian order is a historical anomaly. For them, the state is neither timeless nor natural, and history is replete with alternative models of human political organization, from tribes to kingdoms to empires.[25] Still others contend that Westphalia is a myth altogether. Edward Keene, Andreas Osiander, and others describe 1648 as a figment of the nineteenth-century imagination and reified in twentieth-century academic theories.[26] In fact, the language of the treaties of Münster and Osnabrück does not articulate an international system of states. One scholar even compares the Westphalian world to Narnia.[27]

Despite this debate, the Westphalian paradigm continues to dominate international relations ideas. All major theories—realism and neorealism, liberalism and neoliberalism, constructivism, the English School, critical theory, and so on—still revolve around the primacy of the state. Yet states are no longer the sole authorities in international relations as once conceived under the Westphalian system. Nonstate actors are now also political actors on the world stage, making an international state-centric system impossible. At the same time, alternative and often older conceptions of political order along ethnic, cultural, tribal, and religious lines of identification are reemerging and even eclipsing identity based on nationality. Twentieth-century state-centric theories of international relations can no longer satisfactorily account for these changes, which may explain some of the theoretical incoherence and cognitive dissonance experienced in the post–Cold War era.

An alternative model is needed to comprehend the shifting world we inhabit, one that is not constrained by the state-centric bias we have inherited. As the world reverts to the status quo ante of the Middle Ages, when states did not dominate international politics, it is sensible to adjust with it and adopt a perspective that encompasses this reality. That perspective is termed *neomedievalism*.

8

Neomedievalism

There's never a new fashion but it's old.
—Geoffrey Chaucer

Life at the court of King Roger II of Sicily (1095–1154) might prove surprising to modern readers, who perhaps associate the Middle Ages with ignorance, violence, and suffering—the proverbial "Dark Ages." Life in medieval Sicily was comparatively safe, urbane, and globalized. The architecture of the king's Palazzo Reale in Palermo, like the society surrounding it, was infused with Norman, Arab, and Byzantine influences. Upon entering its doors, a time traveler would hear French, Latin, Greek, Arab, and Hebrew freely spoken on topics ranging from the international silk trade, to the latest news from the distant Levant of the Second Crusade, to the protection of minorities under Roger's laws, which blended Christian Norman law, sharia, and Justinian Roman code. Courtiers swapping scuttlebutt at the portcullis might include Arab geographer Muhammad al-Idrisi, Greek historian Nilus Doxopatrius, and the archdeacon of Catania, who translated Plato's *Meno* and the *Phaedo*, brought from Constantinople, into Latin.

The king himself, though a Norman, spoke fluent Arabic and was fond of Arabic culture. He employed Muslim scholars, poets, and scientists and used Arab troops and siege engines in his campaigns for southern Italy. His chief enemy was not a rival state but the pope, who hired mercenaries to raid Roger's lands in southern Italy. However, Pope Innocent II was not the only nonstate actor with power in Roger's world; he also had to contend with societies such as the Templar knights, semiautonomous cities such as Bari, and families with great reach such as the Bavarian houses of Welf and Babenberg.

This medieval world order, though perhaps more chaotic than our own, did not collapse into anarchy for want of a strong state-centric system. In fact, it was relatively stable, lasting for about a thousand years. Unlike the Westphalian order, medieval sovereignty was fragmented, as different political actors—church, emperor, king, princes, city-states, monasteries, and so on—made overlapping claims of authority over people, places, and things. In the Middle Ages, rulers rarely retained absolute authority within a large territory.

This created divided loyalties. Under the Westphalian order, states demanded that people be patriots first and everything else second; in the Middle Ages, individuals had dueling loyalties to church, kingdom, region, family lineage, ethnic group, monastic order, knightly order, and so forth. For example, a person might self-identify as a Templar knight first, Catholic second, Auvergnese third, and Frenchman fourth. There was no state monopoly of identity and loyalty.

These overlapping authorities and allegiances within the medieval world created a durable disorder, in which a single authority can neither impose greater stability nor cause the system to collapse. A similar situation is developing today. A hundred years ago, "great power politics" in international relations meant interactions between states and states alone. Today states share the world stage with a multitude of nonstate actors: organizations such as the United Nations, nonprofit groups such as Amnesty International, companies such as ExxonMobil, and drug cartels and terrorist organizations. Many of these nonstate actors wield international clout on par with states, making a state-centric system impossible.

The world order may be slowly returning to the status quo ante of the Middle Ages. If so, it would best be described as *neomedievalism*: a non-state-centric, multipolar international system of overlapping authorities and allegiances within the same territory. Do we live in such a world already?

The Neomedieval Imagination

The idea of a "new" Middle Ages might make some instinctively recoil, as it connotes ignorance, stagnation, and barbarism on a continental scale. However, this is unfair; in reality, the medieval era was complex, rich, and vivacious. Part of this misconception stems from the Enlightenment's branding it the *Dark Ages* in a propagandist's ploy to distinguish its ideas from those of the past. Even the term *Middle Ages* is unfortunate, coined well after the age had passed. Certainly, its denizens would not think they were living in the "middle" and believed, as we all do, that they resided at the summit of history. Despite this abuse, the Middle Ages has fueled popular fantasy for centuries, from Arthurian legend to Wagnerian opera to the *Harry Potter* books.

The Middle Ages has also made an appearance in international relations thinking, starting after World War II to the present day. For some, *neomedievalism* means anarchy, as seen in the writings of Leo Gross, Francis Wormuth, Arnold Wolfers, Martin van Creveld, Robert Kaplan, and Alain Minc. These tend to be apocalyptic and ahistorical readings of the past that do not serve the present and would better be dubbed "neobarbarism" or the "New Dark Ages." Yet for others, the Middle Ages represents an alternative model to the Westphalian system, as demonstrated by Philip Cerny, Mark Duffield, Stephen Kobrin, Jörg Friedrichs, and others.[1] This book expands on this school of thought.

Neomedievalism is important because it offers a conceptual lens for understanding the seemingly dissonant and chaotic world order emerging from the ashes of the Cold War that cannot be easily grasped past the conceptual blinders of state-centrism. Rather than rationalizing the paradox in conventional state-centric international relations theory, neomedievalism instead acknowledges the fundamental reorganization and redistribution of power in the system from state to nonstate actors. It embraces the fragmentation of sovereignty and seeks to reorient international relations ideas away from state-centrism and toward an unstructured system of overlapping authorities and allegiances to better comprehend world affairs.

Neomedievalism is a metaphor loosely based on the world order of the European high Middle Ages, but it does not portend a literal return to the medieval period. Nor does it imply Eurocentrism, since the central features of this neomedievalism can easily be found in historical Asia, India, Africa, and elsewhere. The European Middle Ages is merely an illustrative example of this kind of world order, and the label *neomedievalism* does not connote European exceptionalism. If anything, neomedievalism is non-Eurocentric, since it moves away from the primacy of the state, arguably a European invention exported through colonialism. Neomedievalism does not insinuate worldwide atavism. States will not disappear, but they will matter less than they did a century ago. Nor does neomedievalism suggest chaos and anarchy; the global system will persist in a durable disorder that contains, rather than solves, problems.

Hedley Bull's Test for Neomedievalism

One of the greatest interpreters of neomedievalism was Hedley Bull, a seminal scholar of the so-called English School of international relations. Born in 1932, he was a professor at the Australian National University, the London School of Economics, and Oxford University, until his death from cancer in 1985. He addresses neomedievalism in his main work, *The Anarchical Society*, which explores alternative models to the Westphalian system, including what he calls "new medievalism." For this, he imagines a future where "sovereign states might disappear," replaced by "a system of overlapping authority and multiple loyalty."[2]

A neomedieval system would seem to invite instability and even anarchy, but it is balanced and centered, according to Bull, by the dueling universal claims of empire and church, or their equivalents today. In such a world order, no single ruler or state is sovereign in the sense of being supreme over a given territory and its contained population, akin to the modern state. Instead, several authorities—Holy Roman Emperor, pope, prince, city-state, monastic order, guild, and so forth—shared or competed for authority over vassals and resources in a single geographical area. According to Bull, a neomedieval world order could be said to exist "if modern states were to come to share their authority over their citizens, and their ability to command their loyalties, on the one hand with regional and world authorities, and on the other hand with sub-state or sub-national authorities, to such an extent that the concept of sovereignty ceased to be applicable, then a neo-mediaeval form of universal political order might be said to exist."[3] Such a world order characterized by the multiplicity of authorities and allegiances "represents an alternative to the system of states."

Bull looked for evidence of neomedievalism in his day. He proposed five criteria to test for its existence: the technological unification of the world, the regional integration of states, the rise of transnational organizations, the disintegration of states, and the restoration of private international violence. After consideration, he concluded that some elements of neomedievalism existed and that a secular "neomedieval order" might be possible, but overall, he dismissed the idea as lacking sufficient "utility and viability" to displace the state system.

It is not surprising that Bull found little evidence for neomedievalism, since he was writing in the mid-1970s at the height of the Cold War, when global politics was dominated by two superpowerful states and the Westphalian order was at its peak. However, now that the Cold War has ended, it is time to reconsider Bull's initial investigation into neomedievalism and assess whether it is slowly replacing the Westphalian order. Already, strong evidence exists that private international violence is making a comeback in international relations. Bull's other four features of neomedievalism warrant examination.

The Technological Unification of the World

For thirteenth-century Venetians, the world was "flat" in that it was globally connected across boundaries and borders, both natural and artificial. The geography of their imagination saw a planet of endlessly changing trade routes, networks, and opportunities that extended over land and sea. Venetian merchants such as Marco Polo traveled through the known world and beyond by ship or caravan in search of new markets and merchandise ranging from spices and gems to salt and slaves. The world also came to Venice, as it was a hub of international trade and a clearinghouse of goods from Africa, the Middle East, and Western Europe. Such cosmopolitan bustle moved Shakespeare to exclaim through Antonio in *The Merchant of Venice* that "the trade and profit of the city/ Consisteth of all nations."[4]

Venetian trade was synonymous with globalization as the city's traders forged partnerships and complex networks with distant lands that cut across ethnic and religious divisions. Arabs, Jews, Turks, Greeks, and Mongols became trading partners even when they seemed to be political enemies. Cultures, customs, and languages intermingled in ways that endure to this day. For example, the English word *arsenal* comes from the Italian *arzenale*, which can mean a place to store weapons or a dockyard and was the term Venetians used to describe a large wharf in their city renowned as a center of shipbuilding. *Arzenale*, in turn, is derived from the Arabic *dar as-sina'ah*, which literally means "house of manufacture" or "workshop."

Eight hundred years later, the world is "flat" once more, leveled not by ship and caravan but by jet plane and telecommunication. The contemporary technological unification of the world and subsequent globalization are among the most widely studied phenomena of the post–Cold War era. The ability for information to transcend territorial boundaries has diminished the relevance of national borders and the states that control them in ways unimaginable to Bull's generation.

Globalization is driving neomedievalism in several ways. Modern technology and the decrease of state-planned economies have created a single world marketplace linking the fortunes of states and nonstates alike. Overall, this has been good for the world's financial health. According to the World Bank, the gross domestic product (GDP) of the world multiplied by an incredible factor of forty-five over the past four decades, from $1.35 trillion in 1960 to $61.10 trillion in 2008. From 2000 to 2008 alone, world GDP nearly doubled.[5] But when there is an economic crisis in one country, it can affect the world, as seen with the financial collapse of Thailand's currency, which induced the East Asian recession of 1997 or the US subprime mortgage crisis in 2007, which led to a worldwide recession. Nearly everywhere, jobs, production, savings, and investments are connected.

Globalization extends beyond markets and into society itself in what communications theorist Marshall McLuhan labeled the "global village."[6] Modern communications technology is uniting the world and making national borders less relevant and, consequently, states less powerful. For example, the Arab Spring demonstrates that civil dissent in one country can leap to the next in a matter of days, spurred in part by communications technologies. The Internet gives groups such as al-Qaida the ability to recruit terrorists from within the United States, as exemplified by the Washington "DC Five" youth, who traveled to Pakistan to attend a terrorist training camp, or Faisal Shahzad, who attempted to blow up New York City's Times Square. In an era of globalization, states are increasingly challenged to control their borders, eroding the Westphalian distinction between domestic and foreign spheres and producing a world of overlapping authorities and allegiances.

The Regional Integration of States

In the late fourteenth century, Europe had a problem: it had two popes. In 1378, a papal schism over politics rather than theology split the Catholic Church as two men simultaneously claimed to be the true pope, one seated in Rome and the other in Avignon, plunging Europe into strife as kings, princes, priests, abbots, and individuals were forced to choose sides in what became known as the Great Schism. After several decades, a false start at reconciliation at Pisa, and a three-pope schism, resolution was finally achieved at the Council of Constance from 1414 to 1418, which restored the single papacy to Rome in addition to deciding other important church matters.

The Council of Constance was significant for the history of sovereignty and the regional integration of states. It was the first ecumenical council organized along national rather than religious lines and presided over by an emperor instead of a pope. Some view this as the true origins of the state system.[7] Additionally, the famous *Haec sancta* decree stripped the pope of his supreme authority and vested it in a council or assembly of members from different states and church organizations. By pooling their authority, the representatives could overrule any single sovereign, even the pope.

Today the United Nations and other international organizations act analogously to the Council of Constance: they allow states to pool their sovereignty and claim authority over individual member states for the greater good. This trend is increasing, as a century ago, there were about a dozen international organizations, and now there are more than 355. Generally, they are made up of states, maintain formal procedures, and focus on a region, such as the Association of Southeast Asian Nations, or a single policy issue, such as the International Criminal Police Organization (INTERPOL). To Bull, these organizations do not threaten the primacy of states so long as they act as conduits of coordination for transnational problems such as climate change and terrorism.

However, as already seen with the United Nations, after the Cold War's end, some international organizations sought to transform themselves from a world stage for international relations into an actor upon it. The International Criminal Court (ICC) is an example of this. Established in 2002, the ICC is a permanent tribunal at The Hague that prosecutes individuals for genocide, crimes against humanity, and war crimes. By 2017, the ICC might also adjudicate "crimes of aggression," a broad category that entails any action that "constitutes a manifest violation" of the UN charter. This includes trying a head of state whose military goes to war after a formal declaration of war has been issued, signaling a significant departure from Westphalian norms.

The ICC exists to reinforce international law, potentially challenging the domestic laws of states. Its law is sourced from the 1998 treaty known as the

Rome Statute of the International Criminal Court, and its preamble explains that the court's purpose is to "guarantee lasting respect for and the enforcement of international justice."[8] So far, 111 countries are party to the statute, although three of the five veto powers on the Security Council—China, Russia, and the United States—have not signed up. They are concerned that the court's authority would impede their own, restricting their latitude in areas ranging from warfare to domestic law enforcement. This might seem like an overreaction, but it is not. "International justice" is often code for supranational law that seeks to intervene in the domestic affairs of states, or, as Rosalyn Higgins, former president of the International Court of Justice, warns, "the state can no longer protect itself by claiming domestic jurisdiction."[9]

In many ways, the ICC and supranational law function like the medieval church to create overlapping authorities within a single territory. The foundation of church legitimacy was not territory but claims to the moral sphere of individuals' lives. Similarly, supranational law is concerned with the welfare of people within states as realized through human rights, a concept that traces its moral lineage to the church and its notions of natural law. The UN's Universal Declaration of Human Rights serves as the foundational document of human rights and the cornerstone of international organizations' legitimacy as actors within a neomedieval world.

As the self-proclaimed protector of human rights, the ICC claims universal jurisdiction over all people everywhere, just as the church did in the Middle Ages. This creates mixed authorities in the world, pitting state law against supranational law. In some cases, the court may even investigate and try citizens of states that have not signed or ratified the Rome Statute.[10] The ICC also issues arrest warrants for heads of state, such as Sudan's president Omar Al-Bashir or Libya's president Muammar Qaddafi, for actions they undertake within their state's own territory. New doctrines have emerged, such as the Responsibility to Protect (R2P), that demand that the United Nations stage armed interventions in states that fail to respect human rights.[11] Such measures would not be permitted in a strong Westphalian order.

The ICC is not alone. It is representative of a larger trend to create supranational authority that replaces government with governance, as states are increasingly enforcing laws established by international organizations, exemplified by the European Court of Human Rights and the European Union more generally. Contrary to Bull's assumption that pooling state sovereignty does not impugn state power, international organizations have proven to be more than the sum of their parts. They now assert their own authority alongside states within the same territory, producing the conditions of neomedievalism. As Emma Bonino, the senior European Union commissioner, said during the Rome treaty negotiations, "foreign policy may well be the last vanity of nations."[12]

The Rise of Transnational Organizations

In 1338, a diplomatic mission left Europe and embarked on a perilous journey across central Asia to Cathay, today northern China. The envoys' objective was to "carry letters and presents" to the mighty Khan of the Tartars, the Mongol-Chinese emperor, so that they might strike a treaty, enter formal diplomatic relations, and build an embassy at the capital of Armalec.

The diplomacy in question stemmed not from a state but from a transnational actor, the Church. Pope Benedict XII sent John of Marignolli to Cathay after the unfortunate "martyrdom" of their last diplomatic mission, and John proved more capable or luckier, spending several years in Cathay and Manzi, in southern China, acting as a legate to the Khan's court, building churches, converting pagans to Christianity, and ministering to the faithful. The great Khan also maintained an embassy at Avignon, where Pope Benedict XII held his court, and in this way, both political authorities kept diplomatic relations, even though the Church was not a state.

The church was not the sole nonstate authority in Europe at the time. Medieval international society was teeming with transnational organizations: chivalric orders such as the Knights Templar and Knights Hospitaller; merchant and craft guilds ranging from apothecaries to wheelwrights; and mendicant orders such as the Franciscans, Carmelites, Dominicans, and Augustinians, all of which depended directly on the charity of the local population for their livelihood rather than on the church.

Formalized relations between states and transnational actors were not uncommon during the Middle Ages and are becoming increasingly less uncommon today. Bull defines transnational organizations as any organization "which operates across international boundaries, sometimes on a global scale, which seeks as far as possible to disregard these boundaries, and which serves to establish links between different national societies, or section of these societies."[13] As with globalization and international organizations, the expansion of transnational organizations as international political actors has grown exponentially since Bull's time, perhaps beyond what he thought possible. Today such actors fall into three broad categories: nongovernmental organizations (NGOs) such as Oxfam and the Red Cross; multinational corporations such as ExxonMobil and Walmart; and illicit groups such as al-Qaida and drug cartels.

NGOs are international nonprofit groups that operate independently of governments to provide humanitarian services directly to people, and they are increasingly challenging state authority. They are also on the rise. A hundred years ago, there were 1,083 NGOs, and today there are more than 40,000.[14] Like medieval ecclesiastical charities, NGOs derive their legitimacy and power by doing "good works," not in the name of God but instead of human rights.

The universe of NGOs is diverse and defies a single description, with programs in almost every corner of the world, sometimes eclipsing the state in providing social services to populations. In general, there are two types of NGOs, operational and advocacy groups, and each contributes to the neomedieval order in unique ways.

Operational "on the ground" NGOs seek to accomplish good literally from the ground up, such as providing medical care to the world's most needy, as Nobel Peace Prize laureate Médecins sans Frontières does. Operational NGOs challenge state authority by choosing whom to aid and when, independent of state interests and sometimes in violation of them. For example, an NGO might provide medical care to a rebel group. NGOs invoke human rights to justify such arguably treacherous action, and many also claim "humanitarian space," a sort of "no-state sovereignty zone" within a state, which allows them to act freely and remain faithful to their core principles of neutrality, impartiality, and independence. Obviously, this assertion works best in weak states that lack the military forces necessary to throw NGOs out of their space. Regardless, the recent concept of humanitarian space is a direct challenge to Westphalian sovereignty, since it allows NGOs to claim authority beside states within the same territory.

Advocacy NGOs challenge Westphalian sovereignty by acting as watchdogs for states' alleged bad behavior and bringing international pressure to bear on regimes through adroit worldwide media "name and shame" campaigns. For example, Save Darfur and other NGOs helped pressure the UN and the African Union, a regional international organization, to launch a peacekeeping mission in Darfur to end the genocide there. It also ran a number of unflattering full-page ads in the *New York Times* and other influential media outlets that personally demonized top Sudanese officials and demanded that the ICC issue an arrest warrant for Bashir, the president of Sudan. Advocacy NGOs seek to expand the frontiers of supranational law by acting as norm entrepreneurs, promoting concepts of justice that eventually become international law like the Rome Statutes. NGOs have rendered Westphalian authority ambiguous, whether through the "humanitarian space" where NGOs can disregard state sovereignty or through "norm entrepreneurship" which precipitates supranational laws.

NGOs hire PMCs, too. Save the Children, CARE, CARITAS, GOAL, IRC, and Worldvision all hired PMCs to protect their operations abroad. Humanitarian organizations are big business for the private military industry, and companies include ArmorGroup, Control Risks Group, Global Risk Strategies, Erinys, Hart Security, KROLL, Lifeguard, MPRI, Olive, RONCO, Triple Canopy, and Southern Cross.[15] USAID required NGOs that it contracted in Iraq to hire private security. According to Corey Levine, a human rights consultant, "My organization, a small NGO working to build the capacity of Iraq's civil society, was no exception. Approximately 40 percent of our $60 million budget went to protecting the 15 international staff. Our security company was South African."[16]

Large corporations have also joined the ranks of international relations and even employ PMCs. More than $3 trillion flows across national borders each day in today's globalized economy—nearly triple the world's GDP a century ago.[17] This incredible economic growth is propelled by multinational corporations, which are private, for-profit organizations with commercial operations and subsidiaries in two or more countries. In 1960, they numbered 3,500, with an aggregate stock worth $68 billion. By 2000, there were more than 64,000 multinational corporations, worth $7.1 trillion. They account for between 25 and 33 percent of world output, 70 percent of world trade, and 80 percent of international investment. The fifty largest multinational corporations each have annual sales revenue greater than the gross national product of 142 countries, which is about 75 percent of the world's nations. If revenue were counted as GDP, ExxonMobil would rank among the top 30 countries.[18] The rise of multinational corporations has profoundly affected the viability of a state-centric system.

Unlike the East India Companies of the early Westphalian era, today's multinational corporations are not quasi-state-owned enterprises but instead fully private and independent firms. Their foremost allegiance is to their shareholders, who may hail from anywhere in the world, and their chief concern is profit rather than king and country. For example, multinational corporations are increasingly reincorporating outside their home countries to evade taxes in "offshore" low-tax states such as the Isle of Man or the British Virgin Islands, which maximizes shareholder earnings as it garners the wrath of their countries of origin. A US government report found that in 2007, eighty-three of the one hundred largest publicly traded US companies used such tax havens. Worse, from the US perspective, some of these firms, such as Morgan Stanley, Citigroup, and Bank of America, received federal bailout money in 2008 and 2009 that amounted to $700 billion, outraging members of Congress who demanded that the government "shut down these tax dodgers."[19] Tellingly, this has not happened.

Multinational corporations have helped create a world financial system that binds together the economic fates of nations and has created a global economy so strong that no government, even among those with the most powerful economies, can withstand sustained speculation against its currency, imposing significant constraints on national economic policies. States no longer control financial flows across their borders, and it is not possible to regard any one country as having its own separate economy, unless it chooses to live in total isolation as North Korea does. Moreover, states that wish to benefit from the riches of globalization cannot afford to ignore multinational corporations, because they are the gateway to global markets and control the location and distribution of economic and technological capital. This dynamic has given multinational corporations considerable sway within international relations, and many of the Fortune 500 companies are more powerful than most states. It could not be argued that Togo is more influential in world affairs than ExxonMobil.

Multinational corporations employ PMCs, especially the extractive industries. For example, mining giant Freeport McMoRan employs Triple Canopy to protect its sizable mine in Indonesia, Chevron hires Outsourcing Services in the Niger delta, and G4S guards are practically ubiquitous. Often, these PMC personnel are armed with clubs and not guns. International shipping lines are increasingly turning to armed guards to combat pirates, a very medieval problem, off the coast of Somalia, the Strait of Malacca, or the Gulf of Guinea. Maritime PMCs such as Special Tactical Services and Armed Maritime Security place armed contractors on freighters and yachts traveling through these dangerous waters.

Multinational corporations even provide private governance in lieu of weak states, creating overlapping authorities and allegiances. In 2002, the United Nations announced that it had "abandoned" its efforts to rely on governments in weak states to stop the HIV/AIDS epidemic and turned to multinational corporations to provide antiretroviral drugs. This shift in policy was "an acknowledgment that companies have the resources to find health solutions where governments and NGOs are overstretched or failing"[20] and endowed multinational corporations with political authority in the process. That multinational corporations can and do fill in vacuums of sovereignty is a clear indication of their power and the development of neomedievalism.

Illicit groups such as global terrorists, insurgents, drug cartels, and international criminal organizations are a third type of transnational actor on the rise. What makes them illicit is not just their blatant violation of laws but also their wanton use of violence to advance their agendas, whether politics or profits or both.

Terrorism today embraces a neomedieval agenda. In the twentieth century, when the Westphalian system was at its zenith, revolutionaries such as Mao Zedong in China, Ho Chi Minh in Vietnam, Fidel Castro in Cuba, and Che Guevara in Bolivia fought to take over states. In the post–Cold War era, groups such as al-Shabaab in the Horn of Africa, Boko Haram in West Africa, and al-Qaida worldwide fight to leave the state system altogether, abandoning the Westphalian order. Their vision of the future does not entail UN membership but rather a stateless caliphate and society based on their particular vision of Islam. Such a threat is not trivial, and the United States even declared a "war on terror" against such groups, representing a clear departure from the Westphalian threat model of strong states and stronger militaries.

Unlike terrorist groups, which are nominally motivated by ideology, international criminal organizations seek profits and resort to violence—often bloody and horrific—to make their bottom line. Transnational criminal organizations are not new and were a serious threat in the Middle Ages. During the reign of Edward III (1312–1377), robber barons such as Thomas de Lisle, Bishop of Ely, and Sir John Molyns exploited their aristocratic power to run criminal networks that openly engaged in robbery, extortion, and murder in the face of state authorities. Gangs led by noble families such as the Folvilles and the Coterels had free rein over large swaths of England and committed crimes with impunity. In 1326, the Folvilles and their confederates murdered Sir Roger Bellers, a baron of the exchequer. A few years later, they abducted Sir Richard Willoughby, later chief justice of the king's bench, and ransomed him back to the king for thirteen hundred marks, an exorbitant sum at the time. In the heterogeneous political environment of the Middle Ages, the king's law often competed with the robber baron's law rather than subduing it.

A similar situation is developing today. Like al-Qaida, international criminal organizations such as MS-13 in Latin America and D-Company in South Asia are self-governing, operate in a borderless manner, have the capacity to threaten strong states, and are independent political actors in world affairs. Some are so strong that they even co-opt states. Take, for example, the "narco-state," controlled and corrupted by drug cartels. Since the early 1990s, the trend of drug cartels co-opting states has grown, with the Tijuana and Gulf cartels in Mexico and Central America; warlords in Afghanistan, Tajikistan, and the Golden Crescent area; mafias such as the Arkan gang or the Rudaj organization in the Balkans; and South American cartels operating in West Africa. Narco-states are a neomedieval phenomenon, emerging as the Westphalian order declines and correlated with the rise of transnational criminal organizations and other neomedieval threats.

Take, for example, the small West African nation of Guinea-Bissau. It is the fifth-poorest country in the world and rife with corruption, making it an ideal transit hub for drugs moving from Latin America to Europe. Western officials estimate that $150 million of cocaine flows through it per month, equal to the country's annual GDP. This phenomenon is not unique to Guinea-Bissau. In the late 1990s and early 2000s, cocaine seizures in all of Africa rarely exceeded one metric ton a year. Now cocaine transshipments in West Africa range between 60 and 250 tons, yielding wholesale revenues of $3 billion to $14 billion.[21] The profits from cocaine transshipment dwarf the subregion's official resources. Illicit actors have generated a parallel global economy made up of contraband that competes with—and at times is at war with—the legitimate political economy of Bull's society of states.

The Disintegration of States

Unconstrained political rivalries, the proliferation of warlords and mercenaries, weak states, weaker rulers, cowed populations, and little or no rule of law created the maelstrom that was northern Italy in the high Middle Ages. In the absence of a competent civil authority, rulers became tyrants, and people became prey. Florence and Ravenna developed into fortresses, villages grew walls (*castelli*), and the hilltops were adorned with castles to protect the powerful. Bloody vendettas between families such as the Montefeltri and the Malatesti lasted centuries and claimed countless lives, even though no one could recall why there was a vendetta in the first place. The ceaseless wars between states, city-states, the church, and anyone else who could rent or raise an army left the countryside destitute, hungry, and frightened. While passing through hell, Dante is approached by a particularly infamous warlord called Mastin Vecchio, who asks the traveling poet whether his homeland of Romagna is at peace. Dante replies: "Your Romagna is not and never has been without war in the hearts of its despots."[22]

As in Dante's *Inferno* or medieval Romagna, life in a modern failed state—Somalia or Haiti—can be hell, and incidences of state disintegration seem to be on the rise since the Cold War ended. Since Bull's day, entire countries have disappeared, some quietly (Czechoslovakia) and some not (Yugoslavia). Dozens of country rankings exist, and they all agree that the majority of the world's states are weak, failing, or failed.[23] Today about 1 billion people live in a failing or fragile state, and trends indicate that this number will likely increase in the future.

Where state governments are weak, nonstate entities have filled in the authority vacuum and imposed their own independent rule, complete with their own monopoly of force. The violent devolution of Yugoslavia into semiautonomous regions after the end of the Cold War is consistent with the neomedieval process of state disintegration and fragmentation into smaller stateless polities. Many of these new authorities resemble warlords with private armies, such as Zeljko "Arkan" Raznjatovic in the Balkans and Mohamed Farrah Aidid in Somalia; other groups are more ideologically driven, such as Hezbollah in southern Lebanon and some al-Qaida affiliates. What they all share is the ability to create law and enforce order, violently if necessary, creating overlapping authorities and allegiances with the state.

The slums of Jamaica offer an optic into this neomedieval world. Caribbean expert John Rapley observes that where the state has failed to provide essential services, local area leaders, or "dons," step in to supply them, albeit under their independent rule. According to him, Jamaica is not a modern nation-state but a neomedieval one, as he explains:

> The local gang maintains its own system of law and order, complete with
> a holding cell fashioned from an old chicken coop and a street-corner

court. It "taxes" local businesses in return for protecting them, punishing those who refuse to pay with attacks on property and people. It provides a rudimentary welfare safety net by helping locals with school fees, lunch money, and employment—a function that the Jamaican government used to perform. But over the last couple of decades, keen to reduce spending, it has scaled back many of its operations, leaving a vacuum. As one kind of authority has withdrawn, another has advanced.[24]

To forestall this, some states officially permit the limited rule of others within their territory. Political scientists describe this as "legal pluralism," and it arises when different legal ideas, principles, and systems are applied to the same circumstance within a territory. In Kenya, *kahdi* courts are a discrete legal system for Muslims, applying sharia law where government courts use a legal system based on British law. Kenyan Muslims can choose between state and religious courts to resolve disputes. India and Tanzania have similar Islamic courts to address concerns in Muslim communities. In the Philippines, the government recognizes the customary ways of indigenous peoples in the Cordilleras region, especially in the province of Kalinga, where people use the process of *bodong*, or "peace pact," to settle disputes. However, such measures taken by states do not avoid neomedievalism, since it simply sanctions rather than resolving overlapping authorities.

As in the Middle Ages, life in fragile states is marked by fragmented and overlapping loyalties to the ethnic group, religious order, political party, individual leaders, and other political authorities that compete with the central government for fealty. The weakest states in the world are marred by civil war and insurgencies that do not recognize state territorial boundaries or the government in general. The increasing tendency toward state fragility, failure, and disintegration remains a major unmet challenge for the contemporary system—a sign not only of the Westphalian order's decline but of its possible demise.

A Neomedieval State of Affairs

At its core, neomedievalism describes the clash of sovereignty—not just between states but also among nonstate authorities that are de facto peers of states rather than "substate" actors, as traditional political science views them. For example, in the Middle Ages, the contest between church and state authorities provoked strife throughout the era, as exemplified by the investiture controversy in the eleventh and twelfth centuries. It began as a dispute between the Holy Roman Emperor and the pope over control of ecclesiastical appointments, or investitures, of church officials such as bishops and abbots but grew into a wider conflict over authority between a series of popes and kings. Before the conflict, secular authorities had appointed church officials in their lands with the church's grudging approval.

Pope Gregory VII challenged this in 1075, by asserting the *Dictatus Papae*, a collection of canons, or church laws, which decreed that the church was founded by God alone and that therefore the papacy was the sole universal power. This gave it authority to select or remove clergy, move them from see to see, and even depose kings. Henry IV, the Holy Roman Emperor, ignored the pope's decree and sent a letter to Gregory VII calling for the election of a new pope. To make his intentions plain, his letter to the pope opens with "Henry, King not through usurpation but through the holy ordination of God, to Hildebrand, at present not pope but false monk" and concludes with "I, Henry, king by the grace of God, with all of my Bishops, say to you, come down, come down, and be damned throughout the ages."[25]

Thus, war began between factions aligned with the pope and the emperor—Guelphs versus Ghibellines—a conflict that persisted in Italy into the fifteenth century, as portrayed by the dueling Montague and Capulet families in Shakespeare's *Romeo and Juliet*. Opportunistic princes also seized the occasion to rebel against their lieges, exchanging the yoke of the emperor for that of the pope and vice versa. The controversy later spread to other corners of Europe, in England between King Henry I and Pope Paschal II, and also in France. After fifty years of war, the Concordat of Worms in 1122 resolved the controversy with an uneasy compromise. The king had the right to invest bishops with secular authority ("by the lance") in the territories they governed, while the church bequeathed them sacred authority ("by ring and staff"). Consequently, bishops owed mixed allegiances to pope and king.

The investiture controversy is not as archaic as modern readers might imagine, as the clash between sacred and temporal authorities is returning to international relations. For instance, this dueling authority is reemerging in China, which ordains its own bishops for its state-run Catholic church, whom the Vatican then promptly excommunicates. In the words of one Catholic cardinal, "it's war."[26] The foundation of church sovereignty is based not on territory but on claims to the moral sphere of individuals' lives.

Nor is the church the only modern actor challenging states; the human rights regime exerts power over states by making universal claims of authority concerning the welfare of individuals. The term *human rights regime* broadly describes the principles, norms, rules, and decision-making procedures accepted by global actors, such as international organizations and NGOs, that regulate and promote human rights. Not coincidentally, human rights is built on the moral edifice of Western Christian notions of natural law and focuses on the well-being of individuals within states, issuing international laws akin to church canons that can contravene state laws. For example, the Universal Declaration of Human Rights, the R2P doctrine, and the ICC all claim universal jurisdiction alongside states, as did the medieval church, based on the commitment to the rights inherent in every human. The universal claims of "natural," "inalienable," and "human" rights have long been used to curb the authority of states and in some cases rebel against them.[27] Now they arguably exist as a global regime.

Like the church in the Middle Ages, the universal authority asserted by the human rights regime remains controversial. In 1948, Saudi Arabia and South Africa abstained from endorsing the Universal Declaration of Human Rights, a foundational human rights document, for fear that it would challenge their own ability to determine the norms of justice within their borders. Islamic nations contest the universality of human rights, claiming that they do not account for values implicit in sharia. The 1982 Iranian representative to the United Nations, Said Rajaie-Khorassani, argued that "the Universal Declaration of Human Rights, which represented a secular understanding of the Judeo-Christian tradition, could not be implemented by Muslims."[28] This position was formalized in the Cairo Declaration on Human Rights in Islam and adopted by the fifty-six member states of the Organization of the Islamic Conference in 1990. Later, the League of Arab States passed the Arab Charter on Human Rights (2004, entered into force 2008).

Muslim nations are not the only ones questioning the "universality" of human rights. Concerns about human rights overreach led to the Declaration of Indigenous Rights, adopted in Panama in 1984, to safeguard the customs of non-Western peoples. Similarly, the Vienna Declaration on Human Rights in 1993 acknowledges "the significance of national and regional particularities and various historical, cultural, and religious backgrounds" in the face of human rights universalism. The Bangkok Declaration of Human Rights of 1993 asserts that human rights, as generally conceived, do not accord with "Asian values" that oppose some Christian and democratic values. Each of these challenges to the universalism of human rights implicitly proposes a competing world vision of justice and legitimacy that sets the groundwork for a neomedieval environment of multiple authorities and allegiances.

An example of the clash between the universal authority of the human rights regime and Westphalian sovereignty of states is the controversy surrounding the 2010 Nobel Peace Prize. The Nobel committee awarded the prize to imprisoned Chinese human rights activist Liu Xiaobo, "for his long and non-violent struggle for fundamental human rights in China."[29] China, which views him as a criminal, immediately denounced the award as an affront to China's sovereignty, because it challenges the legitimate authority of the state to establish and enforce laws within its territorial boundaries, which is core to the Westphalian order. As Foreign Ministry spokesman Ma Zhaoxu said, "The Norwegian Nobel

Committee, by giving the Peace Prize to a convicted person in China, shows no respect for the judicial system of China" and warned meddling foreigners that "if some people try to change China's political system in this way and try to stop the Chinese people from moving forward, they are obviously making a mistake."[30] Additionally, China formally protested Norway, canceled several planned official meetings, and publicly declared that China-Norway relations had been damaged.

In defense of the award, Thorbjorn Jagland, chairman of the Nobel Committee, boldly asserted a supranationalist position consistent with the human rights regime. He claimed that states are now subservient to the world government embodied in the United Nations and that they must acquiesce to the norms of human rights:

> The idea of sovereignty changed ... during the last century, as the world moved from nationalism to internationalism. The UN, founded in the wake of two disastrous world wars, committed member states to resolve disputes by peaceful means and defined the fundamental rights of all people in the Universal Declaration of Human Rights. The state, the declaration said, would no longer have ultimate, unlimited power. Today, universal human rights provide a check on arbitrary majorities around the world, whether they are democracies or not. A majority in a parliament cannot decide to harm the rights of a minority, nor vote for laws that undermine human rights. And even though China is not a constitutional democracy, it is a member of the UN, and it has amended its Constitution to comply with the Declaration of Human Rights.[31]

The controversy between China and the Nobel Committee is emblematic of the larger shift from an international society of states to a pluralistic global order of multiple authorities, challenging the foundations of the Westphalian order and characteristic of the competing authorities and allegiances that make up neomedievalism.

State sovereignty is retreating on seemingly every front and the Westphalian order with it. Neomedievalism is indeed upon us according to Bull's test. Aside from a handful of strong states in Western Europe, North America, and parts of Asia, an increasing majority of countries are fragile or "disintegrating." Globalization and the technological unification of the world are making national borders, and those who control them, less relevant. The regional integration of states and the international organizations they produce are progressively challenging the sovereignty of states, as have myriad transnational actors, creating overlapping authorities and allegiances within territories. Unlike in Bull's day, the state is no longer the primary player on the world stage; it is merely one among a chorus of actors. This emerging world order heralds a return to the status quo ante of the Middle Ages, or neomedievalism.

Given the relationship between the sovereignty and war, the implications of neomedieval warfare are significant. In the Westphalian order, states have shaped the conduct of war over the past centuries to reduce death and destruction. But who will do this in a neomedieval order? If history is a guide, then the answer is dismal.

9

Neomedieval Warfare

Kill them all, God will know his own.
　　　　—Attributed to Abbot Arnaud Amalric

Sometime in the eleventh century, a Christian sect called the Cathars emerged in Languedoc in southern France. The sect's roots remain a mystery, although it probably originated in Armenia and traveled westward via Byzantine trade routes. Not much is known about Cathar beliefs other than that they were a heretical blend of church doctrine with elements of an ancient Persian religion called Manichaeism and first-century Christian Gnosticism. For example, they believed in reincarnation, a Satan as strong as God, equality of the sexes, veg-etarianism, and pacifism. They also did not believe that priests were required to intercede with God and therefore did not recognize the authority of the church. This got the pope's attention.

In 1209, Pope Innocent III launched a crusade against the Cathars that would look like a war of terror to modern observers. A crusader army consisting of mer-cenary free companies, knights with their retinues, and pilgrims departed from Lyon in July and marched south into Languedoc. Two weeks later, they encoun-tered their first major Cathar stronghold at Béziers, a well-fortified and amply supplied city.

While the pope's army was busy preparing for the siege, a small sortie of armed men from the city snuck into the crusaders' camp seeking mayhem. They got it. A brawl broke out between them and the mercenaries, and, finding themselves quickly outmatched, they beat a hasty retreat to the city walls. Unfortunately for them, the defenders were also preparing for a long siege, and the walls were not fully manned. The mercenaries flooded the gate and swarmed into the streets, with the rest of the crusader army not far behind. The city was doomed.

The crusaders tore through the streets, killing Cathars and Catholics alike. Panic-stricken residents fled to the churches seeking sanctuary but were afforded none, as the crusaders smashed down the doors and slaughtered all inside. Abbot Arnaud Amalric, the papal legate who commanded the crusaders, allegedly ordered, "Kill them all, God will know his own."

Following the holy massacre came the spoils. A dispute arose between the knights and the mercenaries over the division of booty. The enraged knights chased the disorganized and likely drunk mercenaries from occupied houses and seized their plunder. Not to be outdone, the mercenaries burned Béziers to the ground, destroying it and the booty. Estimates of the dead range from seven thousand to twenty thousand, almost all of them civilians. The news of the massacre quickly spread, and many cities and castles surrendered in terror. The crusaders' victory was swift and total.

But the killing did not stop there, as military success does not always induce political victory. Over the next forty-five years, thousands of Cathars were hunted down and massacred, annihilating the sect. A group of zealous monks led by Dominic Guzmán (later Saint Dominic) carried out the systematic proscription and imprisonment of heretics, including the use of torture and execution. Their purpose was to wipe out the last vestiges of resistance; Cathar sacred texts and churches were torched, and believers who refused to recant were publically hanged or burned at the stake. This was the simultaneous birth of the Inquisition and the Dominican order.

The Cathar crusade might seem horrific to modern readers, but how different is it from the genocides of Rwanda and Darfur? Or the massacres in the Balkan, Congolese, or western Africa wars? Or the Sunni and Shia wars of Iraq or Syria? Or the armed conflicts in Sri Lanka, Colombia, or Chechnya? The answer is not much. Given the relationship between war and the state, it is important to consider how the shifting nature of the international system changes warfare and vice versa.

Westphalian versus Neomedieval Warfare

War is timeless; warfare is not. The former describes an activity, one that is bloody, violent, and political and remains the same in the twenty-first century as it was in the twentieth, the nineteenth, and, indeed, the fifth century BC. The latter describes how war is conducted and changes as a result of improved technology, geopolitical conditions, ideology, culture, regime type, and other factors. For example, Caesar's legions and Mao's guerrillas fought differently—warfare. Yet they used organized violence to achieve a political objective—war. There is nothing new about neomedieval war, but neomedieval warfare differs sharply from Westphalian warfare.

In the Westphalian world, war is the exclusive capability and right of states, since they claim the monopoly of force and nonstate actors are outlawed from using violence. Accordingly, Westphalian warfare is generally an interstate affair, fought between states through their national armies like gladiators to violently settle disputes between states. War's objective is the defeat of a rival state or the capture of territory, the measure of sovereign power in a Westphalian system.

Over the centuries, states developed diplomatic protocols regulating interstate affairs such as war and peace. For example, states mark the beginning of armed conflict with an official declaration of war, the victor is often determined by decisive battlefield victories such as Waterloo and Midway, and a formal peace treaty between states denotes war's end. Westphalian warfare is best articulated by Carl von Clausewitz and his book *On War*, written in the 1820s yet still a primary text at war colleges today. The role of the military in international relations is central, because battlefield victory is the ultimate arbiter of political disagreements between nations, and captured in Clausewitz's famous dictum: "There is only one decisive victory: the last."[1]

National militaries also forged customs regarding conflict, later codified into the "laws of war," such as the Lieber Code, the Geneva Conventions, and the Rome Statutes that seek to regulate violence. Examples of this code distinguish between lawful and unlawful combatants, dictate rules of engagement in combat, mandate the humane treatment of prisoners, outlaw hostage taking and some weapons (e.g., triangular bayonets and flamethrowers), and pronounce white flags to signal intent of surrender. World Wars I and II best exemplify the Westphalian way of war, often termed "regular" or "conventional" warfare.

Now this trend is reversing, and "irregular" warfare is more regular than the "regular" warfare. Militaries no longer battle other militaries, and nonstate actors now do the fighting and dying; an estimated 90 percent of casualties today are civilian.[2] War is shifting from interstate to intrastate and is accordingly fought in fragile or failed states that have by definition lost their monopoly of force. In contrast to Westphalian warfare, most fighting today is civil war, ethnic conflict, insurgency, rampant violent crime, warlordism, and general lawlessness.

A review of recent conflict trends confirms this shift away from Westphalian warfare. According to the Center for International Development and Conflict Management at the University of Maryland, the number of internal conflicts has tripled, while the number of interstate wars has dwindled to nearly zero over the past sixty years (see figure 9.1). The top twenty-five "at risk" countries all have at least one active ethnic insurgency or terrorist group within their borders. The report concludes that "the number of conflict recurrences has surged to unprecedented levels. Since the mid-1990s, recurrences outnumber new onsets by significant margins."[3]

Most of today's armed conflicts, like the crusade against the Cathars, are fought between myriad state and nonstate actors for ideological objectives or plunder rather than territory. For example, al-Qaida fights to impose a strict

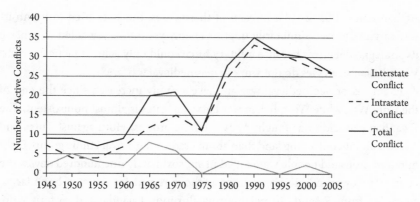

Figure 9.1 Conflict Trends 1945–2005.

interpretation of Islam, and MS-13 fights for control of the illegal drug trade; they do not fight to become a member of the society of states.

The customs of states do not apply to neomedieval actors, and this affects how they fight. Neomedieval wars have no clear beginning, middle, or end; there is no formal declaration of war, battlefield victory to determine the winner, or peace treaty to symbolize conflict's end. Instead, they tend to persist in nebulous perpetuity and can span generations in a lower-intensity yet unending armed conflict that epitomizes durable disorder.

Similarly, neomedieval warfare frequently and flagrantly violates the laws of war. This is to be expected, since such laws were developed by national militaries to fight one another, and neomedieval actors are not signatories to the Geneva Protocols. Consequently, neomedieval warfare blurs the line between civilians and combatants, as in the sacking of Béziers, and today the vast majority of casualties in war are civilian, further evidence of the rise of neomedievalism. In 2003, the European Union estimated that "since 1990, almost 4 million people have died in wars, 90% of them civilians." Oxford economist Paul Collier agrees in a World Bank research report, stating that in modern civil wars, "nearly 90% of the casualties resulting from armed conflict were civilian."[4] Many other individuals and institutions have made similar observations.

Victory is also different in neomedieval warfare. For Clausewitz and the Westphalian way of war, overwhelming force wins the battle that wins the war and ultimately the political objective or national interest. But when Westphalian militaries engage neomedieval foes, they often win every military engagement yet lose the war, because military success does not equal political victory in a neomedieval environment. In other words, the utility of force in neomedieval warfare is low. Examples of this phenomenon are plentiful: France in Algeria (1954–1962); the Soviet Union in Afghanistan (1979–1989); Israel in Lebanon (2006); the United States in Vietnam (1959–1975), Iraq (2003–2011), and

Afghanistan (2001–2014). In each of these cases, the state tried to bomb its way to victory over a militarily inferior enemy yet ultimately failed to achieve its strategic objectives because military force could only achieve tactical results. Westphalian strategies do not work in neomedieval warfare.

Examples of neomedieval warfare have steadily increased since the end of the Cold War, while Westphalian war between states is almost nonexistent. The Rwandan genocide was fought by two ethnic groups, Hutu against Tutsi, and was less about controlling land than about eradicating a rival ethnic group. Eight hundred thousand people were killed in approximately one hundred days.[5] The conflict followed ethnic populations without regard for country boundaries, spreading from Rwanda to neighboring Burundi, Uganda, and eastern Zaire (now the Democratic Republic of Congo). Not present were national armies, Clausewitzian logic, or any regard for the laws of war—in a word, "regular" or Westphalian warfare.

There are numerous other examples of neomedieval warfare since the end of the Cold War: the war in the Balkans, the Sunni and Shia conflict in postinvasion Iraq, the Taliban in Afghanistan, genocide in Darfur, conflicts in the Congo, wars in West Africa, and the civil war in Syria. Drug wars in Latin America pit international and highly organized gangs against one another and society, reaping vast destruction and arguably rendering countries like Mexico a narco-state. Other groups, such as Boko Haram in Nigeria, al-Shabaab in Somalia, and al-Qaida, want to abandon the Westphalian system altogether and establish a caliphate based on their vision of eighth-century Islam.

Additionally, the weak can defeat the strong in neomedieval warfare. In the Westphalian world, weak nations should represent an opportunity or at least not a threat to strong states, most clearly illustrated in the era of colonialism, when strong European states conquered much of the world. Now the opposite is true. Strong states cringe at becoming entangled with weak states. In October 1993, Somali clans armed only with small arms and "technicals"—often pickup trucks with heavy machine guns or antiaircraft guns mounted on the truck beds— defeated the most elite US military forces, consisting of the Army Delta Force, Ranger teams, the 160th Special Operations Aviation Regiment, Navy SEAL Team Six, and Air Force Pararescue–Air Force Combat Controllers. The Battle of Mogadishu, also known to Somalis as the Day of the Rangers, was captured in the book and then the movie *Black Hawk Down*. Following this defeat, the United States left Somalia. The Battle of Mogadishu shows that the Westphalian way of war is not absolute and the hegemony of strong states no longer total.

The defeat also led to broader shifts in US foreign policy. The superpower became reluctant to intervene in weak states, as revealed by its inaction regarding the Rwandan genocide. In *A Problem from Hell*, Samantha Power explains that the "lesson of Somalia" was that the Pentagon now feared that "a small engagement by foreign troops would end up as a large and costly one by Americans."[6] The experience also gave birth to the so-called Mogadishu Line, a foreign policy term denoting the point at which peacekeeping becomes war; it is sometimes used pejoratively to describe strong states' aversion to entering situations in weak states that might drag them into an armed conflict, as with US President Bill Clinton's refusal to mobilize US ground troops to curb the conflict surrounding the Bosnian Serb Army in Bosnia and Herzegovina in 1995 and also his decision to use only airpower in Kosovo during Operation Allied Force in 1999. When ground troops are deployed, they spend the majority of their time conducting force protection of themselves rather than on military expedition, which is questionable military strategy.

Retired British army general Sir Rupert Smith calls these neomedieval conflicts "war amongst the people," because they do not revolve around states. Smith wrote *The Utility of Force* after forty years in the British army and served in East and South Africa, Arabia, the Caribbean, Northern Ireland, Europe, and Malaysia. He commanded the United Kingdom's Armoured Division in the (first) Gulf War, led UN forces in Bosnia in 1995, and commanded British forces in Northern Ireland from 1996 to 1999. He finished his career as the deputy commander of NATO during the Kosovo War. After this distinguished career, he concludes that the Westphalian way of war is dead: "War as cognitively known to most non-combatants, war as battle in a field between men and machinery, war as a massive deciding event in a dispute in international affairs: such war no longer exists."[7]

Private Armies and Contract Warfare

A key feature of neomedieval warfare is the market for force, creating the possibility of contract warfare. Like their *condottieri* ancestors, PMCs are among the new actors waging neomedieval warfare, further blurring the Westphalian distinction between combatant and civilian and that between war and peace. There are no Geneva Protocols or laws of war that clearly regulate armed civilians, leaving their status on the battlefield unclear and challenging the definition of *mercenary* in international law. This question has generated countless academic articles by scholars and international lawyers steeped in the Westphalian tradition of warfare and generally inimical to the trend. On the more practical side, it raises questions about how public armies should interact with private ones, as demonstrated by government initiatives such as the US Commission on Wartime Contracting, international efforts such as the Montreux Document, which aspires to establish best practices for the industry, and the industry's own codes of conduct. However, the challenge remains essentially unresolved, as it was at Béziers and also during Machiavelli's time, and is perhaps unresolvable.

Another consequence is the growing dependency between governments and the industry to win wars. As demonstrated in chapter 2 above, half of US personnel in the Iraq and Afghanistan wars are contractors, and barring mandatory conscription, the superpower cannot wage war without the private military industry. This overutilization of private military organizations alters strategic outcomes in ways national armies do not. For example, in contract warfare, employers, whether Florence in the Middle Ages or the United States in Iraq, are dependent on the industry to deliver victory. The example is most clear with Florence, since the city-state had a relatively weak militia and was almost completely reliant on the services of *condottieri* such as Hawkwood for its military might. The case with the United States is subtler, because the country maintains a potent military, yet it remains true nonetheless.

Despite its strong armed forces, the United States is increasingly dependent on the private military industry to deliver "victory" in modern war. This is because its military is fundamentally structured, trained, and equipped to wage Westphalian warfare, such as defeating the Soviet Union in a World War III scenario, rather than neomedieval enemies such as al-Qaida or the Taliban. For example, US military campaigns proceed in five phases: phase 0 is conflict prevention; phase 1 is the decision to deter or engage the enemy; phase 2 is seizing the initiative to outmaneuver the enemy; phase 3 is decisive operations to defeat the enemy on the field of battle; and phase 4 is postconflict transition and stability operations.[8] In Westphalian warfare, decisive victory occurs on the battlefield in phase 3. Accordingly, during the Iraq and Afghanistan campaigns, the US military concentrated on phase 3 combat operations to win the victory while it contracted out most of the "lesser" phase 0 and phase 4 tasks.

However, in neomedieval warfare, military success in phase 3 matters little. There is no greater metaphor of this than the image of President George W. Bush standing on the deck of the US aircraft carrier *Abraham Lincoln* and declaring "victory" with a large "Mission Accomplished" banner behind him after phase 3 combat operations ended in Iraq, just a few weeks after the invasion began. Few observers today would claim that the United States had accomplished its mission on that brisk day in 2003, and the United States remained embroiled in Iraqi internal warfare well after Bush's departure from the White House.

Victory in neomedieval warfare is dependent on successful phase 0 and phase 4 operations, which often do not involve combat, rather than winning battles in phase 3. It took the Pentagon a few years to learn this lesson in Iraq and Afghanistan, turning away from Westphalian warfare. This strategic paradigm shift is evidenced by the advent of National Security Presidential Directive 44 and the Defense Science Board Task Force on stability operations, which decree phase 4 postconflict and stability operations a strategic imperative on par with combat operations. Similarly, the 2006 Quadrennial Defense Review recognizes that a core military mission should be conflict prevention, or phase 0, to "prevent problems from becoming crises and crises from becoming conflicts."[9] Victory depended more on pre- and postconflict actions than on what happens on a battlefield.

However, the United States soon found itself unable to achieve victory by itself, because its military was tooled for Westphalian war and it lacked the civilian capacity to successful conduct phase 0 and phase 4 operations.[10] To remedy this, President Barack Obama in 2009 announced a "civilian surge" to Afghanistan and established the Civilian Response Corps, but this initiative fizzled, because there was already a robust civilian presence in Afghanistan conducting stability operations: contractors. Tens of thousands of contractors were directing phase 0 and phase 4 operations, while the Civilian Response Corps mustered only one hundred full-time personnel.[11]

Earlier in the campaign, as the military focused on phase 3 combat operations, the private military industry was busy learning skills pertaining to phase 0 and phase 4 operations and selling them back to the government. This made the United States progressively dependent on the private sector for victory. In fact, many of the lessons that informed the army's 2008 field manual on stability operations were drawn from private sector experiences.[12] Of greater concern to the US military is that many of the specialized skills needed for stability operations can now only be found in the private sector and are considered proprietary knowledge. If the government wants to have access to these skills, it *must* hire the companies that perform them, because the military no longer has an internal capability of its own.

Moreover, the country's primary development organization, the US Agency for International Development (USAID), already contracts out the vast majority of its work to the private sector. This led its director, Rajiv Shah, to compare it to the military-industrial complex that President Eisenhower presaged.[13] For instance, the Academy for Educational Development, or AED, was one of USAID's larger partners, managing about $500 million annually in grants and contracts but suspended because of serious mismanagement of funds for programs in Pakistan, causing the firm to go bankrupt in 2011 and pay back $5 million to the government. The United States' overreliance on contractors—both military and civilian—should concern it strategically, since it must rely on the private sector to conduct the stability operations that win neomedieval wars.

The United States is correspondingly vulnerable to strategic defeat when contractors fail. Nisour Square is the clearest case of this, as the tactical failure of Blackwater became a strategic liability for the United States throughout the Middle East. But other examples exist, too. In 2010, the NATO-led International Security Assistance Force (ISAF) mission in Afghanistan determined that PMCs had failed in their contracts to train and mentor the Afghan police.[14]

General Stanley McChrystal, then–commander of ISAF, stated that police were one of the most crucial elements of his campaign plan, yet a US government investigation into police training by PMCs found the program did not "provide the [police] with the necessary skills to successfully fight the insurgency, and therefore, hampers the ability of DOD to fulfill its role in the emerging national strategy."[15] By outsourcing victory and defeat, the United States is increasingly becoming vulnerable to the ebb and flow of contract warfare, just like medieval Florence.

Public versus Private Warrior Ethos

Warrior ethos is vital to why individuals fight and in some cases die. The differing motivations driving public and private warriors have long alienated the two from each other, as demonstrated by the brawl between the knights and the mercenaries following the sack of Béziers that resulted in the city's destruction. Machiavelli is famous for descrying the faithlessness of mercenaries, implying that they have no interests other than profit. Yet many *condottieri* such as Bartolomeo d'Alviano, Gian Giacomo Trivulzio, and Cesare Borgia commanded great respect within Machiavelli's lifetime. This tension is unfolding today, especially within the ranks of the profession itself.

The differences between public sector and private sector warriors are great. Westphalian militaries are highly normative institutions with a cultivated sense of patriotism and self-sacrifice. Like the knights at Béziers, soldiers are supposed to fight for a selfless ideal—God in the case of the knights and country for the soldiers— rather than for personal gain, and they are not allowed to negotiate salaries or working conditions, unionize, or go on strike. The profession maintains an unspoken covenant with the employer, be it church or state, which bequeaths them societal status and often food, housing, clothing, education, health care, and subsidized goods. In exchange, they are expected to protect their employer with their lives.

This "calling" creates a warrior ethos in Westphalian militaries that internalizes concepts such as "service," "duty," "honor," "sacrifice," and "country" into a code of conduct that seeks to distinguish soldiers from every other segment of society, which it terms *civilian*. This creed is imbued in every soldier from the moment he or she enters the ranks; for instance, the motto of the US Military Academy at West Point is "Duty, Honor, Country." Working in the military is called "serving," and many states such as Germany, Iran, and Brazil require mandatory conscription in part to hone the patriotism of their citizenry. As for the knights, the primary incentive of the Westphalian or public sector soldier should be idealism, specifically nationalism.

Private warriors are an affront to this code, because they reject it. Unlike their Westphalian counterparts, PMCs salute something far more palpable and base than the state: profit. Scholar Christopher Coker has long studied warrior ethos and modern wars, and as he explains, "private security companies embrace the norms of the marketplace, with its attachment to the law of supply and demand.... Performance is measured against the standards of the marketplace, such as efficiency and cost. Their relationship with society is highly contractual."[16]

A growing challenge of neomedieval warfare will be reconciling these dueling models of the warrior ethos, the business-oriented view of private armies with the nationalism of public ones, especially when the former is contracted to the latter. The relationship between society and private warriors is still unfolding, and it has the power to change civil-military relationships, what it means to "serve," and ultimately who goes to war and who does not.

Neomedieval warfare has the power to affect the future of international relations. States are losing their monopoly of force, sometimes because it is lost in civil wars, as in Nepal or the Democratic Republic of the Congo, and other times because they allow it, as the United States did by hiring PMCs in Iraq and Afghanistan. Those who control violence can enforce their rule of law, or, as Mao Zedong bluntly said, "Political power grows out of the barrel of a gun."[17] Another concern about neomedievalism is the commodification of conflict, since offering the instruments of war to anyone who can afford them will change warfare, why we fight, and the future of war. If money can buy firepower, then large corporations and ultrawealthy individuals will become a new kind of superpower.

There are at least two directions that the future market for force will take in a neomedieval world. The first is a mediated market for force, where military enterprisers dominate the market and work in close conjunction with their employers, as Wallenstein did with Holy Roman Emperor Ferdinand II during the Thirty Years War. The second is a free market in which mercenaries work for the highest bidder, seek war, and possibly generate it, as was the case in medieval Italy.

These two futures hold different outcomes for the world in terms of peace and security. To explore them, the cases of Liberia and Somalia are instructive. Africa is a useful location, since it is plagued by armed conflict and thus attractive to the industry. In fact, Africa will likely be where the industry ventures next, as supply naturally seeks demand.

In Liberia, DynCorp International acts as a military enterpriser, demobilizing the country's old army and raising a new one for the government after its fourteen-year civil war. The contract for the new army was issued and paid for by the United States, and it is the first time in one hundred fifty years that one state has hired a company to raise another state's armed forces. In the spirit of transparency, the author was a principal architect of this program. Study of this case examines the benefits and dangers of the military enterpriser model and the viability of a mediated market for force.

The second case involves Somalia, a true free market with "lone wolf" PMCs who fight for the highest bidder and become predatory when it suits them. Like medieval Italy, Somalia is an environment of ceaseless conflict and lawlessness. The case study here explores the implications of this and how private military actors heighten or check its instability.

To be clear, neomedievalism is not necessarily a negative phenomenon, nor is contemporary Africa analogous to medieval Europe. In fact, Africa is home to five of the world's fastest-growing economies.[18] However, extreme examples are often the most illustrative, and both cases demonstrate all five characteristics of neomedievalism: the disintegration of states, the regional integration of states, the rise of transnational organizations, the technological unification of the world, and the restoration of private international violence. These cases also offer strategic insights into the future of the private military industry, which is important, because private warfare has the power to shape international relations and the world.

10

Military Enterprisers in Liberia: Building Better Armies

He killed my Ma, he killed my Pa, I'll vote for him!
—Charles Taylor's presidential campaign slogan

In 2005, I joined an assemblage of diplomats, UN officials, local politicians, and reporters at the Liberian presidential palace, once occupied by Charles Taylor, the notorious warlord-turned-president. Bullet holes pocked the walls, and a generator powered the palace. Fourteen years of civil war had left the small West African country of Liberia little but ashes and scars, and it was now home to the largest UN peacekeeping mission in the world. At the time, I worked for a major PMC called DynCorp International.

The new president walked across a makeshift stage and made a declaration that few African heads of state would dare to make: the national army would be demobilized. The army was complicit in the mass atrocities during the war, and a new military was needed if the country wanted a future free of civil war. However, the only thing more dangerous than a rogue military is a threatened one. Similar attempts to decommission army units in neighboring countries such as Côte d'Ivoire triggered more bloodshed, and many feared the same fate in Liberia, a still brittle society.

To great fanfare, ironically provided by the Armed Forces of Liberia (AFL) band, the president made his proclamation, followed by applause. He then stepped off the dais and walked out of the hall to his waiting motorcade. As it pulled away, the band switched its tune from the Liberian national anthem to "Que Será Será."

Razing and raising armies is serious business. Those who wield violence in failed states such as Liberia are de facto authorities, since such a country has no monopoly of force to enforce its rule of law. Warlords are a law unto themselves, and telling them to lay down their AK-47s and become unemployed farmers who obey another's authority is not just political, but it is also extremely dangerous, as they might violently disagree.

However, the Liberian government need not worry about this problem, because the private sector was asked to handle it. The United States paid DynCorp International tens of millions of dollars to demobilize the old army and raise a new one "from the ground up" (the actual language taken from the US government contract), which was why I was there.

DynCorp's contract with the US government in Liberia is a good illustration of how today's private military industry functions within the emerging neomedieval order. The restoration of international private violence is a US-driven phenomenon; hence it makes sense to examine an example of this. Iraq and Afghanistan make poor case studies because such massive undertakings—where the United States pumped billions of dollars into the market for force—are rare. Future contracts will probably occur on a smaller scale, like DynCorp's in Liberia. Also, the private sector took the lead in creating Liberia's military, unlike elsewhere, better demonstrating the benefits and risks of contracting. Lastly, Liberia remains a success story compared to Iraq and Afghanistan, offering important lessons.

DynCorp functioned not as mercenary *condottieri* but rather as a military enterpriser in the tradition of Count Ernest Mansfeld, Louis de Geer, Marquis of Spinola, and Count Albrecht von Wallenstein during the Thirty Years War. Just as these military enterprisers mark the median point in the transition from medieval free market for force to the states' monopoly of it, perhaps DynCorp in Liberia denotes the reverse of this process: it was the first time in two centuries that one sovereign nation hired a private enterprise to raise another sovereign nation's armed forces.

This case has several other merits, too. Liberia is a microcosm of neomedievalism (albeit a worst-case scenario); the case reveals how the United States contracts PMCs; DynCorp is an excellent example of how PMCs provide services under contract to the US government; Africa is a useful location, since the industry will likely seek new markets there once the Iraq and Afghanistan market "bubbles burst"; and building armies is an area that the industry seeks to enter, because it is more profitable than simple executive protection and convoy security. The case exposes some of the inner workings of private military industry, how these companies function, how they alter international outcomes, and how the industry will behave in a larger neomedieval setting in the years to come.

The Siege of Monrovia

"It was really like a fourteenth-century siege. The two rebel armies had surrounded Monrovia with the government's troops inside of Monrovia and the two rebel armies pressing hard outside."[1] This is how John W. Blaney, the US ambassador to Liberia, described the final days of the war in Liberia's capital.

Much of the embassy had been evacuated, mortar fire rained down on the city, and bodies lay strewn in the streets. Packs of child soldiers fought one another, and hapless victims were run down and tortured.

Liberia's war was neomedieval, fought between warlords rather than states. Civilians were both the primary actors and the targets of armed conflict, displacing nearly half the population and destabilizing the region. National armies were either absent or co-opted by warlords, and the Westphalian laws of war were flouted as massacres, torture, rape, child soldiers, looting, and fratricide were the tactics and strategy of war.

At the time, Liberia was more of a kingdom than a state. Beginning with the first coup d'état in 1980, national authority—if it even existed—rarely extended beyond Monrovia. Institutions were anemic, and those who possessed the means of violence served warlords such as Taylor rather than the state. As one Liberian put it, "Ghankay [Charles Taylor] is our law. He understands that the man with the gun is a strongman."[2]

Taylor seized power in 1989, when his troops captured, tortured, and killed the Liberian president, himself a former warlord who came to power in a coup d'état, on international television. A bloody war ensued, claiming hundreds of thousands of lives and displacing 1 million people in a country of about 3 million. The human toll of the fourteen-year war is estimated at 270,000 dead, 320,000 long-term internally displaced people, and 75,000 refugees in neighboring countries. Almost everybody in Liberia was touched by the war: a recent poll shows that 96 percent of respondents had some direct experience of the conflict, and of these, a shocking 90 percent were at one point or another displaced from their homes.[3] The war also spread to its neighbors, and Taylor tried to unseat the president of Sierra Leone, sparking a parallel eleven-year neomedieval war that left 50,000 dead.

Taylor acted the depraved king during his reign. He regularly murdered and mutilated civilians, illegally trafficked "blood" diamonds to enrich himself at the expense of the state, abducted women and girls as sex slaves, and forced children and adults into slave labor and soldiering during the war in Sierra Leone. His militias chased down civilians and asked them if they wanted a long-sleeve or a short-sleeve shirt. For people who said long sleeves, the fighters hacked off their hands at the wrist with a machete. People who said short sleeves had their arms hacked off closer to the shoulder. To this day, people missing one, two, and even four limbs lie on the streets in Monrovia begging for money.

By 2003, the *Economist* predicted that Liberia would be "the world's worst place to live" that year.[4] They were right. That summer, two rebel armies surrounded and sealed off Monrovia. Inside the city, remnants of the AFL still loyal to Taylor ferociously defended it. The fighting was fierce, and all sides committed atrocities. Child soldiers were commonplace, the line between combatants and civilians was blurred, and the laws of war were utterly ignored. Monrovia lay on a small peninsula and was protected on three sides by water, as if by a moat. The battles over the bridges into Monrovia were so intense that the road was paved in blood and brass shells; lampposts, road signs, and nearby buildings were riddled with bullet holes. The siege would not break.

Frustrated by the AFL's resistance, rebels started indiscriminately shelling the overcrowded city with mortars, killing more than one thousand civilians. Liberians described the situation as "World War III" and began piling their dead at the gates of the US Embassy in a macabre plea for help. Monrovia was already a humanitarian disaster, as hundreds of thousands of people had fled the fighting in the hinterlands for the capital, which could not accommodate them all. With no electricity, water, sewage, police, food, or any other accoutrement of modern life, the city became a massive slum of tin shacks, garbage, human waste, disease, and lawlessness. Liberia was once the jewel of West Africa, with three direct Pan Am flights a week from New York City. Now it was apocalyptic.

With global pressure intensifying and rebels at the gates, Taylor finally yielded on August 11, 2003, and fled to Nigeria. He blamed Liberia's problems on foreign meddling and cast himself as the martyr: "Because Jesus died, we are saved today. I want to be the sacrificial lamb. I am the whipping boy. It's easy to say 'It's because of Taylor.' After today, there will be no more Taylor to blame."[5] A few days later, the rebels lifted their siege, and international peacekeepers entered the city, ending the war.

Optic into a New Order

Liberia's violent fall and fragile resurgence illustrate all five characteristics of neomedievalism and shed light on the mechanics of the emerging world order. Liberia is a stark example of state disintegration; as Africa expert Peter Pham observes, "tragically, the recent history of Liberia has been a case study *par excellence* of a failed state."[6] In 1975, Liberia's per capita GDP was greater than those of Egypt, Indonesia, or the Philippines and double that of India. By 2003, it was one of the poorest countries in the world and has remained at the bottom of most international health and development indexes. From 2000 to 2008, 83 percent of the population subsisted on less than $1.25 per day, and in 2008, Liberia had the second-lowest gross national income in the world.[7]

By the time Taylor left the country, Liberia's economic collapse was complete and had been replaced by an illicit economy dominated by warlords trafficking in diamonds, timber, and other natural resources for personal gain at the country's expense.[8] After the war, foreign aid jumped from $106 million in 2004 to $1.25 billion in 2008; Liberia's GDP that year was only $843 million.[9] The country remains totally dependent on global largesse for its survival: five years after the ceasefire, foreign aid still accounts for a stunning 771 percent of government expenditure—the highest percentage of foreign aid to government spending in the world, with Guinea-Bissau a distant second at 221 percent.[10] Not surprisingly, corruption is ubiquitous and so institutionalized that Liberians even have a verb for it—*chopping*—as ministers and executives are expected to chop money off budgets to feed their families and patronize their tribes.

However, Liberia's economic woes are only a fragment of its statehood challenges. There are no functioning public utilities, and most Liberians have no access to electricity, water, sanitation facilities, or health care. Basic infrastructure such as roads and bridges—which aid workers, entrepreneurs, peacekeepers, and Liberians themselves all need, especially in rural areas—are in dire need of repairs. Years of civil war have left a generation of Liberians without a formal education and with a brain drain of those who do. Liberia has no effectively functioning judicial system, leaving it with a culture of impunity: most courts have been destroyed, and trial by ordeal is not unheard of outside the capital.

In another sign of the move toward neomedievalism, states did not manage the situation in Liberia; international organizations did. Liberia's rescuers were not other states, as the Westphalian order demands, but the United Nations and the Economic Community of West African States (ECOWAS), a regional organization. Notwithstanding Blaney's efforts to secure a battlefield ceasefire, the role of the United States was minimal. Its three warships and twenty-three hundred Marines sat off the coast of Liberia and did nothing to stop the fighting; a mere two hundred troops intervened only after Taylor departed. No other state military came to Liberia's aid. By contrast, the ECOWAS peacekeeping mission provided security and humanitarian assistance in the immediate aftermath of the war and was replaced by a larger UN force a few weeks later.

The UN Security Council established an interventionist Chapter VII peacekeeping mission called the UN Mission in Liberia (UNMIL). It was authorized to use "all necessary means" to support the implementation of the ceasefire agreement and the peace process. Led by Jacques Paul Klein, UNMIL was the largest peacekeeping mission in the world at the time, with fifteen thousand blue-helmet peacekeepers. A transitional (and kleptocratic) government was put into place to sate the Westphalian bias for national rule, but in reality, the UN administered the country. Taylor was eventually put on trial for war crimes but not by Liberia. In 2012, an international court at the Hague sentenced him to fifty years in prison for massive human rights violations.

As international organizations rescued Liberia, transnational actors keep it alive on life support. More than four hundred NGOs provide the bulk of services normally associated with the good governance of states: health care, food, shelter, education, security, water, sanitation, sewage, infrastructure, job creation, and general administration. For example, Save the Children provides free health care for 102,399 people, has vaccinated 40,670 children against deadly diseases, has sheltered 15,182 children from violence and abuse, and has helped 56,094 children receive an education.[11] As NGOs provide substantially more public services than Liberia's own government, many on the ground at the time quipped that it was a "republic of NGOs."

Multinational corporations also contributed to Liberia's recovery. After the war ended, Firestone Natural Rubber Company returned to Liberia, where it had operated from 1926 until 1989. According to Firestone, since 2005, it has invested more than $101.75 million to improve conditions in Liberia and "intends to invest tens of millions more." As of 2011, the company had built or renovated 2,200 homes, with an additional 321 under construction. By then, the multinational corporation was operating twenty-six schools, teaching nearly sixteen thousand children, and was running nine health-care facilities, including a hospital. It distributed more than 2.21 million free rubber tree saplings to Liberian farmers to help rebuild the industry and ensure a future for thousands of families in the country.[12] Firestone's actions could prove to be trend-setting. Africa expert Greg Mills notes that low-income countries can prosper when their leaders promote private sector-led development in a "trade not aid" policy.[13]

Underlying and enabling the efforts of both NGOs and multinational corporations is the technological unification of the world, which was involved even in catalyzing the international response. Globalized media streamed arresting images of the war's carnage directly into living rooms across the world twenty-four hours a day, inciting international outrage and demand for humanitarian intervention. This outcry was answered when President Bush declared that "Charles Taylor needs to step down" on CNN, and Kofi Annan, the UN secretary-general, said that Taylor's departure marked "the beginning of the end of the long nightmare of the Liberian people."[14] This sequence of globalized media igniting international uproar and prompting world leaders to take action is a self-feeding cycle sometimes referred to as the "CNN effect."[15] Polling data show that American support for a US peacekeeping mission in Liberia initially increased during media coverage of the war but remained mixed until President Bush announced on CNN that US Marines would be stationed off the coast of Liberia. This galvanized popular support for the policy. Without globalization, the world may have ignored Liberia's plight.

Globalization also facilitated Liberia's recovery. Once peacekeepers were on the ground, information technology and the globalized supply chain nourished the large peacekeeping mission. Satellite telephones, mobile telephone networks, and the Internet allowed for instant coordination between aid workers in the field and those at headquarters in New York, London, Paris, Geneva, Washington, DC, and elsewhere. The global supply chain made it possible to deliver humanitarian aid from around the world to Liberia in a timely manner.

Such aid has accounted for an average of 50 percent of Liberia's total aid, one of the highest shares in all recipient countries in 2004 and behind only Iraq, Sudan, and Somalia. In the months that followed Taylor's departure, $109 million in humanitarian aid was flown, floated, or driven into Liberia; that number jumped to $177 million in 2004.[16] Globalization also spurred the Liberian diaspora community's return and reinvestment in the country: remittances rose from $0 during the war to $1,008,166 in 2009.[17]

Finally, the new private military industry was essential to Liberia's recovery, since it relied on DynCorp International to provide its military, paid for by the United States. The historic choice to outsource the making of a military was almost accidental; necessity drove the decision. Curiously, it was the State Department rather than the Pentagon that issued the contract. The State Department hoped that the US military would raise Liberia's army, but after a brief trip to the country, the DOD balked because of ongoing operations in Iraq and Afghanistan.[18] Consequently, the State Department was left with a Hobson's choice: either outsource the making of the military to a PMC or have no military at all. The State Department chose the former and made history without meaning to.

Buying a New Army

Like almost all things involving the US government, purchasing a foreign army is tediously bureaucratic. During the summer of 2004, the State Department tendered a request for proposal (RFP) to the private sector to rebuild Liberia's armed forces. In the government's contracting system, an RFP is an invitation to bid on a contract, and bids generally consist of two parts: a technical proposal and a cost proposal. The technical proposal explains the company's plan to achieve the objectives outlined in the RFP, and the cost proposal estimates in detail—from airplanes to pencils—the projected cost in time, material, and labor needed to fulfill the contract. Typically, firms dedicate considerable, non-reimbursable resources to crafting detailed proposals and submitting them on time, as the government does not accept late proposals.

Only two companies, DynCorp and Pacific Architects and Engineers (PA&E), were allowed to bid on the RFP for the Liberia army contract, as only they had earlier won a five-year indefinite delivery/indefinite quantity (IDIQ) contract from the State Department to support such efforts in Africa. IDIQs act as large umbrella contracts between the United States and the private sector that, as the name suggests, provide for an indefinite quantity of services during a fixed period of time. The government uses an IDIQ contract when it cannot predetermine the precise amount of supplies or services it will need for complex operations, such as peacekeeping.[19]

IDIQ contracts do not represent a firm order for services. Instead, companies bid to be prequalified for future subcontracts that might arise under the scope of the IDIQ contract. In other words, IDIQs prequalify companies and streamline the process once a task order is issued, as negotiations are already (mostly) prearranged and such contracts are exempt from protest. Because IDIQ contracts are normally large in size and scope, they are usually awarded to multiple firms. In the case of Liberia, those firms were DynCorp and PA&E.

IDIQ contracts work in a relatively uncomplicated way. They stipulate a needed range of services over a period of time, starting with a base year followed by a number of option years, should the United States wish to extend the contract. They also guarantee a minimum and maximum amount of money spent on contracts overall, so that companies have an incentive to bid. The government makes no guarantee regarding the number of task orders it will issue under the IDIQ or the actual amount of expenditure above the guaranteed minimum value, but companies compete vigorously to obtain an IDIQ because it gives them exclusive access to profitable agreements as a "prime" contractor to the government rather than as a subcontractor or "sub" to another firm acting as the prime. Primes become the coveted gatekeepers to lucrative government contracts for the rest of the private sector.

When the government needs services or supplies that fall under the IDIQ, it tenders an RFP, which contains a statement of work (SOW) explaining what the contract entails, to the pool of preselected companies on the IDIQ. Orders placed for supplies are called delivery orders; those for services are called task orders. Once the RFP is issued for either a delivery or a task order, the companies on the IDIQ contract bid for the work. Contracts are typically awarded under a best-value approach, and large orders are usually awarded to multiple firms, while smaller ones are not. Once the government selects its contractors, it issues them a notice to proceed (NTP), which authorizes them to commence work in exchange for payment. The delivery or task order normally requires deliverables from the contractor to the government, such as a delivery schedule and reporting requirements, to ensure accountability.

The IDIQ for Liberia had a five-year period of service, from January 1, 2003, to May 26, 2008, consisting of one base year and four option years, and drew funding from the State Department peacekeeping operations (PKO) account (see annex A). It had a minimum guaranteed expenditure of $5 million and a maximum of $100 million, which was later expanded to $500 million (see annex B). Although only DynCorp and PA&E could bid on the contract, MPRI joined PA&E as a subcontractor on the Liberia assessment mission, given MPRI's background in restructuring military forces and PA&E's lack of it. All in all, the costs of training the AFL by 2009 were an estimated $240.56 million, making it one of the most expensive per capita militaries in Africa.[20]

After the war ended and the United States agreed to rebuild the Liberian military, it considered five options for who should do it and how it should be done: the US military alone, the US military with light contractor involvement, a contractor with light US military involvement, contractors alone, or no one (i.e., abandon the project). To help resolve this, I joined the assessment team as a contractor in 2004.

What we found was a palpably postapocalyptic country with widespread fear of the AFL, disarmed but not demobilized, and the possibility that war could reerupt in the months ahead. In addition to assessing the situation in Liberia, we also considered and rejected the British model of rebuilding military forces in neighboring Sierra Leone, which embeds British soldiers in Sierra Leone military units to mentor them. This was viewed as creating more problems than it resolved. First, placing mentors within existing units to train and equip them is insufficient for wholesale military transformation, which is necessary in failed states where militaries go rogue. Second, the old units were incorporated into the new security forces regardless of quality, experience, capability, and the country's security needs; this created significant problems in quality control and sheer number of forces, which the government of Sierra Leone could not sustain.

Owing to this, it was agreed that the AFL required wholesale security sector reform (SSR) and not just a "train and equip" program. The envisioned end was an all-volunteer, ethnically balanced, properly vetted, professionally trained, civilian-led, and apolitical military capable of "defending the national sovereignty and in extremis, respond[ing] to natural disasters," as called for by the ceasefire agreement.[21]

To accomplish this mission, the team recommended a four-thousand-person force that could be scaled upward over time. It was acknowledged that this small number could not secure Liberia's borders in a Westphalian war, which is about defending territory, but such a war has never occurred there. Moreover, a large force was seen as a threat to security rather than provision of security in Liberia, because unpaid and idle soldiers tend to stage coup d'états. Consequently, the army's size was determined by the government's ability to pay soldiers' salaries regularly and on time instead of troop strength to man the country's borders. Klein even suggested that Liberia abolish its military altogether, quipping that African armies "sit around playing cards and plotting coups."[22]

After the US Department of Defense declined to conduct the program, the State Department turned to the private sector. That summer, it issued an RFP, followed by a SOW that autumn ordering a new Liberian military. It was only seven pages long. The objective and scope were deceptively simple: assist the government of Liberia in recruiting, training, and equipping a new military, starting with two thousand troops.

After reviewing both contractor proposals, the State Department decided to divide the duties between the two firms, giving them different roles based on their expertise. PA&E, a security support company, would build the logistical infrastructure, such as roads and military bases, necessary to support the AFL and then supply the military once it was in place. DynCorp would build the army "from the ground up," which entailed designing, recruiting, vetting, training, equipping, and fielding the new force. It would also create a new Ministry of Defense to manage the military. Absent from the initial plan was the demobilization of the old AFL, which was originally to be conducted by the Liberian government but later fell to DynCorp, owing to the government's inabilities.

The State Department was quite specific about DynCorp's role in raising Liberia's new army. The original SOW called for the complete reconstruction of the Liberian Armed Forces, which it fixed at 2000 troops but scalable to 4300, if funding permitted. It provided guidance on the military's force structure, the Ministry of Defense, and defense policies, but left the details to the company. It specified eight types of weapons the new army should be proficient in and nine missions it should be able to perform. It instructed DynCorp to recruit, vet and train the soldiers, and also procure all necessary weapons, ammunition and equipment for the army. In short, the SOW directed DynCorp to create a "Ft. Benning, GA" for Liberia. Fort Benning is a major US Army base located in Georgia that trains infantry, airborne, rangers, and other soldiers. In other words, the State Department tasked DynCorp to create and run a complete training base capable of raising an army. Incredibly, the SOW commissioning this army was brief—just six pages long—allowing the contractor needed flexibility to conduct a complex operation yet some might find its brevity disquieting for such a mammoth task.

By 2010, Liberia had a small fledgling army. It remains a qualified success compared with efforts in Afghanistan, Iraq, East Timor, Côte d'Ivoire, and elsewhere, where new security forces degenerated into incompetence, sectarian killing machines, or coup d'état makers. What makes Liberia unique is that a corporation raised its army, revealing some of the benefits, complications, and risks of today's private military industry. A brief timeline of the program is included in annex C to provide coherence.

Benefits

Unlike US endeavors in Iraq and Afghanistan or other UN peacekeeping missions, the transformation of the Liberian military was conceived and conducted by the private sector. This was not an entirely bad thing, contrary to some of the dire warnings from skeptics that outsourcing *any* military function is undesirable. DynCorp's profit motive drove it to find innovative, efficient, and effective solutions to thorny security problems, like the *condottieri* before them, and this accounts for some of Liberia's success today.

Innovation: An Engine for Success

Just as the Swiss companies perfected pike warfare and Wallenstein developed unique methods to rapidly generate regiments, PMCs today also innovate in the realm of war. Such ingenuity was all the more important in Liberia, because when DynCorp was hired to rebuild the AFL in 2004, there were no scholarly books, field manuals, or expert practitioners to draw on; DynCorp had to create a safe way to demobilize and rebuild a military in a country recovering from years of war. Some of its innovations yielded more success than similar efforts by the United Nations or the United States; two such examples are examined below.

The first example is human rights vetting of new recruits, which the International Crisis Group, a large NGO, says is "a notable success—the best, several experts said, they had witnessed anywhere in the world."[23] Owing to the AFL's troubled legacy during the civil war, it was agreed that the old AFL should be completely demobilized and rebuilt to ensure systematic human rights vetting of new recruits and also to assure the population that this really was a new AFL. But neither the United Nations nor the United States has developed a systematic method for vetting military recruits in fragile states such as the Democratic Republic of the Congo or Afghanistan, where there are few, if any, public records to check, such as criminal, commercial, governmental, financial, and educational registers. Even verifying a person's identity is difficult in postconflict areas.

Because of this, the United Nations and the United States do not rigorously vet new recruits entering the security forces, despite the fact that, for example, the US Army would never enlist a person into its own ranks without a background check. Yet the United Nations conducted almost no background checks of Liberians entering the police force, nor did the United States conduct significant checks of Iraqis or Afghans joining the military or the police. Consequently, criminals and insurgents have "infiltrated" these forces and corrupted them, ruinously delegitimizing them in the public's eyes. In 2012, one in seven of all NATO deaths in Afghanistan were at the hands of the very Afghan troops the coalition was training.[24]

Presaging this in 2004, DynCorp created a new approach to human rights vetting in postconflict countries that combined common investigative techniques, international best practices, and human rights norms to judge a candidate's character and capacity for a position of trust and to identify potential risks for security reasons. Vetting was embedded within the overall recruitment program for the

Figure 10.1 DynCorp International demobilized Liberia's legacy military and then raised a new one for the country, paid for by the United States government. (Photo: U.S. Department of Defense, U.S. Marine Sgt. Lydia M. Davey).

military, which the company also designed and ran (see figure 10.1). The vetting process utilized three methods: background checks, records checks, and public vetting.

For background checks, DynCorp fielded fact-finding teams, each made up of one Liberian and one international, to interview candidates and their friends, family, associates, and so forth, using a set of standard questions and techniques. The records team collected and analyzed all available public records for verac- ity and completeness. Candidates' names were checked against this database for "red flags" such as identity theft or criminal activities. The team found that some of the best records were kept by regional organizations such as the West African Examination Council and other nongovernmental sources, which cooperated with the vetting program.

Public vetting was a direct appeal to the population to solicit local knowledge of candidates' past wrongdoings. Candidate pictures, names, and hometowns were publicized nationally to afford witnesses and victims an opportunity to identify undesirable candidates anonymously. Candidates were briefed on this procedure during enlistment and signed a release form authorizing DynCorp to broadcast their information. The company used posters, newspaper inserts, radio, and physical facebooks to disseminate the information and invited the public to provide anonymous feedback via telephone hotlines, an e-mail address, or simply walking into an enlistment center. Not surprisingly, public vetting in Liberia attracted many false leads and fraudulent claims aimed at defaming candidates for unrelated reasons, but in a country with few public records, tapping the collective memory of the populace was an important vetting method.

Should a candidate pass all the recruiting and vetting standards, then DynCorp submitted the application to a board, which decided whether or not to accept the individual. This board consisted of a representative each from the Liberian government, the United Nations, and the United States, all with an equal vote. In the first six months of recruiting and vetting, 1,080 candidates were investigated; of these, 335 were accepted. DynCorp had no vote in who was admitted into the new army that it was contracted to create.

DynCorp's success at vetting created unintended problems. In 2006, Liberia's nascent Truth and Reconciliation Commission (TRC) demanded all of the company's vetting records for public hearings. Such a move would have been disastrous for the recruiting and vetting campaign, since no one would volunteer to join if they thought it would land them in front of the TRC. Worse, if the TRC were to use the vetting records as evidence, making them public in the process or leaking them by accident, it would expose the secret identity of witnesses who helped expose candidates with criminal pasts, inviting reprisals and even revenge killings. Sometimes security and justice agendas work at cross-purposes in postconflict countries.

Owing to this, DynCorp refused to hand over the records. The firm did not face resistance from the United States, which deemed that the immediate needs of security outweighed transitional justice. This is an instance when plausible deniability afforded by private companies may have served the employer's interests. It was easier for the PMC to disregard the TRC than the US military, had it been charged with conducting this program, because the US government had publicly supported the transitional justice process whereas the company was silent on the matter.

A second example of innovation is basic training. DynCorp built, staffed, and equipped a military base in Monrovia to train the new army (see figures 10.2, 10.3, and 10.4). After fourteen years of civil war, most Liberians knew how to fire an AK-47 but did not know when or at what. Thus, the original basic training curriculum and first iteration significantly reduced the number of hours AFL recruits spent on the rifle range and added three weeks' worth of civics classes, which taught the laws of war, ethics, Liberian history and the like. It also addressed the problem of low literacy in the ranks by embedding a reading program into the training regime for any recruit needing or wanting it. Finally, it helped overcome neomedievalism, since Liberians often identified first with their tribe and second with their state. DynCorp deliberately recruited an ethnically balanced force and then strove to construct a national identity in basic

Figure 10.2 Liberian soldiers on the rifle range at a base constructed, staffed and equipped by corporations. (Photo: U.S. Department of Defense, Cpl. Cullen Tiernan).

training and beyond with classes on Liberian history, loyalty to the constitution, rule of law, and related topics that imbued a national consciousness and duty to state above all else.

This nontraditional "civics" curriculum was designed in partnership with Liberian lawyers, historians, and educators, in addition to DynCorp staff with backgrounds in international public law and military training. The 120 hours of civics instruction dwarfed all other training, with basic rifle marksmanship coming in a distant second at less than 50 hours. The firm also partnered with international NGOs such as the International Committee of the Red Cross to deliver eight hours of instruction on international humanitarian law and human rights.

This stands in stark contrast to US programs in Iraq and Afghanistan, which essentially clone US Army basic training. Some at the Pentagon were uncomfortable with DynCorp's unorthodox approach to basic training and recommended that the three weeks of civics be dropped, which the State Department did. Owing to this, it is difficult to assess the efficacy of DynCorp's civics program. The US military's reluctance to abandon its doctrine demonstrates that, like the *condottieri* of the Middle Ages, the contractor is only as innovative as the client.

Surge Capacity

In industry parlance, a PMC's ability to rapidly marshal personnel and material resources to a needed location is called surge capacity, and it is a significant private sector advantage over bureaucratically bulky public sector militaries. After the contract was awarded, the DynCorp team went from a skeleton staff to demobilizing an army in three months—fast, compared with the public sector. It can take the US military up to six months or a year to deploy a typical unit, and generating a new unit would take far longer. Smaller and more agile than the US government, DynCorp established a working staff of seventy-three contractors within three weeks of the order.

Further aiding the velocity of hires is the private military sector's ability to hire types of individuals that its public sector counterparts cannot: foreigners. Like all multinational corporations, DynCorp could recruit personnel from around the planet—Canada, Mexico, Australia, Ghana, Germany, the United States, and, of course, Liberia—to create a bespoke staff customized for the mission, something the US military cannot do. Several members had in-depth knowledge of African affairs, having lived, worked, and studied on the continent. Others had expertise in security sector reform. This stands in contrast to public armies that can only recruit citizens from their own country, resulting in ethnocentric approaches and expertise gaps. For example, US troops are not trained in demobilizing foreign forces or human rights vetting; there are no field manuals, training doctrine, or "standard operating procedures" for such tasks in the US military. Furthermore, DynCorp had the flexibility to hire specialists from around the world on short-term contracts to achieve discrete tasks, such as establishing the legal thresholds for vetting or construction-site surveys. Government bureaucracies are far less pliable.

Keeping rapid pace with these hires, logistics experts at DynCorp's headquarters in (at that time) Texas ordered equipment for the program—from pens to trucks to compounds—inexpensively by relying on economies of scale, the global supply chain, and technical expertise in conflict-zone logistics rivaling anything in the Pentagon. In fact, contractors currently handle much, if not most, of the US military's logistical requirements, indicating that its supply chain is already highly privatized.

Free Agent for Effectiveness

In the Middle Ages, the mercenary Varangian Guard was fiercely loyal to the Byzantine emperor and devoted to protecting him. Such fidelity was crucial in a court so insidiously convoluted and treacherous that the word *Byzantine* is used today to describe intractable bureaucratic politics. The secret of the Guard's success was its relative isolation from the intrigues of the court. All its warriors were drawn from the rugged Norse tribes of the north, whom most courtiers and officials perceived as barbarians. As such, Guard members were outsiders rather than stakeholders in the schemes of the court, making them ideal bodyguards. Additionally, as outsiders, they were not beholden to the vested interests of factions within the court and were free to perform their one task with single-minded efficiency and effectiveness.

Like the Varangian Guard, DynCorp was only a stakeholder in its contract and was uninterested in the factionalism within the US government, UN bureaucracy, or Liberian ministries, enabling it to conduct its mission with concentrated effectiveness and avoid becoming entangled in the bureaucratic turf wars and budget battles that can sabotage operational efficacy. Contractors have no long-term interests in their client's organization and can freely make choices that support the program rather than equities back home. This does not suggest that DynCorp could act autonomously in Washington or Monrovia; it could not. But DynCorp managers did enjoy significantly more bureaucratic latitude than their US government counterparts, especially along interagency fault lines of defense, development, and diplomacy. As an institutional outsider, DynCorp could be a free agent for effectiveness in a seemingly Byzantine bureaucracy.

As a private sector actor, DynCorp was not beholden to any country's military doctrine or textbook solutions, and could freely mold existing protocols without fear of institutional reprisal. Substantially modifying orthodox approaches, such as basic training, to fit the needs of a host nation is a departure from the United States' own practice, which, as recent experience suggests, tends to transpose—wholesale—its own military models onto foreign forces without consideration of whether they are appropriate.[25] Not surprisingly, these efforts meet with limited success; US solutions to Iraqi or Afghan problems have made for a poor fit. By contrast, in Liberia, DynCorp used US military concepts as a baseline for innovation rather than as an outright solution.

Additionally, DynCorp's outsider status allowed it to support Liberia's interests in the back offices of the Pentagon and the State Department in Washington, where Liberians could seldom venture. Critics suggest that DynCorp did little or no outreach to Liberians to establish local ownership, but this is untrue: DynCorp's chief interlocutor with Liberian civil society was appropriately the minister of defense, Daniel Chea and later Brownie Samuki.

It became evident during the consultations that Liberians strongly advocated gender equality in the ranks, while the US government did not. Before the civil war, the AFL had an all-female unit called the Women's Auxiliary Corps, which was well respected even in 2005, and during the civil war some of the warlords, such as Black Diamond, were women. Liberians understood that women could be effective warriors. However, the US military holds that women are not fit for combat and therefore should not serve in front-line units, and it initially opposed including women in AFL infantry units.

DynCorp thus became an unwitting arbitrator in a debate between the defense establishments in Washington and Monrovia. As a nominal outsider in the process, DynCorp could credibly present ideas and recommendations to entrenched bureaucracies on both sides of the Atlantic without the burdens of institutional loyalty or prejudice. This helped drive the argument for gender parity, since key managers in DynCorp were persuaded by the Liberians' case. Because the State Department managed the contract, it had the final vote on the matter and opted for gender parity, overruling the Pentagon's desire to impose its own customs on the AFL and a strong bias against women in infantry units. Consequently, in 2005 Liberian women enjoyed greater equality in the ranks than their American counterparts.

Complications

For all the success of the program, few things went as planned. This was partly owing to the complexity of the task and the difficulty of the postwar environment but also to the unique nature of the private military industry. Using private means to achieve public ends can sometimes pit profit motive against policy goals, and this created problems in the public-private partnership among the United States, DynCorp, and Liberia.

Competition for the Worse

In the Middle Ages, free companies hired by the same employer did not always work well together, and the same is true today. The State Department awarded the remaking of the Liberian military to two companies, DynCorp and PA&E, and despite the importance of their shared task, they rarely coordinated. The idea of integrated operations is so critical to success in warfare that the US military even has a word for it—*jointness*—which refers to the ability of separate services, such as the US Army and Marines, to work closely together. The US government has devoted considerable energy to this challenge since the 1980 failed rescue attempt of American hostages in Iran and the subsequent Goldwater-Nichols Act of 1986 to remedy interoperability issues between military services. It is assumed in public sector militaries that different services ought to work well together.

No such assumption exists in the private military sector; PMCs are incentivized *not* to work closely together for a single yet powerful reason—proprietary knowledge—which is not a complication for public armies. Companies do not wish to share trade secrets about how they operate or other sensitive information with their competitors, even when they jointly win a contract, as occurred in rebuilding the AFL. Instead, both firms focused on their discrete tasks, and each assumed the other was competent. DynCorp's job was demobilizing the old force and building a new one; PA&E's assignment was providing newly formed units with logistical and technical life support until they were functionally autonomous (or until the contract expired). This was a flawed solution for a dynamic environment.

This approach became a problem where their mutual roles and competing interests intersected, to the detriment of the AFL. At the end of the contract, the client judged the quality of the new AFL through a grueling multiday field training exercise modeled on the US Army Training and Evaluation Program (ARTEP). Not surprisingly, the client also used the ARTEP to evaluate DynCorp and PA&E, since the AFL's performance reflected on the companies and would affect future contract opportunities with the State Department. This was a frustrating situation for both firms. PA&E had almost no input in the training or force structure of the AFL, yet it was expected to finish what DynCorp started. From DynCorp's perspective, PA&E modified and administered the ARTEP, which allowed its competitor to act as a peer reviewer of DynCorp's work. This created a dysfunctional working relationship that probably detracted from overall contract achievement. Worse, each was likely to blame the other if the State Department complained about the quality of training.

Another deleterious effect of free market competition between firms is leadership selection and training. Today the AFL remains a mostly leaderless army made up of two thousand privates. This is partly because neither firm had full responsibility for leadership selection and training, and it was ultimately neglected in a "tragedy of the commons" dilemma. DynCorp was responsible for the initial training of officers and NCOs, while PA&E would mentor them once they arrived at their home unit. To be fair, developing "instant" senior leadership is extremely difficult and a fundamental challenge of raising armies. In most modern militaries, it takes twenty years to create a colonel and much longer to generate a general. Liberia could not wait that long.

DynCorp's initial plan called for the Liberian government to select leadership through a quarterly or monthly promotion board from among recruits who demonstrated leadership potential in basic training or applicants with relevant experience, such as Liberians serving in the US military or UN peacekeeping missions. Then it was assumed that PA&E would mentor those leaders in the next phase of the program. However, this process yielded few qualified leaders. An alternative was to have a foreigner lead the AFL, which is what the Liberian government chose: the AFL chief of staff was a Nigerian general. However, there was also a third option, not considered by DynCorp, that was very neomedieval: the PMC would lead the army and train Liberian counterparts until they could take control. This might seem outrageous to some, but there is already precedent for it, as Executive Outcomes led client forces into battle during the 1990s. More likely than not, we shall see this again in the future.

Business as Unusual

In the time of the *condottieri*, mercenaries were not the only ones who acted faithlessly, causing catastrophe. During the War of the Eight Saints (1375–1378), for example, a company of Breton mercenaries working for the pope split apart for lack of payment. One faction went north to fight for Pisa, a papal competitor, another stayed with the pope, and a third remained in the local area to loot and pillage.

Sporadic payment remains a problem today for PSCs and PMCs. During the Liberia program, the State Department sporadically paid DynCorp and PA&E, placing the program and indeed the country at risk, as having no army is preferable to having a half-formed one bearing a grudge. At the time, much of the State Department's funding was diverted to help stem the genocide in Darfur. This meant that once the AFL program began, there was no guarantee that it would continue. For example, money for the demobilization of 13,770 legacy soldiers was scarce, delaying their demobilization and placing the entire AFL program in peril. In late April 2006, four hundred to five hundred former AFL soldiers violently protested outside the Ministry of Defense, claiming nonpayment of salary arrears and retirement benefits, and clashed with UNMIL peacekeepers sent to quell the unrest.[26]

Erratic funding to other parts of the program had messy results. The Ministry of Defense reform program was prematurely terminated after the completion of a seventeen-week civil servant training course but before the implementation of a planned five-month mentoring and on-the-job training phase. Consequently, new civil servants went untrained and assumed their official duties in the new ministry without knowing what to do, rendering it incapacitated.[27]

Lapses in client funding and Liberian capacity also created dangerous situations. Training was halted for months owing to lack of payment by the State Department, leaving new soldiers to sit idle while they waited for follow-on recruits to fill out their unit. Making matters worse, in 2006, the new Ministry of Finance still did not have the capacity to pay soldiers, demonstrating that in recovering failed states, all institutions must rise together. This created the dangerous situation of unpaid and disgruntled soldiers that the PMC sought to avoid from the outset.

Meanwhile, those ready to report to basic training were told, "Don't call us, we'll call you," by frustrated program staff. The program then consisted of nearly one hundred international (US and third-country national personnel combined) and several hundred local national staff. Sending the international staff home and furloughing the local staff to save money would cause resentment among the locals, given Liberia's 75 percent unemployment rate, and many of the international staff were specialists who were difficult to replace.

Frustrated and fearing that it might have to leave Liberia for lack of payment, DynCorp urged its client to stabilize the funding stream. The high cost of paying expensive international employees to sit idle in a country where the average person subsisted on $1.25 a day sent a cynical message to the population, already somewhat doubtful about the new AFL. Also, it created a hazardous situation in an unstable state, as DynCorp was unable to store weapons and ammunition safely without an armory, which PA&E was scheduled to build but could not because of lack of payment. Worse, soldiers who completed training would have no military base to report to, as PA&E had yet to complete bases, which could prove a perilous situation for Liberian society and discredit the new military. Weak and erratic funding from the client rather than PMC performance was the main cause of the AFL's slow development. Moreover, this unfortunate situation would seem unlikely had the US Army rather than PMCs run the program, since the US government would be less inclined to default on the US Army.

Who Is Managing Whom?

Just as clients in the Middle Ages sent *provveditori* to watch over *condottieri* in the field, the United States sends contracting officers' technical representatives (COTRs) to oversee contractors, and, as with the *provveditori* before them, the COTR system is plagued with problems. In Liberia, the State Department officials in charge of the program resided in Washington, DC, and not in Africa. Their acting COTR was a lone military officer who worked in the US Embassy's Office of Defense Cooperation (ODC). This individual was responsible for overseeing the entire program and its hundreds of contractors, in addition to other embassy duties.

Several ODC chiefs rotated through the embassy, but few, if any, had significant experience managing multimillion-dollar contracts, handling multibillion-dollar companies, or building militaries wholesale in conflict-affected countries. One ODC chief was a Navy officer with no real experience serving in armies, much less raising them. The lack of qualification was the fault not of the ODC chiefs but of their government: the United States routinely deploys COTRs without adequate training and resources to do their job, as the Gansler report confirms.[28]

The COTR's lack of expertise created asymmetries of information that PMCs can exploit for profit, just as the *condottieri* did with the *provveditori*. Because COTRs are normally less expert than the contractors they oversee, they must rely on the contractors' expert opinions and access to information to make important business decisions on behalf of the government. This encourages moral hazard for contractors, who are incentivized to stall, elongate, or expand their contracts for profit, and they do so by finding additional, billable tasks to accomplish.

Accordingly, they are motivated to steer government officials' decisions toward this goal, influencing foreign policy implementation and outcomes.

Conditions for moral hazard existed in Liberia. An internal State Department investigation revealed weak oversight of DynCorp and other contractors, creating circumstances amenable to exploitation, although the report did not cite any contractor wrongdoing. The inspector general found that embassy personnel who were involved in the program "received no training in managing or evaluating" such contracts. Worse, they discovered that the COTR occasionally "received invoices with vague descriptions, which covered work prior to his arrival in Liberia, or with questionable work descriptions." The investigators also found that the State Department staff responsible for the program in Washington rarely visited Liberia. The report concluded that it "does not believe that such irregular visits assure adequate project oversight for this substantial program which spent $127 million through [fiscal year] 2007."[29]

Outside observers agree. The International Crisis Group found that in Liberia, "oversight structures employed by the US State Department have been shoddy" and recommended that "the State Department, therefore, should radically revamp its oversight system."[30] To be clear, weak oversight conditions do not infer exploitation by DynCorp. But they do demonstrate that such concerns exist when contracting, and this is an important distinction between private and public armies, since the former has a profit motive and the latter does not. This example is representative of a larger problem echoed by many industry critics. The United States has limited regulation of and oversight over the private military industry despite employing it widely. This creates opportunities for abuse by contractors as firms subtly steer client decisions in favor of profit over policy goals, altering strategic outcomes in the process. The objectives of PMCs and their clients will differ, just as those of the *condottieri* and the *provveditori* did in the Middle Ages.

Who Owns What?

As with the *condottieri*, contemporary contractors serve only their paymasters, at the expense of other relevant considerations, such as process ownership. Ownership has become a mantra of the international community vested in developing fragile and failed states; it refers to local political and popular support for foreign assistance programs such as the one in Liberia, and there is a growing consensus among scholars that early local ownership is crucial to program sustainability and legitimacy. The concept is simple enough: a foreign power that wields a heavy hand in transforming another country will likely alienate the very people it aspires to benefit, negating the purpose of the program.

Because the program to recreate the AFL was driven by the United States and its contractors, some scholars assert that it lacks ownership, sustainability, and legitimacy. Morten Bøås and Karianne Stig sum up this collective critique when they claim that the lack of transparency, accountability, and participation of Liberians in the program's decisions led to a paucity of local ownership.[31] Even the US government's own Congressional Research Service questions the balance between foreign support for and national ownership of security in Liberia, and worries that lack of adequate public input has created an AFL where "political legitimacy might be called into question."[32]

Contractors compound the quandary of ownership, because, as Adedeji Ebo reasons, "there is no direct contractual obligation between the security contractor and the institutions and people of the reforming state."[33] Not even the Liberian minister of defense had a copy of DynCorp's contract to transform the AFL that he was to lead, demonstrating a lack of transparency in the process. This created a problematic situation. Liberians were neither an employer nor a signatory to the contract, even though they were the intended beneficiaries of the program. Consequently, the Liberian government had only limited ability to direct DynCorp; the company, in essence, was not accountable to Liberia, even as it was rebuilding its armed forces. For Bøås and Stig, "this clearly represents a democratic deficit in the SSR."[34]

Critics' conclusions may be somewhat overstated. Few Liberians seemed concerned about the US role in transforming the AFL, especially given the urgent need for military reform and the strong historical ties between the two countries. Nor were Liberians troubled by the presence of contractors: there were no riots, protests, violence, or other evidence of widespread PMC rejection. DynCorp's frequent overtures to civil society—almost always through the government of Liberia—were met with general indifference. The Liberian minister of defense had multiple occasions to join DynCorp on its recruitment trips starting in 2006 but chose not to accompany the firm until 2008. Additionally, the government of Liberia—and not DynCorp—determined who was eligible for demobilization benefits and who would be admitted into the new military. This suggests a lack of worry on the Liberian government's part rather than a failure of transparency on DynCorp's, as more recent scholarship confirms: "The Liberian Ministry of Defence, the legislature and civil society have had opportunities to involve themselves more in the reform than they have done, thus suggesting that the reform is not proceeding as such a closed process as previous research on the SSR has argued."[35]

Other problems undermine academic critiques over ownership. Can foreign scholars really speak for Liberians on the question of local ownership? Can outside observers claim that Liberia had no ownership of the AFL program if its government had approved and accepted a gratis program that the United States provided through its contractors? It is self-contradictory to claim that ownership is necessary for program success and that the AFL program lacked it when Liberians have not rejected the AFL and it is a success compared with the Liberian National Police and other elements of the security sector under UN supervision. The International Crisis Group describes progress in Liberia's security sector reform as "uneven": while "the police are still widely considered ineffective and corrupt, . . . Army reform appears to be a provisional success."[36]

Other researchers are more acerbic about the use of a PMC in Liberia. As Mark Malan writes in a monograph for the US Army War College: "In a country and region where recent history has been shaped by warlords and mercenaries, the US Department of State has shown remarkable insensitivity by sending in contractors to shape the new army."[37] Comparing DynCorp to Liberian warlords and mercenaries without supporting evidence is absurd and reveals how ingrained the Westphalian taboo against private military functions remains in academic and policy thinking. Even the International Crisis Group—no apologist for the private military industry—agrees that such interpretations are extreme and declares itself "agnostic" on the issue.[38]

However, despite exaggerations over ownership and the pro-Westphalian zeal of some observers, the concern remains valid. An example of this lack of ownership is the sensitization and recruiting campaign. The first step in creating a new force, unless it is clandestine, is to alert the public. In Liberia, this was challenging, owing to the grim legacy of the former AFL in the war, and to help prepare the populace for this, DynCorp created a public sensitization and recruitment program. To localize this effort, the company hired Liberians to craft effective messages that would resonate with indigenous audiences. DynCorp's role was confined mostly to logistical support and coordination with international community representatives in Liberia.

The sensitization and recruitment campaign involved workshops for civil society, staging rallies featuring senior members of the government, producing radio dramas starring the AFL, placing ads in newspapers, displaying large AFL billboards and murals, and doing recruiting tours in Liberia's hinterlands. DynCorp even commissioned AFL comic books, *Jackie's Adventure* and *Liberia's New Armed Forces*, for free distribution to reach less literate audiences. The company also set up two information booths in downtown Monrovia staffed by Liberians to answer any questions passersby had regarding the new AFL and how to enlist.

Despite DynCorp's efforts to localize the campaign by hiring locals to help design it, many Liberians found it bumbling and even insulting. The use of well-dressed and healthy-looking children on some of the AFL recruiting posters was not well received by a population traumatized by child soldiers. Many asked whether the children on the posters were American, given their health. This demonstrated a lack of cultural sensitivity on the part of the campaign designers, partly because the messages were not thoroughly tested on Liberian focus groups before they went public. Similarly, the comic books received mixed

Figure 10.3 A military policeman stands watch before the Armed Forces of Liberia, a private sector creation. (Photo: U.S. Department of Defense, U.S. Marine Sgt. Lydia M. Davey).

Figure 10.4 Liberian soldiers practice anti-riot skills. (Photo: U.S. Department of Defense, 1st Lt. Mark Lazane).

reactions; they were an effective tool for illiterate audiences but repelled some educated Liberians, who found them infantilizing.

Worse, DynCorp's attempt to combine sensitization and recruitment into a single campaign to conserve resources and time muddled messages and hampered the efficacy of both. In many ways, these two information campaigns are incompatible. The objective of the sensitization program is to alert the public to the new military's formation in the most transparent and neutral manner possible. In contrast, the purpose of recruitment is advocacy by framing information in a highly positive way to encourage enlistment. DynCorp chose to prioritize recruitment over sensitization, which should not be a surprise. After all, it was hired to raise an army, not to facilitate a civil discourse on the role of the new AFL. Too much indigenous criticism of what it was doing could have resulted in the State Department canceling its contract.

Like the *condottieri*, DynCorp sought primarily to please its client—the United States—and not Liberia, whose military it was building. This created incentive structures that explain some of the PMC's behavior in country, such as the weak sensitization campaign. That this program was contracted to the private sector fundamentally altered the relationships among the three main actors: the United States, Liberia, and DynCorp. This distorted the strategic outcome of the program caused by principal-agent challenges.

Akin to the medieval market for force, conducting this operation as a business transaction changed its focus to the entity with the power of the purse, the United States. The United States demanded that the PMC brief it first on all major program decisions, often without the Liberian government's knowledge, allowing it to make important decisions about Liberia's security and influence plans before the Liberian government was even consulted. The State Department finalized and approved DynCorp's plans for demobilization, training, force structure, recruiting, and vetting before they were formally presented to the Liberian minister of defense, often as a fait accompli. This gave the United States a significant—and perhaps undue—advantage in shaping the future of the AFL for its own strategic interests rather than Liberia's ownership.

Risks

The private military industry alters international outcomes by its very presence, just as the *condottieri* did in the Middle Ages. Contemporary military strategists may be tempted to think of PMCs as second-rate auxiliaries for national army units and deploy them accordingly, but such idealizations are dangerously wrong. These companies are fundamentally different in their composition, nature, and purpose from national armies, and this can influence strategic consequences in unexpected ways. Private armies are not swappable substitutes for public ones.

Changing the Tool Changes the Outcome

Private militaries behave differently from public ones because of profit motive. While this can lead to innovation and efficiencies, it also creates conflicts of interest that can alter events, as was the case in the medieval market for force. Principal-agent issues affected events in Liberia. For example, the original contract only encompassed the building of a new army and not the disbanding of the old AFL, which the government of Liberia agreed to do. However, both client and contractor soon discovered that the Liberian government was incapable of doing this, threatening the whole program, which depended on the old army being demobilized before a new one would take its place. The State Department considered cancelling the contract, and this concerned DynCorp.

In early 2005, the company approached the client and discussed the possibility of it conducting the demobilization instead of the Liberian government. The State Department agreed to the company's proposal on two conditions: first, that the firm present a detailed demobilization plan for approval by the State Department, and second, that the Liberian government demonstrate clear political will for the demobilization. By late January 2005, the company had sent a small team to Liberia to achieve this.

Demobilizing armies is deeply political, because warlords are often the de facto law in conflict-affected countries, and putting them out of business is dangerous work, because it reorders who has power and who does not. UNMIL successfully demobilized warlords operating under the aegis of the rebellion while the old AFL—warlords to many—was left to the United States. To set the political groundwork for the demobilization of the AFL and achieve some modicum of consensus for a new AFL, it was necessary to win over stakeholders such as the government of Liberia, UNMIL and other members of the international community helping to rebuild the country, the former rebel groups, civil society organizations, and, of course, the old AFL.

Ideally, this sensitive task would have fallen to the US government, but embassy staffing was thin and overburdened in 2005. The job of engaging stakeholders unofficially fell to DynCorp, creating the sorts of conditions that could, at least theoretically, allow a firm to influence outcomes. Over the next few months, the DynCorp team crafted a detailed plan to demobilize the standing army, but a stickier problem was securing a firm commitment from the government for such a politically dangerous move. Most attempts to demobilize standing African armies end in violence, and given Liberia's past, this seemed probable. Strong shows of commitment are preferable to weak ones, because they would please the client more, leading to a contract's initiation and payment. This would require something more substantial than the Liberian minister of defense talking with the US ambassador over lunch. It would necessitate a more serious commitment, one that the Liberian government could not plausibly deny and would have to own.

Accordingly, DynCorp sought to have a law passed in Liberia mandating the demobilization of the legacy AFL. A law is perhaps an extreme measure but is the strongest possible public commitment from the government of Liberia to the United States and the best chance that the contract would go forward. However, it is also a violation of Westphalian sovereignty, since countries—much less corporations—are not suppose to interfere in the domestic affairs of other countries.

DynCorp had the additional problem of the transitional Liberian Congress, a kleptocratic and dysfunctional body in 2005. The head of state, Gyude Bryant, had the authority to pass executive orders, which possessed the power of law and effectively bypassed the legislative branch. It was possible for Bryant to issue an executive order mandating the demobilization of the legacy AFL. During the spring, the firm engaged select stakeholders to explore options for demobilization, and wielded considerable yet subtle power to affect stakeholder opinions. It could empower stakeholder groups by choosing which ones to meet with or ignore. Similarly, it could influence leadership selection within groups by picking whom to talk to or disregard. The company could set meeting agendas and sequence issues for discussion, affecting outcomes by strategically proposing solutions for stakeholders to adopt. Stakeholder requests deemed unrealistic, not operationally possible, or unprofitable could be overlooked. If present, embassy officials probably did not challenge DynCorp's expert opinions, which is not surprising, since the United States contracted the company for its expertise and also wanted to see the legacy force safely demobilized.

On May 2, DynCorp gave a briefing to the Liberian government's Cluster One committee, which deals with national security issues, outlining two possible courses of action for the demobilization: a "soft" policy option and a "hard" policy option. The soft option entailed a voluntary dissolution of the legacy force, whereby former soldiers would agree to lay down their arms and leave the army in exchange for money. However, it was unclear what would happen to soldiers who refused this deal or if there was even sufficient funding to attract voluntary dissolution. A prudent analysis might find this option risky, since it could fail to demobilize the legacy force, create an indefinite delay of the program, and imperil state security.

Alternatively, the hard policy option recommended that the president exercise his legal prerogative to declare the AFL "demobilized" by a date certain as a matter of law. The advantages of this were clear: financial certainty, finality, and acceleration of the program, outcomes that were important to DynCorp and possibly to Liberia, too. It was reasonable to conclude that the disadvantages

were minor, namely, choosing a demobilization site and possible noncompliance by members of the legacy force, a problem for both soft and hard options.

The brief concluded with a simple decision matrix whereby the company
compared the two options using four criteria: simplicity, time, demobilization costs, and risk of noncompliance. And for each option and criteria, the
firm assigned a score of one (good) or two (bad). Perhaps not surprisingly, the
company's analysis resulted in the hard option winning over the soft one, and
it recommended that the president adopt the hard option by passing an executive order demobilizing the AFL. Two days later the Minister of Defense Daniel
Chea sent a memorandum to the president urging him to sign an executive order
to this effect, underlining key sentences by hand.

Bryant agreed to pass the executive order, and DynCorp immediately drafted
it for his signature. Normally, only Liberian lawmakers possess the privilege
of writing legislation, and it remains uncertain if any lawmakers were aware of
DynCorp's political activities. Before the firm presented the draft to the president, it first furnished a copy to its client for approval, and the State Department
also made edits.

Once Bryant signed Executive Order 5, officially demobilizing the legacy
military, the State Department initiated DynCorp's contract and paid out millions of dollars to begin work. A few days later, Bryant held a national press conference, announced the new law, and realized DynCorp's hard policy option. The
company even took care to prepare the Liberian minister of defense's talking
points for the press conference, which praised the company.

DynCorp had the ability to influence Liberian domestic politics, like a lob-
bying firm, and create the conditions necessary for contract initiation. Clearly,
this is not something a US Army battalion would do, since it lacks profit motive
and the sophistication to influence another country's laws. Had a US military
unit been in charge, it is likely the program would have ended in 2004, when the
US realized the Liberians could not demobilize their old army. As Machiavelli
warned, private armies are not swappable substitutes for public ones, and changing the means of military operations changes the outcome of the campaign.

If You Know How to Build It, You Also Know How to Use It

The most significant fact of DynCorp's work in Liberia is that the private sector
can raise an army at all. Like Wallenstein, the British East India Company, and
other military enterprisers of the past, DynCorp made a military for a client and
did so without external assistance other than payment. The Liberia program was

not a public and private partnership involving a hybrid of US soldiers and PMC personnel working together to transform a foreign military, as has happened in Iraq and Afghanistan. Liberia's armed forces are unique in that they were generated entirely by the private sector. Furthermore, DynCorp would have had an easier job if it had a less finicky client than the US government and a more permissive context than a large UN peacekeeping mission.

If a company can create an army, then it can deploy it, too, because the expertises are linked. This does not suggest that DynCorp secretly desired to deploy the AFL (it did not), only that it possessed the requisite skills to do so, because, like most PMCs, it enlisted most of its personnel from other military, intelligence, or law-enforcement organizations. The military is a profession that can only be taught by its own, and non-military imposters are anathema. For example, a soldier must have years of experience leading troops to be selected as a drill instructor. All of DynCorp's instructors were military veterans, adept at commanding tactical units, and could have easily led the AFL into battle, as Executive Outcomes did in Angola and elsewhere. In some ways, this would have been desirable, since the AFL was essentially an army of entry-level privates by 2010 and in need of tactical leadership.

Another example is arming the AFL. In 2006, DynCorp bought and transported small arms from eastern Europe to Liberia, the first legal arms shipment to the country in more than two decades. The State Department helped arrange the legal aspects of the transfer, while the machinations of the deal itself were left to the firm, knowing what to buy, where to buy, whom to talk to, how to ship it, and so forth. It remains well within the company's grasp to purchase and move small arms around the world without the support of governments. Although DynCorp had no intention of building its own army, taking over the AFL, or illegally supplying weapons to regional actors, the PMC—and others like it— currently possess the ability to do so.

DynCorp acted as a military enterpriser in Liberia, building an army for the client rather than deploying it. The benefits of hiring a private actor for this task are many and include efficiency, innovative approaches, surge capacity, ability to plumb resource pools not accessible to the client, and freedom of action as an "outsider" to stakeholder politics. But contracting also creates complications: poor teamwork between firms, principal-agent issues, asymmetries of information, lack of oversight, difficulties arising from pay problems, and conflicts of interest stemming from the profit motive. There are risks too, notably a company's ability to influence domestic politics, demonstrating that PMCs are a fundamentally different tool from their public sector counterparts. Finally, there remains a disturbing fact: a company that possesses the expertise to raise an army also has the skill to deploy it. DynCorp created a military yet refrained from using it, which is admirable but not the point; that a company could do this at all is astonishing.

Many of these risks were mitigated by the fact that Liberia was a mediated market for force, arbitrated by a strong client with market power and international sway. DynCorp was not a mercenary actor but instead a military enterpriser. Military enterprisers benefit clients without threatening overall security, as mercenaries sometimes do, owing to the monogamous relationship between client and company, aligning long-term interests. DynCorp and the United States worked in a public-private partnership that reduced the dangers posed by private force while reaping the benefits. Like Wallenstein and the Holy Roman Empire, DynCorp was not incentivized to betray the United States, its principal and long-term client. Nor was the US government interested in reneging on its contract with DynCorp, an enduring implementing partner that understood the client's vision, culture, and quirks.

DynCorp's efforts in Liberia are a rare and qualified success in an era of security force assistance failure. Public sector efforts by the United States, the United Nations, and NATO are comparative disappointments, resulting in hollow forces (Afghanistan, Iraq, the Democratic Republic of the Congo, Haiti, Sierra Leone), dangerous renegade units (Iraq, Guatemala), and even coup d'états (Mali, East Timor). By contrast, the AFL is a military that remains loyal to the government, and even deployed a small contingent of peacekeepers to Mali in 2013, ten years after its own civil war ended. As a private sector actor, DynCorp took different approaches to building armies from those of its public sector counterparts, and this accounts for some of its success. This suggests that under the right market circumstances, military enterprisers operating in a mediated market for force could prove to be a powerful tool for stability.

11

Mercenaries in Somalia: A Neomedieval Tale

> Damnation seize my soul if I give you quarters, or take any from you.
> —Pirate Captain Edward "Blackbeard" Teach, before his final battle

"The killing was a message to the owners of the ship who paid no heed to our ransom demands," said Hassan Abdi, a pirate captain operating off the coast of Somalia. The pirates had just killed one crew member and injured another from the cargo ship MV *Orna* that they had hijacked in the Indian Ocean, approximately four hundred nautical miles northeast of the Seychelles in 2010. "More killings will follow if they continue to lie to us—we have lost patience with them."

Like Liberia, Somalia is a worst-case example of neomedievalism, and, while tragic, it clearly shows neomedievalism's five characteristics. Somalia has splintered and dissolved into anarchy owing to decades of conflict and chaos. Mogadishu, the capital, is a viper pit of Islamist militants, clan warlords, factional armies, and rogue fighters who have repelled all foreign interventions, including twenty-five thousand UN peacekeepers in the 1990s. Somalia's ruined cities remain battlegrounds for feuding warlords, and tens of thousands have perished from famine. Religious zealots fight one another in the name of God, mercilessly massacring those who resist salvation. Gunmen of all types—militia, religious, and government—prey upon women and girls as spoils of war, as they rape, rob, and kill with impunity. The lucky ones who escape trek hundreds of miles in search of food, only to end up in crowded, lawless refugee camps, some the size of cities. Somalia is closer to a new Dark Age than to neomedievalism.

Neomedieval Mire

The Horn of Africa is the most tragic example of neomedievalism. At its center is Somalia, a quintessential failed state with the dubious distinction of topping the *Foreign Policy* and Fund for Peace Failed State Index three years in a row. The territory has been without a functional central government since 1991, making it the longest-running instance of complete state collapse in African postcolonial history. Several dozen national peace conferences have been launched to resuscitate Somalia, including many sponsored by the United Nations, but none has succeeded.

While parts of the north have remained relatively peaceful, including much of the self-declared Republic of Somaliland, the region is rife with fighting, kidnapping, murder, crime, and piracy. Since 1991, an estimated three hundred fifty thousand to 1 million Somalis have died as a result of armed conflict or its consequences.[1] Abducting international humanitarian aid workers is practically an industry, and piracy has burgeoned since the second phase of the Somali civil war in 2005, threatening international shipping.

During the 1990s, Somalia disintegrated into at least three semiautonomous areas: Somaliland in the north, Puntland in the northeast, and Somalia in the south. The borders between these informal polities and their neighbors are porous, and tensions remain high. Spillover violence and crime from Somalia threaten the stability of neighboring Ethiopia and Kenya. In an attempt to quell this problem, Ethiopia invaded Somalia in 2006 with troops from Puntland. As Ethiopia's prime minister, Meles Zenawi, explains, the invasion was necessary, because Ethiopia faced a direct threat to its own borders, and "Ethiopian defense forces were forced to enter into war to protect the sovereignty of the nation."[2] Irregular warfare ensued and ended in 2009, when Ethiopian troops withdrew, marking another victory for the clans in southern Somalia.

Similarly, Somali clans clashed near the Kenya border, destabilizing the region. It is estimated that since the start of 2007, violence has killed at least twenty-one thousand people in Somalia and driven another 1.5 million from their homes, many into neighboring countries, helping to trigger one of the world's worst humanitarian emergencies.[3] Over the past twenty years, the Somali refugee camp at Dadaab in Kenya, about one hundred kilometers south of the border, has swelled to nearly three hundred thousand people, making it one of the largest population centers in Kenya and one of the biggest refugee complexes in the world. The United Nations says that Dadaab has ten thousand third-generation refugees, grandchildren of the original arrivals.[4] Overcrowding, lack of shelters, and insufficient food have made matters worse, and the camp is a frequent recruiting spot for Somali warlords and militants.

However, consistent with neomedievalism, Somalia's lack of government does not imply a lack of governance. As with the dons of Jamaica, the lack of a formal central government has given rise to local ad hoc efforts of governance that provide communities with limited public security, dispute mediation, social services, and other political goods. These informal polities range widely in character and effectiveness. The most visible manifestations of these overlapping and competing authorities are Somaliland and Puntland, semiformal and self-declared administrations.

But even these separatist states have sovereignty in name only, for they compete with clan authorities within their territory for authority and allegiance. The Rahanweyn, Hawiye, Darod, Isaaq, and Dir and their subclans all retain a measure of autonomy within Somalia's political mosaic. This "radical localization" of politics transpired in the political vacuum left by the central government's collapse in 1991 and failure of the UN Operation in Somalia (UNOSOM I) in 1992–1993. Somalia expert Ken Menkhaus and researcher John Prendergast describe these independent authorities as "radically localized Somali polities [that] are fluid in structure and authority, overlapping, and situational in nature."[5] Other experts agree that fragmented sovereignty is not unique to Somalia. The rise of informal, localized, and ad hoc authorities that overlap and compete with one another is a growing phenomenon in areas of protracted state failure and an emblem of neomedievalism.[6]

The most significant actors in the Horn of Africa are not states. During the Cold War, Somalia was merely a pawn to the great powers, but as the world changed after the fall of the Berlin Wall, so did the world's interest in Somalia. As the United Nations promoted its muscular vision of a "global transition" to a new world order founded on humanitarian concern rather than the interests of individual states in *An Agenda for Peace*, televisions around the world were flooded with images of dying Somali children, the victims of drought, famine, brutal warlords, and their civil war. Out of a population of 4.5 million people, approximately three hundred thousand died of malnutrition, and at least 1.5 million lives were at immediate risk. Almost 1 million Somalis sought refuge in neighboring countries and elsewhere, creating a massive refugee crisis for the region.[7]

Somalia was an early test case for the United Nations' new world order. By spring 1992, the Security Council established UNOSOM I to provide humanitarian relief in Somalia and monitor the cease-fire of the Somali civil war. Although not a success—hence its sequel, UNOSOM II, one year later—it was a groundbreaking Chapter VII peacekeeping mission that served as a prototype for future missions in the Balkans, Africa, and elsewhere. Following its failure, President George H. W. Bush sent US troops to protect relief workers in the appropriately named Operation Restore Hope. This transitioned into UNOSOM II, but it also failed, and the United Nations withdraw all forces by 1995.

Since then, Somalia has persisted in a state of durable disorder and neomedieval warfare. The forces that defeated the UN were not state militaries but nonstate actors: warlords and their militias. Mogadishu warlord Mohamed Farrah Aidid saw UNOSOM II as a threat to his power, and in June 1993, he attacked the mission, killing more than eighty peacekeepers. Other casualties followed, driving out the United Nations, whereupon Aidid claimed to be the president of Somalia. In neomedieval fashion, competing local warlords, such as Ali Mahdi Muhammad, challenged this claim, and in 1996, Aidid died of a gunshot wound.

Tending to the victims of the internecine fighting is not the society of states but a league of transnational actors: NGOs, which make up the largest international presence inside Somalia. In 1999, they formed a consortium in Nairobi to coordinate their efforts; it now numbers 191 members.[8] It also makes them targets. In 2008, twenty-four aid workers were killed, and another ten remain missing, causing many NGOs to suspend programs and withdraw staff in country. An Amnesty International report found that at least forty Somali human rights defenders and humanitarian workers were killed between January 1 and September 10, 2008, and tersely concludes: "The increasing attacks against humanitarian and civil society workers also testify to the international community's failures in Somalia."[9]

Warlords and their private armies make the laws in much of Somalia's neomedieval landscape, and their presence is ubiquitous (see figure 11.1). One of the most powerful authorities in Somalia is the internationally notorious group al-Shabaab (Movement of Warrior Youth), an Islamic armed group that has successfully waged war against the Somali transitional federal government and its

Figure 11.1 Warlords and their militia are a law unto themselves in Somalia's stateless land. (Photo courtesy of Peter Pham.)

Ethiopian and Ugandan supporters since 2006. In February 2009, the group killed eleven Burundian soldiers who were a part of the African Union peace-keeping mission. The organization also can project force beyond its borders, having launched a coordinated dual terrorist attack in Kampala, Uganda, in July 2010 that killed more than seventy people. Analogous to al-Qaida's 2004 Madrid bombings, the Kampala bombings by al-Shabaab sent a clear strategic message to Uganda to withdraw its troops from the international peacekeeping mission in Somalia.

Globalization is the main reason those outside Somalia know or care about the neomedieval conflict there. NGOs have used globalized media to highlight the humanitarian crisis in the country, bolster their own legitimacy by enacting the human rights agenda, and nettle international organizations and states to do more. Following an especially fraught period of insecurity, drought, and record-high food prices in 2008, some 3.25 million Somalis were in need of emergency aid from outside Somalia. A coalition of fifty-two NGOs banded together to flood international media and world capitals with the message to drum up the needed assistance. In their statement, they echoed the prerogatives of R2P: "The international community has completely failed Somali civilians. We call on the international community to make the protection of Somali civilians a top priority now."[10] World news organizations such as CNN and the BBC even dedicate special watch pages on their websites to al-Shabaab. NGOs' ability to galvanize the global media and mobilize popular support for the humanitarian cause of Somalia is an example of their de facto political power in the international system.

The darker side of globalization has also fostered a bond between al-Shabaab and al-Qaida. The strongest tie between the two groups is ideological. Using the Internet, a senior al-Shabaab leader released a video in September 2008 praising Osama bin Laden and linking Somalia to al-Qaida's global operations. A few months later, Ayman al-Zawahiri, al-Qaida's second-in-command, reciprocated with a video praising al-Shabaab's seizure of the Somali town of Baidoa and assuring followers that al-Qaida would "engage in jihad against the American-made government in the same way they engaged in jihad against the Ethiopians and the warlords before them."[11] The United States added al-Shabaab to its list of foreign terrorist organizations in February 2008 and maintains that senior al-Shabaab leaders have trained and fought with al-Qaida in Afghanistan.

In an example of the technological unification of the world, al-Shabaab uses the Internet to recruit foreign fighters from around the world—including from within the United States and the United Kingdom. From 2007 to 2009, twenty men left Minnesota, California, and Alabama to join al-Shabaab; all but one were of Somali heritage. In June 2010, two US men from New Jersey were arrested at the airport en route to Somalia to join al-Shabaab. They were inspired by the

Yemen-based US cleric Anwar al-Awlaki, who has been described as the "bin Laden of the Internet"; he also inspired US Army Major Nidal Malik Hasan to shoot fellow soldiers at Fort Hood, Texas, killing thirteen people and wounding thirty. US Attorney General Eric Holder calls this a "deadly pipeline that has routed funding and fighters to al-Shabaab from cities across the United States" and represents "a disturbing phenomenon."[12]

In Somalia's continuing armed conflict, none of the major actors is a state. The primary actors are international organizations such as the United Nations, which justifies violence on humanitarian grounds in the guise of Chapter VII peacekeeping missions. Abetting its mandate are transnational NGOs, which provide the bulk of external assistance to the Somalis and also highlight the problem in international politics. The actual battles are waged not between national military units but between UN blue-helmet peacekeepers and militants who serve warlords. Victory is determined as much in the realm of ideology as in physical space.

Al-Shabaab is also a globalized enemy, taking full advantage of the technological unification of the world to resource and recruit its ranks and strike alliances with simpatico groups such as al-Qaida in Afghanistan. The most famous fight between a professional military and nonstate actors was the Battle of Mogadishu, which ended in decisive victory for the low-tech clan militias over the US military's most elite units. The formalized international relations between states as they govern world events have been completely absent from this twenty-year scenario. Somalia represents the antithesis of state-centric international relations theory and demonstrates the emergence of globalized neomedievalism in world affairs.

Pirates and Privateers

In Hedley Bull's day, when the Westphalian order was at an apogee, the notion of pirates threatening the high seas would have seemed like plot fodder for the silver screen. Now it is a fact of life. Piracy off the coast of Somalia threatens international shipping and has reintroduced *pirate* into the lexicon of contemporary global politics.

Since 2005, piracy has become big business in the Horn of Africa, as pirates capture ships in the Gulf of Aden and ransom them and their crews back to the owners for millions of dollars. According to the International Maritime Bureau, in 2010, almost half of the world's pirate attacks occurred off the coast of Somalia, and 92 percent of successful hijackings were Somali, resulting in 948 people taken hostage, a notable increase from 2004, when there were only five recorded attacks in the region. The World Bank estimates that Somali pirates

Figure 11.2 Pirates holding the crew of the Chinese fishing vessel FV *Tianyu* 8 in 2008. (Source: Wikimedia Commons)

cost the world $18 billion annually.[13] The pirates, armed only with light weapons and small boats, can seize large cargo ships, operate two hundred nautical miles offshore thanks to mother ships that act as floating bases, and can take over a ship within fifteen minutes of being sighted by the ship's crew, making it difficult for international patrols to respond in time (see figure 11.2). This is significant because some sixteen thousand ships a year pass through the Gulf of Aden, carrying oil from the Middle East and goods from Asia to Europe and North America, making it one of the most important trade routes in the world.

The security demand caused by pirates has attracted PMC supply. The precursors to pirates in the Gulf of Aden were illegal fishing and toxic waste dumping that exploited Somalia's ungoverned sea space, as pirates later would. A chief security challenge was not rival states but warring clans with ties to illegal fishing profits and the Puntland government. This arrangement evolved into piracy. As Matt Bryden, member of the UN Monitoring Group on Somalia and Eritrea, explains, "By 2003, the fisheries protection racket had become virtually indistinguishable from common piracy."[14]

In 1999, Puntland hired Hart Security to combat this problem and create a local coast guard. The British PMC set up its base in the Puntland city of Bosasso on the north tip of the Horn of Africa, trained a seventy-man armed force, and enjoyed some success even though it had only a single ship. For example, Hart

Security arrested the Spanish fishing vessel *Alabacora Quatro* and successfully extracted an undisclosed amount from its owners. However, as with many *condottieri*, the company and the client ultimately parted ways over payment disputes and weak contract enforcement.

A Somali-Canadian PMC called SomCan Coast Guard replaced Hart. Like Hart, SomCan protected the shipping lanes from illegal fishing vessels and financed its operations by selling fishing permits, with quarterly licenses fetching upward of $50,000. From 2002 to 2005, the firm maintained six patrol boats and four hundred marines and boasted that it arrested thirty fishing ships. SomCan was also faithless to its employer, like many a mercenary of the Middle Ages, and seldom handed over revenue collected from the fishing licenses to Puntland's Ministry of Fisheries.

SomCan also blurred the line between PMC and pirate, preying on the countryside, just as out-of-work mercenaries in the Middle Ages frequently became marauders. For instance, SomCan seized the fishing trawler *Sirichainava 12* and demanded $800,000 for its release. This provoked a strong reaction from states as a joint American and British strike force freed the vessels and captured SomCan's marines, who stood trial in Thailand for piracy and were sentenced to ten years in prison.[15] Curiously, states responded more forcefully against PMCs patrolling the waters rather than the pirates that threatened them, although in this case, the difference is difficult to discern.

Puntland is not the only territory to hire PMCs. Somaliland, just west of Puntland, contracted Nordic Crisis Management to develop security forces for Berbera, its principal port, to reduce insurance costs for shipping. Unlike Hart and SomCan, Nordic Crisis Management did not directly engage illegal fishing vessels or pirates but acted as military enterpriser: training police, conducting risk assessments, and improving security measures at the seaport and the airport. Somaliland hopes these upgrades will attract international investment and act as the gateway to globalization. Another military enterpriser, British PMC Triton International, has also helped to build Somaliland's antipiracy coast guard. According to the firm's chief executive, Simon Jones, its work resulted in more than 120 pirates being captured, prosecuted, and jailed in 2010.[16]

Other firms take a more direct approach and place armed guards on ships, ready to fend off pirate boarders. Known as "embarked security" in the business, these PMCs have more in common with mercenaries than with military enterprisers such as Hart and Triton (see figures 11.3 and 11.4). Examples of these PMCs include Antares World, Protection Vessels International, and ESPADA Marine Services; typically, they deploy a squad of private marines on clients' ships passing through the Gulf of Aden. They also harden the ship by stringing concertina wire around the hull and other protective measures outlined in the Best Management Practices to Deter Piracy (BMP4) guidelines.

Figure 11.3 Armed civilian contractors, known as "embarked security," guard a commercial ship passing through pirate waters. (Courtesy of Port2Port Maritime Security Ltd.)

Figure 11.4 Embarked security being deployed to a freighter by helicopter. (Courtesy of Port2Port Maritime Security Ltd.)

Another PMC, Typhon, offers protection to cargo vessels sailing off the coast of Somalia, but unlike PMCs that put armed guards on board other people's ships, Typhon supplies its own. For a fee, its private navy will escort convoys across pirate-infested waters and establish an exclusion zone of one kilometer around the client ships. Typhon's ships are armed with machine guns and utilize drones and radar to detect pirates. Anthony Sharpe, the company's CEO, says that shipping companies would benefit from reduced insurance premiums: "I have spoken to the underwriters at Lloyds [insurance company] and the expectation is that there will be a 50% to 80% reduction in premiums for customers who use our services."[17]

After the Nisour Square shootings, Erik Prince, founder of Blackwater, left the United States for Abu Dhabi, where he has become a deal maker within the industry, connecting companies with clients and vice versa. He helped the South African PMC Saracen International win contracts from Somalia's beleaguered government to protect its leaders, train Somali troops, and battle pirates and Islamic militants. Saracen was formed from remnants of Executive Outcomes and is managed by Lafras Luitingh, a former officer in South Africa's Civil Cooperation Bureau, a covert government-sponsored hit squad that operated during the apartheid era and is now defunct.

Saracen operates independently of all international and multilateral frameworks in Somalia, and little is known about the firm's intentions other than profit motive. Between May 2010 and February 2011, it trained, equipped, and deployed fighters in an attempt to create one of "the best-equipped indigenous military forces anywhere in Somalia," according to a UN report.[18] Saracen's training camp near Bosaaso was the best-equipped military facility in Somalia after the UN bases in Mogadishu. The company planned to establish a force approximately one thousand strong, equipped with three transport aircraft, three reconnaissance aircraft, two transport helicopters, and two light helicopters. The maritime component of the force would be equipped with one command-and-control vessel, two logistical support vessels, and three rigid-hulled inflatable boats for rapid deployment and intervention.

Using shell companies, Saracen secretly shipped military equipment into northern Somalia on cargo planes, which the UN report declares "the most brazen violation of the arms embargo by a PSC." Worse, the company's presence has aggravated already tense relations in the region, and a UN accused the PMC in several reports of trying to form a "private army."[19] Finally, local authorities and the UN force commander asked the company to leave Mogadishu, which it did.

Suffering from negative publicity, Saracen did what many multinational corporations do in such situations: it rebranded itself, just as Blackwater did after Nisour Square. Luitingh formed a new PMC in Dubai called Sterling Corporate Services with the staff that worked for Saracen. Their employer was the same as Saracen too, the United Arab Emirates, which secretly contracted the PMC to create the "Puntland Maritime Police Force," aimed at preventing, detecting, and eradicating piracy, illegal fishing, and other illicit activity off the coast of Somalia. The Sterling's base included a modern operational command center, a control tower, an airstrip, a helicopter deck, and about seventy tents, which can host up to fifteen hundred trainees.

Sterling is an example of a strong PMC, like Executive Outcomes, as it accompanied Puntland forces on combat missions. The 2013 documentary film *The Project* shows the company in action along with a South African "trainer" acting as a door gunner in one of the helicopters. One of Sterling's employees, Lodewyk Pietersen, was killed while the Puntland Maritime Police Force was conducting an antipiracy operation in Hul-Anod, a district in Iskushuban that pirates use as a base.[20] In June 2012, Sterling abandoned its operations, leaving behind an unpaid but well-armed security force in Puntland.

Sterling Corporate Services is not the only PMC seeking business in Somalia. The State Department contracted DynCorp International to equip, deploy, sustain, and train international peacekeepers from the Ugandan and Burundian contingents.[21] Additionally, it indirectly financed Bancroft Global Development to train African troops to fight al-Shabaab. The firm offers the United States a convenient way to fight its war on terror in Africa without committing its own forces to the battle for fear of becoming entangled in the conflict, an attribute of neomedieval warfare. As Johnnie Carson, the State Department's top official for Africa, explains: "We do not want an American footprint or boots on the ground."[22]

Bancroft's advisers include a retired general from the British marines and a former French soldier who commanded a group of foreign fighters during Côte d'Ivoire's civil war in 2003 and did a stint in the presidential guard of the Comoros Islands. Michael C. Stock, the American head of Bancroft, strongly objects to the term *mercenary* and instead describes Bancroft as an NGO, although it is unclear whether traditional NGOs would recognize Bancroft as such.[23]

Another firm, with backing from Prince, is raising a small army for the United Arab Emirates city of Abu Dhabi. Reflex Responses (R2) is based in the Middle East and boasts that it can provide anything from static armed guards to nuclear security, with "the right people for the right solution at a fair price." Reminiscent of Florence's hiring of Hawkwood, the city paid the firm $529 million to raise an eight-hundred-member battalion of foreign troops to conduct special operations missions inside and outside the country (e.g., Iran), defend oil pipelines and skyscrapers from terrorist attacks, and put down internal revolts.[24] The firm's labor pool is international, with former soldiers from the United States, Europe, Latin America, and South African, but no Muslims, since they might not be willing to kill fellow Muslims. Prince is the first major private military mogul to part ways with the United States, but other individuals and companies will likely follow as US markets dry up, and when they do, they, too, will seek new clients or face bankruptcy.

Over the past twenty years, PMC activity in Somalia has steadily increased on land and sea. Every year, new and unknown PMCs materialize, such as Tacforce International and Specialist Marine Services. Oil companies also hire them. Africa Oil, a Canadian company, hired Pathfinder Corporation to protect its operations in Puntland, and Genel Energy, an Anglo-Turkish company, contracted Olive Group in Somaliland, which has experience protecting oil companies in Iraq.

There are so many maritime PMCs operating in the Gulf of Aden that they have formed their own trade association to look after their industry's interests, like the medieval "confederated *condottieri*." The Security Association for the Maritime Industry (SAMI) estimates that there are more than 180 private security firms hailing from 35 different countries operating in the northwest Indian ocean. Of these, 117 are British, 39 American, 16 South African, and the rest from various EU and British Commonwealth states and also Russia. Steven Jones, maritime director of SAMI, estimates that 36 percent of vessels transiting pirate waters in the Indian Ocean carry guards and maintain a 100 percent success rate at repelling attacks.[25] Other experts estimate that there are at least 2,700 armed contractors on ships, eighteen floating armories are operating in the Gulf of Aden, and forty private armed patrol boats are operating in the Indian Ocean. The most sophisticated of these private navies, Typhon, is outfitting three large boats in Singapore, each with a crew of twenty and capable of carrying forty private marines, a helicopter, and drones.[26]

Even governments are entering the market. The Netherlands, France, Spain, Belgium, and Italy all offer shipping companies the opportunity to hire their troops for security in pirate waters. These "vessel protection detachments" are available to ships registered in each nation or to companies significantly controlled by their citizens. For example, the Netherlands has outlawed the use of PMCs on ships that fly the Dutch flag but will offer its own troops some €400,000 per voyage, half of which must be borne by the ship owner. However, this is five to ten times more expensive than free-market PMCs, and many Dutch ship owners have opted to break the law and hire PMCs.[27] Owing to this market reality, many European governments have reluctantly agreed to legalize or at least tolerate armed guards. One way or another, the counterpiracy fight is becoming a private one.

In terms of "the good, the bad, and the ugly," there is much less to examine than in the Liberia case, because the Somalia market for force is fluid and dynamic. Its market actors are smaller and unsophisticated compared with DynCorp's complex multiyear and multimillion-dollar program. In some ways, this mirrors the past; military enterprisers such as Wallenstein ran huge corporate endeavors while many of the mercenaries of the Middle Ages were fleeting bands of opportunists.

Regarding the "good," private navies are efficient and effective. As Steven Jones puts it, "The benefits are very simple—private security has been able to provide a cost effective and robust form of protection and deterrent to protect seafarers and vessels from pirate attack."[28] From 2008 to 2011, piracy off the Somali coast was the scourge of the commercial shipping industry. However, by 2012, pirate attacks dramatically decreased by about 70 percent, partly because of this industry, and nine out of ten failed attacks by pirates on merchant ships were repelled by maritime PMCs. As the UN notes, this decline in piracy "can largely be attributed to the increasing use of private maritime security companies."[29]

Furthermore, the utility of private military force is high, making PMCs an attractive option to all neomedieval actors. Firms such as Hart Security acted as both traditional mercenary and military enterpriser, competing in the marketplace of force against pirates to establish their client's authority. It is unlikely that Puntland could have afforded its own standing military, making Hart's "rental navy" a high-value proposition. From an international trade perspective, Typhon's armed guards save shipping lines money on insurance premiums, while military enterpriser Nordic Risk Management helped make Berbera more secure, Somaliland's economic lifeline to the outside world. It is possible that these actions increased commerce and exceeded the cost of the PMCs' fees, demonstrating the value of security as commodity.

By 2012, the utility of private force proved so attractive that the International Maritime Organization, the UN's agency for maritime safety, issued guidance on the use of PMCs on ships in pirate waters. The document addresses maritime PMC certification and requirements; management, vetting, and training standards; deployment considerations; and use of force guidance.[30] This astonishing measure bends long-standing Admiralty Law, based on Westphalian sovereignty, and brings it into the neomedieval twenty-first century. Indeed, it could serve as the pilot for updating the UN Convention on the Law of the Sea and customary international law.

Even the US Navy recognizes the value of private maritime force. Rear Admiral (retired) Terence McKnight, the first commander of Combined Task Force 151, the multinational flotilla specifically dedicated to combating Somali piracy, identified the limits of state naval forces and referred to "security teams-privateers" as an option. Vice Admiral Bill Gortney, commander of the US Fifth Fleet, advises that "companies don't think twice about using security guards to protect their valuable facilities ashore. Protecting valuable ships and their crews at sea is no different." Admiral Mark Fitzgerald, commander of all naval forces in Europe and Africa, agrees. Regarding pirate waters, he says "the area is enormous" and that the Navy simply cannot guarantee commercial ships protection against pirates, nor should they. He recommends that ships have armed guards on board: "there's got to be security on these ships and the [private] security detachments that are on some of the large commercial ships have been very effective." Others have argued that privateering would be an ideal vehicle for legal and operational coordination between public and private actors in dealing with piracy.[31]

Perhaps the challenge posed by pirates may give rise to a new age of privateers: for-profit armed ships that are contracted through a "letter of marque" to seek and destroy the client's enemies. This ancient custom was common until the nineteenth century, when the Westphalian order was on the rise, and was abolished by states with the 1856 Paris Declaration Respecting Maritime Law. However, the United States was never a signatory to this treaty, and Article 1, section 8, of the US Constitution authorizes letters of marque. This could quickly resolve the pirate problem worldwide, although it would unleash the market for force on the high seas.

Yet the "good" of private military force may be overshadowed by the "bad." The concept of arming commercial vessels has not been a comfortable fit for many, particularly those who cleave to the Westphalian notion that only states should legitimately wield force. Standards and accountability on the use of deadly force by armed civilians remains a concern, risking relationships between flags and vessels. Other worries exist, too. Who is supplying the guards? What is the quality of their training? How is accountability maintained? The answers to these and other questions remain unknown, since private navies, like their land-based cousins, are opaque and secretive—a situation made worse by the fact that they operate in the middle of the ocean.

Aware of these problems, SAMI has supported standards to assess the performance of its members. It is informing the International Organization for Standardization's (ISO) 28007: 2012 criteria, which provide guidelines for using armed contractors on ships and certify PMCs that abide by these recommended practices. This ISO process forms the potential beginnings of a regulatory scheme for maritime PMCs, and firms such as Port2Port Maritime Security are certified. SAMI is also helping to develop the "100 Series Rules for the Use of Force," which codifies the concept of self-defense and establishes rules of engagement that allow guards to take "necessary and proportionate actions to save people and vessels." However, like the ISOA's voluntary principles for land-based PMCs, monitoring and enforcing this self-imposed regime remains a challenge.

There is also an "ugly" side to this free market for force. Like the *condottieri*, underemployed PMCs often turn predatory, as SomCan did when it seized fishing trawlers for ransom and seldom handed over revenue to its employer. Other observers worry that PMCs such as Saracen and R2 could easily become a law unto themselves, introducing more armed groups into an already war-ravaged region. Finally, what happens to locally trained and equipped private soldiers when foreign PMCs leave? As with so many aspects of the private military industry, the answer is unknown.

Somalia is not alone with pirates and privateers; piracy in the Gulf of Guinea now rivals that in the Gulf of Aden and the Malacca Straits. In 2012, the International Maritime Bureau indicated that there were fifty-eight incidents in the Gulf of Guinea, including ten hijackings, and 207 crew members taken hostage. National navies have proven ineffectual at containing this problem, which is why private ship owners hire PMCs, expanding the market for force. So far, PMCs have been restricted to land and sea forces, but it is conceivable—perhaps probable—that PMCs will use armed drones in the future, making private air forces in addition to private navies and armies.

Medieval Solutions to Modern Problems

All of the above does not mean that Somalia is lawless; a neomedieval durable disorder pervades much of the country, as Somali warlords and armed groups impose order in their own, albeit brutal, manner. Al-Shabaab controls much of southern and central Somalia, including some of Mogadishu, and its influence extends across the Somali borders into neighboring Ethiopia and Kenya. In this area, carved out of the "sovereign" territory of existing states, al-Shabaab maintains the monopoly of force and provides some political goods to the people under its own extreme version of sharia. With the exception of Mogadishu, much of this area is peaceful.

Al-Shabaab also provides governance. In 2008, it began to reach out to the public in a series of town visits that the International Crisis Group describes as "well choreographed, with clerics addressing public rallies and holding talks with local clan elders."[32] They also have handed out food and money to the poor, provided criminal justice through mobile sharia courts, and attempted to settle local disputes. Even Human Rights Watch concedes that "in many areas, al-Shabaab rule has brought relative peace and order that contrasts dramatically with the chaos in Mogadishu."[33]

Horn of Africa expert Andre Le Sage has identified four separate systems of justice in Somalia following its descent into chaos in 1991: the centralized formal judiciary structures created through international peace processes; the traditional, clan-based system known as *xeer*; sharia courts in urban areas, particularly Mogadishu; and civil society and private sector initiatives, including those established by warlords. What makes them essentially neomedieval is that they coexist as "multiple, overlapping and often contradictory sources of law" yet do not descend into anarchy.[34]

For two decades, Somalia has confounded the United Nations and other world powers that continue to look for a Westphalian government to talk to when none exists. A better solution would be to embrace the neomedievalism of the region and work with the various overlapping authorities and allegiances to achieve security, stability, and development.

Longtime Somalia expert Ken Menkhaus recommends establishing it as a "mediated state" and work directly with the ruling elite class rather than ruling institutions. In other words, deal with Somalia as a feudal state rather than a Westphalian one. This different approach to foreign policy in fragile states stems from the Middle Ages, when, as Menkhaus explains, "ambitious monarchs with limited power were forced to manipulate, maneuver, and make deals with local rivals to extend their authority." Those rivals often "mediated" authority as over-powerful purveyors of royal authority, as "private" subjects exercising "public" jurisdiction, or as members of supranational bodies such as the church. This created a situation in medieval France akin to that in neomedieval Somalia: "a nation characterized by parcellized and overlapping jurisdictions, multiple legal codes, and a plethora of internal tariffs and taxes."[35]

Given this reality, a state-building strategy based on neomedievalism may prove more effective than current Westphalian models founded on creating governmental institutions. According to Menkhaus, establishing Somalia as a mediated state would involve creating a limited central government that relies on a diverse range of local authorities to execute core functions of government and mediate relations between local communities and the state. This partner-ship between a weak central government and semiautonomous local authorities might more successfully support stability than conventional Westphalian models of nation building as seen in Iraq and Afghanistan, since it harnesses preexisting local authorities to deliver good governance rather than ignoring or disbanding them—the standard practice in contemporary peacekeeping missions.

Le Sage also recommends an essentially neomedieval approach to Somalia. Specifically, he suggests that Western powers and the United Nations not try to enforce a single justice system within Somalia to the detriment of the others, but instead recognize that the "multiplicity of systems has afforded Somalis options in responding to their predicament of state collapse, and each form of justice has its own advantages."[36]

Precisely how the centralized government can coexist with prevailing local authorities would be uniquely a matter for Somalis to determine, town by town and district by district. Such a process promises to be messy, but there is prec-edent for success. The lawless border region of Kenya, Ethiopia, Somalia, Sudan, and Uganda has produced years of bloodshed rivaling civil war. Unable to police its borders fully, the Kenyan government in the late 1990s partnered with coalitions of local NGOs, traditional leaders, and other civic groups to manage and prevent armed conflict through peace and development committees. Following this, public security and rule of law substantially improved, giving the Kenyan government the capacity to extend its authority into its frontier zones with the help of mediated actors. Similarly, governments and peacekeepers alike increasingly use community policing in fragile states to help provide governance in Afghanistan, the Congo, and Liberia. In this way, neomedieval state building harnesses the overlapping authorities and allegiances of local actors to achieve good governance by working toward a common goal.

Historically, the international community dismisses "subnational" political actors and is especially quick to abandon them once a national government is declared, no matter how feeble. However, in areas where neomedievalism is firmly rooted, establishing a Westphalian state may be unattainable, resulting in state-building failure. Too often, well-intentioned peacekeeping missions attempt to create Westphalian states in neomedieval environments that are doomed to fail, since the two conditions are incompatible, as exemplified by the dismal state-building record in Somalia since 1991. Consequently, Menkhaus concludes, "the problem in Somalia is not that state building itself is doomed to fail; it is rather that the type of state that both external and local actors have sought to construct has been unattainable and has as a consequence repeatedly set up Somali political leaders and their external mediators for failure."[37]

Somalia's governance without government creates a durable disorder that may hold valuable insights beyond its borders. While state-building efforts in Afghanistan and Iraq, along with UN peacekeeping missions around the world, toil in Sisyphean frustration to create Westphalian states where none existed before, an alternative development model based on the realities of neomedievalism might prove more apt. Such a model would recognize the various overlapping authorities and allegiances in a region and work with rather than against them to achieve stability and development. Embracing neomedievalism may be the best way of dealing with weak states and conflict-affected regions.

Both Somalia and Liberia are examples of neomedievalism, albeit highly negative ones. Neomedievalism need not be an adverse condition, but extreme cases help to demonstrate its five characteristics: the technological unification of the world, the regional integration of states, the rise of transnational organizations, the disintegration of states, and the restoration of private international violence. Both cases are stark examples of state disintegration. Tellingly, states did not come to their rescue, as the Westphalian order demands, but nonstates did. The main providers of help are the United Nations, an actor that exemplifies the regional integration of states, and NGOs, actors that are transnational organizations. The main threats to Liberia and Somalia are not states wielding conventional militaries using "regular" warfare strategies but armed nonstate actors such as LURD and al-Shabaab that engage in neomedieval warfare. Undergirding this entire phenomenon is the power of globalization. In Liberia, it was a force for good. For example, the "CNN effect" focused international attention on the crisis and spurred on a peacekeeping mission there. Conversely, in Somalia, globalization made possible an alliance between al-Shabaab and al-Qaida.

A key difference between Liberia and Somalia is their markets for force. Liberia had a mediated market with military enterprisers that worked in a public-private partnership with its employer, the United States, to build an army for Liberia's protection. Conversely, Somalia's free market with mercenaries contributed to instability rather than resolving it. Predatory mercenaries foster ceaseless conflict, worsening security, just like the situation in northern Italy in the high Middle Ages. A future with a free market for force would likely generate more war.

12

Medieval Modernity

The further back you look, the further forward you can see.
—Winston Churchill

The most powerful man in Tirin Kot, a dusty yet strategic stretch of land in southern Afghanistan, is not the provincial governor or the police chief or the commander of the Afghan army. It is Matiullah Khan, the head of a private army contracted by the United States to safeguard the vital NATO supply line from Tirin Kot to Kandahar. War has been good to Matiullah; his Afghan PMC has earned millions of dollars—an astronomical sum in a country as impoverished as Afghanistan—fighting the Taliban alongside American Special Forces soldiers.

Like the *condottieri* of old, Matiullah has a monopoly of force so great that he eclipses the authority of the provincial government. He appoints public officials and doles out government largesse to further his business interests. Also like the mercenaries of the Middle Ages, he is suspected of playing a double game with his employer. NATO commanders appear to ignore reports that he schemes with drug smugglers and the Taliban insurgents he is contracted to combat. It is concurrently difficult for NATO to win with and without him.

Matiullah is not alone. According to Hanif Atmar, the Afghan interior minister, Matiullah is one of at least twenty-three indigenous PMCs working in the area without government license or oversight. Major General Nick Carter, commander of NATO forces in southern Afghanistan in 2010, believes that Afghan PMCs deliberately prolong the fighting for profit: "It would be my expectation that people might create their own demand. It is essential that these highways move freely without extortion and racketeering."[1] Both Hanif Atmar and Carter said they would like to disband Matiullah's private army but cannot control him, making a volatile situation worse.

Private armies are back and not likely to go away. Over the past centuries, rulers first encouraged, then delegitimized, and finally all but eliminated mercenarism. Now it is returning. Since the end of the Cold War, private military actors have reappeared in force, some as military enterprisers and others reminiscent of medieval mercenaries. The future of private warfare seems bright, while the future of war looks perilous.

Four mutually reinforcing trends are emerging in the market for force. The first is the industry's resilience. This multibillion-dollar industry will not simply evaporate once the United States withdraws from Afghanistan. Instead, it will seek new clientele, leading to the second industry trend of proliferation. New customers and companies for private military services are appearing around the world, and the industry is evolving beyond Iraq and Afghanistan. Third, as the industry goes global, it is concurrently indigenizing, or "going native," as Matiullah Khan's private army illustrates. Warlords and others have adopted the PMC model to make a living, and international clients are buying, including the United States. Fourth, the industry is beginning to bifurcate. As Liberia and Somalia demonstrate, the market is developing in two different directions at once; the first is toward a mediated market with military enterprisers, and the second is toward a free market with mercenaries. The trajectory that dominates the market in the coming years is significant, because it will influence stability, as it did in the Middle Ages.

First Trend: Industry Resilience

The private military industry is here to stay. Multibillion-dollar industries do not quickly disappear, and now that the United States has helped legitimize its existence by employing PMCs for more than a decade, others will likely follow suit. Moreover, it will be difficult to curb the industry's growth, as it morphs from an American-based one into something more international.

Currently, many of the big PMCs are headquartered in the United States, and their leadership is American. But, like all multinational corporations, PMCs maintain offices around the world. Should one government, such as the United States or the United Kingdom, impose strict regulations on their trade, they would move offshore. For example, Dubai is a favorite hub for the industry owing to its proximity to markets (i.e., the Middle East and Africa) and its business-friendly laws. This means that as long as there are customers and business safe havens, the industry can evolve more or less unfettered.

Two additional factors are driving the industry's permanence. The first is the internal demographics of giants such as DynCorp, MPRI, Aegis, Triple Canopy, and their peers. Like the medieval free companies, the individuals who staff these large PMCs are mostly international, drawn from nearly every continent. Only a minority of DynCorp employees in Liberia were American. In 2010, the United States conducted a census of private security personnel hired by its military in the Middle East. In Afghanistan, 18,869 individuals worked for PMCs;

of these, only 197 were US citizens. Similarly, in Iraq, only 1,017 of the 11,628 contractors were Americans.[2] The majority of PMC employees are not from the company's country of origin. After working in the industry for several years, these individuals have learned valuable trade knowledge and gained professional connections around the world, and they have the ability to go into business for themselves. If large PMCs downsize, workers in this new class can establish their own PMCs back home, wherever that might be. A decade of PMCs at war has created a new labor pool of *condottieri*.

The second driver is the myriad subcontractors that spin off big PMCs. Global firms such as ArmorGroup typically create or hire local security companies to assist them in fulfilling contracts overseas. Like the international personnel above, these subcontractors, or "subs," have learned the trade craft of the private military industry and will seek out their own clients in those regions, effectively spawning a native market for force in fragile regions, a dangerous prospect. Little is known about these local PMCs in places such as Afghanistan, because NATO generally only monitors the performance of prime contractors, and there is little, if any, vetting or oversight of subs. This has allowed subcontractors to propagate without much scrutiny.

The new international labor pool of private military talent combined with indigenous subcontractors-turned-independent means that the industry is unlikely to dissolve once the United States leaves Afghanistan and other conflict zones. On the contrary, these factors are expanding the industry horizontally and vertically. Horizontally, the industry is laterally growing and globalizing as other international actors follow the US example. Vertically, the industry is indigenizing as native PMCs emerge and mimic their larger international cousins. This effectively offers a spectrum of PMC choices, from local to global, to potential consumers. These concurrent phenomena are examined below.

Second Trend: Industry Proliferation

As the conflict markets in Iraq and Afghanistan dry up, the private military industry is going global in search of new opportunities. Two influences are driving this trend. On the supply side, PMCs are seeking new markets and developing innovative services or face bankruptcy. On the demand side, potential customers are emboldened by the US example of using these firms. The superpower's use of PMCs has fostered their legitimacy and has introduced a new norm in international relations that private force is once again acceptable in war. These factors are causing the industry to go global, well beyond Iraq and Afghanistan, in search of new conflicts, as supply naturally seeks demand and vice versa.

Now that the United States has opened the Pandora's box of mercenarism, private warriors of all stripes are coming out of the shadows to engage in for-profit warfare. Some are military enterprisers like Wallenstein during the Thirty Years War and DynCorp in Liberia, building armies for clients' use. Others are like the mercenaries of medieval Italy or the PMCs in Somalia, offering private armies and navies to those willing to pay. Both reflect a clear regression to the status quo ante of the Middle Ages, when states did not have the monopoly of force and conflict was a commodity.

Like the market in the Middle Ages, this means that the industry will chase conflict, whether it is in fourteenth-century Italy or twenty-first-century Africa, because that is where their profits lie. The rise of a free market for force should be expected, since conflict-affected countries possess the necessary conditions for profit: unconstrained political rivalries, ample resources, tyrannical rulers and cowed populations, the proliferation of militias and mercenaries, and little or no rule of law. In the abstract, it is natural that supply should seek demand and vice versa, yet in reality, introducing an industry vested in conflict into the most conflict-prone regions in the world is vexing, given the possible consequences for the people who live there.

Examples already exist of this trend. Libyan president Muammar Qaddafi hired mercenaries from across Africa to brutally suppress the popular revolt against him, as England's King Henry II did in the twelfth century, albeit more successfully. Like a military enterpriser during the Thirty Years War, the emir of Abu Dhabi paid the PMC Reflex Responses $529 million to build a small army of eight hundred foreign troops to conduct special operations missions inside and outside the country, defend oil pipelines and other infrastructure from terrorist attacks, and put down internal rebellions. In West Africa, both sides in Côte d'Ivoire's civil war in 2011 used mercenaries, mostly from Liberia, who have committed mass atrocities against civilians reminiscent of Hawkwood's destruction of Cesena in 1377.[3] These modern military enterprisers and mercenaries demonstrate that the Westphalian norm against private military forces is eroding and contract warfare is on the rise.

In the coming years, the market will likely become more competitive and expand. Supply of military services probably will diversify as PMCs develop in China, Russia, and elsewhere that have skilled ex-soldiers with access to weapons and an entrepreneurial spirit. For example, large PMCs in Afghanistan will leave behind local subcontractor PMCs following the US withdrawal, perpetuating the market long after NATO has left. No one should assume that the private military industry will remain a singularity of the United States or Western Europe. As the marketplace becomes more crowded, these new PMCs will look to distinguish themselves from their competitors by offering greater combat-oriented services and working for the highest bidder, with scant regard for human rights or international law.

As demonstrated by the *condottieri*, private military supply can create its own demand, either by offering new capabilities previously unavailable or through extortion. Clientele will also diversify as new consumers emerge from the growing cast of neomedieval characters on the world stage: strong states conducting military operations overseas yet not wanting their own "boots on the ground," weak states augmenting their forces, tyrannical governments seeking regime security, UN missions requiring additional peacekeepers, multinational corporations and shipping lines safeguarding their assets, NGOs protecting their humanitarian workers, opposition groups seeking regime change, international criminal organizations craving additional muscle, and the whims of super-rich individuals. As in the Middle Ages, if one actor in a conflict zone hires a PMC, the others may be forced to do the same in a security dilemma, laterally escalating the conflict and widening the market for force in an explosive situation. Contract warfare responds to the demands of the marketplace rather than political dealings.

The current size and scope of the embryonic free market for force remain unknown. Even the approximate number of private military personnel and where they are operating are undetermined, because the firms are notoriously secretive, and no independent organization credibly tracks this information. What is known is meager and generally limited to US employment in Iraq and Afghanistan. According to the Congressional Research Service, a nonpartisan watchdog agency of the US Congress, of the thirty thousand armed contractors operating in the Iraq War, only about a third worked directly for the US government, while the rest served other clients: foreign governments, NGOs, multinational corporations, and international organizations.[4]

This may be the slow beginning of a wider neomedieval market for force. Already, the US military is highly privatized, with contractors making up half of its force structure in theaters of war, and short of a national draft, the country can no longer fight a sustained war without private sector involvement. Many of the security contracts are buried within larger contracts, such as reconstruction projects or aid programs that require security. Reconstruction contractors working for USAID have, in turn, subcontracted with PMCs for protection. In Afghanistan, the situation is more pronounced. Experts estimate that the true number of armed contractors is approximately seventy thousand. Most of these armed civilians work for non-US firms and non-US clients, evidence that the market for force in Afghanistan is expanding beyond the ambit of US security operations.[5]

Conflict markets such as Iraq, Afghanistan, and Africa are attracting new PMCs from around the world, signaling market growth. Chinese PMCs such as Shandong Huawei Security Group seek to protect oil and mining infrastructure in Sudan, Iraq, and Afghanistan. China already has one of the largest domestic private security industries in the world, with more than 4 million authorized private security personnel. It is unclear when the first PMC was created in China, although in 2004, a Ningbo businessman is alleged to have created a company with personnel drawn from China's special forces community and the paramilitary People's Armed Police.[6]

China's entry into the global market is none too late, according to Hu Xiangyun, general manager of Bodyguard Services, who has argued in the Chinese press that China should have entered the foreign market long ago. Revealing his market logic regarding armed conflict, he explains that "the problem is that if China won't open up its market, foreigners can't be expected to open up theirs for China."[7] If China's massive domestic security industry goes global, it will have one advantage over its North American and Western European competitors: price.

Fearing Anglo-Saxon domination of the industry, a bipartisan French parliamentary report has called for the recognition and regulation of PMCs, suggesting that the industry has become too important to ignore. The largest French PMC is GEOS Group, with average annual sales of 40 million euros, followed by Risk & Co at 28 million euros. A visit to post-Qaddafi Libya exposed significant presence of "Anglo-Saxon companies" that threaten French political and commercial interests.[8] A group of French companies—Geodis, GIE Access, Sodexo, and Thales—has formed the Global X company to bid for contracts for UN peacekeeping operations, should it begin outsourcing such activities. Such thinking reveals a market-driven approach toward stability operations.

The private military industry is booming everywhere. Former foes of the industry such as the European Union now employ PMCs such as Argus Security Projects in postconflict Libya, where personnel carry weapons under French diplomatic status. Kenya has turned to British-based XFOR Security Solutions to help ward off Somali pirates from its shores and protect its tourism industry. Russia is drafting legislation establishing a Russian industry based on the American and British model. It would permit Russian PMCs such as the Oskord Security Group to deploy ex-soldiers and police abroad to protect oil, gas, and mineral holdings in conflict zones.[9]

Africa is another market for force in waiting, given its high degree of conflict, natural resources, and commercial interests. DynCorp's work in Liberia and the burgeoning market in Somalia are the beginning of a trend. The profitable Gulf of Guinea has brought oil money and conflict to countries such as Nigeria, which has the second-largest oil reserves in Africa and is one of the top exporters to the United States. The Nigerian government has awarded a ten-year contract worth $130 million for maritime security to fight pirates and insurgents. The awardee, Global West Vessel Special Nigeria, will provide platforms for tracking ships and cargo, enforcing regulatory compliance, and surveillance of the Nigerian

Maritime Domain. The PMC is run by a former commander of a local insurgent group, the Movement for the Emancipation of the Niger Delta (MEND). The most infamous private military expedition in recent years must be Simon Mann's attempted coup in oil-rich Equatorial Guinea in 2004, which could serve as a model of how not to go about overthrowing a country.

Another new market is developing in Latin America, which is ravaged by drug wars. MPRI is training Mexican soldiers in counterinsurgency techniques; DynCorp has job openings there for aviation instructors and mechanics; and Kroll and other antikidnapping specialists protect business executives operating in Mexico. Corporations are not the only ones spending money on private security in Latin America. The United States' annual spending on counternarcotic contracts in Latin America rose by 32 percent, from $482 million in 2005 to $635.8 million in 2009. These contracts went to five primes: Lockheed Martin, Raytheon, ITT, ARINC, and DynCorp, which received the majority of the work.[10] Most of the contracted tasks were not PMC-related but rather private military support functions such as surveillance and aerial spraying to eradicate drug crops.

Perhaps the most anticipated market of all is the United Nations. In the early days of Rwandan genocide, Executive Outcomes met with Kofi Annan, who was then head of the UN Department of Peacekeeping Operations. They discussed the possibility of the PMC staging a humanitarian intervention to arrest the rapidly developing genocide until a larger UN peacekeeping mission could take over. Executive Outcomes said it could have "boots on the ground" in fourteen days, followed in six weeks by a fully equipped, brigade-sized element of fifteen hundred personnel, complete with its own air and fire support. The firm estimated that it could establish "security islands" and refugee safe havens in the region for $600,000 per day over a six-month period ($150 million in total). This is cheap compared with normal UN peacekeeping costs.

(In)famously, Annan refused Executive Outcomes' proposal, later explaining that "the world may not be ready to privatize peace."[11]However, the world was also not ready for genocide, which killed more than eight hundred thousand people in approximately one hundred days, making Annan's Westphalian sentiment an expensive ideology.[12] By the time the UN Assistance Mission for Rwanda (UNAMIR II) arrived in Rwanda, it was too late, and it cost more than five times Executive Outcomes' estimate for its own operation.[13]

The United Nations' strong Westphalian bias against privatized peacekeeping has long made it a critic of the industry. Until recently, the institution was content to avoid this issue altogether, but the persistent shortage of peacekeepers, the legacy of Rwanda, and ongoing mass atrocities in Darfur and the Congo have led many to quietly question the United Nations' unofficial embargo on PMCs.[14] The option of private peacekeepers versus none at all, which is the condition in many parts of the world today, is a Hobson's choice.

Private armies are just the beginning. Already, private forces are manifesting across the five domains of war: land, sea, air, space, and cyberspace. Small private navies such as SomCan patrol the Somali coast, seeking pirates and becoming pirates themselves when convenient. Other PMCs are exploring the use of flying drones, rendering private air forces cheap. While PMCs are not flying through space, there are now private companies that do. This would have been unthinkable a generation ago, and it is conceivable that in another generation, private spacecraft will outnumber national ones in orbit, including armed ones working on behalf of a government or themselves. Finally, cyberspace is already flush with virtual PMCs, offering clients offensive "hack-back" capabilities against intruders, making them the mercenaries of the fifth domain. Contract warfare may one day be available across all five domains of war, changing armed conflict as we know it.

Third Trend: Industry Indigenization

The industry is going native. Matiullah Khan is one of several warlords-turned-PMCs that have emerged from the US war in Afghanistan, adopting the American model of private military contracting. Records in 2010 show that there are fifty-two government-registered PMCs in the country, with twenty-four thousand hired guns, most of them Afghans. However, many, if not most, of the indigenous PMCs operating in the country are not registered at all, and some are little more than profit-seeking militia, akin to medieval mercenaries who plundered the countryside.

The US outsourcing of security has normalized the market for force, inspiring warlords and other conflict entrepreneurs to start their own PMCs. This has resulted in the indigenization of the market. Worse, the United States has inadvertently encouraged this by hiring these homegrown PMCs, such as Matiullah's army. Indigenous PMCs are the next wave of industry growth. In Iraq, fifty-six of the eighty-two PMCs registered with the Ministry of Interior are Iraqi, and they work for a variety of government and private sector clients. In Afghanistan, fifty-two PMCs are licensed to operate, arming about forty thousand civilian contractors. The presence of PMCs became so ubiquitous that in 2010, the Afghanistan government decreed that all PMCs must be disbanded by the end of the year. Tellingly, this drew sharp criticism from the United States, which said that it could not operate without the industry, and the Afghan government backed down, although it did close fifty-four mostly unregistered companies.[15]

Today most of the PMCs operating in Iraq and Afghanistan are local and less picky than their US counterparts about whom they work for and what they do. An example of this is the "Host Nation Trucking" contract. Under this $2.16

billion contract, the US Army hired eight civilian trucking firms to transport supplies to bases in Afghanistan and also required the companies to provide their own security. In some ways, this arrangement worked well: it effectively supplied most US combat outposts across difficult and hostile terrain while only rarely needing the assistance of US troops. However, in 2010 a US congressional investigation revealed that most of the prime contractors hired local Afghan PMCs for armed protection of the trucking convoys. The congressional report, titled *Warlord, Inc.*, found that "the principal private security subcontractors on the [Host Nation Trucking] contract are warlords, strongmen, commanders and militia leaders who compete with the Afghan central government for power and authority. Providing 'protection' services for the United States supply chain empowers these warlords with money, legitimacy, and a *raison d'etre* for their private armies." As with the medieval market for force, the report concluded that these indigenous "private armies" fueled warlordism, extortion, corruption, and likely collaboration with the enemy. It determined that "the logistics contract has an outsized strategic impact on U.S. objectives in Afghanistan."[16]

That same year, a US Senate report confirmed the localization of the industry. In a comprehensive investigation into PMCs, the Senate discovered that the industry was going native, or, as one observer explained, "What used to be called warlord militias are now Private Security Companies."[17] American and British PMCs unwittingly produced the native industry by creating local subcontractors that went into business for themselves. For example, the British PMC ArmorGroup subcontracted two Afghan PMCs that it called "Mr. White" and "Mr. Pink" to provide a guard force. The Senate investigation found evidence that these local PMCs were linked to murder, kidnapping, bribery, and anti-Coalition activities and concluded: "The proliferation of private security personnel in Afghanistan is inconsistent with the counterinsurgency strategy."[18]

Problematically, the only local organizations in conflict-affected states capable of providing private security are warlords, militias, and insurgents, who swell the ranks of the marketplace. The Bagram air base, a strategic military facility in Afghanistan, employs a local PMC run by Asil Khan, a former commander in the Northern Alliance, a guerrilla fighting force. The PMC Afghanistan Navin also supplies a guard force of five hundred men and armed convoy escorts to the air base and is owned by former mujahideen commander Lutfullah. A now-defunct American company, US Protection and Investigations, partnered with Northern Alliance military commanders such as General Din Mohammad Jurat to provide former militia members for protection. Other examples of indigenous Afghan PMCs include Watan Risk Management, Kandahar Security Group, Strategic Security Solutions International, NCL Holdings, Elite Security Services, and Asia Security Group. This model of force provision did not exist before the United States arrived.

In some cases, these native PMCs have restored order yet undermine the very institutions the Americans sought to build—a public police force, a national army, provincial administrations—elements of a Westphalian state. For example, Commando Security is a PMC that escorts convoys between Kandahar and Helmand Province to the west. Ruhullah, the company's chief, is suspected of colluding with the Taliban, like most of his peers. According to one official at the Interior Ministry, "The rule seems to be, if the attack is small, then crush it. But if the presence of Taliban is too big to crush, then make a deal." [19]However, bribing the enemy does not eradicate the problem and perhaps makes it worse. Afghan officials believe that Watan Risk Management secretly pays the Taliban to attack NATO convoys in order to keep the PMC in business. Supply can generate its own demand in a free market for force.

Like medieval mercenaries, this new breed of PMC can prove overly brutal when executing contracts, with little or no concern for human rights. Ruhullah deals ruthlessly with those who impede the flow of his trucks, regardless of whether they are Taliban or civilian. "He's laid waste to entire villages," said one Afghan official. Watan Risk Management and Compass Security were both banned from escorting NATO convoys on the highway between Kabul and Kandahar after a pair of bloody confrontations with Afghan civilians. When asked why NATO would contract these native PMCs, one senior NATO official said, speaking on the condition of anonymity, "I can't tell you about the sub to the sub to the sub."[20] The industry's overutilization of subcontractors has produced an indigenous free market for force, replete with home-grown PMCs that act as mercenaries.

Fourth Trend: Industry Bifurcation

Liberia and Somalia demonstrate that the industry is simultaneously developing along two different tracks, one more desirable than the other for world peace. Both countries are examples of neomedievalism, albeit worst-case scenarios, yet they differ in their market for force. Liberia is a mediated market with military enterprisers, and Somalia is a free market with mercenaries. Consequently, Liberia is more secure and stable than Somalia, and this is instructive for the future.

Liberia is more stable, in part, because it has a mediated market. The United Nations secured the country while DynCorp raised its army in close conjunction with the United States, its employer, and to a lesser extent Liberia and the UN. DynCorp was a PMC in the tradition of military enterprisers such as Wallenstein, who built military forces rather than using them. Whether one is raising an army of two thousand or two hundred thousand, the methods are essentially the same, differing only in scale and scope. The military DynCorp raised was a relative success compared with US efforts in Iraq and Afghanistan or UN experiences in the Balkans, Haiti, Timor-Leste, and the Democratic Republic of the Congo. This public-private partnership in the security sector proved highly effective and provides a model for a world with an effectual private military industry.

By contrast, the neomedievalism of Somalia is analogous to Italy in the age of the *condottieri*: warlordism and ceaseless conflict. Tragically, the country suffers a truly free market for force replete with unscrupulous clients, undisciplined companies, and neomedieval warfare. Overlapping authorities in this case result in anarchy akin to the mythologized "Dark Ages," making Somalia one of the world's most dangerous places.

Comparing these cases shows two possible futures for the industry. The first is Liberia, where security actors operate in a mediated market for force, and the main market actors are military enterprisers that build rather than use military force. The second is Somalia, where a free market for force exists, and market actors are mercenaries that engage in contract warfare. Liberia is more secure than Somalia, implying that PMCs functioning as military enterprisers in a mediated market can have a positive security benefit, while PMCs operating in a free market will likely worsen security conditions.

Military enterprisers represent the median point between a free market for force versus one monopolized by states, since military enterprisers are a hybrid of both: military public-private partnerships. Just as military enterprisers such as Wallenstein were symptomatic of states' gradual monopolization of force, it is not surprising that modern military enterprisers such as DynCorp suggest the current undoing of this monopoly, as the pendulum swings back to a premodern world order.

In a world where the private military industry will likely remain, a mediated market of military enterprisers is preferable to a free market of mercenaries, which can cause war and promote warlordism. However, military enterprisers are not without risks. As shown above, some military enterprisers unwittingly create a local free market for force, giving rise to a new breed of indigenous *condottieri*. Some of them are former subcontractors of larger PMCs, while others are entrepreneurial warlords who have adopted the private military model to win business from those needing security. Some are both. This new kind of mercenary PMC can plague the countryside as their medieval ancestors did.

The unraveling of the state's monopoly of force has begun, not over centuries but over decades. The market for force's trajectory is uncertain; it could develop into a mediated market, which is safer, or a free market, which is dangerous. The market's future depends on what is done now.

What to Do?

The world may be at a crossroads with the private military industry. Left on auto-pilot, the industry may morph into a situation similar to medieval Italy's perpetual contract war. However, other options exist. One response to this conundrum is categorically outlawing private military actors, although this seems unlikely, because the time for such sweeping action is past. A decade of war in Iraq and Afghanistan by the world's superpower has cemented this multibillion-dollar industry onto the international landscape. Efforts to proscribe or heavily regulate big PMCs will simply drive them offshore, while the smaller ones, such as those native to Afghanistan, will go underground. Therefore, it is unlikely that banning the industry will accomplish much.

Another approach is self-regulation. Efforts already exist that aspire to do this, some with the support of the industry, since major PMCs do not wish their brand to be besmirched by roguish companies. One example is the ISOA's voluntary code of conduct, which requires member companies to operate in a responsible manner akin to corporate social responsibility. Industry critics find such self-regulation encouraging but ultimately lacking the transparency and enforcement mechanisms needed to hold PMCs accountable.

An alternative solution would be to regulate the industry. In the United States, every single Defense Authorization Act passed by Congress since 2005 has contained efforts to manage this market. Yet Congress still has not passed comprehensive legislation regarding this industry, despite the multitude of congressional hearings, reports, and cries from civil society groups. Some legislation has been proposed, such as the "Stop Outsourcing Security Act" by Representative Jan Schakowsky (Democrat, Illinois), but these efforts have not mustered enough votes to become law. One reason for this, as demonstrated earlier, is the utility of on-demand force, making PMCs an attractive option even for a military superpower, although the near-term benefits of PMCs may be eclipsed by their long-term liabilities.

Attempts to apply existing laws to the industry have failed because of problems of extraterritorial jurisdiction. The Special Maritime and Territorial Jurisdiction Act (SMTJ) and the Patriot Act both contain provisions that allow the application of federal law to crimes committed by contractors overseas in areas reserved exclusively for the United States' use. This effectively gives the United States extraterritorial jurisdiction to try crimes that are committed by or against American citizens within specific US properties or territories abroad, such as military bases, consulates, and embassies. However, this does not apply to war zones. Can occupied territories in foreign lands truly be called US property? The answer is no, as demonstrated by the so-called Triple Canopy case. On July 8, 2006, PMC employee Jacob Washbourne shot multiple rounds into two

Iraqi civilian cars, unprovoked, according to witnesses. Washbourne was terminated from the company but never faced criminal charges.[21] Foreign war zones
are not US territory, limiting the efficacy of the SMTJ and the Patriot Act as
tools for PMC transparency and accountability.

Others have tried to use the Military Extraterritorial Jurisdiction Act (MEJA)
to impose PMC accountability. The MEJA was passed in 2000 in response to
crimes committed by civilians accompanying the military overseas. It establishes a legal framework for trying contractors abroad in US federal courts for
felonies that are punishable by more than one year in prison. But the MEJA is
not robust enough to enforce accountability and has only been used a few times
since 2000, all for non-PMC-related issues.

Another attempt at stopgap accountability is applying military law, known as
the Uniform Code of Military Justice (UCMJ), to PMC personnel. While such
ideas brief well in Washington, D.C. they do not work in practice. The UCMJ
has no jurisdiction over civilians and is not fully compatible with civilian code,
leaving lawyers bewildered about how it applies to multinational corporations.
For example, can a CEO be thrown into the brig for "conduct unbecoming an
officer and a gentleman" (Article 133 of the UCMJ)? What is required is new
legislation—both domestic and international—to regulate this industry. Yet in
ten years of war, the United States has not taken such action, and the chances of
a timely Geneva Protocol that deals with this issue seem slim.

International efforts are equally frustrated. In 2005, the United Nations
established a working group on the use of mercenaries to "monitor and study
the effects of the activities of private companies... on the enjoyment of human
rights."[22] After five years, it concluded that there is a regulatory legal vacuum cov-
ering the activities of the industry. The group recommended to the UN Human
Rights Council and the General Assembly text for a possible international convention that regulates private military force. It also promotes the Westphalian
notion that only states should have the monopoly of force and cannot outsource
this privilege to the private sector. Furthermore, it envisaged the development
of a national regime of licensing, regulation, and oversight of the industry on a
worldwide scale. States would be compelled to collect and provide this information to the United Nations, which would maintain an international register of
private military actors.[23] However, the proposal has received a cool reception
from member states. In another sign of neomedievalism, many find a binding
instrument with regulatory and oversight mechanisms regarding the use of force
premature and an encroachment on their sovereignty.

In 2006, Switzerland and the International Committee of the Red Cross
launched the "Swiss Initiative" to harmonize industry practices with human
rights norms. The process was consultative in nature and included governments, PMCs, and civil society groups. The governments of the United States

and the United Kingdom underwrote this initiative, which is important, since they employed most of the industry at the time. By 2008, this effort had produced a common understanding regarding the industry's human rights obligations in war zones, which was ratified in Montreux, Switzerland, and known as the Montreux Document. There were 58 original signatory companies, and as of September 1, 2013, there were 708.[24] A parallel effort of the Swiss Initiative is the International Code of Conduct for Private Security Service Providers, which articulates standards for the industry to ensure compliance with international law.

However, the efficacy of the Montreux Document and the International Code of Conduct is questionable, because they are voluntary agreements, not a binding international treaty. Transparency is largely dependent on companies' self-reporting of problems, which is unlikely to happen, because it is bad for business, and enforcement mechanisms are weak. Also, these agreements are limited to trigger-pulling PMCs, while trainers, such as DynCorp in Liberia, and security support companies are excluded. Missing and urgently needed are oversight tools that move beyond the outmoded Westphalian norms inherent in international law such as the Montreux Document and recognize the neomedieval nature of the early twenty-first century.

What Can Still Be Done

The private military industry is not going away, and therefore actions should be taken to harness the good while limiting the bad effects it produces. Instead of relying on weak laws, aspirational codes of conduct, or the forlorn hope of a new Geneva Protocol that deals with these new armed actors, a more practical solution involves fostering a mediated market for force that shuns mercenaries and works only with qualified military enterprisers in public-private partnerships. This would prevent devolution to a free market. A market approach instead of a regulatory one may prove more effective, because in a neomedieval world, no single group of actors, such as states, can collectively impose their will through international law, and consequentially, other methods, like market approaches, must be sought to control this dangerous industry.

A market approach seeks to incentivize desirable practices by making them profitable. A hefty consumer with market power, such as the United States, can drive the market to produce good behavior, or at least acceptable conduct, by manipulating the industry's own profit motive. Market power is the amount of influence that a firm, or in this case a country, has on the industry in which it operates. Firms with market power are said to be "price makers," as they are able to set the price for a good or service while maintaining market share.

The logic is as compelling as it is simple. A customer with market power sets performance standards for the industry, holds companies accountable to those standards, and maintains an index of firms based on performance. Companies that excel get rehired, while those that underperform get replaced, encouraging best practices in the industry through what economist Adam Smith called the "invisible hand" of the marketplace, a metaphor describing the self-regulating behavior of a free market when good behavior is rewarded and bad is expelled.

In the case of the private military industry, the United States had market power, since it was the only significant buyer in the marketplace. This monopsony meant that the country could reasonably dictate prices and standards to PMCs and hold them accountable. Unfortunately, it failed to do so, despite the fact that half its force structure in Iraq and Afghanistan was contracted. There were no unifying performance standards, methods of accountability differed depending on which government office issued the contract, contracts varied widely among companies, they were inconsistently enforced, and there was no government index of company performance. Contracts were frequently renewed for incumbent companies regardless of their competence, as documented in the Gansler report, the Commission on Wartime Contracting, the Special Inspector General for Iraq Reconstruction, the Special Inspector General for Afghanistan Reconstruction, and other government inquiries. Had this megaconsumer used its market power to shape professional norms, set performance standards, and reward best practices when the industry was in its infancy, then things might look very different today. Instead, the industry grew in a haphazard way.

The United Nations may now have the opportunity to shape industry best practices if it decides to outsource some of its peacekeeping. Peacekeeping could become the largest market for private military force in the near future, giving the United Nations market power. The organization will have the opportunity to choose PMC winners and losers for peacekeeping missions, allowing it to determine standards and drive industry behavior, as only a large consumer can do.

This does not suggest that peacekeeping should go onto the auction block or be wholly outsourced to the private sector. Just like "smart sanctions," the world needs "smart privatized peacekeeping" that addresses issues of capability and accountability. To accomplish this, the United Nations must establish a licensing and registration regime that all industry members must observe in order to prequalify for contracts with the organization. This would entail clear standards and policies regulating all industry activities, plus transparent mechanisms of oversight and accountability. As a minimum, this regime should include the following elements: registration criteria, ethical code of conduct, employee vetting standards, mechanisms of transparency and accountability, permissible clients (e.g., sanctioned by the UN Security Council), training and safety standards, contractual standards, and compliance enforcement mechanisms such as audits.

Contract instruments must be in place to ensure swift deployment of PMCs, should a humanitarian catastrophe arise. It would be impermissible to lose a key advantage of PMCs' rapid response and surge capacity to bureaucratic dithering.

The potential benefits that this industry could provide to the United Nations are substantial. Military enterprisers could augment thinning UN peacekeeping forces, either ad hoc or on a more permanent basis. More controversially, strong PMCs with force projection capabilities could also deploy rapidly to arrest tragic situations like genocide, as Executive Outcomes possibly could have done in Rwanda. These PMCs could establish safe havens for civilians and buy precious time for the United Nations to muster a large peacekeeping force from donor countries, which often takes weeks or months. The industry could also provide the United Nations with a quasi-permanent or "on call" military capacity originally envisaged in its inception.

If managed well, such a system would prove a boon to global security as a mediated market for force and forestall the effects of an unrestrained free market, as demonstrated during the era of the *condottieri* and today's Somalia. It would augment understaffed UN missions with qualified peacekeepers, provide a surge capacity for emergency deployments to stop atrocities, permit public scrutiny of the private military industry, allow the United Nations (and the world) to benefit from PMCs' service, and offer a modicum of oversight for this burgeoning industry that is not disappearing. If utilized correctly, PMCs would greatly enhance the United Nations' capacity to ensure peace, security, and governance and, as the UN Charter mandates, "save the future generations." It would also establish the norms that would inform an eventual convention on controlling private military force. To be effective, such a protocol must include the spectrum of neomedieval actors and not just states, since many of these actors now employ force and the state is losing its monopoly.

Some at the United Nations will balk at privatized peacekeeping, as Kofi Annan did during the Rwandan genocide, since it violates Westphalian ideals. But this may be gradually changing. As Sir Brian Urquhart, a retired UN under-secretary-general and considered the founding father of peacekeeping, explains: "It does seem to me that some of these private companies could play an extremely useful role ... there are all sorts of special tasks which possibly these companies are better-trained to perform than a UN force put together at the last minute."[25] In fact, the United Nations has already begun moving in this direction and employs PMCs to protect its operations around the world. In 2012, it introduced guidance for PMCs operating on ships traveling through pirate waters, upending centuries of Admiralty Law that is Westphalian to its core. At present, the UN working group on the use of mercenaries is exploring how the organization should utilize PMCs, and the UN security office has drafted operational guidelines, a model contract, and statement of work for PMCs.[26]

A market approach blended with regulation makes sense, because laws alone are difficult to enforce, and draconian ones will simply drive PMCs offshore, beyond the reach of accountability. Only the United Nations has the potential market power and regulatory heft to shape the industry's future. It is probably too late to ban the industry, for those desiring this, but we do have options: allow the market for force to unfold in a laissez-faire manner, or shape it to extract its benefits while curbing its risks. In other words, accept a free market or nurture a mediated one. The answer is imperative, given the relationship between armed force and sovereignty.

Back to the Future

The reappearance of private armies is a harbinger of a wider trend in international relations: the emergence of neomedievalism. In the modern Westphalian world order, only states can make international law and enforce it through their monopoly of force. That is, only states can use violence "legitimately" to impose their will, leaving nonstate rivals at their mercy. States strictly outlaw mercenaries, because they threaten this monopoly and contest the system.

The erosion of the taboo against mercenarism heralds a shift in this world order, from the state-centric Westphalian system back to the status quo ante of the Middle Ages. The medieval system was not dominated by states but was polycentric in nature, with authority diluted and shared among state and nonstate actors alike. States were just another actor on a crowded world stage, and no one had a monopoly of force to enforce their will. Instead, there was a free market of force, and actors—kings, popes, princes, city-states, rich families, and so on—commonly employed mercenaries to settle disputes in contract warfare.

Neomedievalism describes what a return to a polycentric world order might countenance. Neomedievalism is a non-state-centric and multipolar world order characterized by overlapping authorities and allegiances. It is a metaphor for a global phenomenon and is not intended to be Eurocentric. Nor does it imply worldwide atavism. States will not disappear but will matter less and increasingly compete with other global actors such as the United Nations, NGOs, multinational corporations, politicized ethnic and religious groups, terrorists and transnational criminal organizations, and others for political dominance in world affairs. This was not the situation a century ago, when the rule of states was preeminent. Nor does neomedievalism connote chaos and anarchy; the global system will persist in a durable disorder that contains rather than solves problems.

Already, parallels between the Middle Ages and today are apparent. In 1977, scholar Hedley Bull devised a test to detect the presence of neomedievalism in international relations based on five criteria: the technological unification of the world, the regional integration of states, the rise of transnational organizations, the disintegration of states, and the restoration of private international violence. He found little evidence of neomedievalism in his day, but that was at the height of the Cold War, a very Westphalian period. However, a contemporary examination clearly shows that neomedievalism is on the ascent.

For some, the most disturbing feature of neomedievalism is the restoration of private international violence—mercenarism—and the implications for world peace of contract warfare. The modern equivalents of private military actors are PMCs: expeditionary conflict entrepreneurs structured as multinational corporations that deploy private armies as mercenaries or raise armies as military enterprisers.

Excessive concerns over mercenarism are a Westphalian bias. Those brought up to see war in purely ideological terms, namely, as an armed contest between two or more states, might assume that the commodification of conflict guarantees greater violence, but this overlooks the obvious: some of the bloodiest wars in history, such as World War I and World War II, were fought by states via national armies at the apex of the Westphalian order. And those who fear that mercenaries are more undisciplined and dangerous than national armies ignore the fact that many state militaries have abysmal records of human rights abuse and rapaciousness. Can we honestly say that the national armies of Sudan, Myanmar, Afghanistan, Belarus, Chad, Zimbabwe, Kirgizstan, Yemen, Haiti, and many other states are more professional than PMCs? Public armies are not de facto superior to private ones.

Additionally, the Westphalian belief that war is exclusively the privilege of states does not match historical reality. Throughout most of history, military force was marketized, and waging war with for-profit actors was normal. Wealthy individuals and groups regularly employed private armies to pursue their objectives—political power, wealth, vendetta, glory, and so on—creating a free market for force in which military might was traded as a commodity, and the nationality of suppliers or purchasers meant little. In fact, the private provision of violence was a routine aspect of international relations before the nineteenth century.

As in the Middle Ages, there will be advantages and disadvantages to contract warfare. In terms of economic advantages, on-demand military services generally have greater utility or value than maintaining a full-time standing military, which was very expensive in the Middle Ages and now. Furthermore, private sector innovation can find more efficient and effective ways of achieving war aims, sometimes sparing blood and treasure. Those who worry that PMCs will lead to global Armageddon should not forget that the private military industry, like the *condottieri* of old, require some modicum of law and order to function, such as a reliable banking system, contract enforcement mechanisms, a physical headquarters, a safe base of operations, and other accoutrements of stability. It is not in the industry's interest to have a lawless world.

But the benefits should not disguise the darker side of private warfare, also demonstrated in the Middle Ages. Linking profit motive to killing is morally repugnant to many and may instigate needless death and destruction. Compounding this problem, on-demand military services lower the barriers to waging war, making violence more tempting than peaceful solutions. Once at war, private armies are incentivized to elongate and expand armed conflict for financial gain, a moral hazard inherent to for-profit warfare. Military supply can also generate demand by offering new tactics or technologies previously unavailable to neomedieval actors. They can also create "demand" through racketeering and extortion. A worrisome trend is the development of cheap and accessible military technologies such as robotics and cyber-weapons; the combination of PMCs operating armed drones and using cyber-attacks seems a likely future. As in the Middle Ages, mercenarism can lead to more war.

Privatizing war also changes warfare. Offering the means of war to anyone who can afford it changes why we fight and for what. Moneyed corporations, cartels, and individuals could become a new kind of superpower. Contract warfare also changes how we fight. For example, nonviolent strategies are possible, such as buying out the enemy's mercenaries or retaining all available PMCs in a region so that one is militarily unopposed. A perennial difficulty is enforcing the contract's terms when the client is unarmed and the contractor is armed. A PMC is also incentivized to exploit asymmetries of information between itself and the client for profit and possibly to the detriment of peace. These dilemmas are only the beginning of a brave new world that looks remarkably old.

Just as in the Middle Ages, taming a free market for force is dangerous. A market approach might succeed more than a regulatory one, since onerous laws will simply drive PMCs offshore. Instead, fostering a mediated market for force, perhaps in conjunction with appropriate regulation, will produce better outcomes. A consumer with market power or a consortium of consumers could shape industry behavior by rewarding military enterprisers and shunning mercenaries, thereby avoiding a free market for war. This could potentially harness the industry's benefits and mitigate its threats, domesticating the proverbial dogs of war.

Some may find the "back to the future" aspect of neomedievalism disquieting, but it need not be. The world is not in decline but rather returning to normal, when no single type of political actor dominates the world stage, as states have done in recent centuries. Historically, sovereignty is generally fragmented among different actors, as it was in the Middle Ages, and the past four centuries of Westphalian supremacy by states is anomalous. This also implies that no single actor can monopolize and control force, unleashing the possibility of mercenarism in the world once again. The ensuing free market for force has the potential to change warfare, the distribution of power in global affairs, and world peace. The implications of this are enormous, since it suggests that international relations in the twenty-first century will have more in common with the twelfth century than with the twentieth.

Annex A

IDIQ CONTRACT

UNCLASSIFIED

Peacekeeping/Capacity Enhancement/Surveillance Efforts—African
Continent
S-LMAOM-03-C0034
Section B

SECTION B

SUPPLIES OR SERVICES AND PRICES/COSTS

B.1 The Contractor shall perform any and all services required for Peacekeeping, Capacity Enhancement and Surveillance Efforts within the continent of Africa. The specific projects and scopes of work shall be tasked, via task order, in writing by the Contracting Officer and shall be in conformance with the contract clauses and special conditions contained herein.

The professional services to be provided will include, but are not limited to, logistics, transportation of personnel, training of host country personnel, supply and establishment of field operations/services, maintenance, communications, and any other related service necessary to meet the department's needs, as well as administration and coordination of the various disciplines involved. See Section C for the Statement of Work.

B.2 This is an Indefinite Quantity/Indefinite Delivery contract containing fixed hourly rates. The term of **Contract S-LMAQM-03-C0034** is one base year, with four, 12-month option years to be renewed at the government's discretion. The contract may be renewed by modification under the same terms and conditions as the base year, except as provided in section B.5 Prices/Costs. The actual amount of work to be performed, the time of such performance, the deliverables, and the location of the work will be determined by the Contracting

Officer, who will issue executed task orders to the Contractor. The only work authorized under this contract is that which is performed after receipt of such task orders and a written Notice to Proceed (NTP) from the Contracting Officer. A written NTP may be transmitted by facsimile or electronic mail (e-mail).

B.3 The Contractor shall, upon receipt of a duly executed task order, perform all services as required in this contract and such further requirements as may be contained in task orders for projects described therein. The Contractor shall complete all work and services under this contract within the period of time specified in task orders, except that no task order shall be issued hereunder after the expiration of this contract. Performance, the deliverables, and the location of the work will be task order specific.

B.4 The Government makes no guarantee as to the number of orders or actual amount of services which will be requested above the guaranteed minimum value of **$5,000,000.00** for the life of the contract (1 base year plus all four option years).

B.4.1 If two or more contracts are awarded under this solicitation, the Government reserves the right to compete or assign individual task orders to a particular contractor.

B.4.2 The maximum dollar value for the life of this contract (1 base year plus all four option years) is **$100,000,000.00.**

B.4.3 The minimum value for the contract that is exercised is **$5,000,000.00** for the life of the contract (1 base year plus all four option years).

B.4.4 The minimum dollar value of any awarded task order is **$50,000.00** and the maximum amount of any awarded task order is **$5,000,000.00** (refer to Section I, Contract Clause 52.216-19, Ordering Limitation). These limits may be waived by bilateral agreement between the government and the awarded contractor.

B.4.5 Reserved

B.4.6 The Prime contractor shall not subcontract more than **50%** of the total value of this contract.

B.5 PRICES/COSTS

The Contractor shall provide professional services as directed by individual task orders executed by the Contracting Officer. In establishing the prices for individual task orders, the rates for the required services shall be in accordance with the fixed fully burdened hourly labor rates submitted by the Offeror (see B.5.1).

B.5.1 The Offeror shall submit a Cost Volume that contains unburdened direct hourly rates for each professional category, as well as fully burdened hourly rates for each labor category of each required discipline. The burdened rates shall include direct hourly rates, overhead, G&A, profit, and all employee fringe benefits, such as retirement, withholding for FICA and taxes (NOTE: DBA Insurance is not to be included in the burdened rate), unemployment, workman's compensation, etc. Submit these rates in the form of a chart, detailing each component of the burdened rate. Please include a rate for any category you feel which may be utilized during the performance of Task Orders under this contract. All rates shall be submitted for each of the basic years and each option year. The submission of the option year rates shall not bind the Government to exercising the option year, nor should it be construed by the Offeror as the Government's intention to do so. Submit the same information for all proposed subcontractors, if possible.

B.5.2 Submit a legend depicting the individual labor category and its requirement (e.g., Project Manager—10 to 12 years relative experience, minimum of 4 year degree(s), X certification(s)).

B.5.3 Submit a copy of the most recent audit completed on your company by another Government agency. If a copy cannot be provided, please provide the cognizant agency's name and a contact point.

B.5.4 For cost/price evaluation under this contract, see Section L, M and Appendix I. For evaluation purposes under this contract, the prices submitted in accordance with Appendix I will be analyzed. The rates used in Appendix I will be extracted from the Cost Volume submitted in accordance with B.5.1 and B.5.2 and same shall be affixed to Section B of the resulting contract.

NOTE: Following the completion of negotiations and prior to the award of any Task Order, you will be required, where necessary, and if not waived by the Contracting Officer, to complete a Certificate of Current Cost and Pricing Data.

B.6 COST OF MATERIALS/EQUIPMENT

The cost of any materials or equipment required to be furnished and used in conjunction with the services rendered herein shall be included in the price of each task order unless otherwise noted in the task order.

B.7 TRAVEL

In determining the cost of travel, the terms and conditions of the Federal Travel Regulations/Joint Travel Regulation (FTR/JTR) shall apply to all travel and travel-related matters authorized under this contract; travel and travel-related expenses shall not exceed the maximum allowable under the FTR/JTR. In connection with authorized travel, the following items may be included in the price of the task order:

(i) The cost of domestic economy-class (coach) airfare; (ii) the cost of hotel or housing accommodations, meals, and other incidentals when travel is undertaken; and (iii) miscellaneous expenses incurred in connection with the travel. For international travel, see Section H.14 Reimbursable Expenses.

B.8 GOVERNMENT-FURNISHED PROPERTY

Government furnished property, if provided, will be identified in any issued or executed task order.

B.9 DEFENSE BASE ACT INSURANCE COST

The requirements of the Defense Base Act apply to this contract and any sub-contracts under this contract. The Contractor shall provide Defense Base Act (DBA) insurance coverage in accordance with FAR clause 52.228-03 Workers' Compensation Insurance (Defense Base Act). Rates for DBA will be task order specific.

B.10 DEFINITIONS

In this contract, the terms Contractor or Prime Contractor are used interchangeably unless the context indicates otherwise. Each shall mean the Contractor identified on the cover sheet of this contract.

UNCLASSIFIED

SOLICITATION, OFFER AND AWARD	1. THIS CONTRACT IS A RATED ORDER UNDER DPAS (15 CFR 350)		RATING B2 B4		PAGE OF 1	90 PAGES

2. CONTRACT NO.	3. SOLICITATION NO.	4. TYPE OF SOLICITATION	5. DATE ISSUED	6. REQUISITION/PURCHASE NO.
S-LMAQM-03-C0034	S-LMAQM-03-R0035	☐ SEALED BID (IFB) ☒ NEGOTIATED (RFP)	01/23/2003	

Department of State
e of Acquisition Management (A/LM/AQM/IP)
P.O. Box 9115, Rosslyn Station
Arlington, VA 22219

8. ADDRESS OFFER TO (If other than Item 7)

See Section L.8.1

NOTE: In sealed bid solicitations "offer" and "offeror" mean "bid" and "bidder".

SOLICITATION

9. Sealed offers in original and ___ copies for furnishing the supplies or services in the Schedule will be received at the place specified in Item 8, or if handcarried, in the depository located in **1701 N. Ft. Myer Dr. Arlington, VA** until **16:00** local time **02/24/2003**

CAUTION - LATE Submissions, Modifications, and Withdrawals: See Section L, Provision No. 52.214-7 or 52.215-10. All offers are subject to all terms and conditions contained in this solicitation.

10. FOR INFORMATION CALL:	A. NAME James S. (Steve) Rogers	B. TELEPHONE NO. (Include area code) (NO COLLECT CALLS) (703) 875-7320

11. TABLE OF CONTENTS

✓	SEC.	DESCRIPTION	PAGE(S)			DESCRIPTION	PAGE(S)
✓	A	SOLICITATION/CONTRACT FORM	1			CONTRACT CLAUSES	5
✓	B	SUPPLIES OR SERVICES AND PRICES/COSTS	5			PART III - LIST OF DOCUMENTS, EXHIBITS AND OTHER ATTACH.	
✓	C	DESCRIPTION/SPECS./WORK STATEMENT	5	✓	J	LIST OF ATTACHMENTS	13
✓	D	PACKAGING AND MARKING	2			PART IV - REPRESENTATIONS AND INSTRUCTIONS	
✓	E	INSPECTION AND ACCEPTANCE	3	✓	K	REPRESENTATIONS, CERTIFICATIONS AND OTHER STATEMENTS OF OFFERORS	17
✓	F	DELIVERIES OR PERFORMANCE	3				
✓	G	CONTRACT ADMINISTRATION DATA	4	✓	L	INSTRS., CONDS., AND NOTICES TO OFFERORS	13
✓	H	SPECIAL CONTRACT REQUIREMENTS	12	✓	M	EVALUATION FACTORS FOR AWARD	15

OFFER (Must be fully completed by offeror)

N... m 12 does not apply if the solicitation includes the provisions at 52.214-16, Minimum Bid Acceptance Period.

... mpliance with the above, the undersigned agrees, if this offer is accepted within ___ calendar days (60 calendar days unless a different period is inserted by the offeror) from the date for receipt of offers specified above, to furnish any or all items upon which prices are offered at the price set opposite each item, delivered at the designated point(s), within the time specified in the schedule.

13. DISCOUNT FOR PROMPT PAYMENT (See Section I, Clause No. 52-232-8)	10 CALENDAR DAYS 0 %	20 CALENDAR DAYS 0 %	30 CALENDAR DAYS 0 %	CALENDAR DAYS 0 %

14. ACKNOWLEDGMENT OF AMENDMENTS (The offeror acknowledges receipt of amend- ments to the SOLICITATION for offerors and related documents numbered and dated:	AMENDMENT NO. A001	DATE 05 Feb 2003	AMENDMENT NO. A003	DATE 12 Feb 2003
	A002	11 Feb 2003	A004	20 Feb 2003

15A. NAME AND ADDRESS OF OFFEROR	CODE 1SMB2	FACILITY 1SMB2	16. NAME AND TITLE OF PERSON AUTHORIZED TO SIGN OFFER (Type or print)
DynCorp International LLC 6500 West Freeway, Suite 600 Fort Worth, TX 76116-2167		DUNS: 608-46-1698	Stephen J. Cannon President, DynCorp International LLC

15B. TELEPHONE NO. (Include area code) (817) 737-1513	15C. CHECK IF REMITTANCE ADDRESS IS DIFFERENT FROM ABOVE - ENTER SUCH ADDRESS IN SCHEDULE. ☒	17. SIGNATURE	18. OFFER DATE March 4, 2003

AWARD (To be completed by Government)

19. ACCEPTED AS TO ITEMS NUMBERED N/A	20. AMOUNT $ IDIQ	21. ACCOUNTING AND APPROPRIATION PER TASK ORDER

22. AUTHORITY FOR USING OTHER THAN FULL AND OPEN COMPETITION: ☐ 10 U.S.C. 2304(c) ☐ 41 U.S.C. 253(c)	23. SUBMIT INVOICES TO ADDRESS SHOWN IN (3 copies unless otherwise specified) PER TASK ORDER	ITEM

24. ADMINISTERED BY (If other than Item 7)	CODE	25. PAYMENT WILL BE MADE BY PER TASK ORDER	CODE

26. NAME OF CONTRACTING OFFICER (Type or print) JAMES S. ROGERS	27. UNITED STATES OF AMERICA (Signature of Contracting Officer)	28. AWARD DATE 5/27/2003

Imp... ...t - Award will be made on this Form, or an Standard Form 26, or by other authorized official written notice.

NSN 7540-01-152-8064
PREVIOUS EDITION NOT USABLE

STANDARD FORM 33 (REV. 4-85)
Prescribed by GSA
FAR (48 CFR) 53.214(c)

Annex A   IDIQ Contract (S-LMAQM-03-00034)

   Source: US Department of State, http://www.state.gov/documents/organization/136426.pdf (accessed 21 June 2011).

UNCLASSIFIED

SECTION B
SUPPLIES OR SERVICES AND PRICES/COSTS

B.1 The Contractor shall perform any and all services required for Peacekeeping,. Capacity Enhancement and Surveillance Efforts within the continent of Africa. The specific projects and scopes of work shall be tasked, via task order, in writing by the Contracting Officer and shall be in conformance with the contract clauses and special conditions contained herein.

The professional services to be provided will include, but are not limited to, logistics, transportation of personnel, training of host country personnel, supply and establishment of field operations/services, maintenance, communications, and any other related service necessary to meet the department's needs,.as well as administration and coordination of the various disciplines involved. See Section C for the Statement of Work.

B.2 This is an Indefinite Quantity/Indefinite Delivery contract containing fixed hourly rates. The term of **Contract S-LMAQM-03-C0034** is one base year, with four, 12-month option years to be renewed at the government's discretion. The contract may be renewed by modification under the same terms and conditions as the base year, except as provided in section B.5 Prices/Costs). The actual amount of work to be performed, the time of such performance, the deliverables, and the location of the work will be determined by the Contracting Officer, who will issue executed task orders to the Contractor. The only work authorized under this contract is that which is performed after receipt of such task orders and a written Notice to Proceed (NTP) from the Contracting Officer. A written NTP may be transmitted by facsimile or electronic mail (e-mail).

B.3 The Contractor shall, upon receipt of a duly executed task order, perform all services as required in this contract and such further requirements as may be contained in task orders for projects described therein. The Contractor shall complete all work and services under this contract within the period of time specified in task orders, except that no task order shall be issued hereunder after the expiration of this contract. Performance, the deliverables, and the location of the work will be task order specific.

B.4 The Government makes no guarantee as to the number of orders, or actual amount of services which will be requested above the guaranteed minimum value of **$5,000,000.00** for the life of the contract (1 base year plus all four option years).

UNCLASSIFIED

UNCLASSIFIED

Peacekeeping/Capacity Enhancement/Surveillance Efforts - African Continent
S-LMAQM-03-C0034
Section B

B.4.1 If two or more contracts are awarded under this solicitation, the Government reserves the right to compete or assign individual task orders to a particular contractor.

B.4.2 The maximum dollar value for the life of this contract (1 base year plus all four-option years) is **$100,000,000.00**.

B.4.3 The minimum value for the contract that is exercised is **$5,000,000.00** for the life of the contract (1 base year plus all four-option years).

B.4.4 The minimum dollar value of any awarded task order is **$50,000.00** and the maximum amount of any awarded task order is **$5,000,000.00** (Refer to Section I, Contract Clause 52.216-19, Ordering Limitation.) These limits may be waived by bilateral agreement between the government and the awarded contractor.

B.4.5 **Reserved**

B.4.6 The Prime contractor shall not subcontract more than **50%** of the total value of this contract.

B.5 PRICES/COSTS

The Contractor shall provide professional services as directed by individual task orders executed by the Contracting Officer. In establishing the prices for individual task orders, the rates for the required services shall be in accordance with the fixed fully burdened hourly labor rates submitted by the Offeror (See B.5.1).

B.5.1 The Offeror shall submit a Cost Volume that contains unburdened direct hourly rates for each professional category, as

(The remainder of this page intentionally left blank)

B -2

UNCLASSIFIED

UNCLASSIFIED

well as fully burdened hourly rates for each labor category of each required discipline. The burdened rates shall include direct hourly rates, overhead, G&A, profit, and all employee fringe benefits, such as retirement, withholding for FICA and taxes (NOTE: DBA Insurance is not to be included in the burdened rate), unemployment, workman's compensation, etc. Submit these rates in the form of a chart, detailing each component of the burdened rate. Please include a rate for any category you feel which may be utilized during the performance of Task Orders under this contract. All rates shall be submitted for each of the basic years and each option year. The submission of the option year rates shall not bind the Government to exercising the option year, nor should it be construed by the Offeror as the Government's intention to do so. Submit the same information for all proposed subcontractors, if possible.

B.5.2 Submit a legend depicting the individual labor category and its requirement (e.g., Project Manager - 10 to 12 years relative experience, minimum of 4 year degree(s), X certification(s)).

B.5.3 Submit a copy of the most recent audit completed on your company by another Government agency. If a copy cannot be provided, please provide the cognizant agency's name and a contact point.

B.5.4 For cost/price evaluation under this contract, see Section L, M and Appendix I. For evaluation purposes under this contract, the prices submitted in accordance with Appendix I will be analyzed. The rates used in Appendix I will be extracted from the Cost Volume submitted in accordance with B.5.1 and B.5.2 and same shall be affixed to Section B of the resulting contract.

NOTE: Following the completion of negotiations and prior to the award of any Task Order, you will be required, where necessary, and if not waived by the Contracting Officer, to complete a Certificate of Current Cost and Pricing Data.

B.6 COST OF MATERIALS/EQUIPMENT

The cost of any materials or equipment required to be furnished and used in conjunction with the services rendered herein, shall be included in the price of each task order unless otherwise noted in the task order.

UNCLASSIFIED

UNCLASSIFIED

Peacekeeping/Capacity Enhancement/Surveillance Efforts - African Continent
S-LMAQM-03-C0034
Section B

B.7 TRAVEL

In determining the cost of travel, the terms and conditions of
the Federal Travel Regulations/Joint Travel Regulation (FTR/JTR)
shall apply to all travel and travel-related matters authorized
under this contract; travel and travel-related expenses shall not
exceed the maximum allowable under the FTR/JTR. In connection
with authorized travel, the following items may be included in
the price of the task order:

(i) The cost of domestic economy-class (coach) air fare; (ii)
the cost of hotel or housing accommodations, meals, and other
incidentals when travel is undertaken; and (iii) miscellaneous
expenses incurred in connection with the travel. For
international travel, see Section H.14 Reimbursable Expenses.

B.8 GOVERNMENT-FURNISHED PROPERTY

Government furnished property, if provided, will be identified in
any issued or executed task order.

B.9 DEFENSE BASE ACT INSURANCE COST

The requirements of the Defense Base Act apply to this contract
and any subcontracts under this contract. The Contractor shall
provide Defense Base Act (DBA) insurance coverage in accordance
with FAR clause 52.228-03 Workers' Compensation Insurance
(Defense Base Act).. Rates for DBA will be task order specific.

B.10 DEFINITIONS

In this contract, the terms Contractor or Prime Contractor are
used interchangeably unless the context indicates otherwise.
Each shall mean the Contractor identified on Cover sheet of this
contract.

B -4

UNCLASSIFIED

Annex B

CONTRACT AMENDMENT

UNCLASSIFIED

AMENDMENT OF SOLICITATION/MODIFICATION OF CONTRACT		1. CONTRACT ID CODE	PAGE OF PAGES 1
2. AMENDMENT/MODIFICATION NO. Three (3)	3. EFFECTIVE DATE March 30, 2005	4. REQUISITION/PURCHASE REQ. NO. N/A	5. PROJECT NO. (If applicable)

6. ISSUED BY   CODE

S. Department of State
!ice of Acquisition
.O. Box 9115, Rosslyn Station
Arlington, VA 22219

7. ADMINISTERED BY (If other than Item 6)   CODE

8. NAME AND ADDRESS OF CONTRACTOR (No. Street, county, State and ZIP Code)

DynCorp International, LLC
6500 West Freeway, Suite 600
Ft. Worth, TX 76116-2187

(4) 9A. AMENDMENT OF SOLICITATION NO.

9B. DATED (SEE ITEM 11)

10A. MODIFICATION OF CONTRACT/ORDER NO.

X S-LMAQM-03-C-0034

10B. DATED (SEE ITEM 13)
May 27, 2003

CODE   FACILITY CODE

11. THIS ITEM ONLY APPLIES TO AMENDMENTS OF SOLICITATIONS

[ ] The above numbered solicitation is amended as set forth in Item 14. The hour and date specified for receipt of Offers [ ] is extended, [ ] is not extended.

Offerors must acknowledge receipt of this amendment prior to the hour and date specified in the solicitation or as amended, by one of the following methods:
(a) By completing Items 8 and 15, and returning _____ copies of the amendment; (b) By acknowledging receipt of this amendment on each copy of the offer submitted; or (c) By separate letter or telegram which includes a reference to the solicitation and amendment numbers. FAILURE OF YOUR ACKNOWLEDGMENT TO BE RECEIVED AT THE PLACE DESIGNATED FOR THE RECEIPT OF OFFERS PRIOR TO THE HOUR AND DATA SPECIFIED MAY RESULT IN REJECTION OF YOUR OFFER. If by virtue of this amendment you desire to change an offer already submitted, such change may be made by telegram or letter, provided each telegram or letter makes reference to the solicitation and this amendment, and is received prior to the opening hour and date specified.

12. ACCOUNTING AND APPROPRIATION DATA (If required)

N/A

13. THIS ITEM APPLIES ONLY TO MODIFICATIONS OF CONTRACTS/ORDERS, IT MODIFIES THE CONTRACT/ORDER NO. AS DESCRIBED IN ITEM 14.

[ ] THIS CHANGE ORDER IS ISSUED PURSUANT TO: (Specify authority) THE CHANGES SET FORTH IN ITEM 14 ARE MADE IN THE CONTRACT/ORDER NO. IN ITEM 10A.

[ ] B. THE ABOVE NUMBERED CONTRACT/ORDER IS MODIFIED TO REFLECT THE ADMINISTRATIVE CHANGES (such as changes in paying office, appropriation date, etc.) SET FORTH IN ITEM 14, PURSUANT TO THE AUTHORITY OF FAR 43.103(b).

X C. THIS SUPPLEMENTAL AGREEMENT IS ENTERED INTO PURSUANT TO AUTHORITY OF:
Mutual Agreement of the Parties

[ ] D. OTHER (Specify type of modification and authority)

E. IMPORTANT: Contractor [ ] is not, X is required to sign this document and return 3 copies to the issuing office.

14. DESCRIPTION OF AMENDMENT/MODIFICATION (Organized by UCF section headings, including solicitation/contract subject matter where feasible.)

The purpose of this modification is to increase the five year ceiling amount on subject contract from $100,000,000 to $500,000,000 through the end of the period of performance which is May 26, 2008, if all options are exercised.

Except as provided herein, all terms and conditions of the document referenced in Item 9A or 10A, as heretofore changed, remains unchanged and in full force and effect.

15A. NAME AND TITLE OF SIGNER (Type or print) Timothy J. Crawley VP Contracts Management	16A. NAME AND TITLE OF CONTRACTING OFFICER (Type or print) Edward G. Muller Contracting Officer
15B. CONTRACTOR/OFFEROR (Signature of person authorized to sign)	15C. DATE SIGNED 4/5/05.	16B. UNITED STATES OF AMERICA BY (Signature of Contracting Officer)	16C. DATE SIGNED 7 MAR.05

NSN 7540-01-152-8070
PREVIOUS EDITION UNUSABLE

30-105

STANDARD FORM 30 (REV. 10-83)
Prescribed by GSA
FAR (48 CFR) 53.243

UNCLASSIFIED

Annex B

UNCLASSIFIED

OMB Approved 3705-0043

AMENDMENT OF SOLICITATION/MODIFICATION OF CONTRACT		1. CONTRACT ID CODE	PAGE	OF PAGES
			1	

2. AMENDMENT/MODIFICATION NO.	3. EFFECTIVE DATE	4. REQUISITION/PURCHASE REQ. NO.	5. PROJECT NO. (If applicable)
Four (4)	May 27, 2005	N/A	

6. ISSUED BY	CODE	7. ADMINISTERED BY (If other than Item 6)	CODE
Department of State :e of Acquisition F... Box 9115, Rosslyn Station Arlington, VA 22219			

8. NAME AND ADDRESS OF CONTRACTOR (No. Street, county, State and ZIP Code)	(4)	9A. AMENDMENT OF SOLICITATION NO.
DynCorp International, LLC 6500 West Freeway, Suite 600 Fort Worth, Texas 76116-2187		
		9B. DATED (SEE ITEM 11)
		10A. MODIFICATION OF CONTRACT/ORDER NO.
	X	S-LMAQM-03-C-0034
		10B. DATED (SEE ITEM 13)
CODE	FACILITY CODE	May 27, 2003

11. THIS ITEM ONLY APPLIES TO AMENDMENTS OF SOLICITATIONS

[ ] The above numbered solicitation is amended as set forth in Item 14. The hour and date specified for receipt of Offers [ ] is extended, [ ] is not extended.

Offerors must acknowledge receipt of this amendment prior to the hour and date specified in the solicitation or as amended, by one of the following methods:

(a) By completing Items 8 and 15, and returning _____ copies of the amendment; (b) By acknowledging receipt of this amendment on each copy of the offer submitted; or (c) By separate letter or telegram which includes a reference to the solicitation and amendment numbers. FAILURE OF YOUR ACKNOWLEDGMENT TO BE RECEIVED AT THE PLACE DESIGNATED FOR THE RECEIPT OF OFFERS PRIOR TO THE HOUR AND DATE SPECIFIED MAY RESULT IN REJECTION OF YOUR OFFER. If by virtue of this amendment you desire to change an offer already submitted, such change may be made by telegram or letter, provided each telegram or letter makes reference to the solicitation and this amendment, and is received prior to the opening hour and date specified.

12. ACCOUNTING AND APPROPRIATION DATA (If required)

N/A

13. THIS ITEM APPLIES ONLY TO MODIFICATIONS OF CONTRACTS/ORDERS,
IT MODIFIES THE CONTRACT/ORDER NO. AS DESCRIBED IN ITEM 14.

(C)	A. THIS CHANGE ORDER IS ISSUED PURSUANT TO: (Specify authority) THE CHANGES SET FORTH IN ITEM 14 ARE MADE IN THE CONTRACT/ORDER NO. IN ITEM 10A.
	B. THE ABOVE NUMBERED CONTRACT/ORDER IS MODIFIED TO REFLECT THE ADMINISTRATIVE CHANGES (such as changes in paying office, appropriation date, etc.) SET FORTH IN ITEM 14, PURSUANT TO THE AUTHORITY OF FAR 43.103(b).
	C. THIS SUPPLEMENTAL AGREEMENT IS ENTERED INTO PURSUANT TO AUTHORITY OF:
X	D. OTHER (Specify type of modification and authority) FAR 52.217-09 OPTION TO EXTEND THE TERM OF THE CONTRACT

E. IMPORTANT: Contractor is not required to sign this document and return _____ copies to the issuing office.

14. DESCRIPTION OF AMENDMENT/MODIFICATION (Organized by UCF section headings, including solicitation/contract subject matter where feasible.)

The purpose of this modification is to exercise Option Year Two of subject contract effective May 27, 2005 through May 26, 2006.

Except as provided herein, all terms and conditions of the document referenced in Item 9A or 10A, as heretofore changed, remains unchanged and in full force and effect.

15A. NAME AND TITLE OF SIGNER (Type or print)	16A. NAME AND TITLE OF CONTRACTING OFFICER (Type or print)
	Edward G. Muller Contracting Officer

15B. CONTRACTOR/OFFEROR	15C. DATE SIGNED	16B. UNITED STATES OF AMERICA	16C. DATE SIGNED
(Signature of person authorized to sign)		BY *Edward S Muller* (Signature of Contracting Officer)	May 15, 2005

NSN 7540-01-152-8070
PREVIOUS EDITION UNUSABLE

30-105

STANDARD FORM 30 (REV. 10-83)
Prescribed by GSA
FAR (48 CFR) 53.243

UNCLASSIFIED

UNCLASSIFIED

_A2_

AMENDMENT OF SOLICITATION/MODIFICATION OF CONTRACT	1. CONTRACT ID CODE	PAGE OF PAGES

2. AMENDMENT/MODIFICATION NO. One (1)	3. EFFECTIVE DATE See Block 16c	4. REQUISITION/PURCHASE REQ. NO. N/A	5. PROJECT NO. (If applicable)

6. ISSUED BY CODE	7. ADMINISTERED BY (If other than item 6) CODE

U.S. Department of State
Office of Acquisition Management
P.O. Box 9115, Rosslyn Station
Arlington, VA 22219

RELEASED IN PART
B4

8. NAME AND ADDRESS OF CONTRACTOR (No., Street, County, State and ZIP Code)	( )	9A. AMENDMENT OF SOLICITATION NO.

DynCorp International LLC
6500 West Freeway, Suite 600
Ft. Worth, TX 76116-2187

9B. DATED (SEE ITEM 11)
10A. MODIFICATION OF CONTRACT/ORDER NO. S-LMAQM-03-C-0034
X   10B. DATED (SEE ITEM 13)   May 27, 2003

CODE	FACILITY CODE

11. THIS ITEM ONLY APPLIES TO AMENDMENTS OF SOLICITATIONS

☐ The above numbered solicitation is amended as set forth in Item 14. The hour and date specified for receipt of Offers ☐ is extended, ☐ is not extended.

Offers must acknowledge receipt of this amendment prior to the hour and date specified in the solicitation or as amended, by one of the following methods:
(a) By completing Items 8 and 15, and returning _____ copies of the amendment; (b) By acknowledging receipt of this amendment on each copy of the offer submitted; or (c) By separate letter or telegram which includes a reference to the solicitation and amendment numbers. FAILURE OF YOUR ACKNOWLEDGMENT TO BE RECEIVED AT THE PLACE DESIGNATED FOR THE RECEIPT OF OFFERS PRIOR TO THE HOUR AND DATE SPECIFIED MAY RESULT IN REJECTION OF YOUR OFFER. If by virtue of this amendment you desire to change an offer already submitted, such change may be made by telegram or letter, provided each telegram or letter makes reference to the solicitation and this amendment, and is received prior to the opening hour and date specified.

12. ACCOUNTING AND APPROPRIATION DATA (If required)
N/A

13. THIS ITEM APPLIES ONLY TO MODIFICATIONS OF CONTRACTS/ORDERS, IT MODIFIES THE CONTRACT/ORDER NO. AS DESCRIBED IN ITEM 14.

	A. THIS CHANGE ORDER IS ISSUED PURSUANT TO: (Specify authority) THE CHANGES SET FORTH IN ITEM 14 ARE MADE IN THE CONTRACT ORDER NO. IN ITEM 10A.
	B. THE ABOVE NUMBERED CONTRACT/ORDER IS MODIFIED TO REFLECT THE ADMINISTRATIVE CHANGES (such as changes in paying office, appropriation date, etc.) SET FORTH IN ITEM 14, PURSUANT TO THE AUTHORITY OF FAR 43.103 (b).
X	C. THIS SUPPLEMENTAL AGREEMENT IS ENTERED INTO PURSUANT TO AUTHORITY OF: Mutual Agreement of the Parties
	D. OTHER (Specify type of modification and authority)

E. IMPORTANT: Contractor ☐ is not, ☒ is required to sign this document and return ___3___ copies to the issuing office.

14. DESCRIPTION OF AMENDMENT/MODIFICATION (Organized by UCF section headings, including solicitation/contract subject matter where feasible.)

PLEASE SEE ATTACHED

Except as provided herein, all terms and conditions of the document referenced in Item 9A or 10A, as heretofore changed, remains unchanged and in full force and effect.

15A. NAME AND TITLE OF SIGNER (Type or print) Charles C. CANNON, Jr. VP ITS	16A. NAME AND TITLE OF CONTRACTING OFFICER (Type or print) Colleen M. Kosar Contracting Officer

15B. CONTRACTOR/OFFEROR _(signature)_ (Signature of person authorized to sign)	15C. DATE SIGNED 19 May 04	16B. UNITED STATES OF AMERICA BY _Colleen Kosar_ (Signature of Contracting Officer)	16C. DATE SIGNED 3-99-04

NSN 7540-01-152-8070   30-105   STANDARD FORM 30 (REV. 10-83)
PREVIOUS EDITION UNUSABLE   Prescribed by GSA
                                                        FAR (48 CFR) 53.243

UNCLASSIFIED

UNCLASSIFIED

AMENDMENT OF SOLICITATION/MODIFICATION OF CONTRACT	1. CONTRACT ID CODE	PAGE OF PAGES

2. AMENDMENT/MODIFICATION NO.	3. EFFECTIVE DATE	4. REQUISITION/PURCHASE REQ. NO.	5. PROJECT NO. (If applicable)
Five (5)	See Block 16C	N/A	

6. ISSUED BY	CODE	7. ADMINISTERED BY (If other than Item 6)	CODE
U.S. Department of State. Office of Acquisition P.O. Box 9115, Rosslyn Station Arlington, VA 22219			

8. NAME AND ADDRESS OF CONTRACTOR (No., Street, County, State and ZIP Code)	(✓)	9A. AMENDMENT OF SOLICITATION NO.
DynCorp International, LLC 6500 West Freeway, Suite 600 Fort Worth, Texas 76116-2187		
		9B. DATED (SEE ITEM 11)
		10A. MODIFICATION OF CONTRACT/ORDER NO.
	X	S-LMAQM-03-C-0034
		10B. DATED (SEE ITEM 13)
CODE FACILITY CODE		May 27, 2003

11. THIS ITEM ONLY APPLIES TO AMENDMENTS OF SOLICITATIONS

☐ The above numbered solicitation is amended as set forth in item 14. The hour and date specified for receipt of Offers ☐ is extended, ☐ is not extended.

Offers must acknowledge receipt of this amendment prior to the hour and date specified in the solicitation or as amended, by one of the following methods: (a) By completing Items 8 and 15, and returning _____ copies of the amendment; (b) By acknowledging receipt of this amendment on each copy of the offer submitted; or (c) By separate letter or telegram which includes a reference to the solicitation and amendment numbers. FAILURE OF YOUR ACKNOWLEDGMENT TO BE RECEIVED AT THE PLACE DESIGNATED FOR THE RECEIPT OF OFFERS PRIOR TO THE HOUR AND DATE SPECIFIED MAY RESULT IN REJECTION OF YOUR OFFER. If by virtue of this amendment you desire to change an offer already submitted, such change may be made by telegram or letter, provided each telegram or letter makes reference to the solicitation and this amendment, and is received prior to the opening hour and date specified.

12. ACCOUNTING AND APPROPRIATION DATA (If required)
N/A

13. THIS ITEM APPLIES ONLY TO MODIFICATIONS OF CONTRACTS/ORDERS, IT MODIFIES THE CONTRACT/ORDER NO. AS DESCRIBED IN ITEM 14.

(✓)	A. THIS CHANGE ORDER IS ISSUED PURSUANT TO: (Specify authority) THE CHANGES SET FORTH IN ITEM 14 ARE MADE IN THE CONTRACT ORDER NO. IN ITEM 10A.
X	B. THE ABOVE NUMBERED CONTRACT/ORDER IS MODIFIED TO REFLECT THE ADMINISTRATIVE CHANGES (such as changes in paying office, appropriation date, etc.) SET FORTH IN ITEM 14, PURSUANT TO THE AUTHORITY OF FAR 43.103 (b).
	C. THIS SUPPLEMENTAL AGREEMENT IS ENTERED INTO PURSUANT TO AUTHORITY OF:
	D. OTHER (Specify type of modification and authority)

E. IMPORTANT: Contractor ☒ is not, ☐ is required to sign this document and return _____ copies to the issuing office.

14. DESCRIPTION OF AMENDMENT/MODIFICATION (Organized by UCF section headings, including solicitation/contract subject matter where feasible.)

The U.S. Army Corp of Engineers, North Atlantic Division is hereby authorized to place delivery orders against Contract S-LMAQM-03-C-0034 with DynCorp. The maximum order limitation will not exceed $10,000,000 per order. Only the below named contracting officer is hereby authorized to place orders against subject contract for the U.S. Army Corp of Engineers, North Atlantic Division.

Bethany A. Mills

Except as provided herein, all terms and conditions of the document referenced in item 9A or 10A, as heretofore changed, remains unchanged and in full force and effect.

15A. NAME AND TITLE OF SIGNER (Type or print)	16A. NAME AND TITLE OF CONTRACTING OFFICER (Type or print)
	Colleen M. Kosar Contracting Officer
15B. CONTRACTOR/OFFEROR	15C. DATE SIGNED	16B. UNITED STATES OF AMERICA	16C. DATE SIGNED
(Signature of person authorized to sign)		BY _Colleen M. Kosar_ _(Signature of Contracting Officer)_	8/17/05

NSN 7540-01-152-8070 PREVIOUS EDITION UNUSABLE	30-105	STANDARD FORM 30 (REV. 10-83) Prescribed by GSA FAR (48 CFR) 53.243

UNCLASSIFIED

UNCLASSIFIED

AMENDMENT OF SOLICITATION/MODIFICATION OF CONTRACT	1. CONTRACT ID CODE		PAGE OF PAGES
2. AMENDMENT/MODIFICATION NO. **Six (6)**	3. EFFECTIVE DATE See Block 16c	4. REQUISITION/PURCHASE REQ. NO.	5. PROJECT NO. *(if applicable)*

6. ISSUED BY   CODE | **7. ADMINISTERED BY** *(if other than Item 6)*   CODE

U.S. Department of State
Office of Acquisition
P.O. Box 9115, Rosslyn Station
Arlington, VA 22219

8. NAME AND ADDRESS OF CONTRACTOR *(No., street, county, State and ZIP Code)*

DynCorp International, LLC
6500 West Freeway, Suite 600
Fort Worth, Texas 76116-2187

(✓) **9A. AMENDMENT OF SOLICITATION NO.**

9B. DATED *(SEE ITEM 11)*

10A. MODIFICATION OF CONTRACT/ORDER NO.

S-LMAQM-03-C-0034

10B. DATED *(SEE ITEM 13)*
May 27, 2003

CODE | FACILITY CODE

11. THIS ITEM ONLY APPLIES TO AMENDMENTS OF SOLICITATIONS

☐ The above numbered solicitation is amended as set forth in Item 14. The hour and date specified for receipt of Offers ☐ is extended, ☐ is not extended.

Offers must acknowledge receipt of this amendment prior to the hour and date specified in the solicitation or as amended, by one of the following methods: (a) By completing Items 8 and 15, and returning _____ copies of the amendment; (b) By acknowledging receipt of this amendment on each copy of the offer submitted; or (c) By separate letter or telegram which includes a reference to the solicitation and amendment numbers. FAILURE OF YOUR ACKNOWLEDGMENT TO BE RECEIVED AT THE PLACE DESIGNATED FOR THE RECEIPT OF OFFERS PRIOR TO THE HOUR AND DATE SPECIFIED MAY RESULT IN REJECTION OF YOUR OFFER. If by virtue of this amendment you desire to change an offer already submitted, such change may be made by telegram or letter, provided each telegram or letter makes reference to the solicitation and this amendment, and is received prior to the opening hour and date specified.

12. ACCOUNTING AND APPROPRIATION DATA *(if required)*
N/A

13. THIS ITEM APPLIES ONLY TO MODIFICATIONS OF CONTRACTS/ORDERS, IT MODIFIES THE CONTRACT/ORDER NO. AS DESCRIBED IN ITEM 14.

☐ A. THIS CHANGE ORDER IS ISSUED PURSUANT TO: *(Specify authority)* THE CHANGES SET FORTH IN ITEM 14 ARE MADE IN THE CONTRACT ORDER NO. IN ITEM 10A.

☒ B. THE ABOVE NUMBERED CONTRACT/ORDER IS MODIFIED TO REFLECT THE ADMINISTRATIVE CHANGES *(such as changes in paying office, appropriation date, etc.)* SET FORTH IN ITEM 14, PURSUANT TO THE AUTHORITY OF FAR 43.103(b).

☐ C. THIS SUPPLEMENTAL AGREEMENT IS ENTERED INTO PURSUANT TO AUTHORITY OF:

☐ D. OTHER *(Specify type of modification and authority)*

E. IMPORTANT: Contractor ☒ is not, ☐ is required to sign this document and return _____ copies to the issuing office.

14. DESCRIPTION OF AMENDMENT/MODIFICATION *(Organized by UCF section headings, including solicitation/contract subject matter where feasible.)*

The below named Contracting Officers are hereby authorized to place orders against subject contract for the U.S. Army Corps of Engineers, North Atlantic Division.

Leslie L. Bearden
Theodore M. Kunzog

Except as provided herein, all terms and conditions of the document referenced in Item 9A or 10A, as heretofore changed, remains unchanged and in full force and effect.

15A. NAME AND TITLE OF SIGNER *(Type or print)*	16A. NAME AND TITLE OF CONTRACTING OFFICER *(Type or print)* Colleen M. Kosar Contracting Officer	
15B. CONTRACTOR/OFFEROR *(Signature of person authorized to sign)*	15C. DATE SIGNED	16B. UNITED STATES OF AMERICA BY *Colleen M. Kosar (signature)* *(Signature of Contracting Officer)*	16C. DATE SIGNED 12-12-05

NSN 7540-01-152-8070
PREVIOUS EDITION UNUSABLE   30-105   STANDARD FORM 30 (REV. 10-83)
Prescribed by GSA
FAR (48 CFR) 53.243

UNCLASSIFIED

Annex B   Contract Amendment (raises contract ceiling)
Source: US Department of State, http://www.state.gov/documents/organization/136427.pdf (accessed 21 June 2011).

Annex C

LIBERIA MILITARY PROGRAM TIMELINE

January 2003	DynCorp International (DynCorp) and Pacific Architects and Engineers (PA&E) are both awarded a State Department five-year IDIQ contract to support peacekeeping and security efforts in Africa (contract solicitation number S-LMAQM-03-C-0034; see annex A). Its minimum guaranteed expenditure is $5 million, and maximum is $100 million, later expanded to $500 million (see annex B).
August 2003	Charles Taylor flees Liberia, and 1,000 ECOWAS peacekeepers and 200 US troops arrive. The interim government and rebels sign the CPA. Gyude Bryant is chosen to head the NTGL under the title Chairman rather than President.
September–October 2003	US forces pull out, and UNMIL begins the peacekeeping mission, deploying thousands of troops and encompassing the ECOWAS forces.
December 2003	UNMIL begins DDRR for rebel combatants only. AFL personnel are disarmed, but not demobilized, rehabilitated and reintegrated. After riots at one DDRR site, UNMIL shuts down the program.
January 2004	US sends a six-person SSR preassessment team to Liberia, January 21–29. The United States is responsible for the SSR of the AFL, as agreed to at Accra during peace talks. The State Department is the lead agency within the US government.
February 2004	International donors pledge more than $500 million in reconstruction aid to Liberia.

April 2004	UNMIL commences the DDRR process, and it continues without serious incident. UNMIL also begins SSR for civilian elements of the security sector, such as the Liberian national police. State Department plans a SSR assessment mission to Liberia involving State Department, DOD, and contractors.
May 2004	State Department leads a 10-day assessment mission of SSR for the AFL. The team consists of experts drawn from State Department, DOD, and two contractor teams: DynCorp and PA&E. Additionally, PA&E subcontracts MPRI owing to its PMC expertise (PA&E is a general contractor firm, whereas DynCorp and MPRI are PMCs with relevant SSR expertise). DDR of the AFL is not considered, because the NTGL is responsible for this. A member of the assessment team is murdered in his hotel room while being robbed.
June 2004	DOD determines it cannot conduct the SSR program, and State Department decides to outsource the SSR program entirely to the private sector. Accordingly, it asks both DynCorp and PA&E to submit their assessments and recommendations for SSR.
July 2004	After reviewing the assessments, State Department decides to divide SSR responsibilities between the two companies based on their expertise. DynCorp is responsible for reconstituting the AFL and MOD. PA&E is tasked with constructing most of the military bases and also providing specialty training, equipment, logistics, and base services.
September 2004	State Department tenders a task order RFP and SOW to DynCorp and PA&E entitled "Liberia Security Sector Reform." The SOW states that they must create a 2,000-person military, scalable to 4,300 personnel if funding permits, and a MOD.
October 2004	DynCorp and PA&E submit their proposals to State Department on October 7. State Department awards the task order to both companies, with a division of labor as outlined in July. DynCorp is required to be on the ground initially, with PA&E to follow once sufficient units are fielded. Riots in Monrovia leave 16 people dead; UNMIL says former combatants and AFL veterans were behind the violence.

January 2005	State Department authorizes DynCorp to deploy a small planning team to Liberia to engage stakeholders and design the SSR program. It becomes clear that the NTGL lacks the capacity to conduct DDR of the AFL and State Department asks DynCorp to take on this task. UNMIL imposes a curfew on several southeastern provinces owing to ritual human sacrifices and cannibalism, including the involvement of provincial governors.
February–March 2005	Consultations take place with major stakeholders regarding the mission and composition of the future AFL. This includes civil society, the standing AFL, former warring parties and political factions, UNMIL, the NTGL, civil society through the NTGL, and other entities. A comprehensive recruiting and vetting plan is devised, intended to screen out human rights abusers from joining the AFL.
April 2005	The NTGL releases its AFL Restructuring Policy. Consultations with stakeholders continue. Topics include mission and force structure of the future AFL, location of training bases, sensitization campaign for civil society, and arrears owed unpaid AFL veterans.
May 2005	The demobilization plan is drafted and presented to Chairman Bryant. He signs Executive Order Number Five on May 15, authorizing the full demobilization of all legacy AFL units as of June 30, 2005. State Department issues DynCorp a formal task order for the demobilization of the AFL, releasing full payment to the contractor. DynCorp makes preparations for DDR operations outside of Monrovia and plans to conduct the demobilization, recruiting staff both locally and internationally, and builds up its program (and presence) in Liberia. PA&E is to begin its portion of the program once training commences.
July 2005	DynCorp builds a demobilization site outside Monrovia. The demobilization and reintegration of the legacy soldiers commences. The US government approves DynCorp's blueprint for the new AFL's force structure and TO&E in Washington, D.C. Construction of AFL training facilities starts but is slowed by the heavy rainy season.

September 2005	The NTGL agrees to allow the international community to supervise its finances in an effort to reduce corruption.
October 2005	Recruiting and vetting for the new AFL begins. More than 12,000 applicants will be processed in the two years to come.
November 2005	Ellen Johnson-Sirleaf becomes the first woman to be elected as an African head of state. She takes office the following January.
December 2005	Construction of the new training base remains suspended as Liberia, the United States, and UNMIL debate over its location, costing the program money and time.
January 2006	DDR of 13,770 AFL soldiers finishes. Recruiting and vetting begin at the Barclay Training Center (BTC) in downtown Monrovia. Johnson-Sirleaf is sworn in as president, and the NTGL is no more. Brownie Samukai replaces Daniel Chea as Liberian Minister of Defense.
February 2006	The demobilization of the AFL is successfully completed, perhaps the first time in modern African history that an entire standing military was safely demobilized without significant incident.
March 2006	Johnson-Sirleaf calls for Nigeria to hand over Taylor, which it does. Upon his arrival in Monrovia, he is transferred to the custody of UNMIL and immediately flown to Sierra Leone to stand trial before the UN-backed Sierra Leone Special Court on charges of crimes against humanity.
April 2006	MOD transformation begins at BTC. A violent protest takes place outside the MOD by 400 to 500 former AFL soldiers claiming nonpayment of salary arrears and retirement benefits, and they clash with UNMIL peacekeepers sent to contain the unrest. Taylor appears before the Sierra Leone Special Court.
May 2006	Samukai spends a week in Washington, D.C. with State Department, DOD, and DynCorp to discuss the progress of SSR and formulation of the Liberian National Defense Strategy.

June 2006	State Department issues an updated SOW. DynCorp assists the MOD in a first draft of the national defense strategy. It is written based on the concept of human security, seeking to align the AFL's mission with the goals of development for durable stability and security. Progress is limited because the NTGL, UNMIL, the United States, and others are delayed with the national security strategy. The UN Security Council eases a ban on weapons sales so that Liberia can import small arms for government purposes only. An embargo on Liberian timber exports is lifted shortly afterward. A TRC is set up to investigate human rights abuses between 1979 and 2003. Tensions arise between the TRC and the SSR program as the TRC requests access to SSR vetting records, but the SSR team denies this request, since it might compromise sources and methods, possibly resulting in reprisal killings of victims who spoke to the SSR vetting team on condition of anonymity about human rights abuses of some AFL candidates. The ICC at The Hague agrees to host Taylor's trial.
July 2006	The first class of AFL basic training or IET begins at BTC. It includes 110 candidates, most of whom are selected for their leadership potential to fill the leadership ranks first. The former US Voice of America transmitter site is finally selected as the AFL's main training base, located at Careysburg and rechristened the Sandee S. Ware Military Barracks. DynCorp begins construction once the occupying UNMIL units move offsite. Construction is slowed by the heavy rainy season. DynCorp begins the process of purchasing and importing arms into Liberia for the AFL. Johnson-Sirleaf switches on generator-powered street lights in the capital, which has been without electricity for fifteen years.
August 2006	DynCorp orchestrates the first major shipment of arms, which arrives at Monrovia for the AFL. It is the first legal shipment in more than fifteen years.
November 2006	The first AFL basic training class of 102 graduates. AFL training of future classes is halted owing to US funding shortfalls.

March 2007	After a 17-week SSR program training course, 119 civilian MOD employees graduate. Following this, the MOD reform program is prematurely terminated owing to US funding shortfalls.
April 2007	The UN Security Council votes to lift its ban on Liberian diamond exports. The ban was imposed in 2001 to stem the flow of "blood diamonds," which helped fund the civil war.
May 2007	The United Nations urges Liberia to outlaw trial by ordeal.
June 2007	Taylor's war crimes trial begins at The Hague, where he stands accused of instigating atrocities in Sierra Leone.
September 2007	639 total trained. Owing to budget constraints, State Department shortens IET from 11 weeks to 8 weeks by cutting 3 weeks that were devoted to human rights, civics, and laws of war training.
January 2008	1,124 total trained.
April 2008	1,634 total trained.
September 2008	2,113 total trained.
July 2009	PA&E conducts unit training for the battalions. The TRC lists Johnson-Sirleaf as one of 52 people who should be sanctioned for committing war crimes and places her on a list of people who should be barred from public office. She ignores the TRC.
December 2009	PA&E completes unit training, culminating in an ARTEP to qualify them.
January 2010	DynCorp and PA&E's contract for SSR ends, and a team of 60 US marines begin a five-year mentorship program with the AFL in Operation Onward Liberty. In a new task order (worth $20 million if all options are exercised), DynCorp is selected to provide the AFL with operations and maintenance services. This task order is awarded under the new five-year State Department IDIQ contract called the Africa Peacekeeping Program (AFRICAP), contract solicitation number SAQMMA08R0237. Awardees under AFRICAP include DynCorp International, PA&E Government Services, AECOM, and Protection Strategies Incorporated.

NOTES

1. Peace through Profit Motive?

1. Greystone Ltd. website, http://www.greystone-ltd.com/index.html, accessed April 11, 2009.

2. Understanding the Private Military Industry

1. David Isenberg, "Dogs of War: From Mercenary to Security Contractor and Back Again," United Press International, September 12, 2008; International Consortium of Investigative Journalists, "Making a Killing: The Business of War" (Center for Public Integrity, Fall 2002); James Glanz, "Modern Mercenaries on the Iraqi Frontier," *New York Times*, April 4, 2004.
2. Jeremy Scahill, *Blackwater: The Rise of the World's Most Powerful Mercenary Army* (New York: Perseus, 2008), xxi.
3. Commission on Wartime Contracting in Iraq and Afghanistan, *Transforming Wartime Contracting Controlling Costs, Reducing Risks* (Washington, DC: US Congress, 2011), 45–46.
4. Jennifer Elsea, *Private Security Contractors in Iraq: Background, Legal Status, and Other Issues* (Washington, DC: Congressional Research Service, 2008), 2; P.L.110-181 Sec. 864.
5. Peter W. Singer, *Corporate Warriors: The Rise of the Privatized Military Industry* (Ithaca, NY: Cornell University Press, 2003), 8.
6. Deborah Avant, *The Market for Force: The Consequences of Privatizing Security* (Cambridge, UK: Cambridge University Press, 2005), 15–16.
7. David Shearer, "Outsourcing War," *Foreign Policy*, no. 112 (1998): 73. See also Christopher Coker, "Outsourcing War," *Cambridge Review of International Affairs* 13, no. 1 (1999): 106–107.
8. GAO, Afghanistan Security, "Afghan Army Growing, but Additional Trainers Needed; Long-Term Costs Not Determined," GAO-11-66 (Washington, DC, January 27, 2011); GAO, Afghanistan Security, GAO-12-293R (Washington, DC, February 23, 2012).
9. This typology should not be confused with Singer's self-described "tip of the spear" typology outlined in *Corporate Warriors*. The key differentiator in the present typology is *function*: is the company in a combat, operational support, or administrative support role? This is consistent with the US Army's own typology of its units. A main factor in Singer's typology is *proximity* to the front line. Instead of *PMC*, he uses the term *military provider firm*, which is defined partly based on its closeness to the "front line" within the battlespace. However, few contemporary wars have front lines. For example, the last war the United States fought where there was a front line was the Korean War. Most wars today (e.g., Iraq, Afghanistan, Syria, Mali, northern Nigeria) have no battle lines, making the "tip of the spear" approach limited in an era dominated by unconventional warfare.

3. A Codependency Problem

1. Respectively, "Interview with Doug Brooks," *Frontline*, March 22, 2005, http://www.pbs. org/wgbh/pages/frontline/shows/warriors/interviews/brooks.html, accessed February 25, 2014; "Interview with Peter Singer," *Frontline*, March 22, 2005, http://www.pbs. org/wgbh/pages/frontline/shows/warriors/interviews/singer.html, accessed February 25, 2014.

2. Numbers are in 2010 dollars. "Obligations" occur when US agencies enter into contracts, employ personnel, or otherwise legally commit to spending money. "Outlays" occur when obligations are liquidated. See Moshe Schwartz and Joyprada Swain, *Department of Defense Trends in Overseas Contract Obligations* (Washington, DC: Congressional Research Service, 2011), 1.

3. United Kingdom Central Government and Local Authority Spending, Fiscal Year 2010, http://www.ukpublicspending.co.uk/year_spending_2010UKbn_13bc1n_30#ukgs302, accessed February 14, 2014.

4. Government Accountability Office, *Defense Management: DOD Needs to Reexamine Its Extensive Reliance on Contractors and Continue to Improve Management and Oversight* (Washington, DC: Government Accounting Office, 2008); Moshe Schwartz, *Department of Defense Contractors in Iraq and Afghanistan: Background and Analysis* (Washington, DC: Congressional Research Service, 2010), 5; *Contractors' Support of US Operations in Iraq* (Washington, DC: US Congressional Budget Office, 2008), 13. Data for figure 3.1 are also drawn from Jennifer Elsea, *Private Security Contractors in Iraq: Background, Legal Status, and Other Issues* (Washington, DC: Congressional Research Service, 2008); William W. Epley, "Civilian Support of Field Armies," *Army Logistician* 22 (November–December 1990): 30–35; Steven J. Zamparelli, "Contractors on the Battlefield: What Have We Signed Up For?" *Air Force Journal of Logistics* 23, no. 3 (Fall 1990): 10–19.

5. Steven L. Schooner and Collin Swan, "Contractors and the Ultimate Sacrifice," George Washington University Law School, Public Law and Legal Theory Working Paper 512 (September 2010).

6. Government Accountability Office, *Contingency Contracting: DOD, State, and USAID Continue to Face Challenges in Tracking Contractor Personnel and Contracts in Iraq and Afghanistan* (Washington, DC: Government Accountability Office, 2009); Christian Miller, "Civilian Contractor Toll in Iraq and Afghanistan Ignored by Defense Dept," *ProPublica*, October 9, 2009; Justin Elliott, "Hundreds of Afghanistan Contractor Deaths Go Unreported," Salon.com, July 15, 2010, http://www.salon.com/2010/07/15/afghan_war_contractors_dying, accessed February 14, 2014.

7. *Urgent Reform Required: Army Expeditionary Contracting*, Report of the Commission on Army Acquisition and Program Management in Expeditionary Operations, hearing before the Subcommittee on Readiness and Management Support of the Committee on Armed Services, US Senate (110th Congress, December 6, 2007), 1, 5.

8. Commission on Wartime Contracting in Iraq and Afghanistan, *Transforming Wartime Contracting Controlling Costs, Reducing Risks* (Washington, DC: US Congress, 2011), 1.

9. Christopher Kinsey, *Corporate Soldiers and International Security: The Rise of Private Military Companies* (London: Taylor & Francis, 2006), 4.

10. Quadrennial Defense Review Report, February 2010, http://www.defense.gov/qdr/images/QDR_as_of_12Feb10_1000.pdf, 55–56.

11. Secretary of Defense, "Strategic and Operational Planning for Operational Contract Support (OCS) and Workforce Mix," memorandum, US Department of Defense, January 24, 2011.

12. *Warlord, Inc.: Extortion and Corruption along the U.S. Supply Chain in Afghanistan*, report before the Subcommittee on National Security and Foreign Affairs, US House of Representatives (111th Congress, June 22, 2010), 15; Schwartz, *Department of Defense Contractors*, 8.

13. "Wounded Iraqis: 'No One Did Anything' to Provoke Blackwater," CNN, September 19, 2007, http://www.cnn.com/2007/WORLD/meast/09/19/iraq.fateful.day/index.html, accessed February 14, 2014.

14. Coalition Provisional Authority, Order Number 17 (Revised), Status of the Coalition Provisional Authority, MNF–Iraq, Certain Missions and Personnel in Iraq, June 27,

2007, http://www.iraqcoalition.org/regulations/20040627_CPAORD_17_Status_of_Coalition__Rev__with_Annex_A.pdf, accessed February 14, 2014.

15. Barbara Miller, "Blackwater a Challenge to Iraqi Sovereignty: Al-Maliki," ABC Online, September 24, 2007, http://www.abc.net.au/worldtoday/content/2007/s2041431.htm, accessed February 14, 2014.

16. Joseph E. Stiglitz and Linda Bilmes, *The Three Trillion Dollar War: The True Cost of the Iraq Conflict* (New York: W. W. Norton, 2008), 12. For more information on appropriate cost comparisons, see *Contractors Support of US Operations in Iraq* (Washington, DC: US Congressional Budget Office, 2008), 14.

17. Schwartz, *Department of Defense Contractors*, 9, 12.

18. *Contractors Support of US Operations*, 8.

19. The United States does not formally track these data. Although it is macabre, tracking contractor casualties provides a glimpse of what countries these individuals come from. Christian Miller, "Map: Injuries and Deaths to Civilian Contractors in Iraq and Afghanistan by Country," http://www.propublica.org/special/map-injuries-and-deaths-to-civilian-contractors-by-country-614, accessed February 14, 2014.

20. U.S. Department of Defense, Contractor Support of U.S. Operations in the USCENTCOM Area of Responsibility to Include Iraq and Afghanistan (5A Papers), October 2013.

4. How Did We Get Here?

1. John M. Najemy, *A History of Florence, 1200–1575* (Oxford: Wiley-Blackwell, 2006), 151–155.

2. William Caferro, *John Hawkwood: An English Mercenary in Fourteenth-Century Italy* (Baltimore: Johns Hopkins University Press, 2006), 2.

3. Franco Sacchetti, *Il Trecentonovelle* (Torino: Einaudi, 1970), 528–529. For more on Hawkwood's interesting life, see Caferro, *John Hawkwood*; John Temple-Leader and Giuseppe Marcotti, *Sir John Hawkwood: The Story of a Condottiere*, translated by Leader Scott (London: T. Fisher Unwin, 1889); R. A. Pratt, "Geoffrey Chaucer, Esq., and Sir John Hawkwood," *ELH* 16, no. 3 (1949): 188–193; Kenneth Fowler, "Sir John Hawkwood and the English Condottieri in Trecento Italy," *Renaissance Studies* 12, no. 1 (1998): 131–148.

4. Michael Howard, *War in European History* (Oxford: Oxford University Press, 1976), 29.

5. Geoffrey Parker, *Europe in Crisis, 1598–1648* (Oxford: Wiley-Blackwell, 2001), 17.

6. Howard, *War in European History*, 131.

7. David Parrott, "From Military Enterprise to Standing Armies: War, State, and Society in Western Europe, 1600–1700," in *European Warfare, 1350–1750*, edited by Frank Tallett and D. J. B. Trim (Cambridge, UK: Cambridge University Press, 2010), 85.

8. Sidney B. Fay, "The Beginnings of the Standing Army in Prussia," *American Historical Review* 22, no. 4 (1917): 767.

9. David Blackbourn, *History of Germany, 1780–1918: The Long Nineteenth Century* (Oxford: Wiley-Blackwell, 2003), 17.

10. John A. Mears, "The Emergence of the Standing Professional Army in Seventeenth-Century Europe," *Social Science Quarterly* 50, no. 1 (1969): 115.

11. William Edward Hall, *A Treatise on International Law* (Oxford: Clarendon, 1917), 310.

12. Geoffrey Best, *Humanity in Warfare* (New York: Columbia University Press, 1980), 129. Of course, this etiquette did not extend to nonstate actors. The British did not observe the rules when they blew Indian mutineers from the mouths of cannons. The United States did not observe the rules when it was at war with native American Indians, and of course, the Indians also did not observe them.

13. Nuremberg Trial Proceedings, Vol. 1, Charter of the International Military Tribunal, in the Avalon Project archive, Yale Law School.

14. UN General Assembly, UN Doc. A/CONF.183/9, Preamble, Rome Statute of the International Criminal Court, July 17, 1998, http://www.icc-cpi.int/nr/rdonlyres/ea9aeff7-5752-4f84-be94-0a655eb30e16/0/rome_statute_english.pdf, accessed February 14, 2014.

15. For more on the norm against mercenaries, see Sarah Percy, *Mercenaries: The History of a Norm in International Relations.* Oxford: Oxford University Press, 2007.

16. Daniel Ford, *Flying Tigers: Claire Chennault and His American Volunteers, 1941–1942* (New York: Harper, 2007), 45.

17. Loosely translated, "Long live death! Long live war! Long live the sacred mercenary!"

18. Office of the UN High Commissioner for Human Rights, "Protocol Additional to the Geneva Conventions of August 12, 1949, and Relating to the Protection of Victims of International Armed Conflicts (Protocol I), June 8, 1977," http://www.icrc.org/applic/ihl/ihl.nsf/Article.xsp?action=openDocument&documentId-DC5096D2C036E9C12563CD0051DC30, accessed February 14, 2014.

19. Originally quoted in Geoffrey Best, *Humanity in Warfare* (New York: Columbia University Press, 1980), 375.

20. United Nations, "The Secretary-General Reflects on 'Intervention' in Thirty-Fifth Annual Ditchley Foundation Lecture," Press Release SG/SM/6613, June 26, 1998, part 8, http://www.un.org/News/Press/docs/1998/19980626.sgsm6613.html.

21. Exaggeration over the significance of Executive Outcomes is exemplified by Peter W. Singer, *Corporate Warriors: The Rise of the Privatized Military Industry* (Ithaca, NY: Cornell University Press, 2003); Juan C. Zarate, "The Emergence of a New Dog of War: Private International Security Companies, International Law, and the New World Disorder," *Stanford Journal of International Law* 34 (1998): 75–162; David Shearer, "Outsourcing War," *Foreign Policy*, no. 112 (1998): 68–81; Anna Leander, "The Market for Force and Public Security: The Destabilizing Consequences of Private Military Companies," *Journal of Peace Research* 42, no. 5 (2005): 605–622. For a more balanced analysis of Executive Outcomes, see Herbert M. Howe, "Private Security Forces and African Stability: The Case of Executive Outcomes," *Journal of Modern African Studies* 36, no. 2 (1998): 307–331; Kevin O'Brien, "Private Military Companies and African Security 1990–98," in *Mercenaries: An African Security Dilemma*, edited by A-F. Musah and K. Fayemi, 43–75 (London: Pluto, 2000); Christopher Kinsey, *Corporate Soldiers and International Security: The Rise of Private Military Companies* (London: Taylor & Francis, 2006). For an "inside" perspective, see Eeben Barlow, *Executive Outcomes: Against All Odds* (Alberton, South Africa: Galago, 2007).

22. A complete copy of this contract can be found in Appendix D of Michael Lee Lanning, *Mercenaries: Soldiers of Fortune, from Ancient Greece to Today's Private Military Companies* (New York: Ballantine Books, 2005), 245.

23. Steve Fainaru and Alec Klein, "In Iraq, a Private Realm of Intelligence-Gathering," *Washington Post*, July 1, 2007, http://www.washingtonpost.com/wp-dyn/content/article/2007/06/30/AR2007063001075_pf.html, accessed February 14, 2014.

5. Why Private Armies Have Returned

1. Quoted in John Ranelagh, *Thatcher's People: An Insider's Account of the Politics, the Power and the Personalities* (New York: HarperCollins, 1991), ix; see also Richard Cockett, *Thinking the Unthinkable: Think Tanks and the Economic Counter Revolution, 1931–1983* (New York: HarperCollins, 1995), 174–176.

2. Thomas Frank, "Government by Contractor Is a Disgrace: Many Jobs Are Best Left to Federal Workers," *Wall Street Journal*, November 26, 2008, http://online.wsj.com/news/articles/SB122765980278958481, accessed February 15, 2014.

3. Office of Management and Budget, "The President's Management Agenda: Fiscal Year 2002," http://www.whitehouse.gov/sites/default/files/omb/budget/fy2002/mgmt.pdf, accessed February 15, 2014.

4. Volker Franke and Marc Von Boemcken, "Private Guns: The Social Identity of Security Contractors," *Journal of Conflict Studies* 29 (2009): 10; Government Accountability Office, *Military Readiness: Management Focus Needed on Airfields for Overseas Deployments* (Washington, DC: Government Accountability Office, 2001), 10.

5. Floyd Spence and Eugene J. Carroll, "Q: Is the Military Drawdown Endangering U.S. National Security?" *Insight on the News* 14, no. 36 (1998): 24.

6. On MPRI, see Peter W. Singer, *Corporate Warriors: The Rise of the Privatized Military Industry* (Ithaca, NY: Cornell University Press, 2003), 128. On DynCorp, see "On the Ground: DynCorp and Other U.S. firms Provide U.S. Peace Verifiers to Kosovo," *Newsweek*, February 15, 1999, http://www.highbeam.com/doc/1G1-53865787.html, accessed February 15, 2014. "Peruvian Rebels Assert Role In Downing of a U.S. Copter," *New York Times*, January 24, 1992.

7. Andrew Gilligan, "Inside Lt Col Spicer's New Model Army," *Sunday Telegraph*, November 22, 1998, http://www.telegraph.co.uk/et?ac=001224792737135&rtmo=LKdx333d&a tmo=11/24/98 19&pg.

8. Deborah D. Avant and Lee Sigelman, "Private Security and Democracy: Lessons from the US in Iraq," *Security Studies* 19, no. 2 (2010): 230–265.

9. Carl von Clausewitz et al., *On War* (Princeton, NJ: Princeton University Press, 1976), 75.

10. *Contractors Support of US Operations in Iraq* (Washington, DC: US Congressional Budget Office, 2008), 17.

11. Donald Rumsfeld, "Secretary Rumsfeld's Remarks to the Johns Hopkins, Paul H. Nitze School of Advanced International Studies," http://www.defense.gov/transcripts/transcript. aspx?transcriptid=1361, accessed February 15, 2014.

12. Charity Willard, *The "Livre de Paix" of Christine de Pisan: A Critical Edition* (The Hague: Mouton, 1958), 133.

13. Bernard Bailyn, *The Ideological Origins of the American Revolution* (Cambridge, MA: Belknap, 1992), 356–357. On Hamilton's concerns, see Publius [Alexander Hamilton], "Consequences of Hostilities between States," *Federalist Papers* 8 (November 27, 1787); Publius [Alexander Hamilton], "The Idea of Restraining the Legislative Authority in Regard to the Common Defense Considered," *Federalist Papers* 26 (December 22, 1787).

14. T. X. Hammes, *Private Contractors: The Good, the Bad, and the Strategic Impact* (Washington, DC: National Defense University Press, 2010), 5.

6. The Murky Side of Private Force

1. The duke of Burgundy known as Charles the Bold, also called Charles the Rash, met his end at the Battle of Nancy on January 5, 1477, bringing to a conclusion the Burgundian Wars (1474–1477) between the dukes of Burgundy and the kings of France. A year earlier, Charles had besieged a Swiss garrison at Grandson in Switzerland and promised them safe passage if they surrendered their castle. However, Charles betrayed them and hung or drowned all 412 men in an execution requiring four hours. A year later, at the Battle of Nancy, the Swiss had neither forgotten nor forgiven this perfidy. When Charles's naked and disfigured body was found frozen in a riverbed several days after the battle, only his physician was able to identify him. His head had been cleft in two by a halberd, multiple lances were lodged in his stomach and loins, and his face was so badly mauled by wild animals that he was beyond recognition.

2. Charles Oman, *A History of the Art of War in the 16th Century* (London: C. Oman, 1937), 180.

3. Ibid., 184.

4. The Florentine campaigns against Pisa in 1500 and 1505 were particularly disastrous. In 1505, for example, ten mercenary captains embarrassingly defected to the other side. Not trusting mercenaries, Machiavelli convinced the Florentine authorities to raise a militia instead, composed of citizen soldiers whose loyalty to the state would remain unflappable. However, these farmers-turned-soldiers were no match for professional troops, and the Florentines were soon crushed in 1512. This military disaster resulted in the dissolution of the Florentine Republic, henceforward under papal control, and challenges Machiavelli's claims about the superiority of militias over mercenaries. He wrote *The Prince* to impress the new rulers of Florence and win his old job back, but to no avail. The French regarded the flush Florentines as the epitome of military incompetence. Niccolò Machiavelli, *The Prince and Other Works* (New York: Hendricks House, 1964), 131. On scholarly critique, see Quentin Skinner, *Machiavelli: A Very Short Introduction* (New York: Oxford University Press, 2000), 36–37; Christopher Coker, *Barbarous Philosophers: Reflections on the Nature of War from Heraclitus to Heisenberg* (New York: Columbia University Press, 2010), 139–151; James Jay Carafano, *Private Sector, Public Wars: Contractors in Combat—Afghanistan, Iraq, and Future Conflicts* (Westport, CT: Praeger Security International, 2008), 19; Sarah Percy,

Mercenaries: The History of a Norm in International Relations (New York: Oxford University Press, 2007).

5. William Caferro, "Italy and the Companies of Adventure in the Fourteenth Century," *Historian* 58, no. 4 (1996): 795, 805–806; Jurgen Brauer and Hubert Van Tuyll, *Castles, Battles, and Bombs: How Economics Explains Military History* (Chicago: University of Chicago Press, 2008), 91; Michael Mallett, *Mercenaries and Their Masters: Warfare in Renaissance Italy* (London: Bodley Head, 1974), 27; Charles C. Bayley, *War and Society in Renaissance Florence* (Toronto: University of Toronto Press, 1961), 11.

6. From a bull issued by Pope Urban V on February 17, 1364. Quoted in Caferro, "Italy and the Companies of Adventure," 795.

7. Geoffrey Parker, *Europe in Crisis, 1598–1648* (Oxford: Wiley-Blackwell, 2001), 17.

8. T. X. Hammes, *Private Contractors: The Good, the Bad, and the Strategic Impact*. Washington, DC: National Defense University Press, 2010, 10.

9. However, some research suggests that Americans care just as much about contractor deaths as they do about military personnel deaths. See Deborah D. Avant and Lee Sigelman, "Private Security and Democracy: Lessons from the US in Iraq," *Security Studies* 19, no. 2 (2010): 259.

10. Jennifer Elsea, Moshe Schwartz, and Kennon H. Nakamura. *Private Security Contractors in Iraq: Background, Legal Status, and Other Issues* (Washington, DC: Congressional Research Service, 2008), 41–42.

11. Paul Krugman, *The Return of Depression Economics and the Crisis of 2008* (New York: W. W. Norton, 2009), 63.

12. US Department of Defense, Office of the Inspector General, *DOD Obligations and Expenditures of Funds Provided to the Department of State for the Training and Mentoring of the Afghan National Police* (Washington, DC, 2010). For more information regarding the inadequate levels of training for government officials responsible for managing contractors, see Commission on Army Acquisition and Program Management in Expeditionary Operations, *Urgent Reform Required: Army Expeditionary Contracting* ("Gansler Report"), October 31, 2007, 43; Moshe Schwartz, *Training the Military to Manage Contractors during Expeditionary Operations: Overview and Options for Congress* (Washington, DC: Congressional Research Service, 2008), 4.

13. Doug Brooks, "Write a Cheque, End a War," *Conflict Trends* 3, no. 1 (2000): 33–35.

14. Brauer and Van Tuyll, *Castles, Battles, and Bombs*, 96.

15. "Blackwater USA," hearing before the Committee on Oversight and Government Reform, US House Of Representatives, 110th Congress, October 2, 2007 (statement of Eric Prince).

16. Quoted in Caferro, "Italy and the Companies of Adventure," 801.

7. The Modern World Order: A Brief History

1. "Excerpts from Army Maj. Gen. Eldon A. Bargewell's Report," *Washington Post*, April 21, 2007. http://www.washingtonpost.com/wp-dyn/content/article/2007/04/20/AR2007042002309.html, accessed February 25, 2014.

2. Barbara Miller, "Blackwater a Challenge to Iraqi Sovereignty: Al-Maliki," ABC Online, September 24, 2007. http://www.abc.net.au/worldtoday/content/2007/s2041431.htm, accessed February 25, 2014.

3. Ken Fireman and Robin Stringer, "Blackwater Denies Any Wrongdoing in Shooting Incident," Bloomberg News, September 17, 2007. See also "Memorandum: Additional Information about Blackwater USA," Majority Staff, Committee on Oversight and Government Reform, US House of Representatives, October 1, 2007.

4. "UN Report Describes New Mercenary Activity," *New York Times*, October 17, 2007. http://www.nytimes.com/2007/10/17/world/asia/17iht-mercenaries.1.7923472.html?_r=0, accessed February 25, 2014.

5. Justin Rosenberg, *The Empire of Civil Society: A Critique of the Realist Theory of International Relations* (New York: Verso, 1994), 39; Martin Wight, *Systems of States* (Leicester: Leicester University Press, 1977), 129; Hendrik Spruyt, *The Sovereign State and Its Competitors* (Princeton, NJ: Princeton University Press, 1996), 27.

6. H. H. Gerth, and C. Wright Mills, eds., *From Max Weber: Essays in Sociology* (London: Routledge, 2003), 77–128.

7. Carl von Clausewitz, *On War* (Princeton, NJ: Princeton University Press, 1976), 75, 87.

8. Charles Tilly, "War Making and State Making as Organized Crime," in *Bringing the State Back In*, edited by Peter B. Evans, Dietrich Rueschmeyer, and Theda Skocpol (Cambridge, UK: Cambridge University Press, 1985). Charles Tilly and Gabriel Ardant, *The Formation of National States in Western Europe* (Princeton, NJ: Princeton University Press, 1975), 42.

9. Mancur Olson, *Power and Prosperity: Outgrowing Communist and Capitalist Dictatorships* (New York: Basic Books, 2000).

10. Quoted in Norman Davies, *Europe: A History* (New York: HarperCollins, 1998), 568.

11. In 1949, the International Court of Justice (ICJ) stipulated that "between independent States, respect for territorial sovereignty is an essential foundation of international relations" (ICJ Reports, 1949, 4), and it is "the fundamental principle of state sovereignty on which the whole of international law rests" (ICJ Reports, 1986, para. 263).

12. See also Aram Roston, *The Man Who Pushed America to War: The Extraordinary Life, Adventures, and Obsessions of Ahmad Chalabi* (New York: PublicAffairs, 2009), 182.

13. White House, "President Bush Outlines Iraqi Threat," press release, October 7, 2002.

14. Leo Gross, "The Peace of Westphalia, 1648–1948," *American Journal of International Law* 42, no. 1 (1948): 28, 26. This article was originally published in the *American Journal of International Law* and later included in a book edited by Falk and Hanrieder (1968) is not in bibliography. Please provide full details Richard Falk and Wolfram Hanrieder (1968) and again in a posthumous collection of essays by Gross (1993). In the introduction to this last volume, the editor, Alfred P. Rubin, writes that this essay remains "timeless" and "seminal"; it "popularized the phrase and the notion of a 'Westphalia constitution' for the international order" (Gross 1993, x). This was even though Gross checked for and found little evidence in the language of the treaties to support his claims. For more critique on Gross, see Andreas Osiander, "Sovereignty, International Relations, and the Westphalian Myth," *International Organization* 55, no. 2 (2001): 264–65.

15. Hans Morganthau and Kenneth Thompson, *Politics among Nations: The Struggle for Power and Peace* (New York: McGraw-Hill, 1985), 294.

16. Graham Evans and Richard Newnham, *The Penguin Dictionary of International Relations* (London: Penguin, 1998).

17. See, for example, Philip Kerr, "The Outlawry of War," *Journal of the Royal Institute of International Affairs* 7 (November 1928): 361–368; K. N. Waltz, *Man, the State, and War: A Theoretical Analysis*, rev. ed. (New York: Columbia University Press, 2001); F. W. Wayman and P. F. Diehl, eds., *Reconstructing Realpolitik* (Ann Arbor: University of Michigan Press, 1994); M. E. Brown, O. R. Coté, Jr., S. M. Lynn-Jones, and S. E. Miller, eds., *Theories of War and Peace* (Cambridge, MA: MIT Press, 1998); M. I. Midlarsky, ed., *Handbook of War Studies* (Boston: Unwin Hyman, 1989). A recommended critique of Westphalia that is consistent with this book is Edward Keene, *Beyond the Anarchical Society: Grotius, Colonialism and Order in World Politics* (Cambridge, UK: Cambridge University Press, 2002).

18. Francis Fukuyama, "The End of History?" *National Interest* (Summer 1989): 4.

19. George W. Bush, "The National Security Strategy of the United States of America" (Washington, DC: White House, 2002), 1.

20. Article 2 (4) of the UN Charter stipulates: "All Members shall refrain in their international relations from the threat or use of force against the territorial integrity or political independence of any state." Article 2 (7) stipulates: "Nothing contained in the present Charter shall authorize the UN to intervene in matters which are essentially within the domestic jurisdiction of any state or shall require the Members to submit such matters to settlement under the present Charter; but this principle shall not prejudice the application of enforcement measures under Chapter VII."

21. Boutros Boutros-Ghali, "An Agenda for Peace: Preventive Diplomacy, Peacemaking and Peace-Keeping," *International Relations* 11, no. 3 (1992): 201.

22. Patrik Johansson and Ramses Amer, "The United Nations Security Council and the Enduring Challenge of the Use of Force in Inter-State Relations," Umeå Working Papers in Peace and Conflict Studies No. 3, Department of Political Science, Umeå University (2007), 6.

23. On "states are dead," see Kenichi Ohmae, *The End of the Nation State: The Rise of Regional Economies* (New York: Free Press, 1995). On "states are not dead," see Stephen D. Krasner, "Abiding Sovereignty," *International Political Science Review* 22, no. 3 (2001): 229–251.

24. Phillip Bobbitt, *Terror and Consent: The Wars for the Twenty-First Century* (New York: Alfred A. Knopf, 2008); Robert H. Jackson, *Quasi-States: Sovereignty, International Relations and the Third World* (Cambridge, UK: Cambridge University Press, 1993).

25. Jörg Friedrichs, "The Meaning of New Medievalism," *European Journal of International Relations* 7, no. 4 (2001): 481; S. J. Kobrin, "Back to the Future: Neomedievalism and the Postmodern Digital World Economy," *Journal of International Affairs* 51, no. 2 (1998): 364. For more on the state's historicity, see J. Agnew, "The Territorial Trap: The Geographical Assumptions of International Relations Theory," *Review of International Political Economy* 1, no. 1 (1994): 65; Janice E. Thomson, *Mercenaries, Pirates, and Sovereigns* (Princeton, NJ: Princeton University Press, 1996), 2; and Rosenberg, *The Empire of Civil Society*, 36.

26. Stephen D. Krasner, "Westphalia and All That," in *Ideas and Foreign Policy: Beliefs, Institutions, and Political Change*, edited by Judith Goldstein and Robert O. Keohane (Ithaca, NY: Cornell University Press, 1993), 235; Stephen D. Krasner, *Sovereignty: Organized Hypocrisy* (Princeton, NJ: Princeton University Press, 1999), 82; Keene, *Beyond the Anarchical Society*; Andreas Osiander, "Sovereignty, International Relations, and the Westphalian Myth," *International Organization* 55, no. 2 (2001): 284. See also Benno Teschke, *The Myth of 1648: Class, Geopolitics, and the Making of Modern International Relations* (New York: Verso, 2003).

27. P. Michael Phillips, "Deconstructing Our Dark Age Future," *Parameters* (Summer 2009): 96.

8. Neomedievalism

1. For example, see Rodney Bruce Hall and Frederich V. Kratochwil, "Medieval Tales: Neorealist 'Science' and the Abuse of History," *International Organization* 47, no. 3 (Summer 1993): 479–491; John Gerald Ruggie, "Territoriality and Beyond: Problematizing Modernity in International Relations," *International Organization* 47, no. 1 (Winter 1993): 139–174; Jörg Friedrichs, "The Meaning of New Medievalism," *European Journal of International Relations* 7, no. 4 (2001): 475–501; Stephen J. Kobrin, "Back to the Future: Neomedievalism and the Postmodern Digital World Economy," *Journal of International Affairs* 51, no. 2 (Spring 1998): 361–386; Gregory O'Hayon, "Big Men, Godfathers, and Zealots: Challenges to the State in the New Middle Ages" (PhD dissertation, University of Pittsburgh, 2003), 50; Andrew Gamble, "Regional Blocs, World Order and the New Medievalism," in *European Union and New Regionalism: Regional Actors and Global Governance in a Post-Hegemonic Era*, edited by Mario Telo (Burlington, VT: Ashgate, 2007), 31; Phillip G. Cerny, "Neomedievalism, Civil War and the New Security Dilemma: Globalisation as Durable Disorder," *Civil Wars* 1, no. 1 (1998): 40; Bruce Holsinger, *Neomedievalism, Neoconservatism, and the War on Terror* (Chicago: Prickly Paradigm, 2007), 64; Cristian Cantir and Philip Schrodt, "Neomedievalism in the Twenty-First Century: Warlords, Gangs, and Transnational Militarized Actors as a Challenge to Sovereign Preeminence," paper presented at Annual Meeting of the International Studies Association, New Orleans, 2010, 15.

2. Hedley Bull, *The Anarchical Society: A Study of Order in World Politics* (New York: Columbia University Press, 2002), 254.

3. Ibid., 246.

4. William Shakespeare, *The Merchant of Venice*, edited by Blakemore Evans (Boston: Houghton Norton, 1974), 3.3.30–31.

5. GDP in current US dollars and not adjusted for inflation. See International Bank for Reconstruction and Development, *2010 World Development Indicators* (Washington, DC: World Bank, 2010).

6. Marshall McLuhan, *The Gutenberg Galaxy: The Making of Typographic Man* (Toronto: University of Toronto Press, 1962).

7. Martin Wight, *Systems of States* (Leicester: Leicester University Press, 1977), 131.

8. Statute, Rome. "Rome Statute of the International Criminal Court," *International Legal Materials* 37 (1998): 999–1019.

9. Rosalyn Higgins, "Intervention and International Law," in *Intervention in World Politics*, edited by Hedley Bull (Oxford: Clarendon, 1984), 36. For more of this viewpoint, see Christopher Greenwood, "International Law and the NATO Intervention in Kosovo," *International and Comparative Law Quarterly* 49, no. 4 (2008): 926–934. For an overview of the scholarly debate on sovereignty, see Jennifer M. Welsh, "Authorizing Humanitarian Intervention," in *The United Nations and Global Security*, edited by Richard M. Price and Mark W. Zacher (New York: Palgrave Macmillan, 2004), 177–192.

10. Rome Statute art. 13. For more information on ICC jurisdiction over citizens of nonparties, see Jennifer Elsea, *International Criminal Court: Overview and Selected Legal Issues* (Washington, DC: Congressional Research Service, 2002), 25.

11. At the 2005 UN World Summit, member states included R2P in the outcome document, agreeing to paragraphs 138 and 139, which articulate the scope of R2P and to whom the responsibility actually falls (i.e., nations first, regional and international communities second). In April 2006, the UN Security Council reaffirmed the provisions of paragraphs 138 and 139 in a resolution (S/RES/1674) on the protection of civilians in armed conflict, thereby formalizing its support for the norm. In January 2009, the UN secretary-general, Ban Ki-Moon, released a report called "Implementing the Responsibility to Protect," which further argues for the implementation of R2P. See UN General Assembly, Resolution 60/1, "2005 World Summit Outcome," October 24, 2005, http://www.un.org/summit2005/documents.html; UN General Assembly, A/63/677, "Implementing the Responsibility to Protect: Report of the Secretary-General," January 12, 2009, http://www.unrol.org/files/SG_reportA_63_677_en.pdf.

12. Patricia McNerney, "International Criminal Court: Issues for Consideration by the United States Senate," *Law and Contemporary Problems* 64, no. 1 (2001): 184.

13. Bull, *The Anarchical Society*, 270.

14. Oliver P. Richmond, "The Dilemmas of Subcontracting the Liberal Peace," in *Subcontracting Peace: The Challenges of NGO Peacebuilding*, edited by Oliver P. Richmond and Henry F. Carey (Aldershot, UK: Ashgate, 2005), 20.

15. Peter W. Singer, "Humanitarian Principles, Private Military Agents: Some Implications of the Privatised Military Industry for the Humanitarian Community," in *Resetting the Rules of Engagement: Trends and Issues in Military-Humanitarian Relations*, edited by V. Wheeler and A. Harmer (London: Overseas Development Institute, 2006), 70.

16. Quoted in Yves Engler, "The Mercenaries and the NGOs," *Counterpunch*, August 26, 2010. http://www.counterpunch.org/2010/08/26/the-mercenaries-and-the-ngos/print, accessed February 25, 2014.

17. On trade flows, see Committee on Payment and Settlement Systems, *Progress in Reducing Foreign Exchange Settlement Risk* (Basel, Switzerland: Bank for International Settlements, 2008), foreword.

18. UNCTAD, *Transnational Corporations and World Development* (London: International Thompson Business Press, 1996), ix, 4; UN Conference on Trade, *World Investment Report 1999: Foreign Direct Investment & the Challenge of Development* (Blue Ridge Summit, PA: Bernan, 1999); Peter Willetts, "Transnational Actors and International Organizations in Global Politics," in *The Globalization of World Politics: An Introduction to International Relations*, edited by John Baylis and Steve Smith (Oxford: Oxford University Press, 2001), 356–383; Anthony McGrew, "Globalization and Global Politics," in *The Globalization of World Politics*, 21, 23.

19. *International Taxation: Large US Corporations and Federal Contractors with Subsidiaries in Jurisdictions Listed as Tax Havens or Financial Privacy Jurisdictions* (Washington, DC: Government Accountability Office, 2008); Ryan J. Donmoyer, "83 Percent of Companies Had Tax-Haven Units," *Bloomberg News*, January 16, 2010, http://www.bloomberg.com/apps/news?pid=newsarchive&sid=aK0aqjwsiSCA, accessed February 25, 2014.

20. J. Lamont, "UN Seeks Help from Companies in War on HIV/AIDS," *Financial Times*, August 30, 2002, 1.

21. Stephanie Hanson, "In West Africa, Threat of Narco-States," *Council on Foreign Relations Analysis Brief*, July 10, 2007, i.

22. "Romagna tua non è, e non fu mai, sanza guerra ne' cuor de' suoi tiranni." Dante Alighieri, *The Divine Comedy, Inferno*, rev. ed., translated by Mark Musa (New York: Penguin, 2002), canto XXVII, st. 37–38.

23. For example, see Afrobarometer; Business Environment and Enterprise Performance Survey; Business Environment Risk Intelligence (BERI); the World Bank's Country Policy & Institutional Assessment; State Failure Task Force State Capacity Survey; Global Insight's DRI/McGraw-Hill; European Bank for Reconstruction and Development; the Economist Intelligence Unit; Freedom House; Gallup International; World Economic Forum; Heritage Foundation/Wall Street Journal; Human Rights Database; Latinobarometro; Political Risk Services; Reporters without Borders; Institute for Management Development's World Competitiveness Yearbook; World Markets Online; PriceWaterhouseCoopers's Opacity Index; the World Business Environment Survey; the Fund for Peace Failed State Index; Brookings Institution's Index of State Weakness in the Developing World; the Peace and Conflict Instability Ledger; the Political Instability Task Force (PITF); German Ministry of Development's Listing of Failing States (BMZ).

24. John Rapley, "The New Middle Ages," *Foreign Affairs* (May–June 2006): 95.

25. Internet Medieval Sourcebook, "Henry IV: Letter to Gregory VII, Jan 24 1076," http://www.fordham.edu/halsall/source/henry4-to-g7a.asp, accessed February 25, 2014.

26. Rachel Donadio and Elizabeth A. Harris, "Vatican Excommunicates Chinese Priest Ordained 'Illicitly,'" *New York Times*, July 17, 2011, A9.

27. For example, see the Magna Carta (England, 1215); the Declaration of Arbroath (Scotland, 1320); the Bill of Rights (England, 1689); the Claim of Right (Scotland, 1689); the Declaration of Independence (United States, 1776); the Declaration of the Rights of Man and of the Citizen (France, 1789); the Bill of Rights (United States, 1789–1791); the Universal Declaration of Human Rights (United Nations, 1948); the European Convention on Human Rights (Council of Europe, 1950); the International Covenant on Civil and Political Rights (1966); the International Covenant on Economic, Social, and Cultural Rights (1966); the Canadian Charter of Rights and Freedoms (Canada, 1982); and the Charter of Fundamental Rights of the European Union (European Union, 2000).

28. Cited in David Littman, "Universal Human Rights and Human Rights in Islam," *Midstream* 42, no. 2 (1999): 2–7.

29. Nobelprize.org, "The Nobel Peace Prize 2010 Liu Xiaobo," July 24, 2011, http://nobelprize.org/nobel_prizes/peace/laureates/2010/press.html, accessed February 25, 2014.

30. "China Questions 'True Intentions' of Award of Nobel Peace Prize to Liu Xiaobo," *Xinhua News*, October 12, 2010, http://news.xinhuanet.com/english2010/china/2010-10/12/c_13553857.htm, accessed February 25, 2014.

31. Thorbjorn Jagland, "Why We Gave Liu Xiaobo a Nobel," *New York Times*, October 23, 2010, A21.

9. Neomedieval Warfare

1. Carl von Clausewitz, *On War* (Princeton, NJ: Princeton University Press, 1976), 87.

2. Adam Roberts, "Lives and Statistics: Are 90% of War Victims Civilians?" *Survival* 52, no. 3 (2010): 115–136; see also Martin van Creveld, *The Transformation of War* (New York: Free Press, 1991); Cristian Cantir and Philip Schrodt, "Neomedievalism in the Twenty-First Century: Warlords, Gangs, and Transnational Militarized Actors as a Challenge to Sovereign Preeminence," paper presented at Annual Meeting of the International Studies Association (New Orleans, 2010), 4.

3. J. Joseph Hewitt, Jonathan Wilkenfeld, and Ted Robert Gurr, *Peace and Conflict 2010* (College Park, MD: Boulder Center for International Development and Conflict Management, University of Maryland Paradigm, 2010), 31.

4. Javier Solana, "A Secure Europe in a Better World: European Security Strategy." In *Civilian Perspective or Security Strategy?*, edited by Klaus Schilder and Tobias Hauschild (Paris: European Union Institute for Security Studies, 2003), 5; Paul Collier et al., *Breaking the Conflict Trap: Civil War and Development Policy* (Washington, DC: World Bank, 2003), 17. For a critical examination of this common estimation, see Roberts, "Lives and Statistics."

5. "Rwanda: How the Genocide Happened," *BBC News*, May 17, 2011.

6. Samantha Power, *A Problem from Hell: America and the Age of Genocide* (New York: Harper Perennial, 2003), 366.

7. Rupert Smith, *The Utility of Force: The Art of War in the Modern World* (London: Allen Lane, 2005), 1.

8. Charles F. Wald, "New Thinking at USEUCOM: The Phase Zero Campaign," *Joint Forces Quarterly* 43, no. 1 (2006): 72–75.

9. "Stability operations are a core U.S. military mission that the Department of Defense shall be prepared to conduct with proficiency equivalent to combat operations." US Department of Defense Directive 3000.05, November 28, 2005, updated Septemeber 16, 2009. http://www.dtic.mil/whs/directives/corres/pdf/300005p.pdf, accessed February 25, 2014; National Security Presidential Directive 44: Management of Interagency Efforts Concerning Reconstruction and Stabilization, December 7, 2005, http://www.fas.org/irp/offdocs/nspd/nspd-44.pdf, accessed February 25, 2014; US Defense Science Board, *Institutionalizing Stability Operations within DOD: Report of the Defense Science Board Task Force*, September 2005; *Quadrennial Defense Review*, February 6, 2006, http://www.defense.gov/qdr/report/Report20060203.pdf, 17.

10. I omit counterinsurgency (COIN) strategy from this analysis because of its general incoherence as a strategy. Adopted in Iraq and Afghanistan in 2007 with much enthusiasm at Washington, DC, it has largely failed to deliver on its early promise of victory. The United States leaves those countries in arguably worse shape than when it arrived, despite many years of well-resourced COIN.

11. US Department of State, "Civilian Response Corps Reaches 100 Active Members," April 16, 2010, http://www.state.gov/r/pa/prs/ps/2010/04/140346.htm, accessed February 25, 2014.

12. US Army, *FM 3-07: Stability Operations* (Washington, DC: Department of the Army 2008). The author was a reviewer of this field manual, especially chapter 6 on security sector reform, based on experiences gained in the private military sector.

13. "Remarks by USAID Administrator Dr. Rajiv Shah at the Center for Global Development," USAID.gov, January 19, 2011.

14. Pratap Chatterjee, "U.S. Dyncorp Oversight in Afghanistan Faulted," Inter Press Service, February 27, 2010. U.S. Department of Defense, Office of the Inspector General, *DoD obligations and expenditures of funds provided to the Department of State for the Training and Mentoring of the Afghan National Police* (Washington, DC: 2010), i.

15. T. X. Hammes, *Private Contractors: The Good, the Bad, and the Strategic Impact* (Washington, DC: National Defense University Press, 2010), 9; US Department of Defense, *DOD Obligations and Expenditures of Funds Provided to the Department of State for the Training and Mentoring of the Afghan National Police* (Washington, DC: 2010), 8.

16. Christopher Coker, *Barbarous Philosophers: Reflections on the Nature of War from Heraclitus to Heisenberg* (New York: Columbia University Press, 2010), 150.

17. Mao Zedong, *Quotations from Chairman Mao Zedong* (*The Little Red Book*) (Beijing: Government of the People's Republic of China, 1964).

18. The five fastest-growing African economies by real GDP in early 2011 were also ranked among the fastest in the world: the DRC (tenth in world), Zimbabwe (eleventh), Botswana (thirteenth), Nigeria (sixteenth), and Ethiopia (twentieth). International Monetary Fund, *World Economic Outlook Database* (Washington, DC: IMF, 2011).

10. Military Enterprisers in Liberia: Building Better Armies

1. John Blaney, interview by Ky Luu, Disaster Resilience Leadership Academy, September 11, 2009, http://www.youtube.com/watch?v=cdGGs6QGaCU.

2. Quoted in William Reno, "Reinvention of an African Patrimonial State: Charles Taylor's Liberia," *Third World Quarterly* 16, no. 1 (1995): 109.

3. International Monetary Fund, *Liberia: Interim Poverty Reduction Strategy Paper* (Washington, DC: IMF, 2007), x; IDP Advisory Team Policy Development and Evaluation Service, *Real-Time Evaluation of UNHCR's IDP Operation in Liberia* (Geneva: UN High Commissioner for

Refugees, 2007), 7; UN High Commissioner for Refugees, "Liberia: Regional Operations Profile—West Africa," http://www.unhcr.org/cgi-bin/texis/vtx/page?page=49e484936#, accessed February 25, 2014; International Committee of the Red Cross, *Liberia: Opinion Survey and In-Depth Research* (Geneva: ICRC, 2009), 1.

4. "The World's Worst: Liberia," *Economist*, November, 2002.

5. Stephan Faris, "Charles Taylor Leaves Liberia," *Time*, August 11, 2003. http://content.time.com/time/world/article/0,8599,474987,00.html, accessed February 25, 2014.

6. J. Peter Pham, *Liberia: Portrait of a Failed State* (Georgia: Reed, 2004), 191.

7. In 2008, the UNDP's Human Development Index ranked Liberia 176th of 179 states, and it did not rank Liberia at all in 2003 for lack of data. A Liberian's life expectancy at birth was fifty-six years in 2003 and fifty-nine years in 2010. In 2010, Liberia's adult literacy rate remained at 46 percent, one of the lowest in the world, and the combined gross enrollment in school was only 57.6 percent. The unemployment rate stood at 85 percent. The 2010 Gallup Global Wellbeing Survey puts the country at 141st out of 155 (Gallup, "Global Wellbeing Surveys Find Nations Worlds Apart," http://www.gallup.com/poll/126977/global-wellbeing-surveys-find-nations-worlds-apart.aspx). The 2010 Global Hunger Index ranks Liberia 69th out of 84, which makes it the fifteenth most food-insecure country in the world; Klaus von Grebmer et al., "Global Hunger Index, the Challenge of Hunger: Focus on the Crisis of Child Undernutrition" (Bonn, Dublin, and Washington, DC: Welthungerhilfe, International Food Policy Research Institute, Concern Worldwide, 2010), 17. The UN and the World Bank continue to place Liberia in the lowest category of state strength. Other failed-state indices have ranked Liberia in various versions of "the worst of the worst" category from 2008 to 2010 (no data were available on Liberia during or immediately after the war): the Fund for Peace's Failed State Index; Transparency International's Corruption Perceptions Index; Brookings's Index of State Weakness in the Developing World; the World Bank's Country Policy and Institutional Assessment (CPIA) and International Development Association (IDA) Resource Allocation Index; and Freedom House's World's Most Repressive Societies. See UN Development Program, *National Human Development Report 2006: Liberia* (New York: United Nations, 2006); James Heintz, *A Rapid Impact Assessment of the Global Economic Crisis on Liberia*, (Geneva: International Labour Organization, 2009); Soniya Carvalho, *Engaging with Fragile States* (Washington, DC: World Bank, 2006), 5; World Bank, "Indicators: Data," 2010, http://data.worldbank.org/indicator, accessed February 25, 2014

8. Pham, *Liberia*, 191–192.

9. World Bank, "Indicators: Data."

10. Foreign aid here refers to net official development assistance: World Bank, "Net Official Development Assistance and Official Aid Received (Current US$)," http://data.worldbank.org/indicator/DT.ODA.ALLD.CD?cid=GPD_54, accessed April 16, 2011. Calculation of percentage of foreign aid to government spending: "Percentage of Foreign Aid to Government Spending," *Financial Times*, http://media.ft.com/cms/7398f192-6d99-11df-b5c9-00144feabdc0.swf, accessed February 25, 2014.

11. Save the Children Liberia, http://www.savethechildren.org.uk/en/liberia.htm, accessed February 25, 2014.

12. Firestone, "Liberia Statistics," http://www.firestonenaturalrubber.com/documents/StatSheetNarrative.pdf, accessed February 25, 2014.

13. Greg Mills, *Why Africa Is Poor* (New York: Penguin, 2010), 372.

14. "U.S. Debating Sending Troops to Help Liberian Civil War," CNN (transcript), July 2, 2003; UNIS, "Secretary-General Welcomes Resignation of President Charles Taylor; Hopes Event Marks Beginning of End for Liberia's 'Long Nightmare,'" UN press release SG/SM/8818 AFR/687, August 12, 2003.

15. The concept of the CNN effect holds that globalized media have the power to shape popular opinion in representative governments, which, in turn, influence a state's foreign policy, such as whether to stage a humanitarian intervention. It is named for the popular twenty-four-hour international television news channel Cable News Network, or CNN. For more information on the CNN effect, see Steven Livingston, "Clarifying the CNN Effect: An Examination of Media Effects according to Type of Military Intervention," Research Paper R-18 (Cambridge, MA: Joan Shorenstein Center on Press and Politics, 1997); Eytan Gilboa,

"The CNN Effect: The Search for a Communication Theory of International Relations," *Political Communication* 22, no. 1 (2005): 27–44; Hamid Mowlana, *Global Information and World Communication: New Frontiers in International Relations* (London: Sage, 1997); Michael C. Williams, "Words, Images, Enemies: Securitization and International Politics," *International Studies Quarterly* 47, no. 4 (2003): 511–531; Piers Robinson, *The CNN Effect: The Myth of News, Foreign Policy and Intervention* (London: Routledge, 2002).

16. Based on OECD DAC (constant 2008 prices) and UN Office for the Coordination of Humanitarian Affairs (OCHA) Financial Tracking Service (FTS) data for 2009–2010. See "Liberia Overview," http://www.globalhumanitarianassistance.org/countryprofile/liberia, accessed February 25, 2014.

17. This is still a far cry from prewar levels of $136.2 million in 1986. World Bank, "Liberia—Workers' Remittances and Compensation of Employees," http://www.indexmundi.com/facts/liberia/workers'-remittances-and-compensation-of-employees, accessed February 25, 2014.

18. It may also have something to do with the DOD's general aversion to all things African following the 1993 Somalia disaster.

19. The legal origin of IDIQ contracts comes from the US Federal Acquisition Regulations (FAR), section 16.501(a). There are typically three types of contracts that an IDIQ contract authorizes: fixed-price contracts, time-and-materials contracts, and cost-reimbursement contracts. In a fixed-price contract, the price is not subject to adjustment based on costs incurred, which can favorably or adversely affect the firm's profitability, depending on its execution in performing the contracted service. Fixed-price contracts include firm fixed-price, fixed-price with economic adjustment, and fixed-price incentive. Time-and-materials contracts provide for acquiring supplies or services on the basis of direct labor hours at fixed hourly/daily rates plus materials at cost. Cost-reimbursement contracts provide for payment of allowable incurred costs, to the extent prescribed in the contract, plus a fixed fee, award fee, or incentive fee. Award fees or incentive fees are generally based on various objective and subjective criteria, such as aircraft mission capability rates and meeting cost targets.

20. This US government money was mostly drawn from a mix of fiscal years 2004–2007 international disaster and famine assistance, regional peacekeeping, and foreign military assistance funds. Nicholas Cook, *Liberia's Post-War Recovery: Key Issues and Developments* (Washington, DC: Congressional Research Service, 2005), 6, 18; Nicholas Cook, *Liberia's Post-War Development: Key Issues and US Assistance* (Washington, DC: Congressional Research Service, 2010), 22.

21. AFL mission statement taken from the CPA: Comprehensive Peace Agreement between the Government of Liberia and the Liberians United for Reconciliation and Democracy (LURD) and the Movement for Democracy in Liberia (MODEL) and Political Parties, (August 18, 2003), Part Four, Article VII, para. 2.c.

22. Klein suggested that Liberia could make do with a decent police force and a well-trained border security force of six hundred to seven hundred men. Statement made November 5, 2003. "Liberia: US Hires Private Company to Train 4,000-Man Army," *IRIN Africa*, February 15, 2005, http://www.irinnews.org/report/53038/liberia-us-hires-private-company-to-train-4-000-man-army, accessed February 25, 2014. His opinion may have also been informed by UNMIL's civilian police (CIVPOL) commissioner, Mark Kroeker, who told US State Department personnel that Liberia needed a robust police force and not a military. US State Department, "USG Pre-Assessment Trip to Liberia on Security Sector Reform," January 2004.

23. International Crisis Group, "Liberia: Uneven Progress in Security Sector Reform," *Africa Report* 148 (2009). For more information on this vetting technique, see Sean McFate, "The Art and Aggravation of Vetting in Post-Conflict Environments," *Military Review* (July–August 2007): 79–97.

24. "Green-on-Blue Blues: Afghan Soldiers Increasingly Turn on Their NATO Colleagues," *Economist*, September 1, 2012. http://www.economist.com/node/21561943, accessed February 25, 2014.

25. Until recently, the US military treated the formation of foreign forces primarily as a foreign internal defense (FID) mission. FID is an ill-fitting model for SSR; it is a Cold War concept

informed by Maoist irregular warfare strategy rather than SSR principles. FID employed US Army special forces to covertly train and equip pro-American guerrillas in communist countries (e.g., the Montagnards in Vietnam) and help friendly governments defeat communist insurgents (e.g., El Salvador) in proxy wars between the United States and the Soviet Union. This accounts for the US military's train-and-equip mentality when it comes to SSR, which yields only improved tactical units rather than a transformed security sector. This limited approach is promulgated in Joint Publication (JP) 3-07.1: "Joint Tactics, Techniques, and Procedures for Foreign Internal Defense (FID)"; US Army and US Marine Corps, *FM 3-24/MCWP3-33.5: Counterinsurgency*, chapter 6 (Washington, DC: Department of the Army, 2006); US Army, *FM 3-07: Stability Operations*, chapter 6 (Washington, DC: Department of the Army, 2008). After several years of FID failure in Iraq and Afghanistan, the US military finally drafted more comprehensive doctrine on SSR, called security force assistance: US Army, *FM 3-07/1: Security Force Assistance* (Washington, DC: Department of the Army, 2009). Though a significant improvement, this model does not address the full spectrum of SSR needs, such as vetting, and creates foreign militaries in the image of the US Army, which is inappropriate.

26. Total demobilization costs were approximately $15 million. Cook, *Liberia's Post-War Development*, 22.

27. Thomas Dempsey, *Security Sector Reform in Liberia Part I: An Assessment of Defense Reform*, Issue Paper 2008 (Carlisle, PA: Peacekeeping and Stability Operations Institute, US Army War College, 2008), 3.

28. "Urgent Reform Required: Army Expeditionary Contracting," Report of the Commission on Army Acquisition and Program Management in Expeditionary Operations, hearing before the Subcommittee on Readiness and Management Support of the Committee on Armed Services, US Senate, 110th Congress (December 6, 2007).

29. US Department of State, *Report of Inspection Embassy Monrovia, Liberia Report No. ISP-I-08-20a* (Washington, DC, 2008), 16.

30. International Crisis Group, *Liberia: Uneven Progress*, i, 19, 34.

31. Morten Bøås and Karianne Stig, "Security Sector Reform in Liberia: An Uneven Partnership without Local Ownership," *Journal of Intervention and Statebuilding* 4, no. 3 (2010): 285–303; Louise Andersen, *Post-Conflict Security Sector Reform and the Challenge of Ownership: The Case of Liberia* (Copenhagen: Danish Institute for International Studies, 2006), 286.

32. Cook, *Liberia's Post-War Development*, 26.

33. Adedeji Ebo, "The Challenges and Opportunities of Security Sector Reform in Post-Conflict Liberia," Occasional Paper no. 9 (Geneva: Geneva Centre for Democratic Control of Armed Forces, 2005), 154–155.

34. Michael M. Phillips, "In Liberia, an Army Unsullied by Past," *Wall Street Journal*, August 14, 2007. Bøås and Stig, "Security Sector Reform," 289.

35. Ibid, 289. Other references cited: Adedeji Ebo, "Liberia Case Study: Outsourcing SSR to Foreign Companies," in *No Ownership, No Commitment: A Guide to Local Ownership of Security Sector Reform*, edited by Laurie Nathan (Birmingham, UK: University of Birmingham, 2007); Ebo, "The Challenges and Opportunities," 1–28; Alexander Loden, "Civil Society and Security Sector Reform in Post-Conflict Liberia: Painting a Moving Train without Brushes," *International Journal of Transitional Justice* 1, no. 2 (2007): 297–307.

36. International Crisis Group, *Liberia: Uneven Progress*, i–ii.

37. Mark Malan, *Security Sector Reform in Liberia: Mixed Results from Humble Beginnings* (Carlisle, PA: Strategic Studies Institute, 2008), 69.

38. International Crisis Group, *Liberia: Uneven Progress*, 31.

11. Mercenaries in Somalia: A Neomedieval Tale

1. Global Security, "Somalia Civil War," http://www.globalsecurity.org/military/world/war/somalia.htm, accessed February 26, 2014.

2. Jeffrey Gettleman, "Ethiopia Launches Open War in Somalia," *New York Times News Service*, December 25, 2006. http://www.utsandiego.com/uniontrib/20061225/news_7n25somalia.html, accessed February 26, 2014.

3. Ibrahim Mohamed, "Somali Rebel Groups Clash Near Kenya Border," Reuters, August 26, 2010.

4. UN High Commissioner for Refugees. "Dadaab – World's biggest refugee camp 20 years old," February 21, 2012. http://www.unhcr.org/pages/49c3646c2.html, accessed February 26, 2014.

5. Ken Menkhaus and John Prendergast, "Political Economy of Post-Intervention Somalia," *Somalia Task Force Issue Paper 3* (Washington, DC: Horn of Africa Publications, 1995), 1.

6. Ken Menkhaus, *Kenya-Somalia Border Conflict Analysis* (Washington, DC: USAID, 2005); Koen Vlassenroot and Timothy Raeymaekers, "The Politics of Rebellion and Intervention in Ituri: The Emergence of a New Political Complex?" *African Affairs* 103, no. 412 (2004): 385–412; Georg Lutz and Wolf Linder, "Traditional Structures in Local Governance for Local Development," unpublished report, Institute of Political Science, University of Berne, Switzerland (2004).

7. UN, "United Nations Operations in Somalia (UNOSOM 1) Background" (2003) http://www.un.org/en/peacekeeping/missions/past/unsom1backgr1.html, accessed February 26, 2014.

8. Somalia NGO Consortium, http://www.somaliangoconsortium.org/index.php, accessed February 26, 2014.

9. Amnesty International, *Fatal Insecurity Attacks on Aid Workers and Rights Defenders in Somalia* (London: Amnesty International, 2008), 2.

10. "Somalia: NGOs Urge International Community to Protect Civilians," *IRIN Africa*, October 7, 2008. http://www.irinnews.org/fr/report/80786/somalia-ngos-urge-internatio nal-community-to-protect-civilians, accessed February 26, 2014.

11. Bill Roggio, "Zawahiri Praises Shabaab's Takeover of Southern Somalia," *Long War Journal*, February 24, 2009, http://www.longwarjournal.org/archives/2009/02/zawahiri_praises_ sha.php, accessed February 26, 2014.

12. The Federal Bureau of Investigation, "Fighting Terror: 14 Indicted for Supporting Al Shabaab," August 5, 2010. http://www.fbi.gov/news/stories/2010/august/al-shabaab, accessed February 26, 2014.

13. The actual figures for 2010 (as of December 22, 2010) are as follows: total attacks worldwide, 430; total hijackings worldwide, 49; total Somalia incidents, 210; total Somalia hijackings, 45; total Somalia hostages taken, 948; current vessels held by Somali pirates, 25; hostages held by Somali pirates, 586. International Maritime Bureau, "IMB Piracy Reporting Centre (PRC)," December 22, 2010, http://www.icc-ccs.org/piracy-reporting-centre, accessed February 14, 2014. For more on the rise of pirates in recent years, see Peter Chalk, *The Maritime Dimension of International Security: Terrorism, Piracy, and Challenges for the United States* (Santa Monica, CA: RAND Corporation, 2008); Ken Menkhaus, "Dangerous Waters," *Survival* 51, no. 1 (2009): 21–25; Karl Sörenson, *State Failure on the High Seas: Reviewing the Somali Piracy* (Stockholm: Swedish Defense Research Agency, 2008). The $18 billion number comes from *The Pirates of Somalia: Ending the Threat, Rebuilding a Nation* (Washington, DC: World Bank, 2013), 25.

14. Interview with the author, July 6, 2013.

15. Jay Bahadur, *The Pirates of Somalia: Inside their Hidden World* (New York: Random House, 2011).

16. Simon Jones, "Skulls and Crossroads," *Maritime Security Review*, November 18, 2010. http://www.marsecreview.com/2010/11/1060/, accessed February 26, 2014.

17. Martin Plaut, "Private Patrol Boats to Tackle Somali Pirates," *BBC News*, May 30, 2012. http://www.bbc.com/news/world-africa-18209357, accessed February 26, 2014.

18. UN Security Council, "Report of the United Nations Monitoring Group on Somalia and Eritrea Submitted in Accordance with Resolution 1916" (2010) [S/2011/433], July 18, 2011, 276.

19. UN Security Council, "Report of the Monitoring Group," para. 61–64.

20. "Somalia: Puntland Maritime Police Force Instructor Killed On Duty," Garowe Online, April 28, 2012.

21. Chris Tomlinson, "U.S. Hires Contractor to Back Somalis," *The Associated Press*, March 7, 2007.

22. Jeffrey Gettleman, Mark Mazzetti, and Eric Schmitt, "U.S. Relies on Contractors in Somalia Conflict," *New York Times*, August 10, 2011, A1.

23. Katharine Houreld, "Bancroft Global Development, U.S. Group, Advises African Troops in Somalia," Associated Press, August 10, 2011.

24. International Defense Exhibition & Conference (IDEX), "Reflex Responses Management Consultancy LLC," Abu Dhabi, 2011. http://www.idexuae.ae/page.cfm/Link=21/t=m/goSection=1, accessed August 1, 2011; Mark Mazzetti and Emily B. Hager, "Secret Desert Force Set Up by Blackwater's Founder," *New York Times*, May 14, 2011, A1.

25 Interview with the author, July 16, 2013.

26. James Brown, "Pirates and Privateers: Managing the Indian Ocean's Private Security Boom," Lowy Institute for International Policy, September 12, 2012.

27. Justin Stares, "The International Community Has 'Failed' to Tackle Piracy," *Public Service Europe*, February 28, 2012.

28. Interview with the author, July 16, 2013.

29. In 2012, the number of incidents of attempted attacks decreased dramatically from 237 to 75, a nearly 70 percent drop from the record year of 2011. UN Security Council, "Letter Dated 12 July 2013 from the Chair of the Security Council Committee pursuant to resolutions 751 (1992) and 1907 (2009) concerning Somalia and Eritrea Addressed to the President of the Security Council," S/2013/413 (July 12, 2013), para. 53.

30. International Maritime Organization, *Interim Guidance to Private Maritime Security Companies Providing Privately Contracted Armed Security Personnel on Board Ships in the High Risk Area*, MSC.1/Circ.1443, May 25, 2012.

31. For US Navy quotes, see Terence McKnight, Foreword, in Claude Berube and Patrick Cullen, eds., *Maritime Private Security: Market Responses to Piracy, Terrorism and Waterborne Security Risks in the 21st Century* (New York: Routledge 2012), xix. For Gortney quote, see US Navy, "Super Tanker Attacked in Arabian Sea," no. NNS081117-07, www.navy.mil/, November 17, 2008. For Fitzgerald quote, see Voice of America video, "US Admiral Says Commercial Ships Need Armed Guards," April 22, 2010, http://www.youtube.com/watch?v=NtuJ0VlBVU4. On scholarship arguing for privateering, see Todd Emerson Hutchins, "Structuring a Sustainable Letters of Marque Regime: How Commissioning Privateers Can Defeat the Somali Pirates," *California Law Review* 99 (2011): 819–884; Theodore T. Richard, "Reconsidering the Letter of Marque: Utilizing Private Security Providers Against Piracy," *Public Contract Law Journal* 39/3 (Spring 2010): 411–464; D. Joshua Staub, "Letters of Marque: A Short-Term Solution to an Age Old Problem," *Journal of Maritime Law and Commerce* 40/2 (April 2009): 261–269. For critique, see Patrick Cullen and Claude Berube, eds., *Maritime Private Security: Market Responses to Piracy, Terrorism and Waterborne Security Risks in the 21st Century* (London: Routledge 2012); Christopher Spearin, "Promising Privateers? Understanding the Constraints of Contemporary Private Security at Sea," *Naval War College Review* 67, no. 2 (2014): 97–116.

32. International Crisis Group, "Somalia: To Move beyond the Failed State," Africa Report 147 (2008), 12.

33. Human Rights Watch, "Harsh War, Harsh Peace: Abuses by al-Shabaab, the Transitional Federal Government, and AMISOM in Somalia" (2010), 2.

34. Andre Le Sage, *Stateless Justice in Somalia: Formal and Informal Rule of Law Initiatives* (Geneva: Centre for Humanitarian Dialogue, 2005), 7.

35. Ken Menkhaus, "Governance without Government in Somalia: Spoilers, State Building, and the Politics of Coping," *International Security* 31, no. 3 (2007), 103. The idea of a "mediated state" comes from Michael Barnett and Christoph Züercher, "The Peacebuilders' Contract: How External Statebuilding Reinforces Weak Statehood," in *The Dilemmas of Statebuilding: Confronting the Contradictions of Postwar Peace Operations*, edited by Roland Paris and Timothy D. Sisk (New York: Routledge, 2009), 27.

36. Le Sage, *Stateless Justice*, 8.

37. Menkhaus, "Governance without Government," 105–106.

12. Medieval Modernity

1. Christoph Reuter, "The Warlord of the Highway," *Vice Magazine* (November 2009) http://www.vice.com/print/warlord-of-the-highway-226-v16n11, accessed February 26, 2014; Dexter Filkins, "With U.S. Aid, Warlord Builds Afghan Empire," *New York Times*, June 5, 2010, A1; Dexter Filkins, "Convoy Guards in Afghanistan Face an Inquiry," *New York Times*, June 6, 2010, A1.

2. US Department of Defense, "Contractor Support of U.S. Operations in the USCENTCOM Area of Responsibility, Iraq, and Afghanistan, 4th Quarter FY 2010 Contractor Census," December 15, 2010.

3. According to reports, mercenaries waged a campaign of terror resulting in at least one hundred deaths and causing many hundreds more to flee their homes. Chen Zhi, "Over 100 People Killed in Southwest Cote d'Ivoire," *Xinhua News*, May 11, 2011, http://news.xinhuanet.com/english2010/world/2011-05/10/c_13867888.htm, accessed February 26, 2014; Matthew Russell Lee, "In Cote d'Ivoire Gbagbo Is Using Mercenaries, from Liberia, UN Says, US Unaware," *Inner City Press*, December 20, 2010.

4. Jennifer Elsea, *Private Security Contractors in Iraq: Background, Legal Status, and Other Issues* (Washington, DC: Congressional Research Service, 2008), 3.

5. Moshe Schwartz, *Department of Defense Contractors in Iraq and Afghanistan: Background and Analysis* (Washington, DC: Congressional Research Service, 2010), 3.

6. Susan Trevaskes, "The Private/Public Security Nexus in China," *Social Justice* 34, nos. 3–4 (2007): 38.

7. Ibid., 51.

8. Christian Ménard and Jean-Claude Viollet, *Rapport d'information par la commission de la défense nationale et des forces armees sur les sociétés militaires privées*, Assemblee Nationale, February 14, 2012, www.assemblee-nationale.fr.

9. "Russia Eyes Security Firms to Defend Assets Abroad," Reuters, October 28, 2010.

10. "New Information about Counternarcotics Contracts in Latin America," US Senate Committee on Homeland Security and Governmental Affairs Subcommittee on Contracting Oversight, June 7, 2011.

11. UN, "Secretary-General Reflects on 'Intervention' in Thirty-Fifth Annual Ditchley Foundation Lecture," UN Press Release SG/SM/6613, June 26, 1998, http://www.un.org/News/Press/docs/1998/19980626.sgsm6613.html, accessed February 26, 2014.

12. "Rwanda: How the Genocide Happened," *BBC News*, May 17, 2011.

13. Peter W. Singer, *Corporate Warriors: The Rise of the Privatized Military Industry* (Ithaca, NY: Cornell University Press, 2003), 185–186.

14. "Mercenaries in Africa: The Fog and Dogs of War," *Economist*, March 18, 2004.

15. Heidi Vogt and Rahim Faiez, "Afghan Starts to Close Private Security Firms," Associated Press, October 3, 2010.

16. *Warlord, Inc.: Extortion and Corruption along the U.S. Supply Chain in Afghanistan*, report before the Subcommittee on National Security and Foreign Affairs, US House of Representatives, 111th Congress (June 22, 2010), 2.

17. *Inquiry into the Role and Oversight of Private Security Contractors in Afghanistan*, report with additional views of the Committee on Armed Services, US Senate, 111th Congress (September 10, 2010), i.

18. Filkins, "Convoy Guards."

19. Ibid.; "Convoy Guards."

20. Ibid.; *Warlord, Inc.*

21. Steve Fainaru, *Big Boy Rules* (Philadelphia: Da Capo, 2008), 28–29; Deborah Avant, *The Market for Force: The Consequences of Privatizing Security* (Cambridge, UK: Cambridge University Press, 2005), 17.

22. Permanent Representative of Switzerland to the UN, letter dated October 2, 2008, addressed to the Secretary-General of the Security Council, UN Soc. A/63/467-S/2008/636 (October 6, 2008). Participants included Afghanistan, Angola, Australia, Austria, Canada, China, France, Germany, Iraq, Poland, Sierra Leone, South Africa, Sweden, Switzerland, the United Kingdom, Ukraine, and the United States.

23. UN documents A/HRC/15/25 and A/65/325. See also José L. Gómez del Prado, "A UN Convention to Regulate PMSCs?," *Criminal Justice Ethics* 31, no. 3 (2012): 262–286.

24. International Code of Conduct for Private Security Service Providers, http://www.icoc-psp. org/Home_Page.html, accessed February 26, 2014.

25. "Dogs of War," *Lateline*, Australian Broadcasting Corporation, May 18, 2000, http://www. abc.net.au/lateline/archives/s128621.htm, accessed February 26, 2014. On UN guidance for armed contractors on ships in "high-risk areas," see International Maritime Organisation, *Interim Guidance to Private Maritime Security Companies Providing Privately Contracted Armed Security Personnel on Board Ships in the High Risk Area*, MSC.1/Circ.1443, May 25, 2012.

26. The Working Group on the Use of Mercenaries as a Means of Violating Human Rights and Impeding the Exercise of the Rights of Peoples to Self-Determination was established in July 2005, pursuant to Commission on Human Rights resolution 2005/2. For source documents on UN use of private security, see UN Security Management System Security Policy Manual (Chapter IV, Section I: Armed Private Security Companies), http://www. ohchr.org/Documents/Issues/Mercenaries/WG/StudyPMSC/UNSecurityPolicyManual. pdf, accessed February 26, 2014; UN Security Management System Operations Manual, Guidelines on the Use of Armed Security Services from Private Security Companies, Annex A: Statement of Works, and Annex B: Model Contract, http://www.ohchr.org/Documents/ Issues/Mercenaries/WG/StudyPMSC/GuidelinesOnUseOfArmedSecurityServices.pdf, accessed February 26, 2014.

BIBLIOGRAPHY

Agnew, John. "The Territorial Trap: The Geographical Assumptions of International Relations Theory." *Review of International Political Economy* 1, no. 1 (1994): 53–80.

Al-Baddarin, Bassam. "Al-Qaeda Has Drawn Up a Working Strategy Lasting until 2020." *Al-Quds al-Arabi*, March 11, 2005.

Alighieri, Dante. *The Divine Comedy, Inferno*, rev. ed., translated by Mark Musa. New York: Penguin, 2002.

Alsayad, Nezar, and Ananya Roy. "Medieval Modernity: On Citizenship and Urbanism in a Global Era," *Space and Polity* 10, no. 1 (April 2006): 1–20.

Ambah, Faiza Saleh. "Saudi Women Rise in Defense of the Veil." *Washington Post*, May 31, 2006.

Ames, Glenn J. *The Globe Encompassed: The Age of European Discovery, 1500–1700*. Upper Saddle River, NJ: Prentice Hall, 2008.

Amnesty International. "Amnesty International's Statute." http://www.amnesty.org/en/who-we-are/accountability/statute, accessed February 21, 2014.

———. "Campaign for International Justice." http://www.amnesty.org/en/international-justice/background, accessed September 30, 2010.

———. *Fatal Insecurity Attacks on Aid Workers and Rights Defenders in Somalia*. London: Amnesty International, 2008.

Andersen, Louise. *Post-Conflict Security Sector Reform and the Challenge of Ownership: The Case of Liberia*. Copenhagen: Danish Institute for International Studies, 2006.

Anderson, Benedict. *Imagined Communities: Reflections on the Original Spread of Nationalism*, new ed. London: Verso, 2006.

Anderson, James. "The Shifting Stage of Politics: New Medieval and Postmodern Territorialities?" *Environment and Planning D: Society and Space* 14, no. 2 (1996): 133–154.

Anderson, M. S. *Europe in the Eighteenth Century, 1713–1783*. London: Longman, 1987.

———. *The War of the Austrian Succession, 1740–1748*. London: Longman, 1995.

Ansorge, Josef Teboho, and Nana Akua Antwi-Ansorge. "Monopoly, Legitimacy, Force: DDR-SSR Liberia." In *The Monopoly of Force*, edited by Melanne Civic and Michael Miklaucic, 265–284. Washington, DC: National Defense University Press, 2011.

Arena, Michael P. "Hizballah's Global Criminal Operations." *Global Crime* 7, no. 3 (2006): 454–470.

Arend, Anthony C. *Legal Rules and International Society*. Oxford: Oxford University Press, 1999.

Armstrong, Stephen. *War plc: The rise of the new corporate mercenary*. London: Faber & Faber, 2009.

"Army Adds Charges against Rampage Suspect: 32 Counts of Attempted Murder in Addition to Earlier Murder Charges." Associated Press, December 2, 2009.

Arquilla, John, and David Ronfeldt. *Networks and Netwars: The Future of Terror, Crime, and Militancy*. Santa Monica, CA: RAND Corporation, 2001.

Art, Robert J., and Kenneth N. Waltz. *The Use of Force: International Politics and Foreign Policy*. Lanham, MD: University Press of America, 1983.

Asian Development Bank. "ADB's Approach to Weakly Performing Developing Member Countries." Discussion paper for the Asian Development Fund IX Donors' Meeting, March 2004.

Atwan, Abdel Bari. *The Secret History of Al Qaeda*. Berkeley: University of California Press, 2008.

AUSAid. "Australian Aid: Investing in Growth, Stability and Prosperity." September 2002.

Australian Defence Force. *2005–06 Defence Annual Report*. Canberra, 2006.

Avant, Deborah. *The Market for Force: The Consequences of Privatizing Security*. Cambridge, UK: Cambridge University Press, 2005.

Avant, Deborah D., and Lee Sigelman. "Private Security and Democracy: Lessons from the US in Iraq." *Security Studies* 19, no. 2 (2010): 230–265.

"Awarding Liu Xiaobo Nobel Peace Prize May Harm China-Norway Relations, Says FM Spokesman." *Xinhua News*, October 8, 2010.

Ayoob, Mohammed. "Humanitarian Intervention and State Sovereignty." *International Journal of Human Rights* 6, no. 1 (2002): 81–102.

Badie, Bertrand. *La fin des territoires: Essai sur le desordre international et sur l'utiliti sociale du respect*. Paris: Fayard, 1995.

Bahadur, Jay. *The Pirates of Somalia: Inside their Hidden World*. New York: Random House, 2011.

Bailyn, Bernard. *The Ideological Origins of the American Revolution*. Cambridge, MA: Belknap, 1992.

Bandy, Joe, and Jackie Smith, ed. *Coalitions across Borders: Transnational Protest and the Neoliberal Order*. Lanham, MD: Rowman & Littlefield, 2004.

Barbarossa, Frederick. "Manifesto of the Emperor (Oct. 1157)." In *Select Historical Documents of the Middle Ages*, edited and translated by Ernest F. Henderson, 412–414. London: G. Bell, 1905.

Barlow, Eeben. *Executive Outcomes: Against All Odds*. Alberton, South Africa: Galago, 2007.

Barnett, Michael, and Christoph Züercher. "The Peacebuilders' Contract: How External Statebuilding Reinforces Weak Statehood." In *The Dilemmas of Statebuilding: Confronting the Contradictions of Postwar Peace Operations*, edited by Roland Paris and Timothy D. Sisk, 23–52. New York: Routledge, 2009.

Bartusis, Mark C. *The Late Byzantine Army: Arms and Society, 1204–1453*. Philadelphia: University of Pennsylvania Press, 1997.

Battle in Seattle. DVD. Directed by Stuart Townsend. Redwood Palms Pictures, 2007.

Bauman, Zygmunt. *Globalization: The Human Consequences*. New York: Columbia University Press, 2000.

Bayley, Charles C. *Mercenaries for the Crimea: The German, Swiss, and Italian Legions in British Service, 1854–1856*. Quebec: McGill-Queen's University Press, 1977.

———. *War and Society in Renaissance Florence*. Toronto: University of Toronto Press, 1961.

Bearne, Susanna. *National Security Decision-Making Structures and Security Sector Reform*. Cambridge, UK: RAND Europe, 2006.

Beck, Ulrich. *Risk Society: Towards a New Modernity*. London: Sage, 1992.

———. *What Is Globalization?* Cambridge: Polity, 2000.

Belasco, Amy. *Cost of Iraq, Afghanistan, and Other Global War on Terror Operations since 9/11*. Darby, PA: Diane, 2009.

Bendell, Jem. *Debating NGO Accountability: UN-NGLS Development Dossier*. Geneva: United Nations, 2006.

Benedetti, Carlo. "Islamic and Christian Inspired Relief NGOs: Between Tactical Collaboration and Strategic Diffidence?" *Journal of International Development* 18, no. 6 (2006): 849–859.

Bergesen, Albert. *Studies of the Modern World-System*. New York: Academic, 1980.

Bergreen, Laurence. *Marco Polo: From Venice to Xanadu*. New York: Vintage, 2008.

Berschinski, Robert G. *Africom's Dilemma: The "Global War on Terrorism," "Capacity Building," Humanitarianism, and the Future of US Security Policy in Africa*. Carlisle, PA: Strategic Studies Institute, 2007.

Berube, Claude, and Patrick Cullen, eds., Maritime Private Security: Market Responses to Piracy, Terrorism and Waterborne Security Risks in the 21st Century. New York: Routledge, 2012.

Berzins, Chris, and Patrick Cullen. "Terrorism and Neo-Medievalism." *Civil Wars* 6, no. 2 (2003): 8–32.

Best, Geoffrey. *Humanity in Warfare*. New York: Columbia University Press, 1980.

Best, Steven, and Anthony J. Nocella, Jr., eds. *Terrorists or Freedom Fighters? Reflections on the Liberation of Animals.* New York: Lantern, 2004.

Black, Jeremy. *European Warfare, 1660–1815.* New Haven, CT: Yale University Press, 1994.

Blackbourn, David. *History of Germany, 1780–1918: The Long Nineteenth Century.* Oxford: Wiley-Blackwell, 2003.

"Blackwater USA." Hearing before the Committee on Oversight and Government Reform, US House of Representatives. 110th Congress, October 2, 2007 (statement of Eric Prince).

Blaney, John. Interview by Ky Luu, September 11, 2009. http://www.youtube.com/watch?v=cdGGs6QGaCU.

Blaney, John, Jacques Paul Klein, and Sean McFate. "Wider Lessons for Peacebuilding: Security Sector Reform in Liberia." Policy Analysis Brief. Iowa: Stanley Foundation, 2010.

Bøås, Morten, and Karianne Stig. "Security Sector Reform in Liberia: An Uneven Partnership without Local Ownership." *Journal of Intervention and Statebuilding* 4, no. 3 (2010): 285–303.

Bobbitt, Phillip. *The Shield of Achilles: War, Peace, and the Course of History.* New York: Anchor, 2002.

———. *Terror and Consent: The Wars for the Twenty-First Century.* New York: Alfred A. Knopf, 2008.

Bornschier, Volker, Christopher Chase-Dunn, and Richard Rubinson. "Cross-National Evidence of the Effects of Foreign Investment and Aid on Economic Growth and Inequality: A Survey of Findings and a Reanalysis." *American Journal of Sociology* 84, no. 3 (1978): 651–683.

Boucher, David. *Political Theories of International Relations: From Thucydides to the Present.* Oxford: Oxford University Press, 1998.

Boutros-Ghali, Boutros. "An Agenda for Peace: Preventive Diplomacy, Peacemaking and Peace-Keeping." *International Relations* 11, no. 3 (1992): 201–218.

Boven, Maarten W. van. *Towards a New Age of Partnership (TANAP): An Ambitious World Heritage Project.* Paris: UNESCO Memory of the World, 2002.

Branigan, Tania. "Liu Xiaobo Nobel Win Prompts Chinese Fury." *Guardian,* October 8, 2010.

Brauer, Jurgen, and Hubert Van Tuyll. *Castles, Battles, and Bombs: How Economics Explains Military History.* Chicago: University of Chicago Press, 2008.

Brooks, Doug. "Write a Cheque, End a War." *Conflict Trends* 3, no. 1 (2000): 33–35.

Brown, James. "Pirates and Privateers: Managing the Indian Ocean's Private Security Boom." Lowy Institute for International Policy, September 12, 2012.

Brown, Judith M. *Modern India: The Origin of an Asian Democracy.* Oxford: Oxford University Press, 1994.

Brown, Michael E., Owen R. Coté, Jr., Sean M. Lynn-Jones, and Steven E. Miller, eds. *Theories of War and Peace.* Cambridge, MA: MIT Press, 1998.

Brown, Seyom. *International Relations in a Changing Global System: Toward a Theory of the World Polity.* Boulder: Westview, 1996.

Bull, Hedley. *The Anarchical Society: A Study of Order in World Politics.* New York: Columbia University Press, 2002.

———. *Justice in International Relations: The 1983 Hagey Lectures.* Waterloo, Ontario: University of Waterloo, 1994.

Burbach, R., and W. Robinson, "The Fin de Siècle Debate: Globalization as Epochal Shift." *Science & Society* 63, no. 1 (1999): 10–39.

Bush, George W. *The National Security Strategy of the United States of America.* Washington, DC: White House, 2002.

Bush, George W. "President Salutes Troops of 10th Mountain Division," July 19, 2002.

Butters, Andrew Lee. "Saudi's Small Steps." *Time,* October 19, 2009.

Bybee, Ashley-Louise. "The Narco-Curse in West Africa." *New Voices in Public Policy* 3, no. 2 (2009): 1–22.

Caferro, William. "Continuity, Long-Term Service, and Permanent Force: A Reassessment of the Florentine Army in the Fourteenth Century." *Journal of Modern History* 80, no. 2 (2008): 303–322.

———. "Italy and the Companies of Adventure in the Fourteenth Century." *Historian* 58, no. 4 (1996): 795–810.

———. *John Hawkwood: An English Mercenary in Fourteenth-Century Italy.* Baltimore: Johns Hopkins University Press, 2006.

——. *Mercenary Companies and the Decline of Siena*. Baltimore: Johns Hopkins University Press, 1998.

——. "Warfare and Economy in Renaissance Italy." *Journal of Interdisciplinary History* 39, no. 2 (2008): 169–207.

Campbell, Tom. "A Human Rights Approach to Development of Voluntary Codes of Conduct for Multinational Corporations." *Business Ethics Quarterly* 16, no. 2 (2006): 255–269.

Cantir, Cristian, and Philip Schrodt. "Neomedievalism in the Twenty-First Century: Warlords, Gangs, and Transnational Militarized Actors as a Challenge to Sovereign Preeminence." Paper presented at Annual Meeting of the International Studies Association, New Orleans, 2010.

Caporaso, J. A. "Changes in the Westphalian Order: Territory, Public Authority, and Sovereignty." *International Studies Review* 2, no. 2 (2000): 1–28.

"Captured Mumbai Terrorist Reveals Plot to Slaughter 5000." *Herald Sun*, December 1, 2008.

Carafano, James Jay. *Private Sector, Public Wars: Contractors in Combat—Afghanistan, Iraq, and Future Conflicts*. Westport, CT: Praeger Security International, 2008.

Carr, E. H., and Michael Cox. *The Twenty Years' Crisis, 1919–1939: An Introduction to the Study of International Relations*. New York: Palgrave Macmillan, 2001.

Carsten, F. L. *The New Cambridge Modern History, Vol. 5: 1648–88. The Ascendancy of France*. Cambridge, UK: Cambridge University Press, 1961.

——. *Princes and Parliaments in Germany*. Oxford: Clarendon, 1959.

Carvalho, Soniya. *Engaging with Fragile States*. Washington, DC: World Bank, 2006.

Cerny, Phillip G. "Neomedievalism, Civil War and the New Security Dilemma: Globalisation as Durable Disorder." *Civil Wars* 1, no. 1 (1998): 36–64.

Chalk, Peter. *The Maritime Dimension of International Security: Terrorism, Piracy, and Challenges for the United States*. Santa Monica, CA: RAND Corporation, 2008.

Chatterjee, Pratap. "U.S. Dyncorp Oversight in Afghanistan Faulted." Inter Press Service, February 27, 2010.

"China Protests as Liu Xiaobo Wins Nobel Prize." *RTÉ News and Current Affairs*, October 8, 2010.

"China Questions 'True Intentions' of Award of Nobel Peace Prize to Liu Xiaobo." *Xinhua News*, October 12, 2010. http://news.xinhuanet.com/english2010/china/2010-10/12/c_13553857.htm, accessed February 25, 2014.

Chowdhury, Abdur R. "A Causal Analysis of Defense Spending and Economic Growth." *Journal of Conflict Resolution* 35, no. 1 (1991): 80–97.

Christensen, Jon. "Asking Do-Gooders to Prove They Do Good." *New York Times*, January 3, 2004.

Clark, John. "The Role of Non-Profit Organisations in Development: The Experience of the World Bank." Paper for the International Conference on the Non-Profit Sector and Development, Tsinghua University, Beijing, July 1999.

Clarke, Ryan, and Stuart Lee. "The PIRA, D-Company, and the Crime-Terror Nexus." *Terrorism and Political Violence* 20, no. 3 (2008): 376–395.

Clausewitz, Carl von, et al. *On War*. Princeton, NJ: Princeton University Press, 1976.

CNN. "Al-Shabaab." Accessed November 14, 2010. http://topics.cnn.com/topics/al_shabaab, accessed November 14, 2010.

Coady, C. A. J. "Mercenary Morality." In *International Law and Armed Conflict*, edited by A. G. D. Bradnev, 55–69. Stuttgard: Franz Steiner, 1992.

Coalition for the International Criminal Court. http://www.iccnow.org/?mod=home, accessed October 1, 2010.

Coalition Provisional Authority. Order Number 17 (Revised), Status of the Coalition Provisional Authority, MNF–Iraq, Certain Missions and Personnel in Iraq, June 27, 2007.

Cockayne, James. "Regulating Private Military and Security Companies: The Content, Negotiation, Weaknesses and Promise of the Montreux Document." *Journal of Conflict and Security Law* 13, no. 3 (2008): 401–428.

Cockett, Richard. *Thinking the Unthinkable: Think Tanks and the Economic Counter Revolution, 1931–1983*. New York: HarperCollins, 1995.

Cohen, Marc J., and Tara R. Gingerich. *Protect and Serve or Train and Equip? U.S. Security Assistance and Protection of Civilians*. Washington, DC: Oxfam America, 2009.

Coker, Christopher. *Barbarous Philosophers: Reflections on the Nature of War from Heraclitus to Heisenberg*. New York: Columbia University Press, 2010.

————. *Ethics and War in the 21st Century.* London: Routledge, 2009.

————. *Humane Warfare.* New York: Routledge, 2001.

————. "Outsourcing War." *Cambridge Review of International Affairs* 13, no. 1 (1999): 95–113.

————. *Waging War without Warriors?: The Changing Culture of Military Conflict.* Boulder, CO: Lynne Rienner, 2002.

————. *War and the 20th Century: A Study of War and Modern Consciousness.* Washington, DC: Potomac Books, 1994.

————. *War in an Age of Risk.* Cambridge, UK: Polity, 2009.

Collier, Paul. *The Bottom Billion: Why the Poorest Countries Are Failing and What Can Be Done about It.* New York: Oxford University Press, 2008.

————et al. *Breaking the Conflict Trap: Civil War and Development Policy.* Washington, DC: World Bank, 2003.

Commission on Army Acquisition and Program Management in Expeditionary Operations. Urgent Reform Required: Army Expeditionary Contracting "Gansler Report"), October 31, 2007.

Commission on Wartime Contracting in Iraq and Afghanistan. *Transforming Wartime Contracting Controlling Costs, Reducing Risks.* Washington, DC: US Congress, 2011.

Committee on Payment and Settlement Systems. *Progress in Reducing Foreign Exchange Settlement Risk.* Basel, Switzerland: Bank for International Settlements, 2008.

Comprehensive Peace Agreement between the Government of Liberia and the Liberians United for Reconciliation and Democracy (LURD) and the Movement for Democracy in Liberia (MODEL) and Political Parties." August 18, 2003.

Contamine, Phillipe. *War in the Middle Ages.* Oxford: Wiley-Blackwell, 1986.

Contractors' Support of US Operations in Iraq. Washington, DC: US Congressional Budget Office, 2008.

Cook, Nicholas. *Liberia's Post-War Development: Key Issues and US Assistance.* Washington, DC: Congressional Research Service, 2010.

————. *Liberia's Post-War Recovery: Key Issues and Developments.* Washington, DC: Congressional Research Service, 2005.

Cooper, Robert. *The Post Modern State and the World Order.* London: Demos, 2000.

Crane, David. Statement on International Women's Day. Press release, Special Court for Sierra Leone, Office of the Prosecutor, March 8, 2003.

Creveld, Martin van. "The New Middle Ages." *Foreign Policy* 119 (Summer 2000): 29–69.

————. *The Transformation of War.* New York: Free Press, 1991.

Crosette, Barbara. "UN Chief Wants Faster Action to Avoid Slaughter in Civil Wars." *New York Times,* September 21, 1999.

Cutler, A. Claire. "Critical Reflections on the Westphalian Assumptions of International Law and Organization: A Crisis of Legitimacy." *Review of International Studies* 27, no. 2 (2001): 133–150.

Daragahi, Borzou, and Mark Mazzetti. "U.S. Military Covertly Pays to Run Stories in Iraqi Press; Troops Write Articles Presented as News Reports, Some Officers Object to the Practice." *Los Angeles Times,* August 30, 2005.

Davies, Norman. *Europe: A History.* New York: HarperCollins, 1998.

Davis, Mike. *Planet of Slums.* New York: Verso, 2006.

Defense Science Board. *Institutionalizing Stability Operations within DOD: Report of the Defense Science Board Task Force.* September 2005.

Deger, Saadet. "Economic Development and Defense Expenditure." *Economic Development and Cultural Change* 35, no. 1 (1986): 179–196.

Deibert, Ronald J. "Exorcismus Theoriae: Pragmatism, Metaphors, and the Return of the Medieval in IR Theory." *European Journal of International Relations* 3, no. 2 (1997): 167–192.

Delahunty, Robert J., and John Yoo. "The 'Bush Doctrine': Can Preventive War Be Justified?" *Harvard Journal of Law and Public Policy* 32 (Summer 2009): 843–865.

DeLong, J. Bradford. "Estimating World GDP, One Million BC–Present." May 24, 1998.

Demirovic, Alex. "NGOs: Social Movements in Global Order?" Paper presented at the American Sociological Association Conference, New York, 1996.

Dempsey, Thomas. *Security Sector Reform in Liberia Part I: An Assessment of Defense Reform*, Issue Paper 2008. Carlisle, PA: Peacekeeping and Stability Operations Institute, US Army War College, 2008.

Deng, Francis Mading, Sadikiel Kimaro, Terrence Lyons, Donald Rothchild, and I. William Zartman. *Sovereignty as Responsibility: Conflict Management in Africa.* Washington, DC: Brookings Institution, 1996.

Des Forges, Alison. *"Leave None to Tell the Story": Genocide in Rwanda.* Human Rights Watch, 1999.

Dicklitch, Susan, and Heather Rice. "The Mennonite Central Committee (MCC) and Faith-Based NGO Aid to Africa." *Development in Practice* 14, no. 5 (2004): 660–672.

"Diggin' In: AFL Soldiers Complete FTX." *Military.com*, March 6, 2009.

"Doctrine for Joint Operations." Joint Publication (JP) 3.0, March 22, 2010. http://www.dtic.mil/doctrine/new_pubs/jp3_0.pdf.

"Dogs of War." *Lateline*, Australian Broadcasting Corporation, May 18, 2000. http://www.abc.net.au/lateline/archives/s128621.htm, accessed February 26, 2014.

Donmoyer, Ryan J. "83 Per cent of Companies Had Tax-Haven Units, GAO Says." *Bloomberg News*, January 16, 2010. http://www.bloomberg.com/apps/news?pid=newsarchive&sid=aK0aqjswiSCA, accessed February 25, 2014.

Donnelly, Jack. "International Human Rights: A Regime Analysis." *International Organization* 40, no. 3 (1986): 599–642.

Douzinas, Costas. *The End of Human Rights: Critical Legal Thought at the Turn of the Century.* Oxford: Hart, 2000.

Dower, John W. *Embracing Defeat: Japan in the Aftermath of World War II.* New York: Penguin, 2000.

Duffield, Mark. "Post-Modern Conflict: Warlords, Post-Adjustment States and Private Protection." *Civil Wars* 1, no. 1 (1998): 65–102.

Dull, Paul S. *A Battle History of the Imperial Japanese Navy, 1941–1945.* Annapolis, MD: Naval Institute Press, 2007.

Dunigan, Molly. *Victory for Hire: Private Security Companies' Impact on Military Effectiveness.* Stanford: Stanford University Press, 2011.

Dunn-Marcos, Robin, Konia T. Kolleholn, Bernard Ngovo, and Emily Russ. *The Liberians: An Introduction to Their History and Culture.* Washington, DC: Center for Applied Linguistics, 2005.

Dziedzic, Michael J., and Robert M. Perito. *Haiti: Confronting the Gangs of Port-Au-Prince.* Washington, DC: US Institute of Peace, 2008.

Ebo, Adedeji. "The Challenges and Opportunities of Security Sector Reform in Post-Conflict Liberia." Occasional Paper no. 9. Geneva: Geneva Centre for Democratic Control of Armed Forces, 2005.

———. "Liberia Case Study: Outsourcing SSR to Foreign Companies," in *No Ownership, No Commitment: A Guide to Local Ownership of Security Sector Reform*, edited by Laurie Nathan. Birmingham, UK: University of Birmingham, 2007.

Eco, Umberto. "Travels in Hyperreality" (1990): 61–72.

Economic and Social Council of the United Nations, Resolution 288 (X). "The ECOSOC Statute for Non-Governmental Organisations," February 27, 1950.

Economist. "The State of the State." In *The World in 2010* (2010).

Elgström, Ole. "Norm Negotiations: The Construction of New Norms Regarding Gender and Development in EU Foreign Aid Policy." *Journal of European Public Policy* 7, no. 3 (2000): 457–475.

Elliott, Andrea. "The Jihadist Next Door." *New York Times*, January 27, 2010.

Elliott, Justin. "Hundreds of Afghanistan Contractor Deaths Go Unreported." Salon.com. July 15, 2010. http://www.salon.com/2010/07/15/afghan_war_contractors_dying, accesssed February 14, 2014.

Ellis, Stephen. *The Mask of Anarchy: The Destruction of Liberia and the Religious Roots of an African Civil War.* London: Hurst, 2001.

Elsea, Jennifer. *International Criminal Court: Overview and Selected Legal Issues.* Washington, DC: Congressional Research Service, 2002.

———. *Private Security Contractors in Iraq: Background, Legal Status, and Other Issues.* Washington, DC: Congressional Research Service, 2008.

Engler, Yves. "The Mercenaries and the NGOs." *Counterpunch*, August 26, 2010. http://www.counterpunch.org/2010/08/26/the-mercenaries-and-the-ngos/print, accessed February 25, 2014.

Epley, William W. "Civilian Support of Field Armies." *Army Logistician* 22 (November–December 1990): 30–35.

Evans, Graham, and Richard Newnham. *The Penguin Dictionary of International Relations.* London: Penguin, 1998.

"Ex-CIA Director James Woolsey." Transcript. *Good Morning America*, October 10, 2010. http://abcnews.go.com/US/story?id=92346&page=1, accessed October 24, 2010.

"Excerpts from Army Maj. Gen. Eldon A. Bargewell's Report," *Washington Post*, April 21, 2007. http://www.washingtonpost.com/wp-dyn/content/article/2007/04/20/AR2007042002309.html, accessed February 25, 2014.

Fainaru, Steve. *Big Boy Rules.* Philadelphia: Da Capo, 2008.

Fainaru, Steve, and Alec Klein. "In Iraq, a Private Realm of Intelligence-Gathering." *Washington Post*, July 1, 2007. http://www.washingtonpost.com/wp-dyn/content/article/2007/06/30/AR2007063001075_pf.html, accessed February 14, 2014.

"Faisal Shahzad Made Suicide Video—Al Arabiya Airs Failed Times Square Bomber Tape." *Al-Arabiya*, July 14, 2010.

Farah, Douglas, and Stephen Braun. *Merchant of Death: Money, Guns, Planes, and the Man Who Makes War Possible.* New York: John Wiley, 2007.

Faris, Stephan. "Charles Taylor Leaves Liberia." *Time*, August 11, 2003. http://content.time.com/time/world/article/0,8599,474987,00.html, accessed February 25, 2014.

———. "War Returns to Monrovia." *Time*, July 20, 2003.

Farmer, Brian R. *The Question of Dependency and Economic Development: A Quantitative Analysis.* Lanham, MD: Lexington, 1999.

Fay, Sidney B. "The Beginnings of the Standing Army in Prussia." *American Historical Review* 22, no. 4 (1917): 763–777.

Federal Bureau of Investigation. "Going Global on Gangs: New Partnership Targets MS-13," October 10, 2007. http://www.fbi.gov/news/stories/2007/october/ms13tag_101007, accessed November 20, 2010.

Feld, Werner J., Robert S. Jordan, and Leon Hurwitz. *International Organizations: A Comparative Approach.* Westport, CT: Praeger Security International, 1994.

Ferreira, Francisco H. G., and Martin Ravallion. "Global Poverty and Inequality: A Review of the Evidence." World Bank Policy Research Working Paper. Washington, DC: World Bank, 2008.

Ferris, Elizabeth. "Faith-Based and Secular Humanitarian Organizations." *IRRC* 87, no. 858 (2005): 311–325.

Fidler, David P., and Jennifer M. Welsh. *Empire and Community: Edmund Burke's Writings and Speeches on International Relations.* Boulder, CO: Westview, 1999.

Filkins, Dexter. "With U.S. Aid, Warlord Builds Afghan Empire." *New York Times*, June 5, 2010, A1.

———. "Convoy Guards in Afghanistan Face an Inquiry." *New York Times*, June 6, 2010, A1.

Filkins, Dexter, and Mark Mazzetti. "Contractors Tied to Effort to Track and Kill Militants." *New York Times*, March 24, 2010.

Finckenauer, James. "Meeting the Challenge of Transnational Crime." *Crime and Justice International* 17, no. 48 (2001): 2–7.

Finnemore, Martha. "International Organizations as Teachers of Norms: The United Nations Education, Scientific, and Cultural Organization and Science Policy." *International Organization* 47, no. 4 (1993): 565–597.

Finnemore, Martha, and Kathryn Sikkink. "International Norm Dynamics and Political Change." *International Organization* 52, no. 4 (1998): 887–917.

Fireman, Ken, and Robin Stringer. "Blackwater Denies Any Wrongdoing in Shooting Incident." *Bloomberg News*, September 17, 2007.

Firestone. "Liberia Statistics." http://www.firestonenaturalrubber.com/documents/StatSheet Narrative.pdf, accessed February 25, 2014.

Floud, Roderick, and Paul Johnson. *The Cambridge Economic History of Modern Britain.* Cambridge, UK: Cambridge University Press, 2004.

Foot, Rosemary. *Rights beyond Borders: The Global Community and the Struggle Over Human Rights in China*. Oxford: Oxford University Press, 2001.

Ford, Daniel. *Flying Tigers: Claire Chennault and His American Volunteers, 1941–1942*. New York: Harper, 2007.

Fowler, Kenneth. "Sir John Hawkwood and the English Condottieri in Trecento Italy." *Renaissance Studies* 12, no. 1 (1998): 131–148.

Franco, Celinda. *The MS 13 and 18th Street Gangs: Emerging Transnational Gang Threats*. Washington, DC: Congressional Research Service, 2007.

Frank, Thomas. "Government by Contractor Is a Disgrace: Many Jobs Are Best Left to Federal Workers." *Wall Street Journal*, November 26, 2008. http://online.wsj.com/news/articles/SB122765980278958481, accessed February 15, 2014.

Franke, Volker, and Marc Von Boemcken. "Private Guns: The Social Identity of Security Contractors." *Journal of Conflict Studies Online* 29 (2009). http://journals.hil.unb.ca/index.php/JCS/article/view/15237/24427.

Friedman, Milton. "Public Schools: Make Them Private." *Education Economics* 5, no. 3 (1997): 341–344.

Friedrichs, Jörg. "The Meaning of New Medievalism." *European Journal of International Relations* 7, no. 4 (2001): 475–501.

"From Horror to Hopelessness." Human Rights Watch, March 29, 2009. http://www.hrw.org/en/reports/2009/03/29/horror-helplessness-0?print.

Frontline. Interview with Doug Brooks. March 22, 2005. http://www.pbs.org/wgbh/pages/frontline/shows/warriors/interviews/brooks.html, accessed February 25, 2014.

———. Interview with Peter Singer. March 22, 2005. http://www.pbs.org/wgbh/pages/frontline/shows/warriors/interviews/singer/html, accessed February 25, 2014.

Fuest, Veronika. "Contested Inclusions: Pitfalls of NGO Peace-Building Activities in Liberia." *Africa Spectrum* 45, no. 2 (2010): 3–33.

Fukuyama, Francis. "After Neoconservatism." *New York Times*, February 19, 2006.

———. "The End of History?" *National Interest* (Summer 1989): 3–18.

———. *The End of History and the Last Man*. New York: Free Press, 2006.

———. "History and September 11." In *Worlds in Collision: Terror and the Future of Global Order*, edited by Ken Booth and Tim Dunne, 27–36. New York: Newsweek, 2002.

———, ed. *Nation-Building: Beyond Afghanistan and Iraq*. Baltimore: Johns Hopkins University Press, 2005.

Fulcher, James. *Capitalism: A Very Short Introduction*. Oxford: Oxford University Press, 2004.

Furber, Holden. *Rival Empires of Trade in the Orient, 1600–1800*, 2 vols. Minneapolis: University of Minnesota Press, 1976.

Galula, David. *Counterinsurgency Warfare: Theory and Practice*. Westport, CT: Praeger Security International, 2006.

Gamble, Andrew. "Regional Blocs, World Order and the New Medievalism." In *European Union and New Regionalism: Regional Actors and Global Governance in a Post-Hegemonic Era*, edited by Mario Telo, 21–36. Burlington, VT: Ashgate, 2007.

Garraway, Charles. "Superior Orders and the International Criminal Court: Justice Delivered or Justice Denied." *IRRC* 836 (1999): 785–794.

Gates, Robert M. "A Balanced Strategy: Reprogramming the Pentagon for a New Age." *Foreign Affairs* (January–February 2010): 28–41.

———. "Helping Others Defense Themselves: The Future of U.S. Security Assistance." *Foreign Affairs* (May–June 2010): 2–6.

Gates, Bob, Secretary of Defense. "Strategic and Operational Planning for Operational Contract Support (OCS) and Workforce Mix," memorandum, US Department of Defense, January 24, 2011.

Gerth, H. H., and C. Wright Mills, eds. *From Max Weber: Essays in Sociology*. London: Routledge, 2003.

Gettleman, Jeffrey. "Ethiopia Launches Open War in Somalia." *New York Times News Service*, December 25, 2006. http://www.utsandiego.com/uniontrib/20061225/news_7n25somalia.html, accessed February 26, 2014.

———. "Somalia's Pirates Flourish in a Lawless Nation." *New York Times*, October 31, 2008.

Gettleman, Jeffrey, Mark Mazzetti, and Eric Schmitt, "U.S. Relies on Contractors in Somalia Conflict," *New York Times*, August 10, 2011.

Giddens, Anthony. *Modernity and Self-Identity: Self and Society in the Late Modern Age*. Stanford, CA: Stanford University Press, 1991.

Gilboa, Eytan. "The CNN Effect: The Search for a Communication Theory of International Relations." *Political Communication* 22, no. 1 (2005): 27–44.

Gilligan, Andrew. "Inside Lt Col Spicer's New Model Army." *Sunday Telegraph*, November 22, 1998.

Gilpin, Robert. *The Challenge of Global Capitalism: The World Economy in the 21st Century*. Princeton, NJ: Princeton University Press, 2002.

———. *The Political Economy of International Relations*. Princeton, NJ: Princeton University Press, 1987.

Gilpin, Robert, and Jean M. Gilpin. *Global Political Economy*. Princeton, NJ: Princeton University Press, 2001.

Glanz, James. "Modern Mercenaries on the Iraqi Frontier." *New York Times*, April 4, 2004.

Global Security. "Somalia Civil War," http://www.globalsecurity.org/military/world/war/somalia/htm, accessed February 26, 2014.

Goertz, Gary, and Paul F. Diehl. "Toward a Theory of International Norms: Some Conceptual and Measurement Issues." *Journal of Conflict Resolution* 36, no. 4 (1992): 634–664.

Gómez del Prado, José L. "A UN Convention to Regulate PMSCs?," *Criminal Justice Ethics* 31, no. 3 (2012): 262–286.

Goodrick-Clarke, Nicholas. *The Occult Roots of Nazism: Secret Aryan Cults and Their Influence on Nazi Ideology*. New York: New York University Press, 1993.

Gordon, Glenna. "In Liberia, Sirleaf's Past Sullies Her Clean Image." *Time*, July 3, 2009.

Gottlieb, Gidon. *Nation against State: A New Approach to Ethnic Conflict and the Decline of Sovereignty*. New York: Council on Foreign Relations Press, 1993.

Government Accountability Office. *Afghanistan Security: Afghan Army Growing, but Additional Trainers Needed; Long-Term Costs Not Determined*. Washington, DC: Government Accountability Office, 2011.

———. *Afghanistan Security: Department of Defense Effort to Train Afghan Police Relies on Contractor Personnel to Fill Skill and Resource Gaps*. Washington, DC: Government Accountability Office, 2012.

———. *Contingency Contracting: DOD, State, and USAID Continue to Face Challenges in Tracking Contractor Personnel and Contracts in Iraq and Afghanistan*. Washington, DC: Government Accountability Office, 2009.

———. *Defense Management: DOD Needs to Reexamine Its Extensive Reliance on Contractors and Continue to Improve Management and Oversight*. Washington, DC: Government Accountability Office, 2008.

———. *Foreign Assistance: USAID Relies Heavily on Nongovernmental Organizations, but Better Data Needed to Evaluation Approaches*. Washington, DC: Government Accountability Office, 2002.

———. *International Taxation: Large US Corporations and Federal Contractors with Subsidiaries in Jurisdictions Listed as Tax Havens or Financial Privacy Jurisdictions*. Washington, DC: Government Accountability Office, 2008.

———. *Military Readiness: Management Focus Needed on Airfields for Overseas Deployments*. Washington, DC: Government Accountability Office, 2001.

Government of Liberia. Liberian National Defense Strategy (draft), 2006.

Grace, Nick. "Shabaab Reaches Out to Al Qaeda Senior Leaders, Announces Death Al Sudani." *Long War Journal*, September 2, 2008. http://www.longwarjournal.org/archives/2008-09/shabab_reaches_out_t.php, accessed November 19, 2010.

Graham, Bradley, and Josh White. "Abizaid Credited with Popularizing the Term 'Long War.'" *Washington Post*, February 3, 2006.

Gray, Colin S. "How Has War Changed since the End of the Cold War?" *Parameters* 35, no. 1 (2005): 14–26.

Grebmer, Klaus et al. "Global Hunger Index, the Challenge of Hunger: Focus on the Crisis of Child Undernutrition." Bonn, Dublin, and Washington, DC: Welthungerhilfe, International Food Policy Research Institute, Concern Worldwide, 2010.

"Green-on-Blue Blues: Afghan Soldiers Increasingly Turn on Their NATO Colleagues," *Economist*, September 1, 2012. http://www.economist.com/node/21561943, accessed February 25, 2014.

Greenwood, Christopher. "International Law and the NATO Intervention in Kosovo." *International and Comparative Law Quarterly* 49, no. 4 (2008): 926–934.

Greystone Ltd. Company website, http://www.greystone-ltd.com/index.html, accessed April 11, 2009.

Gross, Leo. "The Peace of Westphalia, 1648–1948." *American Journal of International Law* 42, no. 1 (1948): 20–41.

———. *Selected Essays on International Law and Organization*, edited by Alfred P. Rubin. New York: Springer, 1993.

Guéhenno, Jean-Marie. *The End of the Nation-State*, translated by Victoria Elliott. Minneapolis: University Minnesota Press, 1995.

Gugelberger, Georg, and Michael Kearney. "Voices for the Voiceless: Testimonial Literature in Latin America." *Latin American Perspectives* 18, no. 3 (1991): 3–14.

"Guinea-Bissau Drugs Sanctions Threat." BBC News. http://news.bbc.co.uk/go/pr/fr/-/2/hi/africa/7650063.stm, accessed November 5, 2010.

Hall, Rodney Bruce, and Frederich V. Kratochwil. "Medieval Tales: Neorealist 'Science' and the Abuse of History." *International Organization* 47, no. 3 (Summer 1993): 479–491.

Hall, William Edward. *A Treatise on International Law*. Oxford: Clarendon, 1917.

Hammes, T. X. *Private Contractors: The Good, the Bad, and the Strategic Impact*. Washington, DC: National Defense University Press, 2010.

Hanlon, Querine H. *The Three Images of Ethnic War*. Westport, CT: Praeger Security International, 2009.

Hanson, Stephanie. "Al-Shabaab." Council on Foreign Relations Backgrounder, July 28, 2010.

———. "In West Africa, Threat of Narco-States." *Council on Foreign Relations Analysis Brief*, July 10, 2007.

Hanson, Victor Davis. *Why the West Has Won: Nine Landmark Battles in the Brutal History of Western Victory*. New York: Faber & Faber, 2001.

Hardin, Garrett. "The Tragedy of the Commons." In *Nature's Web: Rethinking Our Place on Earth*, edited by Peter Marshall. Armonk, NY: M. E. Sharpe, 1993.

Harper, Mary. "Profile: Somalia's Islamist 'Lads.'" BBC News, March 21, 2008. http://news.bbc.co.uk/2/hi/7307521.stm, accessed November 14, 2010.

Hartman, Thomas. "Hard Questions for Soft Power." Paper presented at the International Studies Association Annual Convention, San Francisco, 2008.

Hausmann, Ricardo, Laura D. Tyson, and Saadia Zahidi. *The Global Gender Gap Report 2009*. Geneva: World Economic Forum, 2009.

Hay, Colin. "Contemporary Capitalism, Globalization, Regionalization and the Persistence of National Variation." *Review of International Studies* 26, no. 4 (2001): 509–531.

Hedges, Chris. "What if Our Mercenaries Turn on Us?" *New York Times*, June 3, 2007.

Hedgpeth, Dana. "Blackwater's Owner Has Spies for Hire." *Washington Post*, November 3, 2007.

Heintz, James. *A Rapid Impact Assessment of the Global Economic Crisis on Liberia*. Geneva: International Labour Organization, 2009.

Held, David, David Goldblatt, and Jonathan Perraton. *Global Transformations: Politics, Economics, and Culture*. Cambridge, UK: Polity Press, 1999.

Held, David, and Anthony McGrew, eds. *The Global Transformations Reader: An Introduction to the Globalization Debate*, 2nd ed. Cambridge, UK: Polity, 2003.

Herbst, Jeffrey. "The Regulation of Private Security Forces." In *The Privatisation of Security in Africa*, edited by Greg Mills and John Stremlau. Pretoria: South Africa Institute of International Affairs, 1999.

Hertel, Shareen. *Unexpected Power: Conflict and Change among Transnational Activists*. Ithaca, NY: Cornell University Press, 2006.

Hewitt, J. Joseph, Jonathan Wilkenfeld, and Ted Robert Gurr. *Peace and Conflict 2010.* College Park, MD: Boulder Center for International Development and Conflict Management, University of Maryland Paradigm, 2010.

Hiel, Betsy. "Dhahran Women Push the Veil Aside." *Pittsburgh Tribune-Review,* May 13, 2007. http://www.pittsburghlive.com/x/pittsburghtrib/news/middleeastreports/s_507462. html, accessed September 11, 2010.

Higgins, Rosalyn. "Intervention and International Law." In *Intervention in World Politics,* edited by Hedley Bull. Oxford: Clarendon, 1984.

Hirst, Paul, and Grahame Thompson. "Globalization and the Future of the Nation State." *Economy and Society* 24, no. 3 (1995): 408–442.

———. *Globalization in Question: The International Economy and the Possibilities of Governance,* 1st ed. Cambridge, UK: Polity, 1999.

Hobbes, Thomas. *Leviathan.* New York: Oxford University Press, 1998.

Hoffman, Stanley. "Obstinate or Obsolete? The Fate of the Nation-State and the Case of Western Europe." *Daedalus* 95, no. 3 (1966): 862–915.

Holmstrom, Bengt. "Moral Hazard in Teams." *Bell Journal of Economics* 13, no. 2 (1982): 324–340.

Holsinger, Bruce. *Neomedievalism, Neoconservatism, and the War on Terror.* Chicago: Prickly Paradigm, 2007.

Hoogvelt, Ankie M. M. *Globalization and the Postcolonial World: The New Political Economy of Development,* 2nd ed. Baltimore: Johns Hopkins University Press, 2001.

Hopgood, Stephen. *Keepers of the Flame: Understanding Amnesty International.* Ithaca, NY: Cornell University Press, 2006.

Houreld, Katharine. "Bancroft Global Development, U.S. Group, Advises African Troops in Somalia." Associated Press, August 10, 2011.

Howard, Michael. *War in European History.* Oxford: Oxford University Press, 1976.

Howe, Herbert M. "Private Security Forces and African Stability: The Case of Executive Outcomes." *Journal of Modern African Studies* 36, no. 2 (1998): 307–331.

Hughes, Michael. *Early Modern Germany, 1477–1806.* Philadelphia: University of Pennsylvania Press, 1992.

Hufbauer, Gary Clyde, Jeffrey J. Schott, Kimberly Ann Elliott, and Barbara Oegg. *Economic Sanctions Reconsidered: Supplemental Case Histories.* Washington, DC: Peter G. Peterson Institute for International Economics, 1990.

Human Rights First. *Private Security Contractors at War: Ending the Culture of Impunity.* Washington D.C., 2008.

Human Rights Watch. *Harsh War, Harsh Peace: Abuses by al-Shabaab, the Transitional Federal Government, and AMISOM in Somalia.* New York, 2010.

Hutchins, Todd Emerson. "Structuring a Sustainable Letters of Marque Regime: How Commissioning Privateers Can Defeat the Somali Pirates." *California Law Review* 99 (2011): 819–884.

IDP Advisory Team Policy Development and Evaluation Service. *Real-Time Evaluation of UNHCR's IDP Operation in Liberia.* Geneva: UN High Commissioner for Refugees, 2007.

Ife, Jim. *Human Rights and Social Work: Towards Rights-Based Practice.* Cambridge, UK: Cambridge University Press, 2001.

Ignatieff, Michael. "The Attack on Human Rights." *Foreign Affairs* 80, no. 6 (2001): 102–116.

Independent Commission on the Security Forces of Iraq. *The Report of the Independent Commission on the Security Forces of Iraq.* Washington, DC: CSIS, 2007.

International Bank for Reconstruction and Development. *2010 World Development Indicators.* Washington, DC: World Bank, 2010.

International Code of Conduct for Private Security Service Providers. http://www.icoc-psp.org/ Home_Page.html, accessed February 26, 2014.

International Committee of the Red Cross. *Liberia: Opinion Survey and In-Depth Research.* Geneva: ICRC, 2009.

———. "Privatisation of War: The Outsourcing of Military Tasks," May 23, 2006. http://www.icrc. org/web/eng/siteeng0.nsf/htmlall/privatisation-war-230506?opendocument,   accessed April 9, 2009.

International Consortium of Investigative Journalists. "Making a Killing: The Business of War." Center for Public Integrity, Fall 2002.

International Council on Human Rights. *Beyond Voluntarism: Human Rights and the Developing International Legal Obligations of Companies*. International Council on Human Rights Policy, 2002.

International Criminal Court, Office of the Prosecutor. "ICC Prosecutor to Open an Investigation in Libya," March 2, 2011. http://www.icc-cpi.int/NR/exeres/3EEE2E2A-2618-4D66-8 ECB-C95BECCC300C.htm, accessed March 4, 2011.

International Crisis Group. "Liberia: Uneven Progress in Security Sector Reform." Africa Report 148, 2009.

———. "Somalia: To Move beyond the Failed State." Africa Report 147, 2008.

International Defense Exhibition & Conference (IDEX). "Reflex Responses Management Consultancy LLC." Abu Dhabi, 2011. http://www.idexuae.ae/page.cfm/Link=21/t=m/ goSection=1, accessed August 1, 2011.

International Federation of Red Cross and Red Crescent Societies. "Code of Conduct for the International Red Cross and Red Crescent Movement and NGOs in Disaster Relief." http://www.ifrc.org/en/publications-and-reports/code-of-conduct/, accessed September 30, 2010.

International Labor Rights Forum. "Pick All the Cotton: Update on Uzbekistan's Use of Force Child Labor in 2009 Harvest." Washington, DC: 2009.

International Maritime Bureau. "IMB Piracy Reporting Centre (PRC)." December 22, 2010. http://www.icc-ccs.org/piracy-reporting-centre, accessed February 14, 2014.

International Maritime Organization, Interim Guidance to Private Maritime Security Companies Providing Privately Contracted Armed Security Personnel on Board Ships in the High Risk Area, MSC.1/Circ.1443, May 25, 2012.

International Monetary Fund. *Liberia: Interim Poverty Reduction Strategy Paper*. Washington, DC: IMF, 2007.

———. *World Economic Outlook Database*. Washington, DC: IMF, 2011.

International Labour Organization, International Programme on the Elimination of Child Labour. "How IPEC Works with Non-Governmental Organizations." http://www.ilo.org/ ipec/Partners/NGOs/lang--en/index.htm, accessed September 23, 2010.

International Taxation: Large US Corporations and Federal Contractors with Subsidiaries in Jurisdictions Listed as Tax Havens or Financial Privacy Jurisdictions. Washington, DC: Government Accountability Office, 2008.

International Telecommunications Union. "ICT Data and Statistics." http://www.itu.int/ITU-D/ ict/statistics/index.html, accessed August 20, 2010.

Internet Medieval Sourcebook. "Henry IV: Letter to Gregory VII, Jan 24, 1076." http://www. fordham.edu/halsall/source/henry4-to-g7a.asp, accessed February 25, 2014.

"Investing in Prevention: An International Strategy to Manage Risks of Instability and Improve Crisis Response." Prime Minister's Strategy Unit Report to the Government of the United Kingdom, February 2005.

"I Saw It with My Own Eyes": Abuses by Chinese Security Forces in Tibet, 2008–2010. New York: Human Rights Watch, 2010.

Isenberg, David. "Dogs of War: From Mercenary to Security Contractor and Back Again." United Press International. September 12, 2008.

———. "Earth to Government: Less CORS Equal Higher Risk of Fraud," March 1, 2010. http:// www.cato.org/pub_display.php?pub_id=11409.

———. *Shadow Force: Private Security Contractors in Iraq*. Westport, CT: Praeger Security International, 2008.

Ishay, Micheline R. *The History of Human Rights: From Ancient Times to the Globalization Era*. Berkeley: University of California Press, 2008.

Jackson, Robert H. *Quasi-States: Sovereignty, International Relations and the Third World*. Cambridge, UK: Cambridge University Press, 1993.

Jagland, Thorbjorn. "Why We Gave Liu Xiaobo a Nobel." *New York Times*, October 23, 2010, A21.

Jiang, Steven. "China Blanks Nobel Peace Prize Searches," CNN, October 8, 2010. http://arti-cles.cnn.com/2010-10-08/world/china.internet_1_great-firewall-china-proxy-servers?_s=PM:WORLD, accessed October 30, 2010.

Joas, Hans. *War and Modernity: Studies in the History of Violence in the 20th Century*, translated by Rodney Livingstone. Cambridge, UK: Polity, 2003.

Johansson, Patrick. *UN Security Council Chapter VII Resolutions, 1946–2002: An Inventory.* Uppsala: Department of Peace and Conflict Research, 2003.

Johansson, Patrik, and Ramses Amer. "The United Nations Security Council and the Enduring Challenge of the Use of Force in Inter-State Relations." Umeå Working Papers in Peace and Conflict Studies No. 3, Department of Political Science, Umeå University, 2007.

Johns, Gary. "NGO Way to Go: Political Accountability of Non-Government Organizations in a Democratic Society." *IPA Backgrounder* 12, no. 3 (November 2000): 1–16.

"Joint Operation Planning." Joint Publication (JP) 5.0, December 26, 2006. http://www.dtic.mil/doctrine/new_pubs/jp5_0.pdf.

"Joint Tactics, Techniques, and Procedures for Foreign Internal Defense (FID)." Joint Publication (JP) 3-07.1, April 30, 2004. http://www.dtic.mil/cgi-bin/GetTRDoc?AD=ADA434396&Location=U2&doc=GetTRDoc.pdf.

Jones, Simon. "Skulls and Crossroads." *Maritime Security Review*, November 18, 2010. http://www.marsecreview.com/2010/11/1060/, accessed February 26, 2014.

Jouguet, Pierre, and M. R. Dobie. *Macedonian Imperialism and the Hellenization of the East.* New York: Alfred A. Knopf, 1928.

Kaldor, Mary. *New and Old Wars: Organized Violence in a Global Era*, 2nd ed. Stanford, CA: Stanford University Press, 2007.

Kaplan, Robert D. "The Coming Anarchy." In *The Geopolitics Reader*, edited by Simon Dalby, Paul Routledge, and Gerard Toal, 188–196. London: Routledge, 1998.

Keating, Joshua. "How to Hire a Mercenary." *Foreign Policy*, February 24, 2011.

Keeley, James F. "Toward a Foucauldian Analysis of International Regimes." *International Organization* 44, no. 1 (1990): 83–105.

Keene, Edward. *Beyond the Anarchical Society: Grotius, Colonialism, and Order in World Politics.* Cambridge, UK: Cambridge University Press, 2002.

Keohane, Robert O., and Joseph S. Nye. *Power and Interdependence: World Politics in Transition.* Boston: Scott, Foresman/Little, Brown, 1977.

Kerr, Philip. "The Outlawry of War," *Journal of the Royal Institute of International Affairs* 7 (November 1928): 361–368.

Kemp, Anthony. *The SAS: The Savage Wars of Peace, 1947 to the Present.* London: John Murray, 1994.

Kettl, Donald F. "The Transformation of Governance: Globalization, Devolution, and the Role of Government." *Public Administration Review* 60, no. 6 (2000): 488–497.

King, Colbert I. "Saudi Arabia's Apartheid." *Washington Post*, December 22, 2001, A24.

Kinley, David, and Junko Tadaki. "From Talk to Walk: The Emergence of Human Rights Responsibilities for Corporations at International Law." *Virginia Journal of International Law* 44, no. 4 (2004): 931–1023.

Kinsey, Christopher. *Corporate Soldiers and International Security: The Rise of Private Military Companies.* London: Taylor & Francis, 2006.

Kirschke, Joseph. "The Coke Coast: Cocaine and Failed States in Africa." *World Politics Review* part 1 (2008). http://www.worldpoliticsreview.com/article/aspx?id=2629.

Kobrin, Stephen J. "Back to the Future: Neomedievalism and the Postmodern Digital World Economy." *Journal of International Affairs* 51, no. 2 (Spring 1998): 361–386.

———. "Private Political Authority and Public Responsibility: Transnational Politics, Transnational Firms and Human Rights." *Business Ethics Quarterly* 19, no. 3 (2009): 349–374.

Kohnert, Dirk. "Democratization via Elections in an African 'Narco-State'? The Case of Guinea-Bissau." GIGA Working Papers Series (2010).

Kramer, Reed. "Liberia: A Casualty of the Cold War's End." *CSIS Africa Notes* (July 1995).

Krasner, Stephen D. "Abiding Sovereignty." *International Political Science Review* 22, no. 3 (2001): 229–251.

———. *Sovereignty: Organized Hypocrisy.* Princeton, NJ: Princeton University Press, 1999.

————. "Structural Causes and Regime Consequences: Regimes as Intervening Variables." *International Organization* 36, no. 2 (1982): 185–205.

————. "Westphalia and All That." In *Ideas and Foreign Policy: Beliefs, Institutions, and Political Change,* edited by Judith Goldstein and Robert O. Keohane, 235–264. Ithaca, NY: Cornell University Press, 1993.

Krieger, Joel, ed. *The Oxford Companion to Politics of the World,* 2nd ed. Oxford: Oxford University Press, 2001.

Kron, Josh, and Mohammed Ibrahim. "Islamists Claim Attack in Uganda." *New York Times,* July 12, 2010.

Krugman, Paul. *The Return of Depression Economics and the Crisis of 2008.* New York: W. W. Norton, 2009.

Kuhn, Thomas S. *The Structure of Scientific Revolutions.* Chicago: University of Chicago Press, 1996.

Labaton, Stephen. "Bush S.E.C. Pick Is Seen as Friend to Corporations." *New York Times,* June 3, 2005.

Lamont, J. "UN Seeks Help from Companies in War on HIV/AIDS." *Financial Times,* August 30, 2002, 1.

Lane, F. C. "Economic Consequences of Organized Violence." *Journal of Economic History* 18, no. 4 (1958): 401–417.

Lang, Michael. "Globalization and Its History." *Journal of Modern History* 78, no. 4 (2006): 899–931.

Lanning, Michael Lee. *Mercenaries: Soldiers of Fortune, from Ancient Greece to Today's Private Military Companies.* New York: Ballantine Books, 2005.

Lantos, Tom. "Discrimination against Women and the Roots of Global Terrorism." *Human Rights Magazine* 29 (Winter 2002): 7.

Lawrence, T. E. *Seven Pillars of Wisdom.* London: Wordsworth, 1997.

"Leadership of Demobilized AFL Soldiers Assure President Sirleaf of Unwavering Support." Press release, Executive Mansion, February 24, 2010.

Leander, Anna. "The Market for Force and Public Security: The Destabilizing Consequences of Private Military Companies." *Journal of Peace Research* 42, no. 5 (2005): 605–622.

Lebow, Richard Ned. *A Cultural Theory of International Relations.* New York: Cambridge University Press, 2008.

Lee, Matthew Russell. "In Cote d'Ivoire Gbabgo Is Using Mercenaries, from Liberia, UN Says, US Unaware." *Inner City Press,* December 20, 2010.

Leeson, Peter T. "Better Off Stateless: Somalia before and after Government Collapse." *Journal of Comparative Economics* 35, no. 4 (2007): 689–710.

Le Sage, Andre. *Africa's Irregular Security Threats: Challenges for US Engagement.* Washington, DC: Institute for National Security Studies, 2010.

————. *Stateless Justice in Somalia: Formal and Informal Rule of Law Initiatives.* Geneva: Centre for Humanitarian Dialogue, 2005.

Lewis, David. "Qaeda Fuels Security, Criminal Woes in Sahara States." Reuters, February 12, 2010.

Lewis, M. Paul. *Ethnologue: Languages of the World,* 16th ed. Dallas: SIL International, 2009.

"Liberia Overview." http://www.globalhumanitarianassistance.org/countryprofile/liberia, accessed February 25, 2014.

"Liberia: US Hires Private Company to Train 4,000-Man Army." *IRIN Africa,* February 15, 2005. http://www.irinnews.org/report/53038/liberia-us-hires-private-company-to-train-4-000-man-army, accessed February 25, 2014.

Liberian Ministry of Foreign Affairs. *Status of Forces Agreement NTGL/MFA/0212/2-2/05: Arrangement between the Government of the United States of America and the National Transitional Government of Liberia concerning Security Sector Reform in the Republic of Liberia.* 2005.

Liddick, Don. *Eco-Terrorism: Radical Environmental and Animal Liberation Movements.* Westport, CT: Praeger, 2006.

Lindberg, Leon N. *The Political Dynamics of European Economic Integration.* Stanford, CA: Stanford University Press, 1963.

Lindlaw, Scott. "Bush Approves Small Peacekeeping Contingent for Liberia." Associated Press, July 6, 2003.

Lipschutz, Ronnie D. "Reconstructing World Politics: The Emergence of Global Civil Society." *Millennium: Journal of International Studies* 21, no. 3 (December 1992): 389–420.

Little, Peter D. *Somalia: Economy without State*. Bloomington: Indiana University Press, 2003.

Littman, David. "Universal Human Rights and Human Rights in Islam." *Midstream* 42, no. 2 (1999): 2–7.

Livingston, Steven. "Clarifying the CNN Effect: An Examination of Media Effects according to Type of Military Intervention." Research Paper R-18. Cambridge, MA: Joan Shorenstein Center on Press and Politics, 1997.

Loden, Alexander. "Civil Society and Security Sector Reform in Post-Conflict Liberia: Painting a Moving Train without Brushes." *International Journal of Transitional Justice* 1, no. 2 (2007): 297–307.

Lukes, Steven. *Power: A Radical View*, 1st ed. London: Steven Lukes, 1976.

Luna, David M. "Narco-Trafficking: What Is the Nexus with the War on Terror?" Panel presentation, Armed Forces Communications and Electronics Association/Southern Command Conference SOUTH 2008, October 8, 2008.

Luttrell, Marcus, and Patrick Robinson. *Lone Survivor: The Eyewitness Account of Operation Redwing and the Lost Heroes of Seal Team 10*. New York: Little, Brown, 2007.

Lutz, Georg, and Wolf Linder. "Traditional Structures in Local Governance for Local Development." Unpublished report. Institute of Political Science, University of Berne, Switzerland, 2004.

Lynch, Tony, and A. J. Walsh. "The Good Mercenary?" *Journal of Political Philosophy* 8, no. 2 (2000): 133–153.

Lyons, Terrence. "Liberia's Path from Anarchy to Elections." *Current History* 97, no. 619 (1998): 229–233.

Machiavelli, Niccolò. *Art of War*. Chicago, IL: University of Chicago Press, 2009.

Madhani, Aamer. "Cleric Al-Awlaki Dubbed 'bin Laden of the Internet.'" *USA Today*, August 25, 2010.

Mahjar-Barducci, Anna. "African Mercenaries in Libya, Part II," April 1, 2011. http://www.hudson-ny.org/2008/african-mercenaries-libya-2i.

Maier, Charles S. "Democracy and Its Discontents." *Foreign Affairs* 73, no. 4 (July–August 1994): 48–64.

Malan, Mark. *Security Sector Reform in Liberia: Mixed Results from Humble Beginnings*. Carlisle, PA: Strategic Studies Institute, 2008.

Mallett, Michael. *Mercenaries and Their Masters: Warfare in Renaissance Italy*. London: Bodley Head, 1974.

Mandel, Robert. *Armies without States: The Privatization of Security*. Boulder, CO: Lynee Rienner, 2002.

Marcella, Gabriel. *American Grand Strategy for Latin America in the Age of Resentment*. Carlisle, PA: Strategic Studies Institute, 2007.

Marshall, Monty G., and Benjamin R. Cole. *Global Report 2009: Conflict, Governance, and State Fragility*. Vienna, VA: Center for Systemic Peace, 2009.

Martin, Daniel. "Nation States Are Dead: EU Chief Says the Belief That Countries Can Stand Alone Is a 'Lie and an Illusion.'" *Daily Mail*, November 11, 2010.

Masciarelli, Alexis. "Somalia's Kidnapping Industry." BBC News, May 24, 2002.

Matthews, Jessica T. "Power Shift." *Foreign Affairs* 76, no. 1 (January–February 1997): 50–66.

Mattis, James N. "USJFCOM Commander's Guidance for Effects-Based Operations," 2008.

Mayer, Ann Elizabeth. "A 'Benign' Apartheid: How Gender Apartheid Has Been Rationalized." *UCLA Journal of International Law and Foreign Affairs* 5 (2000): 237–338.

Mazzetti, Mark. "Former Spy with Agenda Operates a Private C.I.A." *New York Times*, January 22, 2011.

———. "U.S. Is Still Using Private Spy Ring, Despite Doubts." *New York Times*, May 15, 2010.

Mazzetti, Mark, and Emily B. Hager. "Secret Desert Force Set Up by Blackwater's Founder." *New York Times*, May 14, 2011.

Mazzetti, Mark, and Eric Schmitt. "Blackwater Founder Said to Back Mercenaries." *New York Times*, January 20, 2011.

Mazzitelli, Antoni L. "Transnational Organized Crime in West Africa: The Additional Challenge." *International Affairs* 83, no. 6 (2007): 1071–1090.

McElroy, Damien. "Times Square Bomb Suspect Had Links to Terror Preacher." *London Telegraph*, May 7, 2010.

McFate, Sean. "The Art and Aggravation of Vetting in Post-Conflict Environments." *Military Review* (July–August 2007): 79–97.

McGrew, Anthony. "Globalization and Global Politics." In *The Globalization of World Politics: An Introduction to International Relations*, 3rd ed., edited by John Baylis and Steve Smith, 19–40. Oxford: Oxford University Press, 2005.

McKenzie, Glenn. "Rebels Lift Siege of Liberia's Starving Capital, U.S. Marines Land." Associated Press, August 14, 2003.

McLuhan, Marshall. *The Gutenberg Galaxy: The Making of Typographic Man*. Toronto: University of Toronto Press, 1962.

McNerney, Patricia. "The International Criminal Court: Issues for Consideration by the United States Senate." *Law and Contemporary Problems* 64, no. 1 (2001): 181–191.

Mead, Walter Russell. "America's Sticky Power." *Foreign Policy*, no. 141 (March–April 2004): 46–53.

Mears, John A. "The Emergence of the Standing Professional Army in Seventeenth-Century Europe." *Social Science Quarterly* 50, no. 1 (1969): 106–115.

———. "The Thirty Years' War, the 'General Crisis,' and the Origins of a Standing Professional Army in the Habsburg Monarchy." *Central European History* 21, no. 2 (2008): 122–141.

Media Line. "Aid Workers Begin Quitting Somalia." *Jerusalem Post*, April 13, 2009.

MEJA Expansion and Enforcement Act of 2007, H.R. 2740, 110th Congress (2007).

"Memorandum: Additional Information about Blackwater USA." Majority Staff, Committee on Oversight and Government Reform. US House of Representatives, October 1, 2007.

Ménard, Christian, and Jean-Claude Viollet. Rapport d'information par la commission de la defense nationale et des forces armees sur les sociétés militaires privées. Assemblee Nationale, February 14, 2012.

Menkhaus, Ken. "Dangerous Waters." *Survival* 51, no. 1 (2009): 21–25.

———. "Governance without Government in Somalia: Spoilers, State Building, and the Politics of Coping." *International Security* 31, no. 3 (2007): 74–106.

———. *Kenya-Somalia Border Conflict Analysis*. Washington, DC: USAID, 2005.

———. "Vicious Circles and the Security Development Nexus in Somalia." *Conflict, Security & Development* 4, no. 2 (2004): 149–165.

Menkhaus, Ken, and John Prendergast. "Political Economy of Post-Intervention Somalia," *Somalia Task Force Issue Paper 3*. Washington, DC: Horn of Africa Publications, 1995.

"Mercenaries in Africa: The Fog and Dogs of War," *Economist*, March 18, 2004.

Merle, Renae, and Ellen McCarthy. "The Civilian Contractors: 6 Employees from CACI International, Titan Referred for Prosecution." *Washington Post*, August 26, 2004.

Meyer, John W., and Michael T. Hannan. *National Development and the World System: Educational, Economic, and Political Change*. Chicago: University of Chicago Press, 1979.

Middleton, Roger. *Piracy in Somalia: Threatening Global Trade, Feeding Local Wars*. London: Chatham House, 2008.

Midlarsky, Manus I. *Handbook of War Studies*. Boston: Unwin Hyman, 1989.

Milanovic, B. "Global Income Inequality: What It Is and Why It Matters." *World Economics* 7, no. 1 (2006): 131–153.

Miller, Barbara. "Blackwater a Challenge to Iraqi Sovereignty: Al-Maliki." ABC Online, September 24, 2007. http://www.abc.net.au/worldtoday/content/2007/s2041431.htm, accessed February 25, 2014.

Miller, Christian. "Civilian Contractor Toll in Iraq and Afghanistan Ignored by Defense Dept." *ProPublica*, October 9, 2009.

———. "Map: Injuries and Deaths to Civilian Contractors in Iraq and Afghanistan by Country." http://www.propublica.org/special/map-injuries-and-deaths-to-civilian-contractors-by-country-614, accessed February 14, 2014.

Mills, Greg. *Why Africa Is Poor*. New York: Penguin, 2010.

Milmo, Cahal. "Insurance Firms Plan Private Navy to Take on Somali Pirates." Independent.co.uk, September 28, 2010.

Minc, Alain. *Le nouveau moyen âge*. Paris: Gallimard, 1993.

Mohamed, Ibrahim. "Somali Rebel Groups Clash Near Kenya Border." Reuters, August 26, 2010.

Moorehead, Caroline. *Dunant's Dream War: War, Switzerland and the History of the Red Cross*. London: HarperCollins, 1998.

More, Thomas. *Utopia*. New York: Penguin Classics, 2003.

Morganthau, Hans, and Kenneth Thompson. *Politics among Nations: The Struggle for Power and Peace*. New York: McGraw-Hill, 1985.

Morris, Harvey. "Activists Turn to Blackwater over Darfur." *Financial Times*, June 19, 2008.

Morsink, Johannes. *The Universal Declaration of Human Rights: Origins, Drafting, and Intent*. Philadelphia: University of Pennsylvania Press, 2000.

Morss, Elliott R. "The New Global Players: How They Compete and Collaborate." *World Development* 19, no. 1 (1991): 55–64.

Mowlana, Hamid. *Global Information and World Communication: New Frontiers in International Relations*. London: Sage, 1997.

Muchlinski, Peter. "Human Rights and Multinationals: Is There a Problem?" *International Affairs* 77, no.1 (2001): 31–48.

Mulaj, Kledja. *Violent Non-State Actors in World Politics*. New York: Columbia University Press, 2009.

Murphy, Sean D. *Humanitarian Intervention: The United Nations in an Evolving World Order*. Philadelphia: University of Pennsylvania Press, 1996.

Naidoo, Kumi. "Civil Society Accountability: Who Guards the Guardians." Address at UN Headquarters, New York, April 3, 2003.

Najemy, John M. *A History of Florence, 1200–1575*. Oxford: Wiley-Blackwell, 2006.

Nathan, Laurie, ed. *No Ownership, No Commitment: A Guide to Local Ownership of Security Sector Reform*. Birmingham, UK: University of Birmingham, 2007.

National Counterterrorism Center. "Al-Shabaab." http://www.nctc.gov/site/groups/al_shabaab. html, accessed November 14, 2010.

National Security Presidential Directive 44: Management of Interagency Efforts concerning Reconstruction and Stabilization. December 7, 2005. http://www.fas.org/irp/offdocs/ nspd/nspd-44.pdf.

National Transitional Government of Liberia. AFL Restructuring Policy. 2005.

———. Executive Order No. 5: Demobilization and Retirement of Soldiers. 2005.

———. Ministry of Defense, Operation Order 001: Operation Demobilization. 2005.

"New Armed Forces of Liberia Force Opt Working Brief." Paper presented at the SSR Assessment Mission, Monrovia, 2004.

"Nick Clegg hails 'Axis of Openness' amid Libya Action." BBC News, March 29, 2011.

Nobelprize.org. "The Nobel Peace Prize 2010 Liu Xiaobo," July 24, 2011. http://nobelprize.org/ nobel_prizes/peace/laureates/2010/press.html, accessed February 25, 2014.

Noone, Gregory P. "The History and Evolution of the Law of War Prior to World War II." *Naval Law Review* 47 (2000): 176–207.

"No Pact for Blackwater." Reuters, January 30, 2009.

Norris, Pippa. *Giving Voice to the Voiceless: Good Governance, Human Development & Mass Communications*. New York: United Nations Development Program, 2002. http://hdr.undp. org/en/reports/global/hdr2002/papers/Norris-Zinnbauer_2002.pdf.

Northwestern University. "Government Information." http://www.library.northwestern.edu/ govinfo/resource/internat/igo.html, accessed August 31, 2010.

Nowrojee, Binaifer. "Liberia: Emerging from the Destruction: Human Rights Challenges Facing the New Liberian Government." *Human Rights Watch/Africa*. Washington, DC: Human Rights Watch, 1997.

Nye, Joseph S. *Soft Power: The Means to Success in World Politics*. New York: PublicAffairs, 2004.

Obama, Barack. Remarks by the President at the Acceptance of the Nobel Peace Prize, December 10, 2009. http://www.whitehouse.gov/the-press-office/remarks-president-acceptance-no bel-peace-prize.

O'Brien, Kevin. "Freeland Forces: Exploiters of Old Or New-Age Peacebrokers." *Jane's Intelligence Review* 10 (1998): 42–46.

———. "Private Military Companies and African Security 1990–98." In *Mercenaries: An African Security Dilemma*, edited by A-F. Musah and K. Fayemi, 43–75. London: Pluto, 2000.

O'Connell, Robert L. *Of Arms and Men: A History of War, Weapons, and Aggression*. Oxford: Oxford University Press, 1989.

OECD. "Poor Performers: Basic Approaches for Supporting Development in Difficult Partnerships," DCD/DAC(2001)26/REV1, November 2001. http://www.oecd.org/dataoecd/26/56/21684456.pdf.

Office of Management and Budget. "The President's Management Agenda: Fiscal Year 2002." http://www.whitehouse.gov/sites/default/files/omb/budget/fy2002/mgmt.pdf, accessed February 15, 2014.

O'Hayon, Gregory. "Big Men, Godfathers, and Zealots: Challenges to the State in the New Middle Ages." PhD dissertation, University of Pittsburgh, 2003.

Ohmae, Kenichi. *The End of the Nation State: The Rise of Regional Economies*. New York: Free Press, 1995.

Olson, Mancur. *Power and Prosperity: Outgrowing Communist and Capitalist Dictatorships*. New York: Basic Books, 2000.

Oman, Charles. *A History of the Art of War in the 16th Century*. London: C. Oman, 1937.

"On the Ground: DynCorp and Other U.S. Firms Provide U.S. Peace Verifiers to Kosovo." *Newsweek*, February 15, 1999, http://www.highbeam.com/doc/1G1-53865787.html, accessed February 15, 2014.

O'Regan, David. "Cocaine and Instability in West Africa: Lessons from Latin America and the Caribbean." *Africa Security Brief*. Washington, DC: Africa Center for Strategic Studies, 2010.

Organization for Economic Co-Operation and Development and Development Assistance Committee. *The OECD DAC Handbook on Security System Reform: Supporting Security and Justice*. 2007.

Osiander, Andreas. "Sovereignty, International Relations, and the Westphalian Myth." *International Organization* 55, no. 2 (2001): 251–287.

Palazzo, Guido, and Andreas Georg Scherer. "Corporate Legitimacy as Deliberation: A Communicative Framework." *Journal of Business Ethics* 66, no. 1 (2006): 71–88.

Paley, Amit R., and David S. Hilzenrath. "SEC Chief Defends His Restraint." *Washington Post*, December 24, 2008.

Panarelli, Elizabeth. *Local Ownership of Security Sector Reform*. Washington, DC: US Institute for Peace, 2009.

———. *The Role of the Ministerial Advisor in Security Sector Reform: Navigating Institutional Terrains*. Washington, DC: US Institute of Peace, 2009.

Parker, Geoffrey. *Europe in Crisis, 1598–1648*. Oxford: Wiley-Blackwell, 2001.

———. *The Military Revolution: Military Innovation and the Rise of the West, 1500–1800*. Cambridge, UK: Cambridge University Press, 1988.

Parkinson, F. *The Philosophy of International Relations: A Study in the History of Thought*. California: Sage, 1977.

Parrott, David. "From Military Enterprise to Standing Armies: War, State, and Society in Western Europe, 1600–1700." In *European Warfare, 1350–1750*, edited by Frank Tallett and D. J. B. Trim, 74–95. Cambridge, UK: Cambridge University Press, 2010.

Patterson, Malcolm Hugh. *Privatizing Peace: A Corporate Adjunct to United Nations Peacekeeping and Humanitarian Operations*. New York: Palgrave Macmillan, 2009.

Pegg, Scott, and George Frynas, eds. *Transnational Corporations and Human Rights*. New York: Palgrave Macmillan, 2003.

Pelton, Robert Young. *Licensed to Kill: Hired guns in the War on Terror*. New York: Crown, 2006.

Percy, Sarah. *Mercenaries: The History of a Norm in International Relations*. New York: Oxford University Press, 2007.

Perito, Robert M. "Afghanistan's Police—the Weak Link in Security Sector Reform." In *Revisiting Border between Civilians and Military: Security and Development in Peace Operations and Post-conflict Situations*, edited by Eduarda Hamann, 79–87. Rio de Janeiro: Fundação Konrad Adenauer, 2009.

———. *The Interior Ministry's Role in Security Sector Reform*. Washington, DC: US Institute of Peace, 2009.

Perry, Tony. "Court Upholds Dismissal of Charges in Haditha Case." *Los Angeles Times*, March 18, 2009.

Pfeffer, Jeffrey, and Gerald Salancik. *The External Control of Organizations: A Resource Dependence Perspective*. Stanford, CA: Stanford University Press, 2003.

Pham, J. Peter. "Islamist Extremism's Rising Challenge to Morocco." *World Defense Review*, August 7, 2008.

———. *Liberia: Portrait of a Failed State*. Georgia: Reed, 2004.

Phillips, P. Michael. "Deconstructing Our Dark Age Future." *Parameters* (Summer 2009): 94–110.

Picciotto, Sol. "Rights, Responsibilities and Regulation of International Business." *Columbia Journal of Transnational Law* 42, no. 1 (2003): 131–158.

Pickett, Kate, and Richard Wilkinson. *The Spirit Level: Why Greater Equality Makes Societies Stronger*. New York: Bloomsbury, 2009.

Plaut, Martin. "Private Patrol Boats to Tackle Somali Pirates." *BBC News*, May 30, 2012. http://www.bbc.com/news/world-africa-18209357, accessed February 26, 2014.

Ploch, Lauren. "Africa Command: US Strategic Interests and the Role of the US Military in Africa." Washington, DC: Heritage Foundation, 2010.

Pope Boniface VIII. *Unam Sanctam* (AD 1299). In *Select Historical Documents of the Middle Ages*, edited and translated by Ernest F. Henderson, 435–436. London: G. Bell, 1905.

Powell, William. *The Anarchist Cookbook*. New York: Lyle Stuart, 1971.

Power, Samantha. *A Problem from Hell: America and the Age of Genocide*. New York: Harper Perennial, 2003.

Prange, Gordon W. *Miracle at Midway*. New York: McGraw-Hill, 1982.

Pratt, R. A. "Geoffrey Chaucer, Esq., and Sir John Hawkwood." *ELH* 16, no. 3 (1949): 188–193.

"President Authorizes Defense Ministry to Pay Salary Arrears to Former Soldiers." UNMIL, June 14, 2006.

President's Commission to Strengthen Social Security. "Strengthening Social Security and Creating Personal Wealth for All Americans," December 2001.

Preston, Richard A., Alex Roland, and S. F. Wise. *Men in Arms: A History of Warfare and Its Interrelationships with Western Society*. Westport, CT: Praeger Security International, 1962.

Prevas, John. *Hannibal Crosses the Alps: The Invasion of Italy and the Punic Wars*. Cambridge, MA: Da Capo, 2001.

"Privatization 98." Paper presented at the 12th Annual Report on Privatization and Government Reform, 1998.

Publius [Alexander Hamilton]. "Consequences of Hostilities between States." *Federalist Papers* 8, November 27, 1787.

———. "The Idea of Restraining the Legislative Authority in Regard to the Common Defense Considered." *Federalist Papers* 26, December 22, 1787.

Quadrennial Defense Review. February 6, 2006. http://www.defense.gov/qdr/report/Report20060203.pdf.

Ranelagh, John. *Thatcher's People: An Insider's Account of the Politics, the Power and the Personalities*. New York: HarperCollins, 1991.

Rapley, John. "The New Middle Ages." *Foreign Affairs* (May–June 2006): 95–103.

"Rebels Lift Siege of Starving Monrovia." *RedOrbit.com*, August 14, 2003. http://www.redorbit.com/news/general/14811/rebels_lift_siege_of_starving_monrovia/, accessed April 11, 2011.

Rees, Edward. "External Study: Security Sector Reform (SSR) and Peace Operations: Improvisation and Confusion from the Field." New York: United Nations, 2006.

Reichert, Elisabeth. "Human Rights: An Examination of Universalism and Cultural Relativism." *Journal of Comparative Social Welfare* 22, no. 1 (2006): 23–36.

Reno, William. "Reinvention of an African Patrimonial State: Charles Taylor's Liberia." *Third World Quarterly* 16, no. 1 (1995): 109–120.

Republic of Liberia. "National Policy on Non-Governmental Organizations in Liberia." http://www.emansion.gov/lr/doc/NGOPolicguidelines.pdf.

Reuter, Christoph. "The Warlord of the Highway." *Vice Magazine* (November 2009), http://www.vice.com/print/warlord-of-the-highway-226-v16n11, accessed February 26, 2014.

Rhodes, R. A. W. "The New Governance: Governing without Government." *Political Studies* 44, no. 4 (1996): 652–667.

Richard, Theodore T. "Reconsidering the Letter of Marque: Utilizing Private Security Providers Against Piracy." *Public Contract Law Journal* 39/3 (Spring 2010): 411–464.

Richmond, Oliver P. "The Dilemmas of Subcontracting the Liberal Peace." In *Subcontracting Peace: The Challenges of NGO Peacebuiling*, edited by Oliver P. Richmond and Henry F. Carey, 19–36. Aldershot, UK: Ashgate, 2005.

"Rice Orders Monitoring of Blackwater in Iraq." MSNBC, October 7, 2007. http://www.msnbc.msn.com/id/21162150/, accessed April 23, 2009.

Rife, Rickey L. *Defense Is from Mars, State Is from Venus: Improving Communications and Promoting National Security*. White paper. Carlisle, PA: U.S. Army War College, 1998.

Risse, Thomas. "Global Governance and Communicative Action." *Government and Opposition* 39, no. 2 (2004): 288–313.

Risse, Thomas, Stephen C. Roop, and Kathryn Sikkink, eds., *The Power of Human Rights: International Norms and Domestic Change*. Cambridge, UK: Cambridge University Press, 1999.

Rittel, Horst W. J., and Melvin M. Webber. "Dilemmas in a General Theory of Planning." *Policy Sciences* 4, no. 2 (1973): 155–169.

Rivera, Ray, Alissa J. Rubin, and Sharifullah Sahak. "Deadly Attack by Taliban in Kabul Sought to Kill Head of Blackwater." *New York Times*, January 28, 2011.

Roberts, Adam. "Lives and Statistics: Are 90% of War Victims Civilians?" *Survival* 52, no. 3 (2010): 115–136.

———. *The Wonga Coup: Guns, Thugs, and a Ruthless Determination to Create Mayhem in an Oil-Rich Corner of Africa*. New York: PublicAffairs, 2006.

Roberts, Michael. *The Military Revolution, 1560–1660*. Belfast: Boyd, 1956.

Robertson, Roland. *Globalization: Social Theory and Global Culture*. London: Sage, 1992.

Robinson, Piers. *The CNN Effect: The Myth of News, Foreign Policy and Intervention*. London: Routledge, 2002.

Rodier, Alain. "L'Infiltration d'Al-Qaeda en Afrique." *Centre Français de Recherche sur le Renseignement, Note d'Actualité*, no. 2 (2004).

Roggio, Bill. "Zawahiri Praises Shabaab's Takeover of Southern Somalia." *Long War Journal*, February 24, 2009. http://www.longwarjournal.org/archives/2009/02/zawahiri_praises_sha.php, accessed February 26, 2014.

Rollins, John. *International Terrorism and Transnational Crime: Security Threats, US Policy, and Considerations for Congress*. Washington, DC: Congressional Research Service, 2010.

Rosamond, Ben. *Theories of European Integration*. Basingstoke, UK: Palgrave, 2000.

Rosenau, James N. *Along the Domestic-Foreign Frontier: Exploring Governance in a Turbulent World*. Cambridge, UK: Cambridge University Press, 1997.

Rosenberg, Justin. *The Empire of Civil Society: A Critique of the Realist Theory of International Relations*. New York: Verso, 1994.

Roston, Aram. *The Man Who Pushed America to War: The Extraordinary Life, Adventures, and Obsessions of Ahmad Chalabi*. New York: PublicAffairs, 2009.

Rotberg, Robert, ed. *When States Fail: Causes and Consequences*. Princeton, NJ: Princeton University Press, 2004.

Roth, Ken. "War in Iraq: Not a Humanitarian Intervention." In *Human Rights Watch World Report 2004: Human Rights and Armed Conflict*, 13–35. New York: Human Rights Watch, 2004.

Ruckus Society. "Direct Action Manuals and Checklists." http://www.ruckus.org/section.php?id-82, accessed October 2, 2010.

Ruggie, John Gerald. "Reconstituting the Global Public Domain—Issues, Actors, and Practices." *European Journal of International Relations* 10 no. 4 (2004): 499–531.

———. "Territoriality and Beyond: Problematizing Modernity in International Relations." *International Organization* 47, no. 1 (Winter 1993): 139–174.

Rumsfeld, Donald. "Secretary Rumsfeld's Remarks to the Johns Hopkins, Paul H. Nitze School of Advanced International Studies." http://www.defense.gov/transcripts/transcript.aspx?transcriptid=1361, accessed February 15, 2014.

"Russia Eyes Security Firms to Defend Assets Abroad." Reuters, October 28, 2010.

Russo, Karen, Aadel Rashid, and Ali Mashakheel. "Iraq Status of Forces Agreement Causes More Strife." ABC News, October 22, 2008. http://abcnews.go.com/International/Story?id=6089852&page=1, accessed April 23, 2009.

"Rwanda: How the Genocide Happened," *BBC News*, May 17, 2011.

Samukai, Brownie J., Jr. "A Discussion with Liberia's Defense Minister, Brownie J. Samukai, Jr." US Institute of Peace, Washington, DC, May 11, 2007.

Sandler, Corey. *Henry Hudson: Dreams and Obsession: The Tragic Legacy of the New World's Least Understood Explorer*. New York: Citadel, 2007.

Scholte, Jan Aart. *Globalization: A Critical Introduction*, 1st ed. Basingstoke, UK: Palgrave Macmillan, 2000.

———. "Globalisation: Prospects for a Paradigm Shift." In *Politics and Globalisation: Knowledge, Ethics and Agency*, edited by Martin Shaw, 9–22. London: Routledge, 1999.

Sacchetti, Franco. *Il Trecentonovelle*. Torino: Enaudi, 1970.

Sapone, Montgomery. "Have Rifle with Scope, Will Travel: The Global Economy of Mercenary Violence." *California Western International Law Journal* 30, no. 5 (1999): 36–53.

Santoro, Michael A. *Pfizer: Global Protection of Intellectual Property*. Cambridge, MA: Massachusetts Graduate School of Business Administration, 1992.

Sarkar, Sumita, and Arvind Tiwari. "Combating Organised Crime: A Case Study of Mumbai City." *Faultlines: New Delhi* 12 (2002): 133–176.

Saudi Arabia Market Information Resource and Directory. "Crown Prince Abdullah's Address to the United Nations, September 6, 2000." http://www.saudinf.com/main/x007.htm, accessed September 11, 2010.

Saunders, Alan. *Mercenaries: A History of the Second Oldest Profession*. New York: Acovian, 2010.

Save the Children Liberia. http://www.sasvethechildren.org/uk/en/liberia.htm, accessed February 25, 2014.

Scahill, Jeremy. *Blackwater: The Rise of the World's Most Powerful Mercenary Army*. New York: Perseus, 2008.

Schecter, Anna. "Breakfast with Blackwater: Mia Farrow and Blackwater CEO Prince Met to Discuss a Possible Collaboration." ABC News, August 20, 2008. http://abcnews.go.com/print?id=5617186, accessed April 5, 2009.

Scheye, Eric. *Realism and Pragmatism in Security Sector Development*. Paris: OECD, 2010.

Schreier, Fred, and Marina Caparini. *Privatising Security: Law, Practice and Governance of Private Military and Security Companies*. Geneva: Centre for the Democratic Control of Armed Force, 2005.

Schwartz, Moshe. *Department of Defense Contractors in Iraq and Afghanistan: Background and Analysis*. Washington, DC: Congressional Research Service, 2010.

———. *Training the Military to Manage Contractors during Expeditionary Operations: Overview and Options for Congress*. Washington, DC: Congressional Research Service, 2008.

Schwartz, Moshe, and Joyprada Swain. *Department of Defense Trends in Overseas Contract Obligations*. Washington, DC: Congressional Research Service, 2011.

Schooner, Steven L., and Collin Swan. "Contractors and the Ultimate Sacrifice." George Washington University Law School, Public Law and Legal Theory Working Paper no. 512, September 2010.

Sedra, Mark, ed. *The Future of Security Sector Reform*. Waterloo, Ontario: Centre for International Governance Innovation, 2010.

Sell, Susan K. *Private Power, Public Law: The Globalization of Intellectual Property Rights*. Cambridge, UK: Cambridge University Press, 2003.

Selzer, Stephen. *Deutsche Söldner Im Italien Des Trecento*. Tübingen: Max Niemeyer, 2001.

Sens, Allen G. "From Peace-Keeping to Peace-Building: The United Nations and the Challenge of Intrastate War." In *The United Nations and Global Security*, edited by Richard M. Price and Mark W. Zacher, 141–160. New York: Palgrave Macmillan, 2004.

Shanker, Thom. "Warning against Wars Like Iraq and Afghanistan." *New York Times*, February 25, 2011.

Shearer, David. "Outsourcing War." *Foreign Policy*, no. 112 (1998): 68–81.

———. *Private Armies and Military Intervention*. Oxford: Oxford University Press, 1998.

Sheehan, Michael. *The Balance of Power: History and Theory*. New York: Routledge, 1996.

Shelley, Louise. "Transnational Organized Crime: An Imminent Threat to the Nation-State." *Journal of International Affairs* 48, no. 2 (1995).

Shultz, Richard H., and Andrea J. Dew. *Insurgents, Terrorists, and Militias: The Warriors of Contemporary Combat.* New York: Columbia University Press, 2006.

SIGAR. Special Inspector General for Afghanistan Reconstruction. http://www.sigar.mil/, accessed February 17, 2011.

SIGIR. Special Inspector General for Iraq Reconstruction. http://www.sigir.mil/, accessed February 17, 2011.

Singer, Peter W. *Corporate Warriors: The Rise of the Privatized Military Industry.* Ithaca, NY: Cornell University Press, 2003.

———. "Humanitarian Principles, Private Military Agents: Some Implications of the Privatised Military Industry for the Humanitarian Community." In *Resetting the Rules of Engagement: Trends and Issues in Military-Humanitarian Relations*, edited by V. Wheeler and A. Harmer, 67–80. London: Overseas Development Institute, 2006.

Sixth Annual Report of the President of the Special Court for Sierra Leone. Freetown, Sierra Leone: Special Court for Sierra Leone, 2009.

Skinner, Quentin. *Machiavelli: A Very Short Introduction.* New York: Oxford University Press, 2000.

Slim, Hugo. "By What Authority? The Legitimacy and Accountability of Non-Government Organisations." *Journal of Humanitarian Assistance* 10 (January 2002). http://www.gdrc.org/ngo/accountability/by-what-authority.html, accessed February 26, 2014.

Smith, Adam. *An Inquiry into the Nature and Causes of the Wealth of Nations.* University Park, PA: Penn State Electronic Classics, 2005.

Smith, Rebecca K. "Ecoterrrorism? A Critical Analysis of the Vilification of Radical Environmental Activists as Terrorists." *Environmental Law* 38, no. 2 (2008): 537–576.

Smith, Rupert. *The Utility of Force: The Art of War in the Modern World.* London: Allen Lane, 2005.

Snow, David A., E. Burke Rochford, Jr., Steven K. Worden, and Robert D. Benford. "Frame Alignment Processes, Micromobilization, and Movement Participation." *American Sociological Review* 51, no. 4 (1986): 464–481.

Stares, Justin. "The International Community Has 'Failed' to Tackle Piracy." *Public Service Europe*, February 28, 2012.

Staub, D. Joshua. "Letters of Marque: A Short-Term Solution to an Age Old Problem." *Journal of Maritime Law and Commerce* 40/2 (April 2009): 261–269.

Solana, Javier. "A Secure Europe in a Better World: European Security Strategy." In *Civilian Perspective or Security Strategy?*, edited by Klaus Schilder and Tobias Hauschild. Paris: European Union Institute for Security Studies, 2003.

Somalia NGO Consortium. http://www.somaliangoconsortium.org/index.php, accessed February 26, 2014.

"Somalia: NGOs Urge International Community to Protect Civilians." *IRIN Africa*, October 7, 2008.http://www.irinnews.org/fr/report/80786/somalia-ngos-urge-international-community-to-protect-civilians, accessed February 26, 2014.

"Somalia: Puntland Maritime Police Force Instructor Killed on Duty," Garowe Online, April 28, 2012.

Sörenson, Karl. *State Failure on the High Seas: Reviewing the Somali Piracy.* Stockholm: Swedish Defense Research Agency, 2008.

Spanish Royal Academy. *Diccionario de la Lengua Espanola*, 2 vols. Espasa Calpe Mexicana, 2001.

Spaulding, Oliver L., Hoffman Nickerson, and John Womack Wright. *Warfare: A Study of Military Methods from the Earliest Times.* Manchester, NH: Ayer, 1972.

Spear, J. "Market Forces: The Political Economy of Private Military Companies. New Security Programme." *Fafo Report* 531 (2006).

Spearin, Christopher. "Promising Privateers? Understanding the Constraints of Contemporary Private Security at Sea." *Naval War College Review* 67, no. 2 (2014): 97–116.

Spence, Floyd, and Eugene J. Carroll. "Q: Is the Military Drawdown Endangering U.S. National Security?" *Insight on the News* 14 (1998). http://business.highbeam.com/4977/article-1G1-21161637/q-military-drawdown-endangering-us-national-security, accessed February 26, 2014.

Spotts, Frederic. *Hitler and the Power of Aesthetics.* New York: Overlook, 2003.

Spruyt, Hendrik. *The Sovereign State and Its Competitors*. Princeton, NJ: Princeton University Press, 1996.

Stack, Liam. "New Jersey Men Arrested at JFK on Way to Join Al-Shabab in Somalia." *Christian Science Monitor*, June 7, 2010.

Starr, Harvey, Francis Hoole, Jeffrey Hart, and John Freeman. "The Relationship between Defense Spending and Inflation." *Journal of Conflict Resolution* 28, no. 1 (1984): 103–122.

Statute, Rome. "Rome Statute of the International Criminal Court." *International Legal Materials* 37 (1998): 999–1019.

Stiglitz, Joseph E., and Linda Bilmes. *The Three Trillion Dollar War: The True Cost of the Iraq Conflict*. New York: W. W. Norton, 2008.

"Striking the Appropriate Balance: The Defense Department's Expanding Role in Foreign Assistance," Hearing before the Committee on Foreign Affairs, House of Representatives, 111th Congress, March 13, 2009. Statement of Nancy Lindborg, president, Mercy Corps.

Stoddard, Abby. "Humanitarian NGOs: Challenges and Trends." In *Humanitarian Action and the "Global War on Terror": A Review of Trends and Issues*, edited by Joanna Macrae and Adele Harmer, 25–36. London: Humanitarian Policy Group, 2003.

Stones, E. L. G. "The Folvilles of Ashby-Folville, Leicestershire, and Their Associates in Crime, 1326–1347." *Transactions of the Royal Historical Society* 7 (1957): 117–135.

Strange, Susan. *The Retreat of the State: The Diffusion of Power in the World Economy*. Cambridge, UK: Cambridge University Press, 1996.

Strom, Stephanie, and Lydia Polgreen. "Advocacy Group's Publicity Campaign on Darfur Angers Relief Organizations." *New York Times*, June 2, 2007.

Suchman, Mark C. "Managing Legitimacy: Strategic and Institutional Approaches." *Academy of Management Review* 20, no. 3 (1995): 571–610.

Sundstrom, Lisa McIntosh. "Foreign Assistance, International Norms, and NGO Development: Lessons from the Russian Campaign." *International Organization* 59, no. 2 (2005): 419–449.

Sunstein, Cass R. "Behavioral Analysis of Law." *University of Chicago Law Review* 64, no. 4 (1997): 1175–1195.

———. *The Second Bill of Rights: FDR's Unfinished Revolution and Why We Need It More Than Ever*. New York: Basic Books, 2004.

Szyber, Caroline. "Giving Voice to the Voiceless: A Field Study from India about Capacity Building towards Women in Panchayats as an Instrument for Empowerment." http://www.quotaproject.org/other/Giving_voice_to_the_voiceless.pdf, accessed July 4, 2008.

Temple-Leader, John, and Giuseppe Marcotti. *Sir John Hawkwood: The Story of a Condottiere*, translated by Leader Scott. London: T. Fisher Unwin, 1889.

Tennant, Vicky, Bernie Doyle, and Raouf Mazou. *Safeguarding Humanitarian Space: A Review of Key Challenges for UNHCR*. Geneva: Policy Development and Evaluation Service, 2010.

Teschke, Benno. *The Myth of 1648: Class, Geopolitics, and the Making of Modern International Relations*. New York: Verso, 2003.

"The Non-Governmental Order." *Economist*, December 11, 1999.

"The Responsibility to Protect." Report of the International Commission on Intervention and State Sovereignty. Ottawa: International Development Research Centre, 2001.

Thomas, Hugh M. *The Norman Conquest: England after William the Conqueror*. Lanham, MD: Rowman & Littlefield, 2008.

Thomas, Janet. *The Battle in Seattle: The Story Behind and Beyond the WTO Demonstrations*. Golden, CO: Fulcrum, 2000.

Thomas, Kate. "Liberia Truth and Reconciliation Commission Retracts Controversial Report." Voice of America, July 2, 2009.

Thomson, Janice E. *Mercenaries, Pirates, and Sovereigns*. Princeton, NJ: Princeton University Press, 1996.

"The Threat of Eco-Terrorism." Hearing before the House Committee on Natural Resources, Subcommittee on Forests and Forest Health, 107th Congress, February 2002. Testimony of James F. Jarboe, Counterterrorism Division, FBI.

Tierney, Brian. "Divided Sovereignty at Constance: A Problem of Medieval and Early Modern Political Theory." *Annuarium Historiae Conciliorum* 7 (1975): 238–256.

Tilly, Charles. "War Making and State Making as Organized Crime." In *Bringing the State Back In*, edited by Peter B. Evans, Dietrich Rueschmeyer, and Theda Skocpol, 169–191. Cambridge, UK: Cambridge University Press, 1985.

Tilly, Charles, and Gabriel Ardant. *The Formation of National States in Western Europe*. Princeton, NJ: Princeton University Press, 1975.

Toffler, Alvin, and Heidi Adelaide Toffler. *War and Anti-War: Making Sense of Today's Global Chaos*. New York: Grand Central, 1995.

Torres, Magüi Moreno, and Michael Anderson. "Fragile States: Defining Difficult Environments for Poverty Reduction." PRDE Working Paper, no. 1 (August 2004).

Trease, Geoffrey. *The Condottieri: Soldiers of Fortune*. New York: Holt, Rinehart and Winston, 1971.

Trevaskes, Susan. "The Private/Public Security Nexus in China." *Social Justice* 34, nos. 3–4 (2007): 38–55.

Treverton, Gregory F. *Film Piracy, Organized Crime, and Terrorism*. Santa Monica, CA: RAND Corporation, 2009.

Truth and Reconciliation Commission of South Africa Report, vol. 2. New York: Grove's Dictionaries, 1999.

Turner, Stephen P. *The Cambridge Companion to Weber*. Cambridge, UK: Cambridge University Press, 2000.

The Twentieth Century Atlas—Death Tolls. "Mid Range Wars and Atrocities of the Twentieth Century." http://users.erols.com/mwhite/28/warstat4.htm#Crisis, accessed January 14, 2011.

Tzu, Lao, and James Legge. *Tao Te Ching*. Digireads.com, 2009.

UK Ministry of Defence. "Defence Spending £32.6Bn or $51.84Bn in 2007." http://www.mod.uk/DefenceInternet/AboutDefence/Organisation/KeyFactsAboutDefenceSpending.htm, accessed January 15, 2011.

———. "Table 3a—Strength of UK Regular Forces by Sex." http://www.dasa.mod.uk/applications/newWeb/www/apps/publications/pubViewFile.php?content=170.131&date=2011-05-12&type=html&PublishTime=09:30:00, accessed July 1, 2011.

Ulph, Stephen. "Al-Qaeda's Strategy until 2020." *Terrorism Focus* 2, no. 6 (May 2005). http://www.jamestown.org/ or http://www.turkishweekly.net/op-ed/472/al-qaeda-s-strategy-until-2020.html, accessed February 26, 2014.

UNCTAD. *Transnational Corporations and World Development*. London: International Thompson Business Press, 1996.

UN. "Liberia: Development Challenges Top Agenda as the Nation Recovers from Years of Civil Strife." 2006. http://www.un.org/events/tenstories/06/story.asp?storyID=2100#, accessed April 23, 2011.

———. "The Secretary-General Reflects on 'Intervention' in Thirty-Fifth Annual Ditchley Foundation Lecture." Press Release SG/SM/6613, June 26, 1998. http://www.un.org/News/Press/docs/1998/19980626.sgsm6613.html, accessed February 26, 2014.

———. "United Nations Mission in Liberia's Police Assist in the Development of Security and Rule of Law in Liberia." http://www.un.org/en/peacekeeping/sites/police/field/story_005.shtml, accessed November 12, 2010.

———. "UNMIL Background." http://www.un.org/en/peacekeeping/missions.unmil/background.shtml, accessed April 16, 2011.

———. "United Nations Operations in Somalia (UNOSOM 1) Background." 2003. http://www.un.org/en/peacekeeping/missions/pas/unsom1backgr1.html, accessed February 26, 2014.

———. "UNMIL Background." http://www.un.org/en/peacekeeping/missions.unmil/background.shtml, accessed April 16, 2011.

———. *UN Security Management System Security Policy Manual*. http://www.ohchr.org/Documents/Issues/Mercenaries/WG/StudyPMSC/UNSecurityPolicyManual.pdf, accessed February 26, 2014.

———. *UN Security Management System Operations Manual, Guidelines on the Use of Armed Security Services from Private Security Companies*. http://www.ohchr.org/Documents/Issues/Mercenaries/WG/StudyPMSC/GuidelinesOnUseOfArmedSecurityServices.pdf, accessed February 26, 2014.

UN Conference on Trade. *World Investment Report 1999: Foreign Direct Investment & the Challenge of Development*. Blue Ridge Summit, PA: Bernan, 1999.

UN Development Program. *Human Development Report 1994*. Oxford: Oxford University Press, 1994.

———. *National Human Development Report 2006: Liberia*. New York: UN, 2006.

UN General Assembly. A/46/182, "Strengthening of the coordination of Humanitarian Emergency Assistance of the United Nations," December 19, 1991. http://www.un.org/documents/ga/res/46/a46r/182.htm.

———. A/53/150, "Arrangements and Practices for the Interaction of Non-Governmental Organizations in All Activities of the United Nations System: Report of the Secretary-General," July 10, 1998. http://www.un.org/documents/ga/docs/53/plenary/a53-170.htm.

———. A/63/677, "Implementing the Responsibility to Protect: Report of the Secretary-General," January 12, 2009. http://www.unrol.org/files/SG_reportA_63_677_en.pdf.

———. Resolution 60/1, "2005 World Summit Outcome," October 24, 2005, http://www.un.org/summit2005/documents.html.

———. Resolution 2200A, "International Covenant on Economic, Social, and Cultural Rights," December 16, 1966. http://www2.ohchr.org/english/law/cescr.htm.

———. "The Universal Declaration of Human Rights," December 10, 1948. http://www.un.org/en/documents/udhr/index.shtml.

———. UN Soc. A/63/467- S/2008/636, "Permanent Representative of Switzerland to the UN, letter dated October 2, 2008, addressed to the Secretary-General of the Security Council," October 6, 2008.

UN General Assembly and Security Council. A/63/467–S/2008/636, "The Montreux Document on Pertinent International Legal Obligations and Good Practices for States related to Operations of Private Military and Security Companies during Armed Conflict," September 17, 2008. http://www.eda.admin.ch/etc/medialib/downloads/edazen/topics/intla/humlaw.Par.0057.File.tmp/Montreux%20Document%20(e).pdf.

UN High Commissioner for Refugees. Directory of Non-Governmental Organisations. Geneva: UNHCR, 1992.

———. "Dadaab – World's biggest refugee camp 20 years old," February 21, 2012. http://www.unhcr.org/pages/49c3646c2.html, accessed February 26, 2014.

———. Protocol Additional to the Geneva Conventions of August 12, 1949, and Relating to the Protection of Victims of International Armed Conflicts (Protocol I), June 8, 1977. http://www.icrc.org/ihl/INTRO/470, accessed February 26, 2014.

———. "Liberia: Regional Operations Profile—West Africa," http://www.unhcr.org/cgi-bin/texis/vtx/page?page=49e484936#, accessed February 25, 2014.

UNICEF Innocenti Research Center. *Changing a Harmful Social Convention: Female Genital Mutilation/Cutting*. Florence: UNICEF, 2005.

UNODC. *World Drug Report 2010*. Vienna: UNODC, 2010.

UN Information Service. "Secretary-General Welcomes Resignation of President Charles Taylor; Hopes Event Marks Beginning of End for Liberia's 'Long Nightmare,'" UN press release SG/SM/8818 AFR/687, August 12, 2003.

UN Security Council. "Report of the United Nations Monitoring Group on Somalia and Eritrea Submitted in Accordance with Resolution 1916" (2010), S/2011/433, July 18, 2011.

———. Resolution 1497, S/RES/1497, August 1, 2003.

———. S/PV.5319, Debate Transcript, December 9, 2005.

———. "Letter Dated 12 July 2013 from the Chair of the Security Council Committee pursuant to resolutions 751 (1992) and 1907 (2009) concerning Somalia and Eritrea Addressed to the President of the Security Council," S/2013/413, July 12, 2013.

UN Statistics Division. "Liberia." http://data.un.org/CountryProfile.aspx?crName=Liberia, accessed April 2, 2011.

"UN Report Describes New Mercenary Activity," *New York Times*, October 17, 2007. http://www.nytimes.com/2007/10/17/world/asia/17iht-mercenaries.1.7923472.html?_r=0, accessed February 25, 2014.

USAID. "Fragile States Strategy." January 2005. http://www.usaid.gov/policy/2005_fragile_states_strategy.pdf.

———. "Overview of Activities in Liberia." May 4, 2004.

"US Admiral Says Commercial Ships Need Armed Guards." Voice of America video, April 22, 2010.

"U.S. Ambassador to Liberia Urges Rebels to Leave Capital." *New York Times*, July 28, 2003.

US Army. *FM 3-07: Stability Operations*. Washington, DC: Department of the Army, 2008.

———. *FM 3-07/1: Security Force Assistance*. Washington, DC: Department of the Army, 2009.

———. Regulation 350-1: Army Training and Leader Development, 2007.

US Army and US Marine Corps. *FM 3-24/MCWP 3-33.5: Counterinsurgency*. Washington, DC: Department of the Army, 2006.

US Army Training and Doctrine Command. *TRADOC Regulation 350-6: Enlisted Initial Entry Training (IET) Policies and Administration*. Washington, DC: Department of the Army, 2003.

US Congress. "New Information about Counternarcotics Contracts in Latin America." US Senate Committee on Homeland Security and Governmental Affairs Subcommittee on Contracting Oversight, June 7, 2011.

———. *Warlord, Inc.: Extortion and Corruption along the U.S. Supply Chain in Afghanistan*, report before the Subcommittee on National Security and Foreign Affairs, US House of Representatives, 111th Congress (June 22, 2010).

———. *Inquiry into the Role and Oversight of Private Security Contractors in Afghanistan*, report with additional views of the Committee on Armed Services, US Senate, 111th Congress (September 10, 2010).

"U.S. Debating Sending Troops to Help Liberian Civil War." CNN (transcript), July 2, 2003.

US Defense Science Board, *Institutionalizing Stability Operations within DOD: Report of the Defense Science Board Task Force*, September 2005; *Quadrennial Defense Review*, February 6, 2006, http://www.defense.gov/qdr/report/Report20060203.pdf.

US Department of Defense. Directive 3000.05. November 28, 2005, updated Septemeber 16, 2009. http://www.dtic.mil/whs/directives/corres/pdf/300005p.pdf, accessed February 25, 2014.

———. Contractor Support of U.S. Operations in the USCENTCOM Area of Responsibility, Iraq, and Afghanistan, 4th Quarter FY 2010 Contractor Census, December 15, 2010.

———. Contractor Support of U.S. Operations in the USCENTCOM Area of Responsibility to Include Iraq and Afghanistan (5A Papers), October 2013.

———. *DOD Obligations and Expenditures of Funds Provided to the Department of State for the Training and Mentoring of the Afghan National Police*. Washington, DC: Office of the Inspector General, 2010.

US Department of State. "Civilian Response Corps Reaches 100 Active Members." April 16, 2010, http://www.state.gov/r/pa/prs/ps/2010/04/140346.htm, accessed February 25, 2014.

———. *Report of Inspection Embassy Monrovia, Liberia Report No. ISP-I-08-20a*. Washington, DC, 2008.

US Department of State and Department of Defense. Interagency Assessment of Iraq Police Training: Joint Inspector General Report. Washington, DC, 2005.

US Federal Bureau of Investigation. "Fighting Terror: 14 Indicted for Supporting Al Shabaab," August 5, 2010. http://www.fbi.gov/news/stories/2010/august/al-shabaab, accessed February 26, 2014.

US Financial Management Service, US Department of the Treasury. http://www.fms.treas.gov/index.html, accessed August 22, 2010.

US Institute of Peace. "Guidelines for Relations between U.S. Armed Forces and Non-Governmental Humanitarian Agencies in Hostile or Potentially Hostile Environments." http://www.usip.org/files/resources/guidelines_pamphlet.pdf, accessed October 1, 2010.

"U.S. Military Experts Confront Carnage in Liberia." Associated Press, July 9, 2003.

US Navy. "Super Tanker Attacked in Arabian Sea." No. NNS081117-07, November 17, 2008.

US Social Security Administration. Actuarial Publications. http://www.ssa.gov/oact/STATS/table4a3.html.

"Urgent Reform Required: Army Expeditionary Contracting." Report of the Commission on Army Acquisition and Program Management in Expeditionary Operations. Hearing before the Subcommittee on Readiness and Management Support of the Committee on Armed Services, US Senate. 110th Congress, December 6, 2007.

Vanderheiden, Steve. "Eco-Terrorism or Justified Resistance? Radical Environmentalism and the 'War on Terror." *Politics & Society* 33, no. 3 (2005): 425–447.

Vanderlinden, Jacques. "Le pluralisme juridique: Essai de synthèse." *Le Pluralisme Juridique* (1972): 19–56.

Vardi, Nathan. "Dyncorp Owner Cashes Out of Wartime Investment." Forbes.com, April 12, 2010. http://blogs.forbes.com/streettalk/2010/04/12/dyncorp-owner-cashes-out-of-wartime-investment/, accessed April 18, 2011.

Vasquez, Carlos M. "Direct vs. Indirect Obligations of Corporations under International Law." *Columbia Journal of Transnational Law* 43 (2005): 927–959.

Verdery, Katherine. *What Was Socialism, and What Comes Next?* Princeton, NJ: Princeton University Press, 1996.

Veseth, Michael. *Globaloney: Unraveling the Myths of Globalization.* Lanham, MD: Rowman & Littlefield, 2006.

Vinci, Anthony. *Armed Groups and the Balance of Power: The International Relations of Terrorist, Warlords and Insurgents.* London: Taylor & Francis, 2009.

Vlahos, Michael. *Fighting Identity: Sacred War and World Change.* Westport, CT: Praeger, 2008.

Vlassenroot, Koen, and Timothy Raeymaekers. "The Politics of Rebellion and Intervention in Ituri: The Emergence of a New Political Complex?" *African Affairs* 103, no. 412 (2004): 385–412.

Vlassis, Dimitri. "Global Situation of Transnational Organized Crime, the Decision of the International Community to Develop an International Convention and the Negotiation Process." *Resource Material Series*, no. 59 (2002): 475–494.

Vogel, David. "The Private Regulation of Global Corporate Conduct." *Business & Society* 49, no. 1 (2010): 68–87.

Vogt, Heidi, and Rahim Faiez. "Afghan Starts to Close Private Security Firms." Associated Press, October 3, 2010.

Vuving, Alexander L. "How Soft Power Works." Paper presented at the annual meeting of the American Political Science Association, Toronto, 2009.

Wald, Charles F. "New Thinking at USEUCOM: The Phase Zero Campaign." *Joint Forces Quarterly* 43, no. 1 (2006): 72–75.

Walker, R. B. J. *Inside/Outside: International Relations as Political Theory.* Cambridge, UK: Cambridge University Press, 1992.

Walsh, Nick Paton. "Iraq Bans United States Security Firm Blackwater." *Channel 4 News*, September 18, 2007.

Walton, Clifford. *History of the British Standing Army.* London: Harrison, 1894.

Waltz, Kenneth N. *Man, the State, and War: A Theoretical Analysis,* rev. ed. New York: Columbia University Press, 2001.

Walzer, Michael. *Just and Unjust Wars: A Moral Argument with Historical Illustrations,* 4th ed. New York: Basic Books, 2006.

Ward, William E., and Thomas P. Galvin. "U.S. Africa Command and the Principle of Active Security." *Joint Force Quarterly* 51 (2008): 61–66.

Warlord, Inc.: Extortion and Corruption along the U.S. Supply Chain in Afghanistan. Report before the Subcommittee on National Security and Foreign Affairs, US House of Representatives, 111th Congress, June 22, 2010.

Waters, Malcolm. *Globalization,* 1st ed. London: Routledge, 1996.

Wayman, Frank W., and Paul F. Diehl, eds. *Reconstructing Realpolitik.* Ann Arbor: University of Michigan Press, 1994.

Weber, Max. *The Methodology of the Social Sciences,* translated and edited by Edward A. Shils and Henry A. Finch. New York: Free Press, 1949.

Webster, Camilla. "The Davos Buzz." *Forbes,* January 22, 2008.

Welsh, Jennifer M. "Authorizing Humanitarian Intervention." In *The United Nations and Global Security,* edited by Richard M. Price and Mark W. Zacher, 177–192. New York: Palgrave Macmillan, 2004.

White House, "President Bush Outlines Iraqi Threat," press release, October 7, 2002.

Wight, Martin. *Systems of States*. Leicester: Leicester University Press, 1977.

Willard, Charity. *The "Livre de Paix" of Christine de Pisan: A Critical Edition*. The Hague: Mouton, 1958.

Willetts, Peter. "From Consultative Arrangements to Partnership: The Changing Status of NGOs in Diplomacy at the UN." *Global Governance* 6, no. 2 (2000): 191–212.

———."Transnational Actors and International Organizations in Global Politics." In *The Globalization of World Politics: An Introduction to International Relations*, edited by John Baylis and Steve Smith, 356–383. Oxford: Oxford University Press, 2001.

Williams, Michael C. "The Hobbesian Theory of International Relations: Three Traditions." In *Classical Theory in International Relations*, edited by Beate Jahn, 253–276. Cambridge, UK: Cambridge University Press, 2006.

———. "Words, Images, Enemies: Securitization and International Politics." *International Studies Quarterly* 47, no. 4 (2003): 511–531.

Williams, Phil. *From the New Middle Ages to a New Dark Age: The Decline of the State and US Strategy*. Carlisle, PA: Strategic Studies Institute, 2008.

Wilson, Peter H. "The German 'Soldier Trade' of the Seventeenth and Eighteenth Centuries: A Reassessment." *International History Review* 18, no. 4 (1996): 757–792.

Winnett, Robert. "David Cameron Orders Release of Secret Lockerbie Bomber Documents." *Telegraph*, July 20, 2010.

Winter, Joseph. "Africa—New Front in Drugs War." BBC News, July 9, 2007. http://news.bbc. co.uk/2/hi/africa/6274590.stm.

Wisler, Dominique. "Community Policing?" Paper presented at the UNDP workshop on Community Security and Social Cohesion, Montreux, 2010.

Women in Military Service for America Memorial Foundation. "Statistics on Women in the [US] Military," September 30, 2010. http://www.womensmemorial.org/Press/stats.html, accessed July 1, 2011.

World Bank. "World Bank Group Work in Low-Income Countries under Stress: A Task Force Report." World Bank LICUS Task Force, September 2002.

———. "Indicators: Data." 2010, http://data.worldbank.org/indicator, accessed February 25, 2014.

———. "Liberia—Workers' Remittances and Compensation of Employees," http://www.index-mundi.com/facts/liberia/workers'-remittances-and-compensation-of-employees, accessed February 25, 2014.

———. "Net Official Development Assistance and Official Aid Received (Current US$)." http://data.worldbank.org/indicator/DT.ODA.ALLD.CD?cid=GPD_54, accessed April 16, 2011.

———. *The Pirates of Somalia: Ending the Threat, Rebuilding a Nation*. Washington, DC: World Bank, 2013.

WorldPublicOpinion.org. "Humanitarian Military Intervention in Africa." http://www.americans-world.org/digest/regional_issues/africa/africa4.cfm, accessed April 16, 2011.

"The World's Worst: Liberia." *Economist*, November, 2002.

Wormuth, Francis D. "Return to the Middle Ages." *Western Political Quarterly* 2, no. 2 (1949): 193–207.

"Wounded Iraqis: 'No One Did Anything' to Provoke Blackwater." CNN, September 19, 2007. http://www.cnn.com/2007/WORLD/meast/09/19/iraq.fateful.day/index.html, accessed February 14, 2014.

Wriston, Walter B. *The Twilight of Sovereignty: How the Information Revolution Is Transforming Our World*. New York: Scribner, 1992.

Wyler, Liana Sun, and Nicolas Cook. *Illegal Drug Trade in Africa: Trends and US Policy*. Washington, DC: Congressional Research Service, 2009.

Yergin, Daniel, and Joseph Stanislaw. *The Commanding Heights: The Battle for the World Economy*. New York: Simon & Schuster, 2002.

Yule, Henry, ed. *Cathay and the Way Thither: Being a Collection of Medieval Notices on China*. London: Hakluyt Society, 1866; Cambridge, UK: Cambridge University Press, 2009.

Zacher, Mark W. "The Decaying Pillars of the Westphalian Temple: Implications for International Order and Governance." In *Governance without Government: Order and Change in World*

Politics, edited by James N. Rosenau and Ernest-Otto Czempiel, 58–101. Cambridge, UK: Cambridge University Press, 1992.

Zamparelli, Steven J. "Contractors on the Battlefield: What Have We Signed Up For?" *Air Force Journal of Logistics* 23, no. 3 (Fall 1990): 10–19.

Zarate, Juan C. "The Emergence of a New Dog of War: Private International Security Companies, International Law, and the New World Disorder," *Stanford Journal of International Law* 34 (1998): 75–162.

Zedong, Mao. *On Protracted War*. Beijing: Foreign Languages Press, 1966.

———. *Quotations from Chairman Mao Zedong (The Little Red Book)*. Beijing: Government of the People's Republic of China, 1964.

Zhenmin, Liu. Statement by Ambassador Liu Zhenmin at the Plenary Session of the General Assembly on the Question of "Responsibility to Protect," July 24, 2009.

Zhi, Chen. "Over 100 People Killed in Southwest Cote d'Ivoire." *Xinhua News*, May 11, 2011, http://news.xinhuanet.com/english2010/world/2011-05/10/c_13867888.htm, accessed February 26, 2014.

Zoepf, Katherine. "Talk of Women's Rights Divides Saudi Arabia." *New York Times*, May 31, 2010.

Zucchino, David. "Iraqis Settle Lawsuits over Blackwater Shootings." *Los Angeles Times*, January 28, 2010.

INDEX

239